Voices of Protest

Voices of Protest

Social Movements in Post-Apartheid South Africa

Edited by

Richard Ballard, Adam Habib and Imraan Valodia

UNIVERSITY OF KwaZulu-Natal Press

Published in 2006 by University of KwaZulu-Natal Press
Private Bag X01
Scottsville 3209
South Africa
Email: books@ukzn.ac.za
Website: www.ukznpress.co.za

ISBN 1-86914-089-3

Cover design: Flying Ant Designs
Editor: Sally Hines
Typesetting: Patricia Comrie
Indexer: Judith Shier

Printed and bound by Interpak Books, Pietermaritzburg

Contents

Foreword

IN MY INAUGURAL lecture at the University of Natal in 1997 I reflected on how important any new engagements between academics and progressive social movements was going to be for our future as effective intellectuals and activists, and also for the kind of social, political and economic trajectory we might take as a country. I made the point because of my concerns, even then, that the exciting, albeit problematic era, in which university-based academics had played an integral, often leading role, as policy advisers and experts to social, labour and political movements appeared to be coming to an end. It would be increasingly as technocrats only, I argued, that government would in future turn to academics, and not only to progressive ones either.

Progressive academics in the new South Africa, I suggested, should resist the temptation to respond to the technological and developmental demands of the state and business in narrow technical ways – ways which run counter to the ethos and culture of university life, one of the few remaining sites in contemporary society for a critical and humanistic engagement with issues such as poverty, inequality, oppression, exploitation and democracy. Those academics serious about contributing to critical and effective policy debates and analysis may, as they had done in our decade of liberation, find more socially useful roles to play within the emerging civil society movements of post-apartheid South Africa. The challenge would be to seek actively to do this while at the same time, and wherever possible, to exploit and expand any new spaces opened up at the level of the state by the triumph over apartheid.

As the twentieth century drew to a close, a number of problems emerged that appeared to set back the possibilities for such a bifurcated, synthetic approach. One was that the strategic and political vision, as well as the organisational capacity, of many civil society groups, including the unions, had been badly affected by aspects of the transition. The capacity within, and indeed the willingness of, such organisations to relate to the academic community and to absorb its ideas in dynamic interaction (as the unions did in the 1980s) appeared to have deteriorated. A second was a sense I had then that government had already consolidated within its structures a new, highly loyal and pragmatic economic and technocratic elite, drawn in part from the former progressive economic community, but mainly from the rump of the old apartheid state machinery.

The arguments in the various chapters of this book suggest that these conditions have changed, but in highly complex and uneven ways across old and new social movements, and also between them and the post-apartheid state.

However, it seems to me that whatever the nature and character of state-civil society relations in this country, challenging and important tasks for its progressive social scientists remain. These tasks, in Bellamy Foster's words, could include:

> to advance a politics of the truth; to avoid easy compromises; to address the immediate and long-term needs of the mass of the population and of those who suffer the most severe forms of oppression; to search for the common ground of that oppression; to resist ideological claims that 'we are all in the same boat' in this society; to reject what Mills called the 'crackpot realism' that makes the status quo into a kind of inescapable second nature and closes off the future; to fight market fetishism. In short, to avoid making what Raymond Williams called 'long-term adjustments to short-term problems' (Foster 1990: 286).

This book represents an important, pioneering, dare one say, visionary contribution, to the task of understanding the character of social movements in South Africa, and how these social movements – old and new – relate, if at all, to the state. In a more general sense, the book also allows us to reflect on the nature of some of the key political, social and economic conditions of contemporary South African life.

As someone only marginally involved in this project, as a university bureaucrat, I marvelled at the energy, staying power and commitment of the project leaders and the team of researchers assembled for this ambitious project. Funders and university bosses often expect fast delivery, better to tick off projects as complete, and to claim SAPSE-points and research rewards. It is therefore to the credit of the Ford Foundation and Atlantic Philanthropies, the University of KwaZulu-Natal Research Office, and the School/Centre heads that the project leaders and researchers were left alone to get along with their work with minimal pressure, but maximum support and encouragement, even to the extent of participating in the exciting workshops that took place.

The result is an outstanding collection of rich and nuanced papers by some of the leading scholars, public intellectuals and activists working in this field in South Africa. Beyond its academic value, which I believe will be an enduring one, is its significance as a kind of intervention in the project of South Africa's political and economic reconstruction.

The project was a crucial component of the work of the then newly constituted Centre for Civil Society led by its founding director, Professor Adam Habib. It gave the Centre one significant way in which to carry out its national mandate, among other things, through the way in which it succeeded in attracting to it, and maintaining the commitment of such a large group of people from across the country, both within and outside of the academy. The project was at the same time evidence of the kind of high quality engagement that is possible between the Centre and the School of Development Studies at the University of KwaZulu-Natal, which brought to the table differing, but complementary, traditions of theory and method. It was a collaboration that underpinned growing social connections among such staff who would not otherwise have worked together for such an extended period of time. The Centre and the School were also, through this project, able to give content and substance to the kind of real and dynamic engagement between the academy and civil society which I alluded to in my inaugural, and which I have referred to briefly above.

I wish to recognise publicly the commitment and creativity of the project leaders and editors. Adam Habib, Imraan Valodia and Richard Ballard are both colleagues and close friends; but as the head of School for most of the duration of this project, and as interim-director of the Centre for nearly a year, I can testify to their dedication and creativity in seeing the project through to this important point. It was a great pleasure for me to support this kind of research. Not least, because at the workshops of the project which I attended at Tala Game Reserve and Glenburn Lodge, the nature, character and intensity of the debates among the wide range of participants reminded me so much of earlier moments in our struggle history.

Vishnu Padayachee
Senior professor, School of Development Studies

Reference

Foster, J.B. 1990. 'Liberal Practicality and the US Left'. *Socialist Register*. London: The Merlin Press.

Preface

THIS EDITED VOLUME is being published in the midst of a mushrooming of social struggles against local governments for what is perceived to be their failure at service delivery. How ironic then that its genesis lies in a similar period of heightened social struggles that began a few years after the political transition in South Africa, even before the elation of having overthrown the apartheid state had fully dissipated. Then, as now, some euphorically proclaimed these new struggles and the social movements emerging out of these struggles as the new opposition, the true voice of poor and marginalised South Africans. Others, aligned to the state, questioned the legitimacy and meaning of these struggles. For them, these struggles represented the irresponsible actions of a few activists who did not understand the complexities of post-apartheid reconstruction. This polarised response to the new social struggles is a product of a lack of knowledge of what these movements are and who they represent. So began our desire to undertake a systematic and comprehensive study of emerging social movements in South Africa, a study that lasted three years, and the results of which are reported in this volume.

From the outset, we recognised that the post-apartheid moment is characterised by ebbs and flows in social mobilisation. The sheer diversity and range of these struggles meant that it would be impossible, given our time span and resources, to investigate and tabulate all these struggles. Instead, we had a less ambitious but more intellectually challenging task. We wanted to plough a number of investigative levers into some of the movements that had emerged to understand if there were lessons to be learnt and generalisations applicable about social movements, social mobilisation and social reconstruction in contemporary South Africa. We did not and could not aim to provide a compendium of these struggles.

How did we choose the movements to be studied? By informed intuition. All the movements studied in this volume were in the public eye, in some form or other, when we began this project. As academics, activists, and even citizens of the country, we were cognisant of the diversity of these movements. We thus set out to choose a set of case studies that would reflect the various elements of this diversity including form, scale, ideology and spatial location. We do not see this set as a carefully chosen representative sample whose study could be generalised to the universe of social mobilisation. Rather, they must be treated for what they are: a set of case study reflections, which allow for informed commentaries on the political situation in South Africa, its development models, and on the relationship between civil society and democracy. We also, of course, use the opportunity presented by these case studies to speak to the debates in the global academy for we do believe that despite the methodological concerns in our choice of case studies, this volume does reflect the most comprehensive collection of social movement studies undertaken in the post-apartheid era.

It is also worthwhile noting that we are particularly proud of having brought together the group of scholars and intellectuals that undertook these case studies. These individuals are a diverse lot, ideologically distinct, demographically diverse (although this could have been improved), with different intellectual trajectories, and at various stages in their research careers. Some of us conceive of ourselves as activist scholars, while others are comfortable with simply being academics. All that united us was our combative personalities, which made for intellectually stimulating, if at times, contentious, debates and workshops. But the conversations across ideological and institutional boundaries were the most inspiring moments of our two years together, for they were instrumental, we believe, in the generation of a more probing enquiry and hopefully, a better intellectual product. For that, and for the mature interactions that defined our engagements, credit must be given to this collective group of scholars.

These scholars were asked to answer a number of research questions in relation to specific case studies. What are the social movements, and who is their support base? How are their activities and actions related to the political opportunity structure? Are we witnessing the emergence of a viable left opposition to the ANC? Are all the social movements of the same view? How are South African social movements connected to similar global movements? What does this mean for political power and democratisation in the country?

These questions, which intrigued all of us, became the guiding concerns of this study of social movements in South Africa.

This project would not have been possible without the help of many individuals and organisations. Ashwin Desai helped us to draft the project proposal. Our colleagues in the School of Development Studies and the Centre for Civil Society engaged us and helped us to distil our ideas. In particular, we would like to acknowledge the role that Vishnu Padayachee played in accommodating the needs of the project both in the School and in the Centre. We are grateful to Kanagie Naidoo, who so ably managed our financial reporting, and Helen Poonen for administrative support. The Ford Foundation and Atlantic Philanthropies not only provided the funds for the project, but also engaged with us in the intellectual excitement of this research. We want, in particular, to acknowledge the role of Gary Hawes and Gerald Kraak in making all of this possible. Glenn Cowley of the University of KwaZulu-Natal Press encouraged and supported the publication of this book. Sally Hines was everything you would want from an editor – efficient, insightful and charming. We would like to thank Judith Shier for the hard work she did on the index.

Richard Ballard was just tremendous. We owe him a special gratitude. Not only did he take care of all of the administration and co-ordination tasks with such professionalism and graciousness, he also partnered us in providing leadership and intellectual direction.

But most of all we need to thank the social movement activists. Many of them pushed and criticised, but they always accommodated us and for that we are thankful. It is their generosity of spirit that made this whole project possible. They, of course, cannot be held responsible for the analyses and conclusions in the pages that follow. We alone are responsible for these.

Finally, we shared many of our ideas with our partners, Fatima and Pauline, who as always provided both intellectual and practical support. But we dedicate this book to our kids – Irfan and Zidaan, and Rubina, Zunaid and Aneesa – all very much born in and reflective of the hopes of the new South Africa. It is our aspiration that they will have the pleasure and right to live in a more equitable and humanitarian society. We offer this book in the hope that it may contribute to inspiring the debate, reflection and engagement necessary for the creation of that new world.

Adam Habib and Imraan Valodia

Abbreviations

ABCD	asset-based community development
ABIGALE	Association for Bisexuals, Gays and Lesbians
ADRC	Apartheid Debt and Reparations Campaign
AEC	Anti-Eviction Campaign
AGM	annual general meeting
AIDC	Alternative Information and Development Centre
ANC	African National Congress
APF	Anti-Privatisation Forum
ARVs	anti-retrovirals
AWB	Afrikaner Weerstandsbeweging
CALS	Centre for Applied Legal Studies
CAMS	Coalition Against Military Spending
CBO	community-based organisation
CBRC	Co-ordinating Body of Refugee Communities
CCF	Concerned Citizens Forum
CCG	Concerned Citizens Group
CEC	Central Executive Committee (COSATU)
CEPPWAWU	Chemical, Energy, Paper, Printing, Wood and Allied Workers' Union
Cosancom	Congress for South African Non-Racial Civic Organisations Movement
COSATU	Congress of South African Trade Unions
CRG	Community Research Group

CUSA	Council of Unions in South Africa
DA	Democratic Alliance
DLA	Department of Land Affairs
DRC	Democratic Republic of Congo
EJNF	Environmental Justice Networking Forum
ELA	Earthlife Africa
EMG	Environmental Monitoring Group
ETG	Economic Trends Group
EWT	Endangered Wildlife Trust
FAWU	Food and Allied Workers' Union
FEDUSA	Federation of Unions of South Africa
FEW	Forum for the Empowerment of Women
FOSATU	Federation of South African Trade Unions
FSSC	Financial Service Sector Campaign
GASA	Gay Association of South Africa
GATT	General Agreement on Tariffs and Trade
GEAR	Growth, Employment and Redistribution
GEM	Group for Environmental Monitoring
HIPC	Heavily Indebted Poor Country
HPA	Homeless People's Alliance
IFP	Inkatha Freedom Party
ILO	International Labour Organisation
IMATU	Independent Municipal and Allied Trade Union
IMF	International Monetary Fund
ISP	Industrial Strategy Project
J2000	Jubilee 2000 Coalition
JS	Jubilee South
JSA	Jubilee South Africa
KSG	Khulumani Support Group
LCC	Legal Co-ordinating Committee
LFS	Labour Force Survey
LG	lesbian and gay
LGBTI	Lesbian, Gay, Bisexual, Transgender and Intersex
LPM	Landless People's Movement
LRA	Labour Relations Act
MDM	mass democratic movement
MJC	Muslim Judicial Council

MK	Umkhonto we Sizwe
MP	member of parliament
MPAEC	Mandela Park Anti-Eviction Campaign
MST	Movimento dos Trabhaladores Rurais Sem Terra
NACTU	National Council of Trade Unions
NIA	National Intelligence Agency
NAPWA	National Association of People Living with HIV/AIDS
Narco	National Association of Residents and Civic Organisations
NCGLE	National Coalition for Gay and Lesbian Equality
NDA	National Development Agency
NEC	National Executive Committee
NEDLAC	National Economic Development and Labour Council
NEF	National Economic Forum
NEHAWU	National Education, Health and Allied Workers' Union
NEPAD	New Partnership for Africa's Development
NGO	non-governmental organisation
NIA	National Intelligence Agency
NLC	National Land Committee
NMC	National Manpower Commission
NNP	New National Party
NPO	non-profit organisation
NPPCHN	National Progressive Primary Health Care Network
NT	National Treasury
NUM	National Union of Mineworkers
NUMSA	National Union of Metalworkers of South Africa
OHS	October Household Survey
OLGA	Organisation of Lesbian and Gay Activists
OPHP	Official People's Housing Process
PAC	Pan-Africanist Congress
PAGAD	People Against Gangsterism and Drugs
PCAS	Policy Co-ordination and Advisory Services
PHP	People's Housing Process
POs	participating organisations
RDI	Rural Development Initiative
RDP	Reconstruction and Development Programme
REC	Regional Executive Committee
SACC	South African Council of Churches

SACP	South African Communist Party
SACTU	South African Congress of Trade Unions
SALB	South African Labour Bulletin
SAMWU	South African Municipal Workers' Union
SANCO	South African National Civic Organisation
SANGOCO	South African NGO Coalition
SAPS	South African Police Service
SASCO	South African Students' Congress
SDCEA	South Durban Community Environmental Alliance
SDI	Shack/Slum Dwellers International
SECC	Soweto Electricity Crisis Committee
SECCP	Sustainable Energy and Climate Change Partnership
SEWA	Self-Employed Women's Association (India)
SEWU	Self-Employed Women's Union
SMI	Social Movements Indaba
SMO	social movement organisation
SOMOH	Soweto's Mountain of Hope
SVCC	Steel Valley Crisis Committee
TAC	Treatment Action Campaign
TANs	transnational advocacy networks
TASH	Tenants Association of Sydenham Heights
TCC	Tembelihle Crisis Committee
TRC	Truth and Reconciliation Commission
UCF	United Civic Front
UDF	United Democratic Front
UDM	United Democratic Movement
UNCHS	United Nations Commission for Human Settlements
UNDP	United Nations Development Programme
UNHCR	United Nations High Commission for Refugees
WB	World Bank
WCAR	World Conference Against Racism
WEIGO	Women in Informal Employment Globalising and Organising
WESSA	Wildlife and Environmental Society of Southern Africa
WNC	Women's National Coalition
WSF	World Social Forum
WSSD	World Summit on Sustainable Development
WTO	World Trade Organisation

1

Introduction

From Anti-Apartheid to Post-Apartheid Social Movements

Richard Ballard, Adam Habib, Imraan Valodia and Elke Zuern

A NEW CHAPTER in South African political history was opened on 27 April 1994. It marked the moment when the leaders of South Africa's anti-apartheid social movements entered the corridors of political power. As has happened so often in newly liberated countries, the euphoria of the political transition led many to expect that the need for adversarial social struggle with the state was over. For a while after 1994, this expectation tended to inform much civil society activity and stifled social struggles, but this response was by no means uniform. Some social struggles did take place. Labour struggles, for example, exploded in the immediate aftermath of the first non-racial general elections. Spontaneous social eruptions occurred around the issues of demarcation and crime, but in most cases these quickly dissipated, and state-civil society engagements came to be largely defined by collaborative relations.

This collaborative relationship between the state, on the one hand, and the unions and civics, on the other, was partly facilitated by the new government's attempts to create an enabling political and fiscal environment. Corporatist institutions, such as the National Economic Development and Labour Council (NEDLAC), were established and non-governmental organisations (NGOs) and community-based organisations (CBOs) were given representation in this forum through the establishment of a development chamber. Legislation was promulgated that enabled the registration of NGOs and CBOs. Public funding agencies, such as the National Development Agency (NDA), were established to direct financial resources to the sector, and most importantly, government enabled the sub-contracting of development services to a number of civil society actors, thereby entrenching the collegiate logic of state-civil society relations during the immediate post-apartheid phase.

Unlike in many other transitional societies where the political honeymoon tended to drag on for decades, new social struggles in South Africa emerged surprisingly quickly. Some of these struggles can be traced to the Mandela presidency, even though most of the struggles in the main tended to coincide with South Africa's second democratic election and the ascension to the presidency of Thabo Mbeki. His term of office witnessed the emergence of social struggles on a range of fronts. Three overlapping but distinct types of struggle emerged. Some were directed against various government policies. The classic case here is the Congress of South African Trade Unions' (COSATU) opposition to the Growth, Employment and Redistribution (GEAR) strategy, which represented the post-apartheid government's decision to engage with trade liberalisation and pursue economic growth as the mechanism for facilitating employment, and thereby promote redistribution. Other struggles focused on government's failures in meeting basic needs and addressing socio-economic rights. The most noted examples are the Landless People's Movement (LPM) and the Treatment Action Campaign (TAC) that respectively address the slow pace of land redistribution and government's failure to provide an adequate response to the HIV/AIDS crisis. Finally, some struggles emerged to directly challenge the local enforcement of government policies and to resist government attempts at repression. The Soweto Electricity Crisis Committee (SECC), the Concerned Citizens Group (CCG) and the Anti-Eviction Campaign (AEC) are all attempts to organise poor and marginalised communities to resist local, provincial and national governments' attempts to cut off electricity and water, and to evict residents. The sheer scale and diversity of these social struggles has raised concern in official circles and prompted a number of scholars to turn their attention to this emerging phenomenon (Bond 2000; Marais 1998).

How do we understand these contemporary social struggles? Some studies have collectively referred to them as social movements (Desai 2002), but, is this a fair description? Definitions of social movements abound. Charles Tilly suggests that 'the proper analogy to a social movement is neither a party nor a union but a political campaign. What we call a social movement actually consists in a series of demands or challenges to power-holders in the name of a social category that lacks an established political position' (1985: 735–6). Elizabeth Jelin provides more form to this definition when she defines movements 'as forms of collective action with a high degree of popular participation, which use non-institutional channels, and which formulate their demands while simultaneously finding forms of action to express them, thus establishing themselves as collective subjects, that is, as a group or social category' (Jelin 1986 quoted in Escobar and Alvarez 1992: 15). We also understand these social movements to largely exist within that sphere defined as civil society: 'the organised expression of various interests and values operating in the triangular space between the family, state, and the market' (Habib and Kotze 2002: 3; Habib 2003).

Social movements are thus, in our view, politically and/or socially directed collectives, often involving multiple organisations and networks, focused on changing one or more elements of the social, political and economic system within which they are located. This then suggests that we should perhaps be circumspect about categorising all of South Africa's contemporary struggles as social movements; some may not be popularly located or do not sufficiently establish a collective identity. While these definitional questions can be instructive, we do not wish to dwell upon them here. This volume employs the social movements frame as an entry point to explore the social base of these collectivities, the strategies they employ, and the implications of their choices for both development and democracy in South Africa. From this perspective, we turn to consider the questions and insights offered by social movement theories before addressing the context and implications of collective action in South Africa.

A Survey of Social Movement Theories

Investigations of social movements commonly build upon three central aspects relevant to our understanding of mobilisation: the structure of opportunities and constraints within which movements may or may not develop; the networks, structures and other resources that actors employ to mobilise supporters; and the ways in which movement participants define or frame their movement. Analyses of political opportunities, mobilising structures and framing processes include a wide range of theoretical perspectives from structural materialist approaches to mobilisation to constructivist understandings of identity. They therefore work together to bridge approaches to 'old' and 'new' social movements, bringing together movements for liberation, independence and freedom that often sought revolutionary change and the overthrow of the state with the 'self-limiting radicalism' of 'new' social movements (Cohen 1985: 664) which demanded greater equality and rights without challenging the structure of formally democratic states and the market economy. This three-pronged approach also offers important insights into the so-called 'new-new' (Della Porta 2003) transnational movements that press for alternative globalisations and in so doing challenge powerful transnational and global political and economic structures. In this way, these three aspects of social movement inquiry productively accommodate the analysis of significantly different movements across time and space.

As a first step, structuralist discussions of political opportunity seek to understand the contexts within which mobilisation is more or less likely. Approaches to political opportunity incorporate the insights from theorists of collective behaviour (Oberschall 1993; Smelser 1971) by pointing to the importance of broader structural openings and instabilities to which actors may respond. Political opportunity theorists also underline Piven and Cloward's central insights into the importance of institutions to both 'create and limit opportunities for mass struggles' (1979: xv). They therefore work to connect broader structural and institutional configurations to the prospects for movement activity and the rise and decline of protest cycles, but importantly do so without reducing the presence of movement activity to structural conditions.

Tarrow offers a fairly concise definition of political opportunity structure: 'consistent – but not necessarily formal, permanent or national – dimensions of the political environment that provide incentives for people to undertake collective action by affecting their expectations for success or failure' (1994: 85). McAdam expands on this by identifying four dimensions of political opportunity which most authors employing the term agree upon: 'The relative openness or closure of the institutionalised political system; the stability or instability of that broad set of elite alignments that typically undergird a polity; the presence or absence of elite allies; the state's capacity and propensity for repression' (1996: 27). Changes in political opportunity structure would therefore include shifts in any one or more of these four dimensions. It is important to stress that state actors can provide opportunities through their engagement or disengagement, and that forms of engagement clearly vary; for example, while a participatory corporatist system may open opportunities, a co-optive corporatist structure will work to diminish them. Finally, not only elites but also counter-elites play crucial roles in defining political openings.

Political opportunity theorists also point to the formation of protest cycles that begin with an increase in structurally created political opportunities, which are then expanded by movements as they successfully mobilise, offering greater opportunities for the creation of new movements. In this way, political opportunity is not simply given but is also strongly affected by the actions of collective actors. Protest cycles are expanded by heightened mobilisation and rapid innovation as different actors learn from and improve upon existing models of collective action. Either increasing popular acceptance of many of the claims made by the participants or increasing state repression may spell the end of a cycle of heightened protest. Alternatively, disillusionment, frustration and even boredom on the part of the movement participants may lead to a decline in protest and possibly the disappearance of formerly popular movements (Castells 1983; Tarrow 1994; Zuern 2001). Political opportunity approaches consequently offer significant contributions to the study of social movements by highlighting the opportunities for action and suggesting the possible forms that movements will take as they respond to the context in which they organise. Opportunity structures cannot, however, explain the rise of new movements on their own.

Movements also build upon existing human and material resources. The investigation of mobilising structures, which has grown out of resource mobilisation theory (McCarthy and Zald 1973), rationalist accounts of collective action (Olson 1965), moral economy approaches (Thompson 1971) and political process models (Tilly 1978; McAdam 1982), has underlined the need to consider not only material resources but also the formal and informal networks upon which movements are built. These networks include those that develop along class, ethnic, racial, religious and gender lines, as well as those that transcend these distinctions.

This second branch of inquiry investigates how social movement organisations are formed, what local networks they build upon, what existing institutions they employ, and what access they have to political and material resources. This conception of resources also includes established repertoires of contention, essentially the means of claim making (Tilly 1986: 4) which range from peaceful sit-ins and letter-writing campaigns to acts of vandalism or violent attacks upon individuals or state institutions. Though these resources exist for new movements to employ, new movements often innovate within existing repertoires. During different periods, under different regimes, various forms of protest dominate. As repertoires become outdated, social actors work to change them in response to changes in their own interests and organisations as well as the overall relationship between state and society. The changes are, however, extremely gradual; in the interim, repertoires may actually constrain action (Tilly 1986; Zuern 2001).

Analysts who employ mobilising structures as part of a broader inquiry, work to avoid the central criticisms levelled against earlier, more narrowly defined, approaches. Melucci, for example, notes that theories based purely on resource mobilisation 'tend to explain how, but not *why* social movements emerge and develop', adding 'resource mobilisation approaches view collective action as "data" which is merely given' (1989: 3). Political opportunity approaches offer some insight into the question of 'why?', but largely from the perspective of factors external to the movements themselves. In short, it is necessary to investigate the very process by which movements define themselves in order to fully understand the 'why' of movement mobilisation and organisation.

This third area of social movement studies is based on identity-oriented paradigms that stress the importance of social relationships for any under-standing of movement activity; they therefore bring cultural frames including shared meanings, symbols and discourses into the analysis (Lichbach 1998: 407). Analysts of new social movements such as Touraine (1981) and Melucci (1989) have underlined the importance of framing, by focusing on subjective elements such as identity, status and values. Melucci reminds us that the same experiences and behaviour can be viewed in different ways; meanings depend upon systems of reference (1985: 794). These shared meanings, defined as framing processes by Snow and others (Snow et al. 1986), are central to any understanding of social movement activity. Even the structuralist account of Piven and Cloward (1979) and the relative deprivation theory expounded by Gurr (1970) point to the central importance of a shared feeling of grievance in order for mobilisation to occur. The oversight in these theories has been to assume that such collective framings simply appear without investigating their very construction.

McAdam, Tarrow and Tilly argue: 'For a growing school of "constructionists", social movements were *both* carriers of meanings and makers of meaning, that, by *naming* grievances and expressing new identities, constructed new realities and made these identities collective' (1997: 149; italics in original). Insights from the study of so-called 'identity-based' movements, such as those focusing on women's and gay rights, were incorporated into the study of social movements more generally to work to address questions of collective identity, consciousness and solidarity that earlier models had difficulty solving. The inclusion of these approaches underlines the importance of definitions of community, shared meanings and transcripts (Scott 1985) for any account of collective action.

Scholars from numerous perspectives have worked to bridge these three central aspects and often divisions in the study of social movements (Cohen 1985; Della Porta and Diani 1999; Lichbach 1998; McAdam, McCarthy and Zald 1996; McAdam, Tarrow and Tilly 1997, 2001). While different authors allocate varying degrees of attention to underlying structural factors, it is quite clear that no movement can be understood without some investigation of the material structure within which it formed. Opportunity structures work either to limit collective action, as in highly representative or repressive systems, or to encourage such behaviour, especially under conditions where there is a clear definition of a repressive system (for example, apartheid, around which many could rally in opposition). The establishment or presence of solidarity networks is clearly required for the 'production of meaning and the mobilization of resources' (Della Porta and Diani 1999: 22) that enable popular protest. Finally, the production of shared beliefs and collective identities form the necessary, but not sufficient, basis for all social movements.

Before moving on to an investigation of the underlying structural conditions, both domestic and transnational, affecting recent movement activity in South Africa, it is necessary to add two more important innovations and challenges to this three-pronged perspective on movement activity. First, until relatively recently, most scholars of movements have focused upon domestic contexts and movements rather than transnational actors, constraints and opportunities. Keck and Sikkink (1998), however, have importantly drawn attention to transnational advocacy networks. A growing scholarship, following in their footsteps, furthers this inquiry by focusing on the development of transnational organisations and movements, particularly those challenging neo-liberal discourses of globalisation (for example, Clark 2003; Cohen and Rai 2000; Della Porta and Tarrow 2005; Florini 2000; Keane 2003; Khagram, Riker and Sikkink 2002; Klein 2001; O'Brien et al., 2000). These scholars have pressed researchers and activists to define opportunities, networks and identities which transcend national boundaries, and that work to connect the 'local' to the 'global'.

Second, McAdam, Tarrow and Tilly (2001) have worked to define a more dynamic approach to movement activity and collective action more generally. This approach seeks to move the focus of inquiry from one of understanding political opportunities and threats, mobilising structures and framing processes to a framework within which greater emphasis is placed upon the very mechanisms and processes that bring about contentious action by connecting these factors. This results in a more dynamic and complex framework which effectively focuses on processes such as boundary activation (defining 'us' and 'them'); diffusion (the transmission of ideas and approaches to new populations); brokerage (the linking of previously unconnected actors and sites); radicalisation (the move to more extreme tactics or agendas); social appropriation (the appropriation of previously non-politicised sites or activities into sites of mobilisation); category formation (creation of a new social category); object shift (change in perceptions and relations among actors); and certification (validation of actors by an external authority). Such a framework challenges researchers to draw connections between various processes to better understand social movements and collectivities in motion.

This dynamic framework, along with the three-pronged approach outlined above with the crucial addition of transnational and global opportunities, actions, identities and constraints, offers a host of questions, approaches and mechanisms for researchers to consider when investigating popular responses to the political and socio-economic context in South Africa. In order to employ these insights, it is necessary to begin by defining the broader framework of opportunities and constraints to investigate globalisation as it manifests itself in South Africa.

Globalisation and Marginalisation in South Africa

The term globalisation has come to dominate discourses of social, economic and cultural developments in contemporary society. Given the multifaceted processes that are often merged under its rubric, the term defies clear and precise definition. Most analysts begin by pointing to the economic dimensions of globalisation, including the dramatic increases in international trade and finance, the growing importance of multi-national corporations in the international economy, and, more generally, the growing interconnectedness of many parts of the world. This growing interconnectedness has been characterised over the last three decades by the increasing importance of new technological advances, which have dramatically reduced the costs of international transactions, thereby promoting the increased movement of capital, goods and services and, to a certain extent, people. It is important to also recognise that the integration of the global economy has led to a rapid proliferation and spread of new information and communications technologies.

The forces unleashed by globalisation have had a fundamental impact on the production system, which itself has become globalised. The shift from Fordist to post-Fordist production strategies has led to the outsourcing of suppliers and the relocation of price-sensitive products to low-cost production regions where labour is cheap. These changes in the production system have in turn fostered fundamentally reconfigured labour markets, forcing a rapid growth in new forms of informal, contract and part-time working arrangements across the globe (see Standing 1999).

The economic definitions highlight some of the key features of globalisation – the importance of trade, the growing importance of multi-national corporations, the extent and ease of international capital flows, the importance of the spread of technologies and ideas, and the globalisation of production – but say very little about hierarchies of power and social relations. Others in the social sciences, however, emphasise the importance of the compression of time and space as key dimensions of globalisation (see Harvey 1989; Giddens 1984). Distinguishing between place and space, where the former signifies the idea of locale or geographical location and the latter is structured by social relations, globalisation involves the increasing disconnection from place and connection to space. Globalisation is thus defined as 'the intensification of worldwide social relations which link distant localities in such a way that local happenings are shaped by events occurring many miles away and vice-versa' (Giddens 1990). Mittelman extends this conception of globalisation to emphasise the political dimensions of globalisation and the responses to it. He views globalisation thus:

> As experienced from below: the dominant form of globalisation means historical transformation: in the economy of livelihoods and modes of existence; in politics, a loss in the degree of control exercised locally – for some, however little to begin with – such that the locus of power gradually shifts in varying proportions above and below the territorial state; and in culture, a devaluation of a collectivity's achievements or perceptions of them (2000: 6).

The strength of Mittelman's concept is that it provides a framework for an analysis of how agents may respond to globalisation and therefore of the politics of globalisation. Gillian Hart expressly argues against seeing globalisation as 'an inexorable force of nature' (2002: 50) and suggests that even critical readings of globalisation have been disabling for the way in which they have promoted ' "the global" as the site of active primacy' (2002: 294). She advocates a recognition of local politics as a mechanism both to challenge and engage with globalisation. These innovations allow us to view globalisation not only in economic terms but also as a multifaceted process with power relations that produce powerful forces supporting its further entrenchment and also discontents that sometimes coalesce into counter movements.

In this way, globalisation has been linked to marginalisation, a term used in the literature on poverty and social policy to encompass the disadvantages of individuals, households, social groupings, or spatial areas, in terms of some social, economic, cultural or political activities or processes. Marginalisation is most often linked closely to a lack of material resources and poverty and associated with powerlessness and lack of representation and freedom.

What, then, is the impact of globalisation? There is now a large economic literature that empirically explores the effects of globalisation (see, for example, Dollar and Kraay 2000; World Bank 2002; Stiglitz 2002; Sala-i-Martin 2002; Rodrik 1999). This empirical literature, complicated as it is by a range of measurement controversies, does not address the fundamental issues at play. This is largely because answers to this question too often take a homogenous form. For its proponents, globalisation is a necessary development that will enable society to maximise its wealth and bring prosperity to all. For its critics, it is an ominous development that increases exploitation and oppression and plunges societies into the depths of poverty and immiseration. Both these perspectives contain at least a kernel of truth, but their essential weakness is that they speak only to one side of a multifaceted process, which has differential effects among and within nations.

What then are these differential effects? To state the obvious: globalisation has both winners and losers. These winners and losers do not correspond to the neat national-international divide that is so often reflected in left-leaning nationalist literature. The beneficiaries and victims of globalisation are present in both the industrialised and the developing world. This should not be surprising. After all, the defining element of globalisation is its integrative character: the erosion of national boundaries and the increasing drift to a spatially unified universe. Its effects are thus global. Recognition of this, however, must not be interpreted to mean that the effects are uniform across the globe. Indeed, since social structures vary across spatial contexts, the impact of globalisation differs dramatically across regional and national contexts. Peasant-based societies, for instance, are far more adversely affected by the disciplining effects of globalisation than are societies with a high preponderance of skilled workers concentrated in knowledge-based industries.

Globalisation has transformed social structures by reorganising the industrial sector and forcing a large percentage of organised workers into the informal economy; it also reconfigured the class alliances of the post-Second World War period (see Marglin and Schor 1992). In this new era, the domestic bourgeoisie was reconfigured into an alliance with international capital. As a result, domestic labour was thrown onto the defensive and forced into a rear-guard battle to protect the gains won in an earlier phase of the accumulation process (see Held and McGrew 2002). The primary beneficiary of this state of affairs was capital, although this was not universally the case (Habib and Padayachee 2000). This enhanced the negotiating power of finance capital and multi-national corporations, in particular *vis-à-vis* other social actors as a result of the increasing availability of investment sites across the world. The primary institutional casualty of this process was the nation state. Previously it served to condition and constrain capital in its quest for profit. Now capital, with its control over investment and the availability of an overabundance of investment sites, served as a constraining influence on the nation state. Increasingly, it demanded less regulation and more market-oriented policies as a cost for its investment. As the years rolled on, the nation state began making significant concessions in this regard.

Labour, as a social actor, has lost the most as a result of this process of globalisation. The enhanced power of capital, the increasingly subservient status of the nation state, and the transformation in the industrial economy unleashed by globalisation all has taken its toll. Large numbers of workers, particularly in vulnerable industries, have been thrown out of work or into casual labour. Gains won in the earlier accumulation phase around the social wage have largely been rolled back. And the influence of labour over the state has declined dramatically, making it almost impossible to turn the political tide. Of course the effects on labour have not been equally distributed, but labour as a social category has experienced a net loss in influence, members and control over and share of society's resources.

Ironically, as we noted in the previous section, one sector to have benefited from globalisation, or at least from some aspects of it, is the activist layer of social movements spawned in this period (Lambert and Webster 2004: 86; Taylor 2004). The technological and communication revolution has not only made it easier for capital to do business, but has also enabled activists from across the ideological spectrum to wage their struggles. E-mail and cheaper global travel enables activists from different parts of the world to communicate much more easily. The Internet and satellite television facilitate the universalisation of struggles, in particular because the citizenry in the industrialised countries are more easily made aware of the oppression, exploitation and immiserising conditions to which other parts of the world are subjected. As a result, in the last two decades, United States and European corporates such as Nike and Shell have been held accountable for their labour conditions and environmental records in other parts of the world through consumer boycotts and other forms of protest in the US and Europe. International financial agencies, in particular the International Monetary Fund and the World Bank, are continually confronted with street demonstrations at their annual general meetings; these protests are overwhelmingly populated by activists and citizens from the industrialised world. Seattle, Genoa and the range of international consumer boycotts launched against a diverse set of multi-national corporations for everything from the Palestinian struggle to child labour practices would not have been possible without the increasing integration of the world through globalisation (Byers 2000).

South Africa serves as a textbook example of how globalisation plays itself out in the semi-industrialised world. Capital has been the primary beneficiary as productivity and the return on investment dramatically improved in the last decade. The state has been largely constrained by domestic and foreign capital and has, as was indicated earlier, made significant concessions at the macro-economic policy level (Michie and Padayachee 1997). Labour has been the principal loser in this process. COSATU's influence on its alliance partner, the African National Congress (ANC), has been steadily eroding throughout the transition years. Large numbers of organised workers have been retrenched, casualised and/or forced into the informal economy, leading to a further expansion of the burgeoning underclasses. Some workers have done well. Senior managers and certain categories of skilled workers (including professionals) have experienced rising incomes, but they constitute a tiny proportion of the overall labour community that has been on the defensive for most of the last decade (Nattrass 2003).

One distinctive feature of the South African case is that the globalisation process was simultaneously accompanied by a political transition from apartheid to a democratic order. The substantive compromise of this transition was the incoming regime's support for neo-liberal economic policies in exchange for capital's acceptance of black economic empowerment and some affirmative action. The result has been a globalisation process tinged by colour. Black entrepreneurs have become the primary beneficiaries as they have been included in new investment from both foreign and domestic capital, and have been provided with concessionary loans by the state and/or its financial agencies. Skilled black personnel have benefited enormously as the corporate sector has scrambled to meet equity targets in their managerial and staffing structures. Black managers and workers have been prioritised in public sector employment, but black has also been the colour of most of the victims of this neo-liberal globalisation, an unfortunate legacy of the overlap of race and class categories bequeathed by apartheid.

The net effect of this simultaneous coupling of economic globalisation with the democratic transition, what Samuel Huntington (1991) called the Third Wave, has been devastating. According to the Report of the Committee of Inquiry into a Comprehensive System of Social Security for South Africa (2002: 19), unemployment stands at 36 per cent for the overall population and at 52 per cent for African females. Poverty is pervasive and, according to a recent committee of enquiry for the Department of Social Welfare, stands at an astounding 45 to 55 per cent. About 10 per cent of African people are malnourished and at least 25 per cent of African children are stunted (Everatt 2003: 77). Evidence suggests that key indicators, such as unemployment and the number of households without a breadwinner, are deteriorating (Everatt 2003). The level of inequality is also getting worse. South Africa has always been one of the most unequal societies in the world, and the incoming ANC government in 1994 committed itself to addressing this problem. Yet despite the post-apartheid regime's rhetorical commitment to redistribution, the Gini coefficient continued to rise throughout the ANC's first two terms of office (Report of the Committee of Inquiry into a Comprehensive System of Social Security for South Africa 2002: 27). One factor worth noting, however, is that the racial profile of inequality is changing. This is reflected in the fact that the size of the African component in the richest income decile rose from 9 per cent in 1991 to 22 per cent in 1996. The racial profile of the poorest has, however, remained black, leading many commentators to conclude that the present economic dispensation benefits only a tiny elite within the African population. The predicament of the losers in this transition is perhaps most graphically captured in the words of Emma Makhaza in the poverty hearings hosted by the South African Human Rights Commission, the NGO Coalition and the Commission on Gender Equality:

> I am having seven children and nothing to depend on. I am making bricks and sometimes it rains and then I can't do it. And I collect food and take it to people. I fetch wood and collect cans of cold drink and sell them. When I am without food then I go next door and if they don't have then the children will have empty stomachs and I cry. Yesterday I left with my children fast asleep because they will ask me what we are going to eat. I am very thin because when I bought a bucket of mielie meal, I won't eat at all if I am thinking of the children. They say: Mum you are going to die (Commission of Gender Equality et al. 1998: 17).

The Reinvention of Social Movements in Post-Apartheid South Africa

One of the most striking features of social movements in post-apartheid South Africa is that many of them are new, and a number of them emerged from the late 1990s. This is striking, in particular, because South Africa's recent political history is so integrally tied to social movements. Although some may be accused of romanticising the extent and effectiveness of civic and trade union organisation in South Africa during the apartheid era, it would be fair to say that, compared to many other countries, there has since the 1970s been a heightened level of social organisation in the country, especially in urban areas. Social movements in South Africa played a vital part in precipitating and defining the terms of the transition to democracy and indeed the liberation movement was arguably one of the quintessential social movements of the twentieth century (see Figure 1.1, block 1). Opposition to apartheid was, as a result of apartheid itself, necessarily extra-parliamentary. Banned political parties, such as the ANC and Pan-Africanist Congress (PAC), along with the United Democratic Front (UDF), COSATU, NGOs, civics and churches, formed a collective mass of democratic energy, which – in combination with economic difficulties, external political pressure and changing geo-political circumstances – resulted in the negotiated revolution of the early 1990s.

Yet, in a country whose politics were defined by an ultimately overwhelming anti-government movement, there is only limited institutional continuity between the movements of the 1980s and those of the late 1990s. The key explanation for the newness of today's generation of social movements is that old avenues of opposition were absorbed into the post-apartheid government, thus leaving opponents of the government without a 'voice' with which to express or a mechanism to organise opposition (see Figure 1.1, block 2). This marked a change in the political opportunity structure and the repertoires of contention, as well as the activation of new boundaries and therefore new sets of political actors.

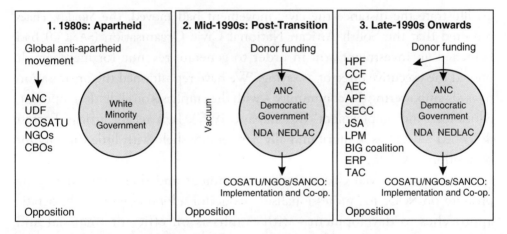

Figure 1.1:   The reinvention of South Africa's social movements.

As we argued earlier, in the immediate aftermath of the political transition of 1994, state-civil society relations changed from the adversarial opposition that characterised apartheid politics, to a more collaborative and development-oriented focus. Unlike the previous government, which did not have international or domestic legitimacy, this was now a democratically elected government that was seen to be 'working on the problem' of poverty and deprivation rather than creating or exacerbating it. Patience was exercised, and although social conditions remained difficult for the poor, communities were not inclined to mobilise (Desai 2002: 1).

Furthermore, even if communities had wanted to mobilise, the institutional environment that historically enabled this had all but disappeared. The organisational mechanisms that had been used to express opposition to government prior to the transition – the UDF, ANC, civics, NGOs – were either now part of the government or operating in close collaboration with the government:

> . . . key activists [took] key jobs in parliament and other government structures. Generally, there was deep confusion in that the civics' mainly oppositional role to the state was now deemed inappropriate, as they were urged to move from 'resistance to reconstruction' (Lumsden and Loftus 2003: 19).

To illustrate the distance the civic movement had moved, the *Sunday Times* reported that the South African National Civic Organisation (SANCO) had launched an investment arm in order to generate revenue for members. It quoted the executive director as saying: 'We have repositioned the organisation towards empowering the community – with the emphasis on skills development, education, and employment' (Kobokoane 1997). In a recent article, Forrest described SANCO as a 'moribund ally', an 'empty shell' with little capacity for opposition (2003: 9).

NGOs, too, moved closer to the government and there was 'increasing pressure on NGOs to "professionalise" – code for adopting more technocratic approaches to development – with emphasis on efficient financial and management systems, and the ability to effect swift delivery' (Marais 1997). Boulle alluded to the danger that NGOs and CBOs were 'falling into the trap of being restricted to delivery' (1997). The mid- to late 1990s could arguably be described as a hiatus in popular and radical activity during which proponents of social justice attempted to internalise their programmes within the state through the drafting of the new constitution, the alleviation of poverty through welfare, and the implementation of policy to redress inherited inequalities.

There were, however, divergent opinions both within the state and civil society on the best development path. As welfarist solutions of the Reconstruction and Development Programme were increasingly seen to be trumped by pro-growth approaches as articulated in the 1996 GEAR strategy, opposition has been expressed through the re-invigoration of civil society and the development of a new generation of CBOs, which seek to challenge the emerging pro-growth consensus.

> These new, emerging CBOs are different from their traditional counterparts. Often they command greater technical capacity and expertise, and slot into networks with larger NGOs. One example is People's Dialogue and its community-based structures like the Homeless People's Federation . . . As well, their rising expertise implies a gradual break in their former dependency on 'struggle NGOs'. Most importantly, they do not shy away from taking government on (Anonymous 1997).

The Homeless People's Federation (the community-based organisation which is part of the Homeless People's Alliance) was indeed the forerunner to a host of significant social movements that were subsequently established (see Figure 1.1, block 3). The TAC (1998), Concerned Citizens Forum (1999), Anti-Eviction Campaign, Anti-Privatisation Forum, Soweto Electricity Crisis Committee (2000), the Landless People's Movement, Coalition of South Africans for the Basic Income Grant (2001), and the Education Rights Project (2002), amongst others, have re-constituted a vibrant civil society.

Contemporary social movements are by no means unitary and uniform. A quick scan of the issues they represent indicates a massive diversity of concerns: land equity, gender, sexuality, racism, environment, education, formal labour, informal labour, access to infrastructure, housing, eviction, HIV/AIDS treatment, crime and safety, and geo-politics. Many movements suggest that they draw from class-based ideologies with notable self-descriptions as: anti-neoliberal, anti-capital, anti-GEAR, anti-globalisation, anti-market, and pro-poor, pro-human rights, socialist and Trotskyist. However, while the material improvement of poor people's lives is at the core of many of these movements, they are by no means limited to demands for delivery or indeed to the concerns of the poor. Some also speak to legal rights, social and environmental justice, and stigmas and discrimination of certain categories of people rooted in everyday society and culture. Furthermore, the acknowledgement of second-generation rights in the constitution allows for material gains to be constructed as rights, and there is increasing blurring between class-based and rights-based struggles.

In addition to issues, social movements vary according to geographic scale. On one end of the continuum, the Concerned Citizens Forum is a largely Chatsworth-based movement focusing its work on Durban. At the national level, the TAC is strongly represented throughout the country, although it may be more active in urban areas. Jubilee South Africa, on the other end of the continuum, is a local office of a global movement. Local initiatives often overcome the constraints of their geographic focus by affiliating with movements elsewhere in the country or world, as was seen in the way Durban's Self-Employed Women's Union with 2 000 members modelled itself on the Self-Employed Women's Association with 700 000 members in India. These and many similar institutions are linked through the global organisation of Streetnet, launched in Durban in 2002. Along with a variation of scale, movements also vary in size. According to Forrest (2003), the National Association of People Living with HIV/AIDS claims a membership of 200 000 to 300 000. Others may have memberships of just a few hundred, or memberships that are difficult to determine as a result of their structural form.

Institutional shape is also a dimension of variation. As we have seen, some are local branches of international movements. Others, such as the National Land Committee, describe themselves as independent NGOs, and yet still others are associations and networks of existing organisations such as the Coalition of South Africans for the Basic Income Grant. Finally, some still choose not to formalise their structure at all and prefer to remain unregistered and informal.

This diversity amongst contemporary social movements in terms of issues, size, institutional form and tactics creates important methodological challenges. Is it fair to say that in all cases we are dealing with the same 'unit of analysis' and that all movements are necessarily of the same category? Can all of these social struggles necessarily be defined as social movements? How do we understand social movements within the global and national context? What are the implications of such movements for democracy in South Africa?

In an effort to address these questions and understand the significance of these movements, a case study methodology was adopted. The research process involved bringing together scholars and activist intellectuals, from a diverse set of ideological backgrounds, to investigate these movements, the social background of their membership and leadership, their operations and decision-making processes, their goals and strategies, and finally their social and political significance. The research generated a voluminous set of information, all of which would be impossible to capture in the pages that follow. The chapters of this volume, then, each of which focuses on an individual social movement, must be treated as analytical summaries of more micro-directed and empirically detailed reports published elsewhere. They are conceptually brought together in a concluding chapter, which reflects both on the political significance of these movements for development and democracy in South Africa, and on the debates in the global academy around social movements, social mobilisation and social reconstruction. It should go without saying that the analysis and conclusions in the pages that follow are founded on the World Social Forum's ambition that a better world is possible and are offered as a contribution to the struggle for the creation of that future.

References

Anonymous. 1997. 'Compromising Positions: Are NGOs Bent out of Shape or Just Learning the Ropes'. *Development Update* 1 (1).

Bond, P. 2000. *Elite Transition: From Apartheid to Neoliberalism in South Africa*. London: Pluto Press.

Boulle, J. 1997. 'Putting the Voluntary Sector Back on the Map'. *Development Update* 1 (1).

Byers, M. 2000. 'Woken up in Seattle'. *London Review of Books* 22 (1).

Castells, M. 1983. *The City and the Grassroots: A Cross-Cultural Theory of Urban Social Movements*. Berkeley and Los Angeles: University of California Press.

Clark, J. (ed.). 2003. *Global Civic Engagement: Civil Society and Transnational Action*. London: Earthscan.

Cohen, J. 1985. 'Strategy of Identity: New Theoretical Paradigms and Contemporary Social Movements'. *Social Research* 52 (4): 663–716.

Cohen, R. and S. Rai (eds). 2000. *Global Social Movements*. London: Athlone Press.

Commission on Gender Equality, South African Human Rights Commission and the South African NGO Coalition. 1998. *The People's Voices: National Speak Out on Poverty Hearings, March to June 1998*. Johannesburg.

Della Porta, D. 2003. 'Globalisation and Social Movements: Hypotheses from Research on the Protest against the G8 in Genoa'. Paper presented at the European Consortium for Political Research Conference 2003 in Marburg, Germany, 18–21 September.

Della Porta, D. and M. Diani. 1999. *Social Movements: An Introduction*. Malden, MA: Blackwell Publishers.

Della Porta, D. and S. Tarrow. 2005. 'Transnational Processes and Social Activism: An Introduction'. In D. Della Porta and S. Tarrow (eds), *Transnational Protest and Global Activism*. Oxford: Rowman and Littlefield Publishers.

Desai, A. 2002. *We Are the Poors: Community Struggles in Post-Apartheid South Africa*. New York: Monthly Review Press.

Dollar, D. and A. Kraay. 2000. 'Growth is Good for the Poor'. Policy Research Working Paper No. 2587. Washington: World Bank.

Escobar, A. and S. Alvarez (eds). 1992. *The Making of Social Movements in Latin America: Identity, Strategy and Democracy*. Boulder: Westview Press.

Everatt, D. 2003. 'The Politics of Poverty on South Africa'. In D. Everatt and V. Maphai (eds), *The (real) State of the Nation*. Johannesburg: Interfund.

Florini, A.M. (ed.). 2000. *The Third Force: The Rise of Transnational Civil Society*. Washington DC: Japan Center for International Exchange, Tokyo/Carnegie Endowment for International Peace.

Forrest, D. 2003. 'Social Movements: "Ultra-left" or "Global Citizens?"' *Mail and Guardian* 31 February: 9–11.

Giddens, A. 1984. *The Constitution of Society: Outline of the Theory of Structuration*. Cambridge: Polity Press.

———. 1990. *The Consequences of Modernity*. Cambridge: Polity Press.

Gurr, T. 1970. *Why Men Rebel?* Princeton: Princeton University Press.

Habib, A. 2003. 'State-Civil Society Relations in Post-Apartheid South Africa'. In J. Daniel, A. Habib and R. Southall (eds), *State of the Nation 2003–2004*. Pretoria: HSRC.

Habib, A. and H. Kotze. 2002. 'Civil Society, Governance and Development in an Era of Globalisation'. In O. Edigheji and G. Mhone (eds), *Governance in the New South Africa*, Cape Town: University of Cape Town Press.

Habib, A. and V. Padayachee. 2000. 'Economic Policy and Power Relations in South Africa's Transition to Democracy'. *World Development* 28 (2): 245–64.

Hart, G. 2002. *Disabling Globalization: Places of Power in Post-Apartheid South Africa*. Pietermaritzburg: University of Natal Press.

Harvey, D. 1989. *The Condition of Postmodernity*. Oxford: Blackwell.

Held, D. and A. McGrew. 2002. *The Global Transformations Reader*. Cambridge: Polity Press.

Huntington, S. 1991. *The Third Wave: Democratisation in the Late Twentieth Century*. London: University of Oklahoma Press.

Keane, J. 2003. *Global Civil Society?* Cambridge: Cambridge University Press.

Keck, M. and K. Sikkink. 1998. *Activists Beyond Borders: Transnational Activist Networks in International Politics*. Ithaca, NY: Cornell University Press.

Khagram, S., J. Riker and K. Sikkink (eds). 2002. *Restructuring World Politics: Transnational Social Movements, Networks and Norms*. Minneapolis, MN: Univeristy of Minnesota Press.

Klein, N. 2001. *No Logo*. London: Flamingo.

Kobokoane, T. 1997. 'SANCO Accepts the Civility of Profit'. *Sunday Times, Business Times* 13 April.

Lambert, R. and E. Webster. 2004. 'Global Civil Society and the New Labour Internationalism'. In R. Taylor (ed.), *Creating a Better World: Interpreting Global Civil Society*. Bloomfield, CT: Kumarian Press.

Lichbach, M.I. 1998. 'Contending Theories of Contentious Politics and the Structure-Action Problem of Social Order'. *Annual Review of Political Science* 1. Berkeley: University of California: 401–24.

Lumsden, F. and A. Loftus. 2003. 'Inanda's Struggle for Water Through Pipes and Tunnels: Exploring State-Civil Society Relations in a Post-Apartheid Informal Settlement'. CCS Research Report.

Marais, H. 1997. 'The RDP: Is there Life after Gear?' *Development Update* 1 (1).

———. 1998. *South Africa: Limits to Change: The Political Economy of Transformation*. London: Zed Books.

Marglin, S. and J. Schor. 1992. *Golden Age of Capitalism: Reinterpreting the Postwar Experience*. Oxford: Oxford University Press.

McAdam, D. 1982. *Political Process and the Development of Black Insurgency, 1930–1970*. Chicago: University of Chicago Press.

———. 1996. 'Conceptual Origins, Current Problems, Future Directions'. In D. McAdam, J.D. McCarthy and M.N. Zald (eds), *Comparative Perspectives on Social Movements: Political Opportunities, Mobilizing Structures, and Cultural Framings*. New York: Cambridge University Press.

McAdam, D., J.D. McCarthy and M.N. Zald (eds). 1996. *Comparative Perspectives on Social Movements: Political Opportunities, Mobilizing Structures, and Cultural Framings*. New York: Cambridge University Press.

McAdam, D., S. Tarrow and C. Tilly. 1997. 'Toward an Integrated Perspective on Social Movements and Revolution.' In M.I. Lichbach and A.S. Zuckerman (eds), *Comparative Politics: Rationality, Culture and Structure*. New York: Cambridge University Press.

———. 2001. *Dynamics of Contention*. New York: Cambridge University Press.

McCarthy, J. and M.N. Zald. 1973. *The Trend of Social Movements in America: Professionalization and Resource Mobilization*. Morristown, NJ: General Learning Corporation.

Melucci, A. 1985. 'The Symbolic Challenge of Contemporary Movements'. *Social Research* 52 (4): 789–816.

———. 1989. *Nomads of the Present*. Philadelphia: Temple University Press.

Michie, J. and V. Padayachee. 1997. *The Political Economy of South Africa's Transition*. London: Dryden Press.

Mittelman, J. 2000. *The Globalization Syndrome: Transformation and Resistance*. Princeton, NJ: Princeton University Press.

Nattrass, N. 2003. 'The State of the Economy: A Crisis of Employment'. In J. Daniel, A. Habib and R. Southall (eds), *State of the Nation 2003–2004*. Pretoria: HSRC.

Oberschall, A. 1993. *Social Movements: Ideologies, Interests and Identities*. London: Transaction Publishers.

O'Brien, R., A.M. Goetz, J.A. Scholte and M. Williams. 2000. *Contesting Global Governance: Multilateral Economic Institutions and Global Social Movements*. Cambridge: Cambridge University Press.

Olson, M. 1965. *The Logics of Collective Action*. Cambridge, MA: Harvard University Press.

Piven, F. and R. Cloward. 1979. *Poor People's Movements: Why They Succeed and How They Fail*. New York: Pantheon.

Report of the Committee of Inquiry into a Comprehensive System of Social Security for South Africa. 2002. *Transforming the Present: Protecting the Future*. Pretoria: Department of Social Development.

Rodrik, D. 1999. 'The New Global Economy and Developing Countries: Making Openness Work'. Policy Essay No. 24. Washington DC: Overseas Development Council.

Sala-i-Martin, X. 2002. 'The Disturbing "Rise" in Global Income Inequality'. NBER Working Paper w8904.

Scott, J.C. 1985. *Weapons of the Weak: Everyday Forms of Peasant Resistance*. New Haven: Yale University Press.

Smelser, N. 1971. *Theory of Collective Action*. New York: The Free Press.

Snow, D.A., E.B. Rochford Jr, S.K. Worden and R.D. Beneford. 1986. 'Frame Alignment Processes, Micromobilization, and Movement Participation'. *American Sociological Review* 51: 464–81.

Standing, G. 1999. *Global Labour Flexibility: Seeking Distributive Justice*. London: Macmillan.

Stiglitz, J. 2002. *Globalisation and its Discontents*. New York: Norton.

Tarrow, S. 1994. *Power in Movement: Social Movements, Collective Action and Politics*. New York: Cambridge Press.

Taylor, R. 2004. 'Interpreting Global Civil Society'. In R. Taylor (ed.), *Creating a Better World: Interpreting Global Civil Society*. Bloomfield, CT: Kumarian Press.

Thompson, E.P. 1971. 'The Moral Economy of the English Crowd in the Eighteenth Century'. *Past and Present* 50.

Tilly, C. 1978. *From Mobilisation to Revolution*. Reading, MA: Addison-Wesley.

———. 1985. 'Models and Realities of Popular Action'. *Social Research* 52 (4): 717–47.

———. 1986. *The Contentious French*. Cambridge, MA: Harvard University Press.

Touraine, A. 1981. *The Voice and the Eye: An Analysis of Social Movements*. Cambridge: Cambridge University Press.

World Bank. 2002. 'Globalization, Growth and Poverty: Building an Inclusive World Economy'. *Policy Research Report*. Washington: World Bank.

Zuern, E. 2001. 'South Africa's Civics in Transition: Agents of Change or Structures of Constraint?' *Politikon: South African Journal of Political Studies* 28 (1).

2

Seeking the High Ground

The Treatment Action
Campaign and the Politics of Morality[1]

Steven Friedman and Shauna Mottiar

IN 2001, WHEN multi-national corporations were meant to be invincible, demonstrators pressured international pharmaceutical firms into abandoning court action seeking to prevent the government from importing cheaper generic medicines (TAC 2001). In 2003, the government succumbed to pressure and sanctioned a plan to distribute anti-retroviral medication (ARVs) to people living with HIV/AIDS (TAC News Service 2003a).

The common thread between these events was the Treatment Action Campaign (TAC): it was responsible for the 2001 demonstrations and played a pivotal role in a campaign to win access to ARVs for people infected with HIV and AIDS. The second victory helped confirm the TAC's iconic status internationally and at home. The TAC and its chair, Zackie Achmat, were nominated for the Nobel Peace Prize (TAC News Service 2003b). It has also been cited repeatedly as a model of a social movement that has won gains for its constituency: it was reportedly a model for a campaign by the South African Council of Churches and National Land Committee for the expropriation of land from absentee landlords (Kindra 2001).

The TAC is a movement that campaigns for affordable treatment for people living with HIV and AIDS. It was launched on 10 December 1998, International Human Rights Day, to 'campaign for greater access to treatment for all South Africans, by raising public awareness and understanding about issues surrounding the availability, affordability and use of HIV treatments'. The TAC says it also 'campaigns against the view that AIDS is a "death sentence"'.[2] It is regarded by many as the most successful of the South African social movements since it is seen to have led the campaign that pressured the cabinet into approving the roll-out of ARVs to people living with AIDS and to have played a role in pressuring international pharmaceutical companies into abandoning their court case against the importation of generic drugs.

Is the TAC a model for social movements? Are its methods effective? Has it developed ways of winning gains that could be adopted by others demanding social equity? And does the TAC offer an approach that enables the poor to claim the rights promised by democratic citizenship?

These questions have ramifications well beyond the important question of how people infected with HIV/AIDS can be heard. Unlike a previous wave of democratisation, the current international spread of democracy has not reduced social inequality: the poor have been unable to use democratic rights to win effective egalitarian policies because changes in the labour market, which exclude them from the formal workplace, have deprived poor people of traditional means of organisation (Friedman 2002). There is, therefore, a pressing need for approaches that enable the poor and weak to use democratic freedoms to win greater equity. The TAC's experience may shed light on possibilities for effective social activism in current circumstances.

The Political Environment

The opportunities and constraints that face social movements are determined not only by their efforts but also by the external environment. Social movement theorist Sidney Tarrow thus proposes the notion of a 'political opportunity structure' to describe 'dimensions of the political environment which either encourage or discourage people from using collective action'. The most salient changes in opportunity structure result from the opening of access to power, the availability of influential allies and cleavages within elites: changes within states provide the openings that 'actors can use to create new movements' (Tarrow 1994: 18).

In post-apartheid South Africa, two dynamics could offer opportunities for collective action in social movements: changes in the political environment and in social conditions. The key change in the political opportunity structure is democratisation since 1994. This opened up opportunities by reducing the threat of repression – and creating opportunities for influence, such as the use of the constitutional court or engagement with government. But it also ended a key reason for popular action, apartheid. On the second score, the growth of social movements is frequently linked to government macro-economic policy that is said to have worsened social conditions, creating new rationales for collective action (Interview, McKinley, 25.05.04).[3] How applicable are these explanations to the TAC?

The environment has changed, creating new opportunities and constraints. But there are strategic continuities: 'Many of us with activist backgrounds are doing old things in a new environment' (Interview, Heywood, 29.03.04). The constitutional court is seen as a resource: but, while the rights that make a court challenge possible now were not available before 1994, the courts were used under apartheid by unions and by activists contesting residential segregation and influx control. And, while an activist accuses the TAC of over-reliance on the law, he acknowledges that the 'TAC has managed to find a balance between (using the courts) and the masses in the streets' (Interview, Desai, 19.05.04). The use of international solidarity, broad alliances and civil disobedience also show continuities with tactics under apartheid.

But despite considerable conflict with the government, the TAC now has allies as well as opponents within it (Interviews, Mthathi, 19.02.04; Heywood, 29.03.04). Another key asset, the support of people who are strategically placed in society, is also a product of a post-apartheid opportunity structure. And apartheid's end has opened the space of activism on HIV/AIDS because it can no longer be seen as a diversion from the anti-apartheid struggle.

Democratisation has also created new strategic challenges for social movements. Winning and retaining public opinion is of greater concern now than during the anti-apartheid struggle when support could often be assumed. The legitimacy of the government and popularity of the ruling party are new realities that activists forget at their peril: 'A major tactical error would be to lose support among our members as other social movements have done when they are seen to be threatening democratically elected leaders' (Interview, Achmat, 19.02.04; see also Chance and Mbali 2004). The TAC is unusual among social movements in its appreciation of the need to change strategic calculations to accommodate formal democracy.

It is harder to see the TAC as a response to government failure to improve the conditions of the poor: it was originally envisaged as a vehicle to challenge pharmaceutical companies, not the government (Interview, Heywood, 29.03.04). But government's failure to address the needs of poor people living with HIV and AIDS may well have created opportunities for activism and enhanced support for the TAC.

The issue on which some of these considerations crystallised is the 2003 civil disobedience campaign in response to government failure to sign an agreement consenting to an AIDS treatment plan. Mthathi recalls: 'Civil disobedience was a difficult decision because it was historically used against a government most people did not support. There were fears that it would make us politically vulnerable if we seemed anti-government' (Interview, Mthathi, 19.02.04). COSATU did not participate because 'we felt our members would see this as an attempt to overthrow the government. It also placed them at risk' (Interview, Mpolokeng, 17.05.04). Decisions that would have been straight-forward before democracy became complicated under democratic conditions.

The TAC leadership opted for disobedience because it judged that the campaign could be conducted in a way that would not lose it the moral high ground: 'We were forced to enter into a civil disobedience campaign because we had exhausted all other means. We recognise the legitimacy of the state and are fully prepared to take the consequences of breaking the law' (Interview, Achmat, 19.02.04). It was essential that the campaign be conducted in a manner that showed that the TAC behaved non-violently and accepted the consequences of defying legitimate laws. The methods used were also underpinned by the TAC's concern to maintain a moral consensus in its support: 'We found ourselves engaging with police officers on HIV issues in their families and communities' (Interview, Achmat, 19.02.04). The calculation appears to have been vindicated: the campaign is seen in the TAC as a success and is credited with achieving the cabinet decision to 'roll out' ARVs (although the evidence for this is inconclusive).

The campaign may indicate the challenges and potential rewards of a democratic environment. It shows that, in a democracy, careful strategic calculations are needed if social movements are to maintain a successful coalition. But it shows too that, if the need to retain the support of key allies and the public is taken seriously, social movements can win major gains under democratic conditions without sacrificing the mobilisation that is their lifeblood.

The TAC and the Government

The relationship between social movements and governments depends to a degree on the nature of the political system – and on the movements' perceptions of it.

Where a political system is hostile to social movements, the relationship will be adversarial – relations between the apartheid state and resistance organisations are an example. Even where movements use levers provided by the system, this will not mean co-operative engagement with government: it may produce what students of the labour movement call 'militant abstentionism' (Buhlungu 2000: 90; Von Holdt 2003). Some social movement approaches exhibit this. The state is seen as an enemy (Ngwane 2003) and the system solely as a source of inequity (Vally 2004). The TAC's approach assumes a more complicated relationship in which co-operation and conflict are employed together. Behind this is an assumption that 'we can win gains from this system – far-reaching reform is possible' (Interview, Heywood, 29.03.04).

This is particularly so since the cabinet decision to approve an ARV 'roll out'. Ensuring that it is implemented is a key TAC goal – its statements on the 'roll out' insist that it is an enthusiastic partner with government in this venture. A critic suggests that 'joining with government to provide ARVs will cost the TAC its independence' (Interview, Desai, 19.05.04). But the TAC and government leaders know the 'roll out' is not the unfolding of a voluntary government strategy but a reluctant response to pressure. Nor has the government displayed great enthusiasm for partnership with the TAC. Given this, the TAC's intention to make the 'roll out' succeed is primarily a means to hold the government to its promise. This could entail further confrontation and court action (Interviews, Achmat, 19.02.04; Geffen, 19.02.04). It is not an abandonment of mobilisation for change but an intention to pursue the battle by other means. The TAC leaders acknowledge, as many movements that have won policy changes know, that, where concessions are reluctantly made to campaigns by governments, ensuring that they do what they say they will do is as much a challenge, if not more of one, than winning the concession.

That said, its strategy on the 'roll out' does indicate an approach to engagement with the government unusual in South African social movements. The TAC's primary goal is not to help the government but to ensure ARVs for people with AIDS. While this may require continued campaigning, it will entail co-operation as well as conflict. The TAC wants the 'roll out' to work, for it gains little if government fails, much if it succeeds. The issue-based incrementalism that the TAC pursues creates an interest in strengthening government that is rare among social movements. Mthathi observes: 'The TAC's relationship with government will always be difficult. But we would like to be engaging more constructively' (Interview, Mthathi, 19.02.04).

The government may vastly exaggerate the threat posed to it by social movements – a senior government politician is said to have told TAC activists it feared being overthrown by the TAC's campaign (Interview, Geffen, 19.02.04)! The government, suggests an activist, 'sees the TAC as political competition' (Interview, Kunene, 24.03.04). This may reflect a wider government fear of 'populist' movements that causes it to overstate their power (Interview, Political Analyst, 29.06.04). But when authorities implement the 'roll out', the TAC's activities become an important resource to them. Just as the Social Development ministry has discovered that mobilising civil society organisations can help ensure that people access the social grants to which the law entitles them, so might a government official concerned to ensure effective 'roll out' come to see the TAC as a resource. Social movement activism can also be an important resource for governments on issues on which they share goals championed by the movements. As long as the TAC relies on government delivery to achieve its goals, they will remain, to a degree, mutually dependant, regardless of the conflict between them.

Making sure that concessions won by campaigns are implemented poses significant challenges to movements concerned with winning gains rather than acting only as vehicles of resistance. The delicate strategic challenge of knowing how to combine co-operation and conflict, partnership and challenge, poses far more complicated dilemmas than the politics of winning the concession.

The TAC does not see the government as a monolith and has allies within it. It has lobbied sympathetic cabinet members, even during open conflict (Interview, Mthathi, 19.02.04). Several interviewees suggested relations with their provincial health departments were good (Interviews, Mpongose, 12.12.03; Mkhutyukelwa, 28.01.04; Ramothwala, 18.03.04; Xaba, 02.12.03) in contrast to tension with national government. A strategy based on using every possibility for engagement with the government clearly presents challenges: 'On the one hand we are offering help to the minister of health and on the other we are saying she is mad' (Interview, Geffen, 19.02.04). But influence depends on accepting the challenge.

The TAC's mode of engagement with government, in which co-operation and conflict are intertwined, is not simply born of convenience. It does also recognise that, while the power of democratic governments could be used against the grassroots, they are elected and so cannot be dismissed as 'enemies of the people'. The TAC's approach concedes that alliances with democratic government are possible and that co-operation and confrontation can be complementary strategies.

The Bigger Picture: The TAC and the Redistribution of Power and Resources

A key function of social movements is said to be the vehicle they offer the poor for exercising power, albeit in a limited sphere (Desai 2002). Does the TAC empower the poor and marginalised? Does it enhance the deepening of democracy and the redistribution of resources?

TAC leaders insist that it gives people, particularly the most powerless, a sense of their ability to become active citizens: 'Our members are not used to thinking of themselves as people with agency and power. Participation in the TAC makes them aware of what they can do' (Interview, Heywood, 29.03.04). The TAC has also become a vehicle for grassroots initiatives (Interview, Mambo, 28.01.04). The TAC's role in fighting the stigma of HIV/AIDS and giving people living with it a sense of efficacy is itself an important contribution to changing roles in society. And basic information on the virus and how to cope with it helps participants take control of a vital aspect of their lives.

The level of grassroots participation suggests that the TAC is doing far more than providing a vehicle for people to find medical relief from a deadly condition – although even that may empower its members (Interview, Geffen, 19.02.04). It offers members an opportunity to become active citizens rather than passive subjects (Mamdani 1996). And this is empowering them to become more active in the TAC. 'Branch members used to keep quiet in meetings but are beginning to participate actively – it started small but then grew' (Interview, Kunene, 24.03.04). The TAC aids democratisation by ensuring that people are better able to participate as democratic citizens.

Winning in the courts is also said to 'facilitate empowerment' of members (Interview, Mvotho, 18.02.04). Gains are thus paramount: 'We do not just want a voice, we want to win our demands' (Interview, Geffen, 19.02.04). At the TAC as well as in the union movement during the 1970s and 1980s, gains are a means by which grassroots people become more aware of their capacity to change their world. There is, however, a widespread view among TAC activists that it needs to deepen its roots in society: 'we are working to make the TAC more visible in the communities' (Interview, Mvotho, 18.02.04). Similarly, there are plans for grassroots members to play a greater role.

The TAC is pursuing a redistributive agenda, albeit one that its critics feel is not thoroughgoing enough. It has, with its allies, pressed multi-national companies to make medication available at lower prices or to give up their right to exclusive supply to manufacturers of generic medicine in exchange for a royalty (Interview, McKenna, 28.04.04). It has also prompted the government to agree to use its resources to provide ARVs to people who cannot afford them. The TAC, despite its focus on an issue not automatically associated with poverty eradication, is working, with some success, towards the redistribution of social power and resources.

The Politics of the Moral High Ground

The TAC's senior leadership readily acknowledges that it has not won major gains because of organised strength in numbers. While it has a larger membership and more organised structure than most other social movements, its leaders and activists in other movements agree that its power lies elsewhere. But where?

Achmat is specific on the TAC's prime source of strength – morality. 'The TAC is not a numbers game. It is more about the ability to create a moral consensus. The button we were aiming to push (in planning civil disobedience) was that the government is morally weak. Morality is usually left to the churches but we all have a duty to be moral. The left needs to give a sense of morality to politics' (Interview, Achmat, 19.02.04). Morality is thus a principle and an important weapon. The 'politics of the moral high ground' is a key resource for the TAC because winning the moral argument gains it and its cause substantial support and weakens its opponents. A company executive notes: 'Whatever we might feel about their campaign, the TAC and other activist organisations did persuade us to see the need for a middle ground between our need for returns on investment and the poor's need for medication' (Interview, McKenna, 28.04.04).

Analyses that assume an irreconcilable conflict between those who wield power and those over whom they wield it imply that the weak can gain power only by forcing the powerful to concede it. Even if a compromise is possible, this can be seen purely as the outcome of a 'game' in which actors use their strategic resources to wield power over their opponents.[4] But the TAC's experience suggests that persuading a range of audiences that the actions of a power-holder are immoral is itself a vital source of power.

At first glance, this is trite: all movements that make redistributive demands seek to portray their denial as immoral. The difference lies in the way in which morality is understood and the uses to which it is put. If redistribution can be gained only by rallying the powerless to seize power from the powerful, movements might see morality as a convenient 'weapon' that can rally their constituency to their cause (since other social interests are assumed to be beyond moral appeal). But in this view, morality is a tactic used for a specific purpose and is not central to the movement's manner of operating.

The TAC's objective has been far more ambitious. Seeking a 'moral consensus' assumes that it is possible to win support, including among constituencies that may be hostile to redistribution, by using moral argument. Thus a government could be morally weak because important constituencies on which it relies are persuaded that its conduct or position on an issue is immoral. Being seen as immoral may also be damaging simply because humans prefer to feel their actions are moral – why else would authoritarians surround themselves with people who assure them they are moral? The TAC approach assumes, therefore, that a small movement with limited organisational power can compensate by appealing to a sense of compassion and fairness across many of the social barriers that are often assumed to impede a common morality. Since morality in this view is an indispensable resource, it must become a permanent part of the movement, not a tactic to be used or discarded depending on circumstance. Paradoxically, morality may be most effective as a strategy when it is not seen as a strategy, but as an indispensable element of a struggle for rights or entitlements.

This has important strategic implications. If morality is an integral part of how a movement operates, it must become essential to all activity – from financial management and internal decision-making to the way in which campaigns are designed – since losing the moral high ground would be to lose one of the movement's reasons for existence. This means accepting constraints that do not apply when morality is seen only as an occasional strategic device.

The politics of the moral high ground requires that tactics be evaluated not only by whether they enhance the movement's ability to force others to do what it wants them to do, but by whether they retain the 'moral consensus' which underpins its work. 'Tactics which show militancy but alienate people destroy that consensus' (Interview, Achmat, 19.02.04). As the civil disobedience campaign shows, this does not mean avoiding all militancy. But action must be morally justifiable beyond the core of committed activists. Thus one activist notes that the TAC's first step in fighting a campaign would be to communicate with government. 'If this didn't work we would consider litigation and failing this we would turn to demonstrations and protest' (Interview, Mthethwa, 03.12.03).

It could be argued that moral consensus was possible only because of the issue on which the TAC organises. In this view, the denial of medication to people infected with a deadly virus morally offends even those who would oppose broader social change. Certainly, health issues are amenable to the politics of the moral high ground: 'Business is far more vulnerable to moral attack on medicines and health issues. Many people see making a profit out of illness as immoral, no matter how much we show that without us people would not have effective medicine,' pharmaceutical executive Kevin McKenna observes (Interview, 28.04.04). But HIV/AIDS may not be the automatic source of consensus that those who hold this view suggest.

So broad has the moral consensus underpinning HIV and AIDS become that its considerable potential to be divisive has been ignored. A moral assault on the TAC position, which began by picturing the demand for ARVs as an attack on intellectual property rights needed for the fight against disease, could have been accompanied by an attempt to portray people living with HIV and AIDS as the cause of their own infection. The racial element in attitudes to HIV/AIDS – racists tend to stigmatise it as a 'black disease' – may have given the government a powerful incentive not to stigmatise victims but might also have given sections of international opinion a reason to see HIV/AIDS much as bigots see conflict in Africa, as a sign of the primitivism of Africans. So the fact that denying treatment to people with AIDS is seen by world opinion as morally repugnant – a key pressure impelling the government to concede the 'roll out' – can be attributed to the effectiveness of the moral campaign waged by a variety of organisations and movements, into which the TAC effectively tapped. It was hardly inevitable that HIV/AIDS would be seen so widely as a cause for sympathy. Activism made it so. If that is acknowledged, the potential for morality to become a key element of campaigns in many other policy areas may be substantial.

The TAC experience shows that the politics of the moral high ground can help win single-issue demands. It does not say the same about wider redistributive programmes. But there are few demands for greater equity on which moral appeals are likely to be ignored by everyone excepting a social movement's constituency. The moral high ground may, therefore, be available to social movements on a wide range of issues, as long as each is approached separately. This implies a need for movements to engage in strategic thinking on potential recruits to a moral consensus – and to analyse potential for recruiting allies beyond their normal constituency for each demand.

Thinking Alliances

Allied to the politics of the moral high ground in the TAC's armoury is a stress on alliances. Alliance politics is not simply a matter of gratefully accepting the support of those who agree. It requires, firstly, rejection of a purism that insists on working only with natural allies: it assumes that common ground can and should be found with those who differ. Secondly, it needs an acknowledgement that alliances – like morality – are rarely cost-free. Where it entails reaching out to those who have different interests or goals, the politics of alliances requires compromises. In the TAC's situation, this is so even in the case of a like-minded ally such as COSATU. Its unwillingness to support civil disobedience disappointed some in the TAC. Nevertheless, concessions were made to retain it as an ally. COSATU says the campaign was called a 'protest' in an attempt to dispel the impression that it was a rebellion against government authority and it was agreed that COSATU's failure to participate would not jeopardise the alliance (Interview, Mpolokeng, 17.05.04).

The TAC- COSATU alliance is a natural 'fit', given their similarity in approach and that some of COSATU's members are affected by HIV/AIDS (Interview, Mpolokeng, 17.05.04). But some TAC alliances required adjustment on each side – such as that with the Catholic Church opposing condoms, which are considered essential by the TAC to curb the spread of HIV/AIDS. In this case, the alliance acknowledges difference and seeks co-operation despite it. Alliance politics does not mean suppressing 'controversial' opinions – Mthathi has insisted on raising the occupation of Iraq in donor meetings (Interview, Heywood, 29.03.04) and Achmat called for the defeat of President Bush at meetings in the United States (Schindler 2003). But it may be necessary for the TAC to adjust its actions and strategies to maintain allies. Achmat insists that his activist past taught 'the development of united fronts despite differing views' (Interview, 19.02.04). The concern to form alliances seems to have become ingrained: in Khayelitsha, local organisers plan to seek co-operation with youth and religious groups, schools and business (Interview, Mvotho, 18.02.04). A social movement activist says a positive aspect of the TAC's performance has been its ability to use the media: 'Even when they brought in drugs illegally, they got media support' (Interview, Desai, 19.05.04). While the media are not a TAC ally, strategy presumably must take into account a need not to alienate them.

A penchant for alliances does not mean working with everyone on any terms. The TAC, in its initial phase, fought heated battles in the AIDS Consortium, the network that brings together all sources of AIDS activism in South Africa, to establish treatment as a key goal against those who favoured an exclusive stress on prevention. The TAC is also accused of refusing to work with other social movements because it fears their militancy will jeopardise its attempts to build winning coalitions (Interview, Desai, 19.05.04). The TAC insists it is not afraid of their militancy but believes that their tactics and approach will not yield change. Almost by definition alliances entail conflict and co-operation, a strategic appreciation of who, on any given issue, is an opponent as well as an ally.

The TAC leadership approaches issues in a way that can be described as 'thinking alliances'. Indispensable to the planning of any campaign is considering where support can be sought from significant constituencies, including unlikely ones. Thus, one rationale behind the People's Health Campaign is the expectation that the middle class has a strong interest in health reform (Interview, Achmat, 19.02.04). Whether or not this is vindicated, it demonstrates an approach that assumes that, without the support of key constituencies, a campaign will be pushed to the fringes of the policy debate. Chances of success, therefore, depend on attracting the support of influential allies. Absolutely indispensable is a refusal to assume that a constituency is beyond reach of a campaign unless thorough analysis indicates this – as well as avoidance of purism in selecting or rejecting potential allies for particular campaigns. And this assumes a politics that sees winning particular issues and demands as desirable.

This propensity to 'think alliances' is particularly important when we consider current constraints to redistributive politics. Mainstream development approaches, by insisting that anti-poverty programmes be targeted so that the 'non-poor' do not benefit, politically isolate the poor and may create conflicts between the poor and less poor, thereby obstructing alliances in support of redistributive programmes (Friedman 2002). Since the poor and marginalised lose influence when they are isolated, strategies are likely to strengthen the voice of the poor only if they transcend isolation. The more campaigns for social equity are restricted to weak sections of society forced to act on their own, the likelier it is that they will be ignored. Since none of the constituencies pressing for equity are majorities, only coalitions can win gains. In principle, the TAC, by 'thinking alliances', is opening new potential frontiers for effective action against inequality by raising the possibility that, on most issues, those campaigning for change can find allies and so win a seemingly unwinnable campaign. While the days in which the poor, organised into unions and labour parties, could win redistributive social programmes by forming durable electoral alliances (Przeworski 1987) may be over, issue-based alliances may be more possible than they seem.

Hands Across the Sea: The International Dimension

The TAC's most strategically important alliance may have been the ones formed with international allies. International support has been important in two ways. It placed pressure on pharmaceutical companies because their head offices abroad feared being portrayed as unsympathetic to the poor (Interview, McKenna, 28.04.04). And the fact that the TAC and other organisations secured international opposition to government policy on ARVs must, given government sensitivity to international opinion, have played a role in winning the 'roll out'. A background in Trotskyite activism taught him 'an understanding of international solidarity', according to Achmat (Interview, 19.02.04).

This is important because, while globalisation is frequently seen as a constraint to collective action for equity, it may be a resource. The claim that states are unable to chart their social and economic policy directions lacks compelling evidence (Friedman 2002). However, advances in communications technology have ensured that ideas and information can travel more quickly than ever. An environment in which a company official can face immediate unfavourable publicity in the North because of actions in Africa offers considerable scope for activists. International solidarity has also given the TAC access to information it has been able to use to campaign more effectively (Interview, Achmat, 19.02.04). A key feature of international alliances in the era of electronic communication is that they can be sustained without significant resources – 'we don't need a direct presence abroad to build international support' (Interview, Morgan, 01.04.04).

But international alliances are also not cost-free. In the same way that the anti-apartheid movement discovered that its international allies felt entitled to a veto over compromises, such as the ANC decision to lift sanctions in the early 1990s, so, it appears, did some TAC allies. 'When we agreed with two drug companies on a formula which made cheaper medicine available while recognising some of their concerns, our allies said we should have taken them to the competition tribunal' (Interview, Morgan, 01.04.04). The TAC leadership insists that alliances need not erode its autonomy: 'We are always careful in our contact with international organisations to stress that we are involving ourselves as equals and are not being told what to do' (Interview, Achmat, 19.02.04). Like the ANC in the 1990s, the TAC has made compromises opposed by international allies. And, while at least one cross-national alliance did collapse as a result of strategic differences, most continue despite them.

The TAC is seeking to broaden its international base by strengthening a Pan-African network of AIDS treatment activists. Passing on experience in coalition building is a key goal since it believes that, in many African countries, treatment activism is restricted to people living with HIV/AIDS and that this isolates it and renders it ineffective. One rationale is a need to share its experience and resources. But solidarity also enables regional pressure for treatment. The network engages the secretariat of the Southern African Development Community and African Union, potentially creating new momentum towards treatment in South Africa and other countries. And the regional focus concentrates on international equity issues such as global trade regulation and its effect on the availability of anti-AIDS drugs. South African trade negotiator, Xavier Carrim, 'says we have made his life easier' (Interview, Morgan, 01.04.04).

This last observation raises the possibility again that activism can be an asset as well as a challenge to African governments, strengthening pressure for a fairer international economic order. While there are few examples of governments seeing independent activism as a resource 'it is too pessimistic to say that activist-government co-operation is impossible', Morgan insists.

International activism remains a key resource for the TAC. It has won it significant gains. But cross-national activist networks have not managed yet to make inroads into what are seen as structural inequities in the international system that militate against adequate treatment for people living with AIDS in Africa. A campaign against the US administration's AIDS policy may indicate that these issues are being pursued with increased vigour (TAC News Service 2004b).

Beyond Race?

Is the TAC able to transcend the politics of race? While left social movement activists might insist that, in the struggle for justice, common interests override racial identity, that is not the view of the Landless People's Movement's Andile Mngxitama: 'To date, what has often happened in these social movements in South Africa is that historically dominant voices – primarily white-left intellectuals – have been the main mediators of the identity and aspirations of the poor . . . we are witnessing the re-inscription of racial domination . . .' (Mngxitama 2004).

That race could be a source of division within the TAC occurred to Health Minister Manto Tshabala-Msimang, who launched a racial attack on the TAC national treasurer Mark Heywood.[5] It occurred also to Thandoxolo Doro, national organiser of the National Association of People Living with HIV/AIDS (NAPWA), who, at a meeting in March 2004, is said to have attacked Heywood and a white member of the AIDS Consortium. A consortium statement questioned NAPWA's motives (TAC News Service 2004a). But, even if these claims are accurate, the power of race may lie precisely in the reality that people can use it to hide questionable motives.

Given this background, it is significant that the attempt to introduce racial division into the TAC has failed thus far. Heywood insists that black members have enthusiastically supported him against these attacks (Interview, 29.03.04). This seems confirmed by the fact that race did not emerge as an issue, overtly or in veiled reference, in any of our interviews at all levels of the TAC.

This does not necessarily mean that the TAC has defied the laws of South African political gravity by 'transcending race'. If circumstances emerged in which grassroots frustration could be linked to the prominent role of white activists, racial sentiments might surface. But, thus far, like the union movement and other activist organisations, the TAC's experience seems to show that people in a society with South Africa's history of racial division can co-operate across race barriers in search of a common interest in social equity.

As Mngxitama's critique implies, however, this does not mean the TAC can afford to assume that, in this environment, 'colour-blindness' is possible: failure to take seriously a history of racial disadvantage could privilege whites whose access to resources gives them a dominant position. If that were allowed to continue unfettered, black frustration would be probable. The TAC is aware of this – it is committed to developing grassroots leadership and recognises that race must play a role in appointments. The TAC has not 'transcended' race, but it is managing it thus far. Continued success will depend on nurturing black leadership.

What is New?

Is the TAC a model for 'new social movements'? This depends on whether it can be seen as 'new' – or, indeed, a social movement. For, if it is, in the eyes of some, the most successful of these movements, it is also different to most others. Activists in other movements say the chief divide lies in its failure to situate its campaign in a critique of government macro-economic policy (Interviews, Desai, 19.05.04; McKinley, 25.05.04). Its frequent use of the law is also seen as distinguishing. It is criticised because it 'seems to work within the corridors of power'. It is seen to rely too heavily on 'a bureaucracy of full-time personnel who could become the decision-makers' (Interview, Desai, 19.05.04) and to distance itself from other social movements: 'They seem to see us as wild troublemakers – they need to recognise that we could work together' (Interview, McKinley, 25.05.04).

But the difference may be more fundamental than differing attitudes – it may lie in the reality that the TAC, unlike many other movements, engages with the post-apartheid system and accepts that rights can be won within it. To use the law implies that it is not inherently biased against the poor. To lobby politicians implies that those who demand equity can find allies in mainstream politics. To help the 'roll out', albeit in a way which may require confrontation, implies that the government can, with prodding, meet the needs of poor people living with HIV/AIDS.

Many social movement intellectuals would be more inclined to endorse this view: 'The post-apartheid state is primarily the guardian and protector of . . . dominant economic interests and the guarantor of capitalist property relations . . .' (Vally 2004). While this view does not necessarily exclude the possibility of reform, it does deny a central element in the TAC's approach – the assumption that engagement with the post-apartheid system within its rules can redistribute power to the poor. Logically, then: 'It seems increasingly unlikely that open confrontation with the repressive power of the post-apartheid state can be avoided' (Desai 2002: 147). In this view, engaging with the state is futile since the problem is not that poor people have failed to assemble the power they need to influence the state, but that it can never be influenced by the poor.

The TAC's strategy of engaging with and winning incremental gains from the state sets it apart from many other social movements, even if it is not unique (Habib 2003: 18). It also categorises it as a civil society association, one that 'interact(s) with the state but (doesn't) want to take it over' (Chazan 1993: 14). This describes a form of engagement with the democratic state that is held to enrich democracy since citizens claim the right to be heard through their associations. It also describes the TAC's approach to democratic government. There is no contradiction between being a social movement and operating in civil society: 'When civil society networks join forces on a scale and over a time span significant enough to force through more fundamental change, they can be classified as social movements' (Edwards 2004: 33; see also Habib 2003). And so we best understand the TAC as a social movement that chooses to operate in civil society.

Seeing social movements as a type of civil society association that relies on mobilisation is not what many champions of 'new social movements' have in mind. For them, social movements are defined by more than mobilising people. Two broad criteria are said to distinguish them – their agenda and mode of operation. On their agenda, one study emphasises that they intentionally seek a far-reaching restructuring of society (Zirakzadeh 1997). Similarly, social movements are defined as 'politically and/or socially directed collectives . . . focused on changing one or more elements of the social, political and economic system . . .' Another definition sees them as 'purposive collective actions whose outcome in victory, as in defeat, transforms the values and institutions of society' (Castells 1997: 3).

The movements may be seen as vehicles of fundamental change – 'the torch-bearers of the new socialist revolution' (Mngxitama 2004). Activist Trevor Ngwane thus talks of the need to 'fight with your own national bourgeoisie' (Ngwane 2003). Alternatively, intellectuals may see them not as attempts to overthrow the existing order but to create an alternative within it (Desai 2002; Centre for Civil Society 2004). Neither view sees movements as a means of winning gains from the state by engaging with it in that mixture of conflict and co-operation employed by the TAC as it operates in civil society.

But the weakness of defining social movements by their aims is revealed when we apply it to the TAC. It is unclear why a movement seeking subsidised electricity for the poor is pressing for structural change, and one which wants poor people to enjoy free AIDS medication is not. And defining social movements by how radical the describer believes them to be is arbitrary. If the TAC is a social movement because it seeks to change the distribution of resources in society, most of civil society would be included. If social movements are characterised by something other than reliance on mobilisation, this something must be more fundamental than their demands.

Social movements are therefore distinguished by some in their mode of action. 'This movement . . . is about creating new forms of organisation . . . It is about creating and enacting horizontal networks instead of top-down structures like states, parties or corporations . . . it does not seek to solicit hegemony as a part of civil society . . .' Instead, it seeks to 'reinvent daily life as a whole' (Desai 2002). For others, refusal to engage in mainstream politics is vital: 'Social movements . . . result from protests against predominant social structures. This implies a natural opposition to established politics' (cited by Sachs 2003: 24) – 'the vote is meaningless unless we can run our own economy' (Desai quoted in Kingsnorth 2003: 121).

Added to this is a suggestion that new forms of action are being employed – so new that they are defined only in the negative. Social movements are thus not an advocacy network, not a labour movement – indeed, not anything the author is willing to define (Waterman 2003: 28). Another view is more descriptive, talking of 'largely atomized and prolonged mobilization with episodic collective action, and open and fleeting struggles without clear leadership, ideology or structured organization' (cited by Fakir 2004: 143). Others talk of multiple, hybrid forms of action. But, while definition is often vague, the consensus is that social movements offer a new form of activism (Cock 2003: 21) – one in which the rules of civil society engagement do not apply.

If this is what defines social movements, the TAC does not fit since its strategies are entirely consistent with those of civil society organisations as understood here. It too seeks to engage with the state without taking it over and employs the methods of civil society engagement – lobbying and coalition building, public protest and legal action: organisations that mobilise people are firmly within civil society if they also engage with the state to win concessions. Nor is civil disobedience incompatible with operating in civil society: openly and non-violently breaking the law to draw public attention to a perceived injustice is compatible with the loyalty to the state and willingness to respect its rules associated with civil society. But if we understand social movements as associations that mobilise people, the TAC clearly qualifies. Thus its activists want it to be seen as a social movement since they associate the term with advocacy and are adamant that the TAC will always remain 'a campaigning organisation' (Interviews, Heywood, 29.03.04; Morgan, 01.04.04; Mthathi, 19.02.04). The TAC is, clearly, a social movement. But it is hard to see in what way it is 'new'.

Much more is at stake than definitions. The stress on 'new' social movements assumes that 'classic' democratic modes of engagement with the state cannot deliver gains for the poor, and that something new is needed. But if the most successful of the 'new' movements is not 'new', the TAC demonstrates that mobilising in the traditional way in civil society can yield real gains for the poor and marginalised and that no new approach is needed. While its stress on the moral high ground, its use of alliances and its tactical flexibility are all-important assets that may provide useful pointers to more effective action for equity in the current environment, none suggest that a significantly new form of activism has emerged. The lesson of the TAC's experience, then, is that it remains possible to use the rights guaranteed and institutions created by liberal democracy to win advances for the poor and weak. The claim that a new form of action is needed is not vindicated by the TAC's experience.

But this too must be qualified. The TAC's experience has much to teach about how social movements or civil society organisations can win single-issue battles. It cannot point to strategies for more fundamental change because that has not yet been its goal. Whether this approach can win the sustained policy changes and programmes that will enable the poor and marginalised to claim their place as full citizens remains untested. But, by suggesting that the possibility of winning allies across divides is greater than we may think, that 'globalisation' provides unprecedented opportunities for cross-national action, and that the politics of the moral high ground and its assumption that all humans have a moral sense and are vulnerable to shame can be effective, it has held out the possibility that organisations of the poor that apply these lessons can make an impact on the structure of inequality as well as its symptoms.

Notes

1. This chapter is an abbreviated version of 'A Rewarding Engagement?: The Treatment Action Campaign and the Politics of HIV/AIDS' which can be accessed on the website of the Centre for Civil Society, University of KwaZulu-Natal and 'A Moral to the Tale: The Treatment Action Campaign and the Politics of HIV/AIDS' (see CCS Research Report 27, http://www.ukzn.ac.za/ccs/

default.asp?3,45,10,2061 and long research report available at http://www.nu.ac.za/ccs/files/
FRIEDMAN%20MOTTIER%20A%20MORAL%20TO%20THE%20TALE%20LONG%20VERSION.PDF.
Information on the informal workings of the TAC can be found in those papers and will not be
repeated here.

2. 'About TAC'. www.tac.org.za.
3. A more nuanced view is offered by, for example, Bhorat (2003). Clearly, however, many people
    continue to live in dire poverty, creating potential fuel for activism.
4. For an analysis that blends both perspectives see Przeworski (1987).
5. The Minister said people 'come with busses and go to commissions where they wait for the white man
    to tell them what to do . . . Our Africans say: Let us wait for the white man to deploy us; to say to us:
    toyi-toyi (protest) here' (MassiveEffort.org 2003).

References

Bhorat, H. 2003. 'The Post-Apartheid Challenge: Labour Demand Trends in the South African Labour
    Market, 1995–1999'. Working Paper 03/82, August. University of Cape Town: Development Policy
    Research Unit.

Buhlungu, S. 2000. 'Trade Union Organization and Capacity in the 1990s: Continuities, Changes and
    Challenges for PPWAWU'. In G. Adler and E. Webster (eds), *Trade Unions and Democratization in
    South Africa, 1985–1997*. New York: St Martin's Press.

Castells, M. 1997. *The Information Age: Economy, Society and Culture. Volume II. The Power of Identity*. Malden,
    MA: Blackwell.

Centre for Civil Society. 2004. 'Finding Ferial's Rebellion'. 29 June. ccs-l@lists.ukzn.ac.za.

Chance, K. and M. Mbali. 2004. 'Chance/Mbali on limits to invoking "false consciousness"'. 2 July. ccs-
    l@lists.nu.ac.za.

Chazan, N. 1993. 'Discussion: Governability and Compliance during the Transition'. In R. de Villiers
    (ed.), *Governability during the Transition*. Johannesburg: Centre for Policy Studies.

Cock, J. 2003. 'Local Social Movements: Some Questions from the "Back Alleys" of South Africa'. *South
    African Labour Bulletin* 27 (6) December.

Desai, A. 2002. *We Are the Poors: Community Struggles in Post-Apartheid South Africa*. New York: Monthly
    Review Press.

Edwards, M. 2004. *Civil Society*. Oxford: Polity.

Fakir, E. 2004. 'Institutional Restructuring, State-Civil Society Relationships and Social Movements'.
    Development Update 5 (1) April.

Friedman, S. 2002. 'Equity in the Age of Informality: Labour Markets and Redistributive Politics in South
    Africa'. *Transformation* 50.

Habib, A. 2003. 'State-Civil Society Relations in Post-Apartheid South Africa'. *South African Labour
    Bulletin* 27 (6) December.

Kindra, J. 2001. 'TAC Model for Land Campaign'. *Mail and Guardian* 14 December.

Kingsnorth, P. 2003. *One No, Many Yesses: A Journey to the Heart of the Global Resistance Movement*. New York:
    The Free Press.

Mamdani, M. 1996. *Citizen and Subject: Contemporary Africa and the Politics of Late Colonialism* Princeton:
    Princeton University Press.

MassiveEffort.org. 2003. 'Red Tape Delays AIDS Grant to South Africa'. 17 April. http://www. massiveeffort.org/showstory.asp?id=1227.

Mngxitama, A. 2004. 'Let Black Voices Speak for the Voiceless'. *Mail and Guardian* 22 June.

Ngwane, T. 2003. 'Interview'. *New Left Review* 22 (July–August).

Przeworski, A. 1987. *Capitalism and Social Democracy*. Cambridge: Cambridge University Press.

Sachs, M. 2003. ' "We don't want the fucking vote": Social Movements and Demagogues in South Africa's Young Democracy'. *South African Labour Bulletin* 27 (6) December.

Schindler, P. 2003. 'South African AIDS Activists Share their Experience and Hope'. Gay City News, *CCS-l digest* 1 (1019) 17 November (ccs-l-request@lists.nu.ac.za).

TAC News Service. 2003a. 'TAC Welcomes Cabinet Statement Committing to Antiretroviral Treatment Rollout'. 8 August. moderator@tac.org.za.

———. 2003b. 'TAC Responds to American Friends Service Committee Nobel Peace Prize Nomination'. 2 December. moderator@tac.org.za.

———. 2004a. 'Condemn the Threats by NAPWA Against AIDS Activists'. 30 March. moderator@tac.org.za.

———. 2004b. 'Invest in Health Not War'. 14 June. moderator@tac.org.za.

Tarrow, S. 1994. *Power in Movement*. Cambridge: Cambridge University Press.

Treatment Action Campaign (TAC). 2001. 'An Explanation of the Medicines Act and the Implications of the Court Victory'. TAC Statement on the Court Case, 24 April.

Vally, S. 2004. 'The Political Economy of State Repression in South Africa'. *CCS-l digest* 1 (1169) 15 March (ccs-l-request@lists.nu.ac.za).

Von Holdt, K. 2003. *Transition from Below: Forging Trade Unionism and Workplace Change in South Africa*. Pietermaritzburg: University of Natal Press.

Waterman, P. 2003. 'The International Call of Social Movements'. *South African Labour Bulletin* 27 (6) December.

Zirakzadeh, C. 1997. *Social Movements in Politics: A Comparative Study*. New York: Longman.

Interviews

Achmat, Zackie. TAC Chairperson. 19.02.04.

Desai, Ashwin. Researcher and Activist, 19.05.04.

Geffen, Nathan. TAC National Manager, 19.02.04.

Heywood, Mark. TAC Treasurer, 29.03.04.

Kunene, Xolani. TAC Gauteng Organiser, 24.03.04.

Mambo, Rosemary. Co-ordinator, Thatnusizo Support Group, Inanda, 28.01.04.

McKenna, Kevin. Boehringer Ingelheim, 28.04.04.

McKinley, Dale. Anti-Privatisation Forum, 25.05.04.

Mkhutyukelwa, Bongi. Treatment Literacy Co-ordinator, TAC KZN, 28.01.04.

Morgan, Njogu. TAC International Co-ordinator, 01.04.04.

Mpolokeng, Jacqui. HIV/AIDS Co-ordinator, COSATU, 17.05.04.

Mpongose, Gugu. Deputy Chairperson TAC KZN PEC and provincial representative to the TAC NEC, 12.12.03.

Mthathi, Sipho. TAC Deputy Chair and National Treatment Literacy Co-ordinator, 19.02. 04.

Mthethwa, Nkosi. Chair TAC KZN PEC, 03.12.03.

Mvotho, Bulelani. TAC Khayelitsha District Organiser, 18.02.04.

Political Analyst, 29.06.04.
Ramothwala, Pholokgolo. TAC Gauteng Provincial Co-ordinator, 18.03.04.
Xaba, Zakhele. Secretary TAC KZN PEC, 02.12.03.

3

Dynamics of a 'Mini-Mass Movement'

Origins, Identity and Ideological Pluralism in the Soweto Electricity Crisis Committee

Anthony Egan and Alex Wafer

YOUNG MEN ILLEGALLY reconnect the electricity supplies of householders and shop-owners in Soweto – on one occasion they even reconnect a police station. Twenty-five thousand people march from Alexandra Township to Sandton to protest the way in which the Johannesburg World Summit on Sustainable Development has seemingly been 'hijacked' by 'the rich and powerful'. Activists from Soweto meet with comrades from Chatsworth and delegates from the Indian Dalit Peoples' Movement and join in a march in Durban that is larger than the 'official' African National Congress/Tripartite Alliance rally at the World Conference Against Racism. The annual general meeting of two allied movements in Diepkloof combine populist socialism and religious revivalism. And 87 activists – many of them elderly pensioners – are arrested after shots are fired when the protesters try to disconnect the mayor of Johannesburg's electricity, becoming in the process 'the first political prisoners of neoliberalism' in the eyes, at least, of the international resistance movement to globalisation (Resist 2002).

These historical snippets and snapshots of struggle illustrate in brief many of the themes and issues, personalities, alliances and collective contentious actions of a small but significant social movement organisation (SMO) of protest, the Soweto Electricity Crisis Committee (SECC). While fundamentally focused on a limited issue – provision of affordable (where possible free) electricity to the poor of Soweto – the SECC discourse and praxis links access to services to a critique of economic globalisation and advocacy for democratic socialism. Though largely under-researched (except Alexander 2003; Kingsnorth 2003; Desai 2002; McInnes n.d.), it has had an uneven yet disproportionate impact on South African society precisely through its ability to network with like-minded organisations and activists.

Yet such a story is only partly complete. The SECC is not one organisation: it is a highly complex and heterogeneous movement, containing variously moments of strong cohesion and survivalist solidarity, as well as a series of tensions and cleavages; small and imprecise in size, it manages to mobilise considerable public and media attention (hence Cerruti's clumsily poetic idea of a 'mini-mass movement' [2002: 45]); organised into over twenty branches across Soweto, it seems at times almost anarchic in structure; born and sustained out of a 'new left' ideology, it remains pluralist, comprising anarchists, ANC supporters and everyday church-goers. In an attempt to understand it more clearly, this chapter will explore some of these tensions through considering the origins of the SECC, the competing identities and ideologies that are forged through the SECC, and the strategies and logistics of mobilising a 'mini-mass movement'.

Roots and Branches: Origins and Membership of the SECC

If it were possible to define a single moment when the SECC emerged, then it might be the protests that accompanied the launch of Igoli 2002, the policy package launched by the mayor of Johannesburg in 1999 aimed at making the Johannesburg Metro Council financially viable. Development in South Africa underwent a shift in emphasis after 1996 when the Growth, Employment and Redistribution strategy (GEAR) replaced the Reconstruction and Development Programme. The RDP had emphasised a relatively progressive set of welfare-oriented policies, and against 'apartheid created infrastructure disparities' (RDP 1995). In the extension of electricity and water services, the RDP proposed free lifeline tariffs, cross-subsidisation from areas with higher rates bases, and a National Electricity Fund underwritten by government (RDP 1995). Tariff structures were to reflect 'relative affordability' (RDP 1995). Crucial to the success of the RDP was the 'democratisation of the state and society' (RDP 1995); local governments were to be responsible for delivery of services, for drawing up programmes to extend service networks, and for engaging local communities in dialogue. Interestingly, Bond has argued that the process of 'depoliticising civil society' was begun even in the RDP, with the assumption that local government is the most effective tool of delivery (Bond 2000: 92–3).

After 1996, ANC policy shifted progressively towards the more growth-oriented GEAR policy that sought to balance social development, the demands of joining a highly competitive global market and the often conflicting stakeholder interests of the ANC's supporters (Friedman 2001, 2004), and regarded by some as a 'neo-liberal inspired policy package' (Bond 2000). These shifts in policy have had unequal impact in terms of benefiting the majority of South Africans. The poorest 50 per cent of South Africans continue to receive only 3.3 per cent of the national income and 45 per cent are considered poor to very poor (Terreblanche 2003; Department of Social Development 2002).

Local government service provision in water and electricity has shifted to a policy of cost recovery, backed up by the threat and exercise of disconnection of defaulters. This is allegedly because such policies maintain sustainable and affordable pricing regimes in the industry (Clark and Drimie 2002). Recent research has suggested that far from a culture of non-payment among various defaulters, many South Africans simply cannot pay for electricity and water (Bond et al. 2002; McDonald and Pape 2002; Khunou 2002; Fiil-Flynn 2001).

In Johannesburg this policy shift was manifested in Igoli 2002. Following the 1997 budgetary crisis of the Johannesburg Metropolitan Council, service delivery was re-organised into self-contained 'utility' companies (such as City Power) that would have to make themselves financially viable. It was partly as a response to this process that the SECC was born. For his opposition to Igoli 2002, SECC figurehead Trevor Ngwane was dismissed from his post as ANC councillor in Pimville, Soweto (Haffajee 2001). He was subsequently involved in 'a series of workshops [in Soweto] on the energy crisis' (Ngwane 2003: 46), out of which emerged the primary organised constituency of the SECC. At the same time, in downtown Johannesburg, a series of protests were organised around the Urban Futures conference held at the University of the Witwatersrand in June 2000. Here, a number of activists linked up with academics and staff of the Centre for Applied Legal Studies (CALS) and the Municipal Services Project. This would forge the SECC's public profile under the auspices of an umbrella body, the Anti-Privatisation Forum (APF). The SECC became 'one of the most active members' of the APF (Interview, Ngwane, 2003), combining conventional protest actions with illegal reconnections ('Operation Khanyisa'). Within six months, the SECC had reconnected over 3 000 households (Ngwane 2003: 47).

The different origins of the SECC suggest something of the different identities and constituencies that make up the organisation. Almost at once one sees two emerging strands: the politically organised and articulate members such as Ngwane who form the leadership core, and the 'survivalist' members in Soweto who make up the membership at the local branch level. To suggest that this poses a fundamental and deep-seated cleavage would be an over-statement. There is a common issue that gives the SECC cohesion, and the more ideologically sophisticated leadership are by and large the sons and daughters of these 'survivalist' branch members. Yet it does suggest a site of possible tensions within the organisation, and it poses specific challenges for mobilising a 'mini-mass movement'.

Reflecting its complex origins, the structure of the SECC has maintained from the start a heterogeneous membership, with varying degrees of commitment to and engagement in the organisation. Core activists, such as Ngwane, no longer hold official positions of leadership in the SECC but nonetheless are seen as its 'public face'. The (mostly young male) illegal reconnectors operate deep in the communities and illegally reconnect electricity supplies for those who have been disconnected for defaulting. Rank-and-file SECC branch members (mostly elderly women, the 'grannies of Soweto') participate in the various branches, some of them holding positions on the executive, and take part in the marches and protests, and sporadically get sent on training workshops with SECC partner organisations.

Publicly the heart of the SECC is the small core of activists who operate from a little office at the Careers Centre community hall near Baragwanath Hospital. Officially, office bearers are elected annually at the AGM, and include many newer members. Yet the founding members still maintain a large degree of influence in the leadership structure, often because they commit time and energy to maintain the momentum of the SECC, which at times threatens to splinter into its branches. Not formally its chairperson, and having no formal office, in fact not even a card-carrying member of the organisation, Trevor Ngwane is nevertheless often regarded as *de facto* spokesperson of the SECC (Ngwane 2003: 47), particularly at international meetings of anti-globalisation activists such as the World Social Forum (Bond 2003). Although the SECC would not collapse 'if Trevor [Ngwane] got killed by a bus tomorrow' (Interview, Cerruti, 2004), his role, together with his comrades within left intellectual circles, sections of the trade union movement and a number of grassroots activists, has been crucial to the SECC. Ngwane is clearly by virtue of his academic background a 'traditional' intellectual, but he has tried to develop a cadre of grassroots 'organic intellectuals' to complement the 'traditional intellectuals' in the movement. He is certainly a highly innovative leader with a strong flair for the dramatic (Alexander 2003).

This small core of activists, working on a single computer from the office at the Careers Centre, arrange meetings, compile and distribute pamphlets to the local branches, organise recruitment initiatives and speak on behalf of a diverse and often elusive constituency. The channels of communication between the intentionally semi-autonomous branches (cf. SECC n.d. [c.2004]) and the Careers Centre office are never direct, often comprising a text message to a cell phone that may or may not still exist. Apart from attending mass meetings and marches, most of the branch-level membership is seldom involved in the other aspects of the SECC beyond their own branch structure. A continuing source of frustration for the leadership is the lack of communication not only with the Careers Centre offices, but also between the branches themselves (SECC 2004a).

Given the informality of the SECC's membership structures, one must rely on impressions to try to gauge its size. Trevor Ngwane's estimate that there are about 7 000 active SECC members (2003: 47) seems somewhat optimistic. One possible way of considering numbers is to look at attendance at recent AGMs – Peter Alexander's estimate for 2003 was around 110 present on the first day and 80 on the second day (Alexander 2003: 9). Similar numbers could be found in 2004. The problem with these figures is that there is considerable overlap in membership between the SECC and APF (particularly among leadership). Nor indeed can we reliably judge the SECC size on such 'events' as the march on Sandton (somewhere between 20 000 and 25 000 demonstrators), which was a broad-based action comprising a range of new social movements as well as sympathisers and, in all likelihood, people who joined the march out of curiosity. SECC members themselves admitted that some branches are stronger than others, with some recording attendances at meetings of 50 to 100 members or associates, while others often have less than 10 members. If, based on the recent AGM Organisers' Report (SECC n.d. [c.2003/4]), there are about 32 branches spread across Soweto, the best case scenario for 'membership' might be between 1 600 and 3 200 members. If half the branches are inactive or have a handful of members, the numbers might drop to about 1 000 active members. There is a realistic understanding that involvement in the SECC fluctuates according to its level of campaigning, which from the evidence seems to suggest waxing and waning cycles of protest.

Having said this, one place where the SECC does come together as a coherent movement is in the mass demonstrations outside council offices in downtown Johannesburg. This is a definitive public profile of the SECC: the highly evocative image of several hundred pensioner-aged women, dressed in full SECC regalia, brandishing umbrellas and whistles, marching through the streets of downtown Johannesburg. It is in this moment of the march, perhaps more than anywhere else, that the SECC is the SECC. For a few fleeting moments there is unity in the crowd. The symbolic value of closing the street for half the day is not insignificant in forging group cohesion and identity within the SECC, if not presenting an immediate threat to those in power.

Another structural problem is that apart from the SECC leadership and the illegal reconnectors who are mostly young men, there are few youth active at the branch level. In the post-1994 city, many Soweto youth seem 'apolitical' or 'depoliticised':

> . . . [T]he youth of today is politically ignorant. You know, they like drugs, they like nice times. They are not politically conscious, because they believe the struggle is over. Everything is fine, we have democracy (Interview, Activist 1, 2004).

Even for those youth who are more politically conscious, the bread and butter issues of the branch-level members, such as evictions and electricity cut-offs, do not capture the imagination, as do more personal aspirations like mobility (Interview, Activist 2, 2004). This points to an issue of competing identities within the SECC, and a significant cleavage in the organisation. Even at the mass rallies and marches this is noticeable. By the end of the marches downtown, some who started the march have disappeared, scattered in different directions along the way; most conspicuous by their absence at the end of marches are the mostly young men from Tembelihle and Orange Farm, 'informal' communities on the outskirts of Soweto, and even more marginal than the township communities of Soweto.

What is clear is that the majority of SECC members are middle-aged to elderly women, which is seldom reflected in its elected leadership profile. Though the 'grannies' are certainly taken seriously by the organisation, which conducts all its meetings in vernacular languages rather than English, there remains an element of male domination in the SECC. This is quite the opposite at the branch level, where the most active members on a day-to-day level are the 'grannies' of Soweto, and most of the active branch structures are headed by these old women.

> It is because it is them who get affected most of the time. To live depends on granny's pension. When rates go up the first person who is going to get affected is granny (Interview, Activist 3, 2004).

One of the SECC leadership suggests that 'the councillors target old ladies', alluding to the threat of evictions and attachment of property that accompany the drive to install prepaid meters, or to extract arrears payments (Interviews with a number of activists from 2002–04). Many old women capitulate in the face of such threats, scared to lose even the little that they have.

> The ANC took the grannies to town to give them food parcels so that they agree in everything that they said to them. On Wednesday [councillor] Kunene said the police will come and people will put pre-paid like it or not. Kunene is still a child . . . the councillor is fighting for his pocket (Interview, Activist 3, 2004).

Given its small size and geographical specificity, can we accurately call the SECC a social movement? The SECC is certainly a social protest organisation, an alternative to the established political representation system that 'mediates' between state and citizens in a context where the established system is seen to fail a significant section of the citizens (Jenkins and Klandermans 1995), drawing on a non-elite base and offering a vision of a new social order, while engaging in politically confrontational and disruptive tactics (Zirakzedeh 1997: 4–5). To clear up such theoretical confusions as 'mini-mass movements', it might be more useful to speak of social movement organisations that collectively constitute a 'social movement' (cf. Touraine 1981; Tilly 1984). Touraine (1981: 77) defines a social movement as 'the organized collective behaviour of a class actor struggling against his class adversary for the social control of historicity in a concrete community': social movement as collective action by a group of social movement *organisations* (SMOs) and a greater diversity of ideological positions within a coalition (as one saw at the recent Genoa protests, cf. Andretta and Mosca 2004) helps to account for such phenomena as non-affiliated supporters and bourgeois intellectuals within SMOs (often figures outside the broad social class of the SMO membership). This perspective helps us to reconcile the SECC's size, structural disjuncture between leadership and rank-and-file, with its clear importance within a network of likeminded organisations.

A network of SMOs engages in a variety of relationships of competition and co-operation (non-competitive co-operation; competitive co-operation; neutrality; and sometimes factionalism) (Della Porta and Diani 1999: 124–7; cf. Diani 1995; Zald and McCarthy 1980). The SECC clearly operates within a network of associate organisations under the co-ordinating banner of the APF (Ngwane 2004). Other grassroots groups openly align themselves with the SECC, such as the Tembelihle Crisis Committee (TCC) and the Small Farms Water Crisis Committee. They have largely emerged in response to the same concerns: evictions, service delivery and cut-offs (Interview, Activist TCC, 2004), with no official membership structure, and wield no effective power yet try to listen to and fight for their community. Such localised groups stretch from Cape Town to Durban to Nelspruit through the 'network umbrella' of the APF. This networking is not simply within South Africa but linked to the anti-globalisation resistance community. Thus, although the SECC is small, poor and (as we suggest below) ideologically pluralist, it has received global coverage through its leaders' participation in a range of international forums. It remains to be seen how the cleavages of age and gender play themselves out within the organisation.

Mobilisation and Repression: The SECC versus the State

In 2002, the SECC chose to boycott the debt moratorium process, initiated in the wake of widespread grassroots refusal to pay arrears electricity charges. The SECC had helped to mobilise resistance to collections by Eskom, the national electricity supplier. After much pressure the state and Eskom offered to make concessions. The SECC did not participate in the negotiation process. The South African National Civic Organisation (SANCO) criticised the SECC for this decision.

> No movement can be in an endgame all the time. Communities will do what needs to be done in terms of their lives improving, not for some ideological end (Donovan Williams quoted in *Mail and Guardian* 5 April 2003).

The SECC retorted that the ANC and its allies such as SANCO have 'used the levers of state to pry what they see as *their* grassroots base from interlocutors' (Ngwane quoted in *Mail and Guardian* 5 April 2003). Yet within SECC leadership circles there is acknowledgement that the decision not to be a part of the process was an unfortunate one. The SECC is consistently outspoken in its critique of government policies, employing a number of contestational strategies. Although 'any [movement] is constructed through political action' (Laclau 2003: 30), the strategic choices suggest much about the nature of a movement. Mobilisation and contestation take a range of shapes and forms, and have at times proved definitive for the SECC.

The SECC has developed notoriety for outspoken critique of globalisation and neo-liberalism. In August 2001, SECC members attended the World Conference Against Racism (WCAR) in Durban. The most dramatic moment in the conference for the SECC and its allies was the unofficial march on 31 August in Durban by the social movements, the largest during the WCAR. This event would be repeated at the Johannesburg World Summit on Sustainable Development the following year – dubbed the W$$D by activists. New alliances were formed with progressive labour movements (particularly the South African Municipal Workers' Union, SAMWU) and the SECC participated in wider struggles over water ('Operation Vulamanzi') and housing ('Operation Buyel'ekhaya'), removing and destroying pre-paid meters in Soweto (Ndaba 2003), and expanded their campaign to include all basic services beyond electricity – water, housing, healthcare, transport and education, with forays into protests against rising food prices.

But if the SECC has had a 'defining moment', it has been the events surrounding what became known as the case of the 'K87'. On 6 April 2002, nearly 100 SECC members, many of them pensioners, arrived at the mayor of Johannesburg Amos Masondo's Kensington home to present a petition and protest against power cuts. When the crowd tried to disconnect the mayor's electricity, an altercation with bodyguards turned into a minor riot and two people were wounded. Police arrested 87 people after the incident, including SECC leader Trevor Ngwane and SAMWU organiser Rob Rees. Smaller opposition parties such as the United Democratic Movement (UDM) and Pan-Africanist Congress (PAC) saw it as an understandable if regrettable result of government's failure to fulfil its electoral promises of access to power for the poor. SAMWU also condemned the state's handling of the incident, as did many local and global activist groups. Through the Internet, socialist and broader anti-globalisation groups called on their members to express their solidarity with the 'Kensington 87' (or K87) and lobby the South African government for their speedy release (SAPA 2002a; Salayedwa 2002; Martorell 2002; SAMWU 2002). Released on bail from Diepkloof Prison a few days later, the trial dragged on for almost a year, until 5 March 2003, when it was dismissed because the testimony of Masondo's bodyguard was ruled unreliable, self-contradictory and incredible. If anything his actions had probably caused most of the disturbance (APF 2003). For its part, the SECC and its allies used the trial and publicity as a vehicle to communicate its anti-privatisation, anti-cut offs message to a wider public. After his release on bail, Trevor Ngwane reaffirmed the SECC's commitment to marches, protests, boycotts and illegal reconnections of electricity and to hold the ANC to its 2000 election promises of free water and electricity for the poor (SAPA 2002b).

Another form of contestation consistently pursued throughout the period under discussion (2000–04) has been illegal reconnection. The high number of reconnections has been the major means of mobilising support. Strict professionalism and integrity in this respect is maintained because part of the performance of this work, the theatre or spectacle of the reconnection, is about extending the solidarity and support of the SECC. As one connector said, 'you learn not to do it in the dark . . . everybody must see who was there . . . don't hide yourself' (Interview, Illegal Reconnector 1, 2004). Such civil disobedience, seen by the state as criminality, is part of the SECC's repertoire of contention, and does much to maintain the SECC's public profile of community service and dissent: 'We turned what was a criminal deed from the point of view of Eskom, into an act of defiance' (Ngwane 2003: 47).

However, in areas where knowledge of the SECC is limited, where the sense of community is weak, or where (like Orlando West Extension) people are slightly wealthier and more able to pay for services, the reconnectors have often found hostility. Some fear 'trouble' with the authorities and Eskom, or the inconvenience of temporary loss of power during reconnections. In such circumstances there is less likelihood of establishing a grassroots-based movement. As one reconnector remarked, 'they put themselves high, because they pay. They think you will make a problem for him . . . but if you do it right, he will realise that we are there to help, not to destroy' (Interview, Illegal Reconnector 2, 2004).

Of course these offer no automatic guarantee of success, however one might choose to measure success. As noted at the March 2004 AGM, failures, weaknesses and perceived threats revolved around sustaining activism and keeping branch commitment to the goals of the SECC. Members, it seems:

> become involved in various activities but fail to report back to the executive and the forum. Activities are therefore not used to allow the organisation to grow but [as an] individual thing. The organisation also needs to develop a mechanism of dealing with the problems from the structures (SECC 2004b).

But this might suggest that the SECC leadership have less power to speak on behalf of their constituency than is acknowledged. The semi-autonomy of the branches may weaken the movement's ability to co-ordinate and maintain a sense of accountability, but it may also reflect the reality of how people in communities construct and contest identity. In this regard, the recent rumours that some of the reconnectors have been charging money to perform reconnections is not insignificant. While publicly claimed as a political action, in the context of economic marginalisation and high unemployment many of the reconnectors regard their work as a job, and an access to resources. The report hints at this division between the 'political' leadership and its 'de-politicised' branches, a tension highlighted by the SECC's concern that many of its supporters remain politically loyal to the ANC.

It is therefore interesting to consider that the SECC has been systematically vilified by the ANC. At the peak in the 2000–01 cycle of cut-offs and illegal reconnections, then Minister of Public Enterprise Jeff Radebe, while proposing a number of reforms to electricity service delivery – punishment of corrupt Eskom officials, streamlined billing, an amnesty for those who reported illegal reconnections and a willingness to set aside 50 per cent of residents' arrears – launched a stinging attack on the SECC as representing part of a 'criminal culture' with a radical anti-ANC agenda (Radebe 2001). His voice echoed many in the ANC who saw, and see, groups like the SECC as not only opponents of its public policies but also the challengers to the ANC Alliance's 'historic right' to represent the masses, particularly the working class. ANC and South African Communist Party (SACP) discourse on the new social movements is rooted in denunciations of a supposed 'ultra left', whose position is unrealistic, 'undermining' the 'progressive' policies of the government (Nzimande 2003; ANC Political Education Unit 2002; Makhaye 2002; Moleketi and Jele 2002). Trevor Ngwane's status as a former ANC member in bad standing, a 'dreadlocked demagogue' (Kindra 2003; Tankiso 2003), adds to the hostility.

The SECC has certainly caught the attention of government and the ANC at local level. Though the government has denounced the movement as criminals, the ANC at the grassroots has perhaps taken closer note. The ANC has, at least semi-officially, noted the need to revive SANCO as a community-based lobbying organisation, revitalise ANC and SACP branches and encourage local councillors to be seen to be 'delivering' lest the SECC, APF and its associates consider entering directly into the realm of contesting local council elections. One ANC commentator, though fiercely hostile to the SECC and Ngwane, presciently avoiding the 'criminal' and 'rent a mob' rhetoric of the ANC in government, noted that 'history bears testimony to the fact that to spark a wave of disenchantment does not require big numbers' (Tankiso 2003).

Identity and Ideology: Inclusions and Exclusions

The culture of the SECC, the symbolic expressive aspects of social behaviour (Wuthnow 1987), those parts of its 'action system' that generate collective identity (Melluci 1995) incorporates its beliefs, values, artefacts, symbols and rituals. Similarly, SECC ideology (in a Weberian rather than classically Marxist sense as the symbolic expression of political behaviour) is that of an SMO within overlapping layers of culture (urban, African, township, new social movement, protest, and left intellectual cultures to name broad categories) that in turn creates its own multi-discursive, disjunctive culture within its membership. Within the SECC, at the level of political culture and ideology there appears to be a series of shifts. Desai (2003a) argues that the 'poors'

> have come to constitute the most relevant post-1994 social force from the point of view of challenging the prevailing political economy. The community movements have challenged the very boundaries of what for a short while after the demise of the apartheid state was seen exclusively as 'politics'.

What Desai tries to do here and elsewhere (see, for example, Desai 2002), is link organisational ideology and grassroots political culture. What we have seen with the SECC is to a large degree a less conscious link: the unintentional disjuncture between a sophisticated critique of neo-liberal globalisation and cost-recovery processes, which only occasionally coincides with a grassroots communal-family 'ideology' of survivalism and identities of daily material realities, linked at times to popular religiosity.

There is little evidence that SECC members at the branch level see themselves as part of a general resistance to neo-liberalism or the vanguard of a populist new left alternative to the ANC – most SECC members after all voted for the ANC in the 2004 general election, as the SECC/APF leadership implicitly acknowledged by not calling explicitly for a stayaway. In contrast to the political and academic backgrounds of some of the founding members of the SECC, the majority of branch-level members are probably less educated. They articulate their concerns as immediate and material, related to their daily lives rather than abstract ideas about privatisation and globalisation. In fact, one concern of the leadership is to educate the branches about these concepts, and to show how these ideas do impact upon peoples' daily lives (Interview, SECC Organiser, 2004).

> They know something of that [privatisation and globalisation] at the APF. I am still a learner. I cannot tell somebody about it. I can say I am getting help for the level that I am at. Whatever I hear I will cram it . . . it is my pleasure to see that nobody is living in darkness (Interview, SECC Branch Member, 2004).

In Soweto, electricity is important because 'life is hard without it' (Interviews, various SECC activists, 2004). In the context of post-apartheid Soweto, and promises made by the Metro mayor for affordable basic services for all, electricity is understood to be a right that is due to the grannies of Soweto, most of the members that make up the SECC. In this respect, electricity is symbolic of what it means to have dispensed with apartheid. For most SECC members at branch level, trying to survive and make 'Granny's [monthly R1 000.00] pension' keep eight people alive, the branches are the primary expression of discontent, and reflect the everydayness of post-apartheid Soweto. The SECC branch meetings take place in local school halls or community centres. These are places that people are generally familiar with, and may have some significance other than simply being local spaces to gather. They are places to which people can and must walk, and the journey itself is often an important activity itself; members sometimes meet up along the way and discuss anything from electricity cut-offs to family dramas. The fact that it affects 'us all' is the glue that binds members. The meetings affirm and reiterate the daily lives of those that are involved and make up the branch, and act in some way as a support network for people in the local community.

Many of the branch members of the SECC are church-goers, and there is often an invocation of similar language to talk about the SECC and the church. Certainly, the church occupies an important place for many of the branch members, and in the Chiawelo branch, the meetings are held in a local church.

> Most mornings I go to church. If I don't I feel something. After church
> I can meet my friend, maybe go to a meeting . . . SECC is physical; church
> is spiritual. In prayer, they say pray and God will help those who do
> practical things (Interview, SECC Branch Member, 2004).

Branch meetings usually begin with prayers and hymns are interspersed with 'struggle' songs (sung with great gusto and familiarity). And many grassroots activists express their anger at their conditions as well as their sense of enthusiasm for the SECC in religious terms. However, unlike in the anti-apartheid period, protest rooted in popular religiosity has not created a new political 'theology of reconnection'. This may be because most 'progressive' theologians are still picking over the bones of the Truth and Reconciliation Commission for their inspirations. Others may have moved on to more 'serious' stuff, and a few are now in government. The lived religious spirituality of ordinary SECC activists (and their counterparts in other SMOs) has yet to be given written symbolic expression. Many of the local churches in Soweto are selling salvation in the afterlife, and do not provide a context for political and community mobilisation, as they did in the 1980s.

There is a further popular element, of looking backwards to the anti-apartheid struggle, the tradition of UDF/COSATU community mobilisation before the ANC 'sold out' to the World Bank and International Monetary Fund (IMF). 'Struggle' culture, including many of its cultural artefacts and symbols (including music, songs and the distinctive SECC T-shirt that uncannily and possibly deliberately resembles the SACP/COSATU T-shirt) has been re-appropriated. 'The ANC taught us how to protest,' explains Ngwane about the sense of satisfaction that many of the old ladies took from cutting off the mayor's electricity in April 2002 (Interview, Ngwane, 2003). This performance is a significant weapon in the repertoire of the SECC, having cut off many local councillors in the past (Interviews, various SECC activists, 2004). Yet there is also a sense of frustration and despondency at times. 'We fought for this before,' claimed one informant, 'why must we fight again?' (Interview, Activist 3, 2004). This reference to the struggles of the 1980s is a source of cultural continuity and an assertion of popular legitimacy, but may backfire on the SECC by further alienating it from sympathetic elements within the Tripartite Alliance (Barchiesi 2004: 35).

Although supposedly pursuing the 'dream of socialism' (SECC n.d. [c.2004]: section 1.2), the leadership's own ideology is complex. If anything it is multi-layered, self-consciously non-sectarian, welcoming members of all or no political parties into the fold: the underlying issues revolve around what Desai (2003b) calls 'the politics of the immediate', a politics of survival for the poor that unites the 'grannies of Soweto' with the illegal re-connecters with Trevor Ngwane and his APF comrades. This is not surprising, given the diversity of its membership. Such a politics of respect and recognition of diversity within communities expresses what Desai (2003b) has dubbed the essence of the South African 'new left'. As Flacks (2004: 145) notes:

> Ideologically committed activists frequently have taken leadership in single-issue causes and campaigns while, at least initially, seeing those causes as mere steps towards more ultimate ends, rather than ends in themselves.

The dominant daily SECC discourse seems more rooted in notions of economic rights and the South African Constitution, claiming legitimacy in terms of their existence as the 'pensioners of Soweto' (Field notes, February 2004). There is no right to free electricity in the Bill of Rights, though according to a study by CALS there may be some grounds to challenge electricity pricing under the constitution (Roux and Vahle 2002). It remains unclear how successful the SECC would be in such a constitutional challenge. The chairperson's report, having savaged 'bourgeois politics', argued that, once the SECC and other movements had built up a more solid political base in Soweto, a shift to participation in elections might occur (SECC 2004b). This would be a new direction for the SECC and APF, and a great risk. Could it succeed in the face of a hegemonic

ANC? With the networks forged by the leadership with other social movement organisations, such a party might offer an alternative to current political parties (McKinley 2004; Harvey 2002a, 2004). The unknown factor is how far the SECC could take its diverse and illusive constituency, and whether the many 'poors' of Soweto would in fact choose such an alternative.

Conclusion

> [. . . social] movements are 'plural and diversified', 'un-representable and unpredictable', and 'express a qualitatively new level of the struggle, a level in which life itself is the stake' . . . which threaten not only state control but also the established left's understanding of struggle and politics (Greenstein 2003).

The leadership of the SECC tends to understand their role as providing localised resistance to the ideology of 'cost recovery' and neo-liberal policies in South Africa. In this regard, the SECC has been somewhat successful in so far as it has built a public profile on consistent critique of government policy, and turned the electricity crisis into a political issue. This, despite its fairly small size, loose structure and disjuncture between its base and leadership. Such strategic resourcefulness can (sometimes at least) overcome institutional power. Drawing on a combination of leadership and sound organisation, rooted in deliberation among members, using resources to mobilise multiple constituencies, and based on strict accountability, Ganz (2004: 177) argues that:

> [o]rganizations can compensate for lack of economic, political, or cultural resources with creative strategy, a function of the motivation, access to a diversity of salient information, and heuristic facility with which their leadership teams interact with their environment . . . People can generate the power to resolve grievances not only if those with power decide to use it on their behalf, but also if they can develop the capacity to outthink and outlast opponents – a matter of leadership and organization.

Yet the SECC remains a diverse and heterogeneous organisation. Spread over twenty branches across Soweto, and containing within it a broad set of ideological and cultural origins, it is unclear how the cleavages of age, gender and political identity will play themselves out within the organisation. Moreover, the relationship between the SECC and other organisations remains tentative. The relationship with the APF represents the solidification of a 'new left' political identity at the level of leadership, but the impact at the branch level, where issues are expressed far more in material immediacy, remains lukewarm. The SECC consistently berates government economic policies publicly, but has so far been unable to mobilise support for contesting local elections. In the meantime, the SECC continues to exist in its most potent form at the branch level, organised around local campaigns of resistance and the everyday realities such as illegality, church and electricity.

References

Alexander, P. 2003. 'Anti-Globalisation Movements, Identity and Leadership: Trevor Ngwane and the Soweto Electricity Crisis Committee'. Paper for the South African Sociological Association, 27 June – 1 July, Durban.

ANC Political Education Unit. 2002. 'Contribution to the NEC/NWC Response to the "Cronin Interview" on the Issue of Neoliberalism'. Pamphlet. September.

Andretta, M. and L. Mosca. 2004. 'Understanding the Genoa Protest'. In R. Taylor (ed.), *Creating a Better World: Interpreting Global Civil Society*. Bloomfield, CT: Kumarian Press.

APF. 2003. 'There is No Case Against the Kensington 87!'. Anti-Privatisation Forum Press Statement, 8 April. http://www.apf.org.za/htm/030123.htm.

Banda, C. 2003. 'Eskom Writes off R1.4bn for Joburg Townships'. *The Star* 1 May.

Barchiesi, F. 2004. *Classes, Multitudes and the Politics of Community Movements in Post-Apartheid South Africa.* Centre for Civil Society Research Report No. 20. Durban: University of KwaZulu-Natal.

Bodibe, O., P. Craven and V. Mda. 2002. 'The Politics of Paranoia'. *Mail and Guardian* 1 November.

Bond, P. 2000. *Elite Transition: From Apartheid to Neoliberalism in South Africa*. Pietermaritizburg: University of Natal Press.

——. 2001. *Against Global Apartheid: South Africa Meets the World Bank, IMF and International Finance*. Cape Town: University of Cape Town Press.

——. 2002a. 'An Answer to Marketization: Decommodification and the Assertion of Rights to Essential Services'. *Multinational Monitor* 23 (7/8). http: //multinationalmonitor.org/mm2002/02july-aug/july-aug02corp3.html, 29 October 2003.

——. 2002b. *Unsustainable South Africa: Environment, Development and Social Protest*. Pietermaritzburg: University of Natal Press.

——. 2003. 'Two Trevors Go to the Forums: Soweto Embraced By Brazil – Pretoria Shunned in Switzerland'. *The Sowetan* 7 February.

——. 2004. *Talk Left, Walk Right: South Africa's Frustrated Global Reforms*. Pietermaritzburg: University of KwaZulu-Natal Press.

Bruggemans, C. 2003. *Change of Pace: South Africa's Economic Revival*. Johannesburg: Witwatersrand University Press.

Cerruti, C. 2002. 'Masondo, somyagazisa malele: Masondo we'll shake you while you sleep – a favourite song in our cell'. *South African Labour Bulletin* 26 (3): 44–5.

Clark, A. and S. Drimie. 2002. *Energy Sustainability for South Africa's Poor.* Cape Town: HSRC.

Daniels, G. 2001a. 'Soweto Power Cuts to be Challenged. *Mail and Guardian* 6 April.

———. 2001b. 'Electricity Crisis Deepens'. *Mail and Guardian* 8 June.

Della Porta, D. and M. Diani. 1999. *Social Movements: An Introduction.* Oxford: Blackwell.

Department of Social Development. 2002. *Transforming the Present – Protecting the Future: Report of the Committee of Inquiry into a Comprehensive System of Social Security for South Africa.* Pretoria: Government Printers.

Desai, A. 2002. *We are the Poors: Community Struggles in Post-Apartheid South Africa.* New York: Monthly Review Press.

———. 2003a. 'Neoliberalism and Resistance in South Africa'. *Monthly Review* 54 (8) January. http: // www.monthlyreview.org/0103desai.htm.

———. 2003b. 'The New Tools of Liberation in South Africa: Interview with Ashwin Desai'. *Z Magazine* 16 (3) March. http: //zmagsite.org/Mar2003/wrenprint0303.html.

Diani, M. 1995. *Green Networks: A Structural Analysis of the Italian Environmental Movement.* Edinburgh: Edinburgh University Press.

Fiil-Flynn, M. 2001. 'The Electricity Crisis in Soweto'. Queen's University Municipal Services Project Occasional Papers Series No. 4.

Fine, B., and Z. Rustomjee. 1996. *The Political Economy of South Africa: From Minerals-Energy Complex to Industrialisation.* Johannesburg: Witwatersrand University Press.

Flacks, R. 2004. 'Knowledge for What? Thoughts on the State of Social Movement Studies'. In J. Goodwin and J.M. Jasper (eds), *Rethinking Social Movements: Structure, Meaning, and Emotion.* Lanham: Rowman and Littlefield.

Friedman, S. 2001. 'Equality in the Age of Informality: Labour Markets and Redistributive Politics in South Africa'. Unpublished paper, University of Cape Town.

———. 2004. 'An Act of the Will: Manuel and the Politics of Growth'. In R. Parsons (ed.), *Manuel, Markets and Money: Essays in Appraisal.* Cape Town: Double Storey.

Gamson, W. 1990. *Strategy of Social Protest.* Homewood, ILL: Dorsey Press.

Gamson, W. and A. Modigliani. 1989. 'Media Discourse and Public Opinion on Nuclear Power: A Constructionist Approach'. *American Journal of Sociology* 95 (1): 1–37.

Ganz, M. 2001. 'The Power of Story in Social Movements'. Unpublished paper for the Annual Meeting of the American Sociological Association, Anaheim, California, August.

———. 2004. 'Why David Sometimes Wins: Strategic Capacity in Social Movements'. In J. Goodwin and J.M. Jasper (eds), *Rethinking Social Movements: Structure, Meaning, and Emotion.* Lanham: Rowman and Littlefield.

Gramsci, A. 1971. *Selections from the Prison Notebooks.* London: Lawrence and Wishart.

Greenstein, R. 2003. *State, Civil Society and the Reconfiguration of Power in Post-Apartheid South Africa.* Centre for Civil Society Research Report No. 8. Durban: University of KwaZulu-Natal.

Haffajee, F. 2001. 'From Seattle to Soweto'. *New Internationalist* 338 (September). http: //www.newint.org/ issue338/from.htm.

———. 2004. 'Fact, Fiction and the New Left'. *Mail and Guardian* 11 June.

Harvey, E. 2002a. 'Getting to Grips with a New Workers' Party'. *South African Labour Bulletin* 26 (1): 15–19.

———. 2002b. 'A Taste of the Jackboot of the New Ruling Elite?'. *South African Labour Bulletin* 26 (3): 41–3.

———. 2004. '. . . but not without Cosatu'. *Mail and Guardian* 14 May.

Jenkins, J.C. and B. Klandermans. 1995. 'The Politics of Social Protest'. In J.C. Jenkins and B. Klandermans (eds), *The Politics of Social Protest: Comparative Perspectives on States and Social Movements*. London: UCL Press.

Khunou, G. 2002. '"Massive Cut-offs": Cost Recovery and Electricity Services in Diepkloof, Soweto'. In D.A. McDonald and J. Pape (eds), *Cost Recovery and the Crisis of Service Delivery in South Africa*. Cape Town and London: HSRC and Zed Books.

Kindra, J. 2001a. 'The Rich should Subsidise the Poor'. *Mail and Guardian* 8 June.

———. 2001b. 'Crisis as Eskom faces R1bn in Electricity Arrears'. *Mail and Guardian* 28 September.

———. 2003. 'Dreadlocks and Demagogues'. *Mail and Guardian* 4 July.

Kingsnorth, P. 2003. *One No, Many Yesses: A Journey to the Heart of the Global Resistance Movement*. London: The Free Press.

Laclau, E. 2003. 'Can Immanence Explain Social Struggles?'. In P. Passavant and J. Dean (eds), *Empire's New Clothes: Reading Hardt and Negri*. London: Routledge.

Makhaye, D. 2002. 'Left Factionalism and the NDR: The ANC Must Respond to Professionals of the Left'. *ANC Today* 29 November. http: //www.anc.org.za.

Martorell, J. 2002. 'Soweto Activists Arrested in Demonstration against Electricity Cut-offs'. *In Defence of Marxism* 10 April.

McAdam, D. 1982. *Political Process and the Development of Black Insurgency*. Chicago: University of Chicago Press.

McDonald, D.A. and J. Pape (eds). 2002. *Cost Recovery and the Crisis of Service Delivery in South Africa*. Cape Town and London: HSRC and Zed Books.

McInnes, P. n.d. 'Making the Kettle Boil: Socio-Economic Rights and Community Struggles for Affordable Water and Electricity Services in Soweto'. MA thesis, University of the Witwatersrand (in progress).

McKinley, D.T. 1997. *The ANC and the Liberation Struggle: A Critical Political Biography*. London: Pluto Press.

———. 2004. 'New Power to the People . . .'. *Mail and Guardian* 14 May.

Melluci, A. 1995. 'The Process of Collective Identity'. In H. Johnston and B. Klandermans (eds), *Social Movements and Culture*. London: UCL Press.

Moleketi, J. and J. Jele. 2002. 'Two Strategies of the National Liberation Movement in the Struggle for the Victory of the National Democratic Revolution'. Discussion document. Johannesburg: ANC.

Ndaba, B. 2003. 'Electricity Meters Ripped Out in Soweto'. *The Star* 14 November.

Ngwane, T. 2003. 'Sparks in the Township: Interview with Trevor Ngwane'. *New Left Review* 22 (July/ August): 37–56.

———. 2004. 'Organisational Report of the APF for the Year 2003'. 10 September. http: //www.apf.org.za/ article.php3?id_article=47.

Nzimande, B. 2003. 'New Possibilities for a Progressive Global Politics'. *Umsebenzi* March. http:// www.sacp.org.za.

Radebe, J. 2001. 'Speech of Jeff Radebe, Minister of Public Enterprises, at the Workshop on Service Delivery Framework held at Megawatt Park Conference Room'. 30 November. http:// www.polity.org.za/html/govdocs/speeches/2001/sp1130.html.

RDP. 1995. *The Reconstruction and Development Programme*. Pretoria: Government Printers.

Resist. 2002. 'The First Political Prisoners of Neo-Liberalism'. *Resist* August. http: //www.resist.org.uk/ reports/background/soweto.html.

Roux, T. and R. Vahle. 2002. *Electricity Rights in Soweto: An Analysis of Possible Legal Arguments*. Johannesburg: Centre for Applied Legal Studies, University of the Witwatersrand.

Salayedwa, A. 2002. 'Attack on Mayor's House'. *Business Day* 8 April.

SAMWU. 2002. 'Union Demands Release of SAMWU Organiser and Soweto Electricity Crisis Committee Protesters'. South African Municipal Workers' Union Press Statement 8 April. http: //nologo.org/ newswire/02/04/12/1647204.shtml.

SAPA. 2002a. 'Angry Mob Trashes Jo'burg Mayor's Home'. 8 April.

———. 2002b. 'Fight for Free Water, Electricity in Soweto not over'. 16 April.

SECC. 2004a. 'SECC Overall Struggle'. Soweto Electricity Crisis Committee/Anti-Privatisation Forum, 3rd Annual General Meeting, Diepkloof Hall, 6 March.

———. 2004b. 'Chairperson's Report'. SECC/APF 3rd Annual General Meeting, Diepkloof Hall, 6 March.

———. n.d. [c.2004]. 'Constitution of the Soweto Electricity Crisis Committee'.

———. n.d. [c. 2003/4]. 'SECC Organiser's Report'.

Tankiso, Cde. 2003. 'Beyond Dreadlocks and Demagogy'. *Umrabulo* 18 June. http: //www.anc.org.za/ ancdocs/pubs/umrabulo/umrabulo18/beyond.html.

Terreblanche, S. 2003. *A History of Inequality in South Africa 1652–2002*. Pietermaritzburg: University of Natal Press.

Tilly, C. 1978. *From Mobilization to Revolution*. Reading, MA: Addison-Wesley.

———. 1984. 'Social Movements and National Politics'. In C. Bright and S. Harding (eds), *Statemaking and Social Movements*. Ann Arbor: University of Michigan Press.

Tilly, C., L. Tilly and R. Tilly. 1975. *The Rebellious Century*. Cambridge, MA: Harvard University Press.

Touraine, A. 1981. *The Voice and the Eye: An Analysis of Social Movements*. Cambridge: Cambridge University Press.

Wuthnow, R. 1987. *Meaning and Moral Order: Explanations in Cultural Analysis*. Berkeley, CA: University of California Press.

Zald, M. and J.D. McCarthy. 1980. 'Social Movement Industries: Competition and Cooperation Among Movement Organizations'. In L. Kriesberg (ed.), *Research in Social Movements: Conflict and Change* Volume 3. Greenwich, CT: JAI Press.

Zirakzedeh, C.E. 1997. *Social Movements in Politics: A Comparative Study*. London and New York: Addison-Wesley Longman.

Interviews

Numerous interviews were conducted over an eighteen-month period, with activists, local branch members and illegal reconnectors, as well as members of associated organisations. In the light of the need to protect the confidentiality of our subjects, we decided, with a few exceptions, to preserve their anonymity and not to specify the dates or places where they were interviewed. Only those quoted in this chapter are listed below. No subjects were interviewed outside the Greater Johannesburg (Johannesburg-Soweto) area.

Activist 1. SECC, 2004.

Activist 2. SECC, 2004.

Activist 3. SECC, 2004.

Activist. Tembelihle Crisis Committee, 2004.

Branch Member. SECC, 2004.

Cerruti, Claire. Activist with Keep Left, 2004.

Illegal Reconnector 1. SECC, 2004.

Illegal Reconnector 2. SECC, 2004.

Ngwane, Trevor. Founding member of Soweto Electricity Crisis Committee/Organiser for the Anti-Privatisation Forum, 2003.

4

Upstarts or Bearers of Tradition?

The Anti-Privatisation Forum of Gauteng[1]

Sakhela Buhlungu

THE ADVENT OF democracy has resulted in the proliferation of movements representing a wide range of constituencies and interests in South Africa. Many of these movements were formed or operate outside the auspices of the former liberation movements and other civil society organisations of the struggle era. For this reason, some observers and activists have styled them 'new social movements' to underline the fact that they represent new constituencies facing new issues in post-apartheid South Africa. One of these 'new' social movements is the Anti-Privatisation Forum (APF), an umbrella organisation that has gained prominence since its formation in 2000. This chapter examines the organisational and political trajectory of the APF over the first five years of its existence.

Social Movements and Social Change in South Africa

The struggle for liberation in South Africa was fought on different fronts by a multiplicity of social forces organised into different organisations and movements. Indeed, the South African struggle differs from struggles on the rest of the African continent in two fundamental respects. On the one hand, it differs from those struggles where the liberation movements remained legal and were so dominant in the struggle that they crowded out or absorbed civil society movements. This observation applies to liberation movements during the late 1950s and the 1960s. The dominant discourse at the time was the construction of liberation, movement-led 'state-centred development coalitions' (Beckman 1998) oriented towards winning state power. During the political transition and after independence even those movements that operated outside the orbit of the liberation movements were either absorbed or marginalised.

On the other hand, South Africa differs from those countries where liberation movements were outlawed but continued in exile or underground or where they opted for this route even though they were not banned. In the majority of such cases, the preferred method of achieving change was the armed struggle and all other efforts were subordinated to it. This approach was most common among liberation movements in countries that achieved freedom from the 1970s onwards. Once again, the dominant discourse was a statist one with the main liberation movement at the helm.

In explaining the political trajectory of these and other countries, Frederick Cooper (1996) has argued that what this represented was a tension between political projects (in the form of liberation movements) and social projects (in this case labour movements). He argues that this tension is useful for understanding why African countries ended up with the kind of liberation they got, namely, 'politically assertive and socially conservative regimes focused on their control of the coercive, patronage, and symbolic apparatus of the state, distrustful of and hostile to the continued influence of social movements that had once helped challenge the colonial state, fearful of groups that might make claims' (Cooper 1996: 5).

While it may be possible that South Africa will follow this trajectory, a notable difference with South Africa is that the banning of the liberation movements created spaces within which new movements and struggles emerged *independently* of the banned movements. Three phases of struggle can be delineated and, significantly, all activists and movements that emerged during these phases positioned themselves to the left of the dominant liberation movements, particularly the ANC and the Pan-Africanist Congress (PAC). The first was the emergence of the Black Consciousness movement organisations in the late 1960s and early 1970s. The second phase began with the Durban strikes in 1973 and the unions that were formed in the wake of those strikes. The third phase of independent mobilisation began in 1976 with the student uprisings that began in Soweto. Many activists who started off independently later went on to join one or the other of the liberation movements. But a pattern was set during these three phases whereby the absence of the liberation movements created spaces for independent political mobilisation. In all three instances, the liberation movements were forced to react and belatedly seek to reassert their hegemony or to compromise and accept the legitimacy of other political currents.

The above suggests that in South Africa there is a tradition of independent mobilisation that emerges to contest with the dominant liberation movements for hegemony. This is often achieved by mobilising around those issues that the liberation movement seems incapable of addressing. In all cases, such contestation seeks to appropriate the mantle of the struggle and to position the new movements to the left of the liberation alliance. Although the ANC has reasserted itself as the leading party of liberation, it has not succeeded in delegitimising the role and struggles of movements that emerged during these three phases.

Thus, the emergence of the APF (and other movements) should be seen as the continuation of a pattern of independent mobilisation at times when the national liberation movement is absent or failing to act on issues that affect a significant constituency. This approach helps us look beyond the 'ultra-left' label that has been so easily thrown at the APF and other new movements.

The National and Global Context

In 1998, two years after the adoption of GEAR (Growth, Employment and Redistribution) by the ANC government, many activists in South Africa still believed trade unions would lead the struggle against neo-liberal globalisation. A labour support organisation exhorted workers to 'join in the struggle against globalisation' (ILRIG 1998: 39). But unions were slow in responding to the challenge. According to Congress of South African Trade Unions' (COSATU) president Willie Madisha, COSATU has been weak since the unveiling of GEAR in 1996 and only recently did it start opening its eyes (Interview, Madisha, 14.10.03). It was in this context that the new social movements emerged.

The APF was established on the 6 July 2000 at the University of the Witwatersrand in Johannesburg, but the founding conference was held on the 10th floor of COSATU House in September that year. The formation of the movement followed a chain of events that unfolded out of the Urban Futures conference held at the University of the Witwatersrand in July of that year. Up to that point, left-wing activists outside of the Tripartite Alliance were uncertain about how to proceed and were thus searching for political relevance in a context where left-wing ideas were no longer fashionable. Those inside the ruling alliance organisations were facing greater marginalisation. However, the immediate post-GEAR period did not give rise to militant social movement politics. Although the Treatment Action Campaign (TAC) was formed soon after the adoption of

GEAR (December 1998), its leaders and activists did not present it as a left organisation.

A crucial impetus for social movements in South Africa that provided coherence to left activists and social movements was the emergence of the so-called anti-globalisation movement, first in Seattle in 1999, and later in other cities in North America and Europe. Activist circles across the world, including those in South Africa that were feeling rather rudderless, were buoyed by these events and found them convenient as reference points in the anti-globalisation struggle (Wainwright 2003).

At about the same time, managerial and government strategies of cost-cutting and retrenchment were proceeding unabated and the effects were particularly severe for growing numbers of the working class. In Johannesburg two developments, namely, the Johannesburg City Council's Igoli 2002 plan and Wits University's Wits 2001, were seen by activists as a manifestation of the cost-cutting economic regime that was unfolding since the adoption of GEAR. In addition, the Igoli 2002 plan also represented the introduction of cost-recovery in municipal service provision. According to McDonald (2002) cost recovery in publicly-owned service providers necessarily seeks to 'recoup the full cost of production' and may even aim to extract profit.

By 2000, a year after the second democratic election, the ANC's strategy of using patronage for political management and co-option of union and communist leaders was proving extremely effective. Despite protestations by COSATU leadership that the ANC was shifting to the right and that the union movement had become marginal in shaping policy formulation and implementation (COSATU 1996), in 1999 yet another crop of union leaders was drawn into political and other career opportunities controlled by the ruling party. In addition, the ANC had succeeded in building a political aspiration among unionists at various levels. As John Appolis, former regional secretary of the Chemical, Energy, Paper, Printing, Wood and Allied Workers' Union (CEPPWAWU)[2] has argued, there has emerged a 'symbiotic relationship between the trade union bureaucracy and the ANC leadership which has nothing to do with politics but is related to self-preservation by the elite' (Appolis 2003).

In this context the formation of the APF was the result of co-operation by three broad but not homogeneous groupings of the left. First there were left activists within the ANC/SACP/COSATU Alliance who felt a sense of frustration, particularly after the adoption of GEAR by the ruling party. However, in most cases this did not translate into a challenge of the increasingly hegemonic political and economic positions of the ruling party. Indeed, where there was an attempt to do this, such as in Trevor Ngwane's criticism of the cost-recovery model in local government (Ngwane 2003), Dale McKinley's criticism of the leadership, or John Appolis's criticisms of COSATU's participation in the Alliance, such expression of dissent was dealt with ruthlessly. Trevor Ngwane was expelled from the party and therefore lost his position as an ANC local government councillor for Pimville in Soweto. McKinley was expelled from the South African Communist Party (SACP) and Appolis was dismissed from his job as the regional secretary of CEPPWAWU. It is worth mentioning at this point that none of the activists in this group were senior leaders in the Alliance.

At the same time, many left activists outside the Alliance, mostly young, were also searching for relevance, particularly in light of developments in the anti-globalisation movement elsewhere in the world. Many of these were student or youth activists, while others worked in various non-governmental organisations. Some belonged to remnants of socialist groups such as the Marxist Workers' Tendency, which had faded out of the political scene after 1994.

The third grouping comprised working-class activists from communities that were looking for answers in a context where retrenchments and cost recovery had combined to destroy their livelihoods and limit their access to basic goods and services. An example is the membership of the Soweto Electricity Crisis Committee (SECC), an affiliate of the APF. As Ngwane explains, the membership of the SECC is made up of residents who are 'working class residents or unemployed, with lots of grannies as heads of households' (Ngwane 2003).

During its five years of existence, the Forum has been forced to adapt rapidly to changing political and economic circumstances in South Africa. This dynamism is a feature of all social movements, which implies that the movement must be 'continually engaged in attracting and holding supporters by reframing the undertakings of problem, solution and action' (Drakeford 1997: 74).

A Post-Apartheid Social Movement

Although the APF has received considerable media coverage in recent years, little is known about the Forum's history, structures, social base and where it operates. The first important fact is that the APF is a forum, not an organisation. This means it is very loosely structured and allows for flexibility and autonomy for the constituent organisations and groups. But this is also a weakness as it limits the ability of the Forum to be decisive. These structural issues can be traced back to its formation in 2000. The organisations that constituted the APF when it was formed were the South African Students' Congress (SASCO); the South African Municipal Workers' Union (SAMWU); the National Education, Health and Allied Workers' Union (NEHAWU); the COSATU Wits Region; the Pimville community (mostly represented by Trevor Ngwane); 'left-wing' individuals and groupings such as Keep Left and the Democratic Socialist Movement; and the Johannesburg district of the SACP. The Independent Municipal and Allied Trade Union (IMATU) also played an important role in the early years.

A protest by members of these organisations and other unaffiliated individuals at the Urban Futures conference at the University of the Witwatersrand triggered a chain of events that resulted in the formation of the APF. The conference was jointly organised by the University and the Johannesburg City Council. Both institutions had embarked on restructuring exercises (the City Council's Igoli 2002 and the University's Wits 2001), which entailed massive retrenchment of workers. The protest and the events that followed brought together disparate groupings of the left who had been cast aside by the ANC/SACP/COSATU juggernaut and communities who, up to then, had not found a voice loud enough to publicise their plight.

At the founding conference Sibongile Radebe (SASCO) and John Appolis were elected co-chairs of the new forum. This choice underlined the important role that the students played in the early years of the APF. But in 2001 the COSATU Regional Executive Committee decided to withdraw from the forum and so Appolis's role changed to that of a 'community activist'. From around that time several other organisations and their representatives 'faded out' of the APF without making a formal announcement (Interview, Appolis, 05.05.04). Apart from IMATU, most of these were Tripartite Alliance organisations. In the case of NEHAWU and SAMWU, this happened after their struggles, against Wits 2001 and Igoli 2002 respectively, had been lost.

Despite the presence of formal organisational representatives, from the early years the APF and its activities were driven by individual activists, particularly those that media and information officer Dale McKinley calls the 'core activist group'. This was particularly the case in 2000 and 2001 when the Activist Forum emerged as an 'activist vanguard' driven by the 'suburban left' (Interview, Hlatshwayo, 27.05.04). What made matters worse was the withdrawal of several founding organisations and the fact that meetings of the Forum were held in the evenings and most representatives of township-based communities could not attend because of transport and other problems.

From early 2002, some activists began to argue against the Activist Forum and in favour of a more structured and grassroots model of organisation. Later that year the Forum was disbanded and a membership model was adopted that sought to reprioritise communities. A co-ordinating committee was revived as a key structure of the organisation. Three categories of membership were identified, namely, community groups such as the SECC, the Johannesburg Inner City Forum and the Katlehong Concerned Residents, political groups such as Keep Left, Bikisha and the Socialist Group, and individual members.

Today the APF has 21 organisational affiliates and 4 political groups, which works out to a 'support base'[3] of about 10 000 individuals. Several hundred of these are 'core activists' (Interview, McKinley, 13.10.04). Most of these affiliates and members are based in Gauteng, while a few are in Northwest Province. But the organisational affiliates tend to be extremely uneven in terms of size and effectiveness. The SECC is by far the largest, with a claimed membership of between 7 000 and 8 000. Nevertheless, the bias in favour of community groups is aimed at strengthening the grassroots character of the Forum and restricting the role of individuals.

Some remarks about the social characteristics of APF members and activists are apposite at this juncture. Firstly, the members of APF affiliates generally come from marginal and vulnerable sections of society. In particular, they are drawn from the unemployed and pensioners as well as some at the bottom end of those in employment, and the APF is one of the few organisations available that offers these people a voice and a sense of solidarity. However, the APF and its affiliates do not seem to have made serious inroads in terms of organising employed workers, casual and full-time. Secondly, there is a significant presence of older members and pensioners (Trevor Ngwane affectionately calls them 'the grannies of Soweto') and young (teenage and early twenties) people who are still at school or are unemployed. SECC chairperson, Tebogo Mashota, says pensioners constitute a significant proportion of APF membership because 'they are the ones who pay the bills'. As recipients of the government's old age pension, they are often the sole breadwinners and leaders of their households. Both categories are the ones who bear the brunt of job loss and cost-recovery policies of the local state.

Thirdly, the majority of APF members are women. Women carry the burden of providing for families and caring for the weak and are therefore the first to feel the pinch of free market policies. Finally, the APF draws its community group membership exclusively from black townships, informal settlements and run-down sections of the inner cities in Gauteng. Thus, similar to other 'new' social movements, the Forum's constituency are 'the poors' (Desai 2002).

By contrast, most leaders and key activists do not come from the same social backgrounds as the members. Most are articulate young and middle-aged men and women with relatively high levels of formal education. Several of them have tertiary educational qualifications and possess a range of skills. They are predominantly male and there is a significant representation of racial groups other than black among them. These activists and leaders are drawn from different generations, some being relatively recent activists, while others have a longer record of political involvement. But all of them come from outside the mass ANC/SACP/COSATU Alliance fold or were inside but marginal.

Repertoires of Resistance

Although the APF has been in existence for more than five years now, there remains considerable ambiguity regarding the identity of the movement and its members. Many members are still ANC (and to a lesser extent COSATU) members and thus political identities are not always clear. This raises questions not only about the 'newness' of formations such as the APF, but it also alerts us to the fact that the Forum is not as homogeneous as it is often made out to be.

The Forum uses a wide range of methods of struggle to try to achieve its objectives. The organisational report of the APF that reviewed its activities for 2003 identified three clusters of activities, namely,

- mass activities: marches, pickets, demonstrations;
- raising public awareness and influencing public opinion: media statements, interviews, submissions, cultural expression; and
- building organisation: meetings, education and solidarity activities (APF Gauteng 2004a).

The campaigns and struggles of the APF and its affiliates are driven by a focus on basic needs, principally water, electricity, housing and education (APF Gauteng 2004b). This focus is the basis for the cohesion and solidarity that the movement has maintained since its inception. Also, focusing on these needs provides the movement with perhaps the most powerful weapon against the ANC as it enables movement activists to expose the failures of the government on issues that are closest to people's hearts. The basic needs approach also shows that not only is the movement trying to model itself on the emerging unions of the early 1970s (by focusing on bread and butter issues to mobilise), it has also been trying to position itself as the bearer of the struggle tradition and to appropriate the symbolism of the militant struggles of the 1970s and 1980s. 'Are we on the eve of a new 1973–1976, which ushered in a new phase of more sustained mass struggles?' asked John Appolis rhetorically in a recent assessment of the state of the new social movements (Appolis 2004: 38). Another variation of the same theme is the attempt to project the APF and other movements as the 'radical' alternative to the 'sell-out' leadership of the Alliance.

COSATU's failure to provide leadership, consistent resistance to neo-liberalism and a coherent alternative to capitalism has left working class communities to fight water and electricity cuts and evictions on their own. As a result of COSATU's paralysis, its own membership and structures have, with few exceptions, failed to throw their weight behind working class community resistance. A vacuum has resulted that is partially being filled by the APF (Hamilton 2002: 17).

The APF's frequent resort to militant mobilisation is another indication of the movement's desire to inherit the mantle of militancy that was once worn by other movements, including those in the Tripartite Alliance, during the struggle against apartheid. Some of the more spectacular examples of militant mobilisation include several instances of the destruction of pre-paid water meters and water and electricity reconnections, the march on mayor Masondo's house in 2002 and the march on the constitutional court in 2003. But the biggest protest action for the APF and its fraternal organisations under the banner of the Social Movements Indaba was the 31 August 2002 march during the World Summit on Sustainable Development (WSSD). This march, which is held up by the movements as a watershed event in post-apartheid South Africa, overshadowed the official Tripartite Alliance and proved politically embarrassing for its leaders. COSATU president, Willie Madisha, acknowledges this embarrassment and argues that the new social movements have real grievances, particularly in those areas where the government has not been successful. 'The reality is that these movements are growing in South Africa and around the world,' he claims (Interview, Madisha, 14.10.03).

Sometimes the use of militant rhetoric and action simultaneously with more conventional methods creates the impression that the APF is ambivalent towards the democratic order and its institutions. While there are some who question the legitimacy of the new state because of its bourgeois underpinnings, there is also a strong lobby favouring participation in the system. This ambivalence came to the fore in the run-up to the national elections in April 2004. Eventually the movement resolved not to oppose national elections in principle, but decided not to participate. In addition, it urged those members and affiliates who wanted to vote not to vote for the ANC and 'other bourgeois parties' (APF Gauteng 2004b).

However, it would appear that many in the movement are more favourably disposed towards participating in local government elections. During a public discussion at the May Day celebration in 2003, many APF members argued that the best way of defeating neo-liberalism was for the APF to contest the municipal elections under its own name. According to McKinley, the current position is that the APF will not contest the 2006 municipal elections but that each community organisation is autonomous and therefore free to contest if it so decides.[4] The SECC has already taken a decision to contest the elections in Soweto. But Mashota says the organisation is developing elaborate checks and balances to ensure accountability and to counter careerism (Interview, Mashota, 13.10.04). Notwithstanding these plans, the APF will have to contend with new contradictions within its ranks as only a few of the community groups are strong enough to win seats. Will this give rise to new fault-lines within the movement between, say, those who manage to find a foothold inside the system and those who don't? Also, will this give rise to tensions between community organisations on the one hand, and the political activist groupings that, according to McKinley, prefer non-collaboration with state institutions, on the other (Interview, McKinley, 13.10.04)?

Relations with Other Organisations and Movements

Many members of the new movements have a history of activism or membership in the 'traditional struggle organisations' such as the ANC, COSATU, the SACP and the South African National Civic Organisation (SANCO). Their decision to join to these movements was a response to the government's policy of economic liberalisation, commodification of basic needs and services and cost recovery in a context of massive job losses and absence of social protection. From the beginning, the approach of the new movements towards the ANC government was militant condemnation and opposition. More difficult to explain are the hostile relations between the APF and the SACP and COSATU, both of whom are critical of neo-liberalism. Equally puzzling is the failure of other organisations of the working class (such as SANCO, the National Council of Trade Unions [NACTU] and the Federation of Unions of South Africa [FEDUSA]) to find common cause with the APF.

The emergence and subsequent widening of the rift between the APF and most of its founder organisations is also complex. The president of SAMWU, Petrus Mashishi, argues that his union initiated the APF and COSATU launched it, but the problem is that the Forum was 'hijacked' by others. Then it started acting like a political party and opposing the government. This created problems within the union as some leaders were accused of forming a party under the guise of the APF. For this reason the union's anti-Igoli 2002 campaign collapsed and the leadership decided to sort out the internal problems rather than pursue the campaign. Mashishi says that the union was conducting research to see if the Igoli 2002 plan has delivered the promised benefits. If not, the union will revive the campaign (Interview, Mashishi, 19.05.04).

Others in the Tripartite Alliance support the argument that the APF is now in the hands of anti-ANC and anti-government elements that are determined to subvert the 'national democratic revolution'. Explaining the federation's position, a 2002 COSATU political discussion paper made a distinction between 'ultra-left groups' on the the one hand, and 'the rest of civil society', on the other:

> We cannot work closely with the ultra-left groups because we differ on basic principles. Still, as they have requested, we should meet with them and explain our position. At the same time, COSATU should consider developing broader and more structured relationships with the rest of civil society, especially the churches, youth, student groups, TAC, women's groups and many of the civil society formations in SANGOCO [South African NGO Coalition] (COSATU 2002).

ANC researcher Michael Sachs sees the anti-government discourse as the work of 'demagogues' in movements such as the APF and the Landless People's Movement (LPM) who enjoy negligible political support (Sachs 2003: 23). But there is a different way of explaining the political fallout between the APF and organisations associated with the Tripartite Alliance that avoids conspiracy theories. Firstly, the ANC and its Alliance partners are intolerant of new centres of popular mobilisation because these have the potential to undermine its support. One of its approaches to movements that operate outside its compass is to demonise and marginalise them by labelling them as the 'ultra left', and this includes critics within COSATU and the SACP.

Secondly, the rift also widened because of a combination of naivety, arrogance and poor political judgement on the part of some leading activists in the APF. There is a notion that because their cause is a just one, the masses would come by their thousands to join the APF. Some believe that patterns of spectacular mass mobilisation and resistance in the emerging anti-globalisation movement will soon be reproduced in South Africa, thus hastening the loss of credibility by the ANC government. The WSSD moment in 2002 reinforced this view. The result was that sustainable alliance building was neglected in favour of political grandstanding and posturing that antagonised not only the leadership of the Tripartite Alliance but large sections of the membership as well (see Hamilton 2002).

Thirdly, since its inception COSATU has been a major actor in civil society, often claiming to speak on behalf of not only their members but working class communities in general. The emergence of the APF threatened this 'big brother' role as the Forum had the potential of usurping COSATU's leadership of the fight against privatisation and exposing its vacillation in its dealings with the ANC government. APF chairperson, John Appolis, argues that the problem is that when COSATU leaders talk about working with social movements, they are talking about 'giving social movements direction. In other words, social movements must get subordinated to the positions that they [COSATU] hold. There is no genuine attempt to listen and learn' (Interview, Appolis, 05.05.04).

Finally, the approach and the rhetoric of the APF are too radical for some within the Alliance who have their sights set on positions of power and privilege in politics and business. The APF blames the Tripartite Alliance for the lack of co-operation between itself and COSATU, while the latter blames the Forum for its apparent anti-government position (see Mantashe and Ngwane 2004). But the Forum and its leadership have not given up on trying to reach out to COSATU members, encouraging them to engage in joint action with the APF.

Workers and shop stewards – encourage your federation and trade unions to link with community struggles against privatisation. Our struggle is littered with examples of alliances between trade unions and community organisations, against a common enemy – the privatisation plans of the ANC government (APF Gauteng n.d.).

This view in the APF is based on three assumptions about the present and the future of working-class organisation and struggle and Ngwane, national organiser of the APF, captured all these in a recent article. Firstly, many in the APF believe that, in Ngwane's poetic terms, 'the leadership [of COSATU] has captured the bodies of the workers but their souls are wondering around. One day they will connect with other bodies'. Secondly, many acknowledge that the political role of the new social movements will always be limited because of their small membership and their dependence on donor funding. Finally, all APF activists accept that the organised working class remains a 'key component of any alternative left strategy' (Ngwane 2003).

What is intriguing is that the APF does not have relations with the two politically non-aligned union federations, namely FEDUSA and NACTU. Neither the APF nor the federations have made moves to forge close links. Indeed, former NACTU general secretary, Cunningham Ngcukana, is contemptuous of APF leaders and intellectuals. 'How can you listen to Trevor Ngwane about international financial institutions when he does not know how the system works?' he asks (Interview, Ngcukana, 14.08.03).

But the APF has good relations with most of the 'new social movements'. It has worked well with them in the past, particularly through the Social Movements Indaba, a broader forum that brings together most of the new social movements to co-ordinate joint action. But its relations with the TAC, which is closer to COSATU, seem to be cordial but aloof. A key difference between the two is the fact that the TAC has a critical, but engaged, relationship with the ANC government. Many of the TAC members are active members of the ANC.

A recent assessment of APF activities argues that the voice of the new social movements has 'reverberated throughout South Africa like the voice of the prophets'. The report then goes on to assert that the mass media and communities often treat these movements as the 'conscience of the nation' (APF Gauteng 2004b). While it is true that the media covers some of the more spectacular activities of the movements, they often do so in a way that reinforces the notion of these movements as the mindless 'ultra left'. Too often the nuances of APF positions are left out in media accounts of the organisation and only the sensational aspects come through.

Even those members and activists of the traditional struggle organisations that are on the left of the political spectrum are wary of associating with the new social movements. The one exception is Winnie Madikizela-Mandela who in 2001 wanted to join the SECC and the SECC raised the matter at the APF meeting for a decision. Two positions emerged and 'after a lot of debate for and against this' the matter was left to the SECC to decide upon (APF Minutes of meeting 30 July 2001). At that time Madikizela-Mandela, who was once associated with SANCO and informal settlement communities, was facing fraud allegations. Her application for SECC membership was unsuccessful.

Relations with State Institutions

Recently, the APF's ambivalence towards state institutions was shown by the different positions towards engagement in electoral politics and the position taken around the time of the march to the constitutional court. In broad outline, there are two extreme positions in this debate, with several others occupying the middle ground. On the one extreme, there are those who see the state as a bourgeois institution that cannot provide relief to the working class. Their solution is an intensification of the struggle for socialism. On the other extreme are those who see the present state as a legitimate one. The only problem is seen to be the policies of the present ruling party. The solution is to contest elections and choose left candidates. The political groupings tend to hold the former positions, while community groups and activists tend to hold the latter. Of course, in reality there are many other complex positions that do not fit neatly into this characterisation.

The question of whether or not South Africa is a repressive state has come up often in APF debates. Repression is seen as part of neo-liberalism and some point to the arrest of protesters to prove this point. The APF organisational report for 2003 makes reference to the 'intimidation of individuals and activists', the 'surveillance of members' by the National Intelligence Agency (NIA), the regular 'banning' of marches and demonstrations, the detention of APF activists in 'Mbeki's overcrowded and filthy jails' and 'state repression' (APF Gauteng 2004a).

For their part, most state institutions are hostile to the 'ultra left' and seek to close down spaces for the existence of radical movements such as the APF. Furthermore, the APF has no relations with unions that organise workers in state institutions such as the police force, the civil service, metro police services and even private security companies, which are often used against APF protesters.

Financial, Intellectual and Organisational Resources

The APF is not financially self-sufficient because the majority of its members cannot pay subscriptions as they are pensioners or are unemployed. It depends entirely on donations from others and patterns of funding have not changed much over the last five years. A portion of its financial and material resources comes from individual members of the core activist group. These are in the form of cash or the use of personal phones, cars, computers and other resources that these activists possess. In some cases activists employed by better-resourced organisations often use such resources (such as photocopiers, e-mail, telephones and computers) for the benefit of the APF. However, the bulk of the organisation's funding comes from the main sponsor, the United Kingdom-based War on Want, as well as other organisations such as Oxfam (Canada), the South Africa Development Fund, the Polaris Institute and the Public Citizen, which have provided once-off financial support. Others such as the Education Rights Project have made contributions in kind, in this case material support for the APF's education campaign. The War on Want funding has been on the basis of a three-year cycle (ending in 2004) and in the 2003/04 financial year this donation was R638 739 (APF Gauteng 2004a). The Forum is proud of the fact that it 'enjoys a very good relationship' with War on Want and the core funding has enabled it to run meetings, education and training workshops, and campaigns and to set up an administrative infrastructure. At the end of 2004, the APF was preparing a motivation for a new funding cycle by War on Want (APF Gauteng 2004a).

Intellectuals play a crucial role because as 'idea workers', they help movements to invent discourses about 'what should be or could be' (Garner 1996). Another scholar has also argued that during a movement's formative years the influence of certain individuals or groups is 'decisive in crystallising certain strands and providing impetus for particular courses of action' (Drakeford 1997: 65). McKinley argues that in any organisation the role of intellectuals is often out of proportion to their actual numbers because they have skills and the APF is no exception. But the organisation has now been restructured and things are getting to a point where the intellectuals can only play a 'background supportive role' (Interview, McKinley, 13.10.04). Virginia Magwaza, a member of the SECC and an APF activist, also acknowledges that intellectuals have an important role to play and have built the APF by opening up political spaces and contributing resources. Her concern is that communities tend to depend on intellectuals instead of using their presence as an opportunity to learn so that they are in a position to assume leadership positions themselves (Interview, Magwaza, 15.10.04).

But other activists who prefer to remain anonymous are more critical of the role played by the intellectual core. One argues that unlike the Black Consciousness movement in the 1970s, the APF has not produced organic intellectuals and neither has it a coherent ideology nor an intellectual platform, such as a newspaper, to convey its position. The activist also argues that there is an 'unchanging intellectual division of labour' within the APF and the new social movements in general. Andile Mngxitama has raised similar concerns with regard to all the new movements:

> (H)istorically dominant voices (primarily white left intellectuals) have been the main mediators of the identity and aspirations of the poor of South Africa. In a sense we are witnessing the re-inscription of racial domination in the service of a 'greater good' – to hold back the tide of neo-liberal attack on black bodies (Mngxitama 2004: 3).

The similarity in the role played by intellectuals in the new social movements with the one they played in the unions that emerged after 1973 is striking (see Buhlungu 2004).

Organisations such as the Municipal Services Project, the Alternative Information and Development Centre (AIDC), the Freedom of Expression Institute, the Workers' Library and Museum and Khanya College have also, from time to time, provided intellectual, moral and material support to the APF and its affiliates. Khanya College provides education and training for APF affiliates and member communities. Its programme co-ordinator, Oupa Lehulere, argues that his organisation has been 'at the coalface of the formation of all the new social movements' and this includes providing a printing service for most of the movements and working with community organisations by providing infrastructure support and education (Interview, Lehulere, 19.05.04). Khanya also produces a regular journal that tracks the history of the movements, publishes official documents and records their struggles.

Some within the APF also have intellectual contact with groups outside the country. Some of this contact takes places through e-mail and the Internet and is in the form of discussion groups, exchange of documents and information about struggles in the broad anti-globalisation movement. One of the outcomes of these various processes of intellectual exchange is that there is continual learning and refining of strategies. The different methods of struggle used by the movement are a combination of methods used at different historical moments by different movements in South Africa and globally. Some of the methods of organising and mobilisation are drawn from struggles of the young union movement in the 1970s and 1980s and the militant civic movement in the 1980s. Some also aspire to achieve some kind of ungovernability as it prevailed in the 1980s, while others seek to achieve Seattle-type modes of protest as shown by this resolution taken in preparation for the Durban World Conference Against Racism in August 2001:

> The APF will send busloads of comrades to Durban, SANGOCO funds permitting, with the aim of disrupting the main conference in the spirit and practice of Seattle . . . There must be liaison with other organisations in particular the Concerned Citizens Forum in Durban and our international comrades (APF Minutes of meeting 30 July 2001).

Global Links

The APF regards itself as part of a global anti-globalisation movement fighting against the dominant discourse and practice of neo-liberalism. For this reason, it has endeavoured to maintain links with like-minded activists and organisations from other parts of the world. APF activists have attended seminars, conferences and other gatherings in various parts of the world organised by its fraternal organisations. In addition, the Forum participates actively in the activities of other international forums such as the African Social Forum and the World Social Forum. It is worth noting also that all international links of affiliates are made through the APF.

Most of these global links are mediated by the individual members as well as members of the political groups in the APF, both of whom tend to have more extensive international contacts than community activists. For a variety of reasons, including the background of these globally-connected activists, these links tend be oriented, in the first instance, towards developed countries, particularly those in Europe and North America. If the political activists in the APF are the main point of international contact for the organisation, then electronic communications are the main vehicle for such links. In this regard the vast majority of APF members are disadvantaged and therefore remain dependent on those with the resources and who speak English, the language through which these interactions are conducted.

Conclusion

A question that is often raised by activists and observers is whether the new social movements have 'achieved a "permanent" presence on the political map of South Africa' and whether their struggles are leading to a new phase of sustained mass struggles (see Appolis, 2004). For the APF, this question is particularly pertinent given its fragility as a result of a small membership and lack of resources.

The political hegemony of the ANC/SACP/COSATU Alliance remains unchallenged and the APF does not seem to have made any inroads into eroding the support of this political current. The Forum is aware of this and argues that the ANC manages to have the following it has because it has 'anti-apartheid struggle credentials and a great store of political capital in the person of Nelson Mandela and other struggle luminaries' (APF Gauteng 2004a). By contrast, the APF does not have in its ranks any 'struggle luminaries' and has been extremely unsuccessful in re-appropriating some of the political capital and symbolism of the anti-apartheid struggle. To stand a chance of attracting support away from the ruling 'liberation movement', an oppositional movement needs to contest and appropriate the political capital and symbolism of the liberation struggle. Meanwhile, the perception among sections of the organised working class is that the ANC government is 'delivering' in certain areas. They are therefore willing to give it more time to deliver to those areas where it is weak.[5]

The above is related to the fact that not only is the APF failing to attract unionised workers and others in the formal sector of the economy, it also has not made any inroads in organising workers in precarious forms of employment (casual, subcontracting, etc.), the self-employed and those in the informal sector.

In trying to model itself on the union movement that emerged in the wake of the 1973 Durban strikes and attempting to 'reclaim the militant traditions of May Day and the Durban strikes of 1973' (APF Gauteng 2003), the APF ignores the fact that the existence of democratic, legitimate institutions today makes the context vastly different from the one in the apartheid era. Not only does democracy create an expectation that all individuals should process their grievances through these institutions, but also the use of political identity frames such as 'enemy' or 'sell-out' against an elected government and its officials could strengthen the view that the movement is 'anti-democratic' (see Sachs 2003; Haffajee 2004).

In addition, unlike movements in the 1970s and 1980s, new movements in the democratic environment can no longer take public sympathy for granted. They have to earn it, sometimes by engaging in activities that are not conventional in APF circles, for example, attracting the youth, many of whom believe that 'politics is a dirty game and all politicians are liars' (Interview, Mashota, 13.10.04). Furthermore, democracy has created opportunities for upward social mobility for a few, particularly those who are young and skilled, and an illusion that upward mobility is available to everybody who takes advantage of the available opportunities.

At present the balance of power within the movement favours the non-collaborationists. Over the last few years the movement has become increasingly radical and in 2003 it adopted socialism as a goal. This radicalisation is to a large extent a function of the movement operating outside established institutions. However, this is likely to change if some of its affiliates win some seats in the municipal elections in 2006. If this happens, it would also reverse the existing balance of forces within the APF and give the pragmatists more influence over the policy direction of the movement.

The APF and its affiliates remain extremely small and fragile. However, they give us an idea of what Karl Polanyi (1957) had in mind when he spoke about a 'double movement'. If the emergence of neo-liberalism represented the move of the pendulum towards the right, then the formation of the APF and other 'new social movements' suggests that the pendulum could be swinging in the opposite direction and a new counter-hegemony may be emerging. But, as the APF is discovering, the task of building a counter-hegemonic movement from scratch in a post-colonial society entails more than pointing out the shortcomings of the existing social order. It also implies that the emerging movement should be able to turn dissatisfaction with the existing order into a coherent programme for an alternative social order. It is too early to say if the APF will survive, let alone present an alternative to the existing social order.

Notes

1. This chapter is about the Anti-Privatisation Forum (APF) of Gauteng. At the moment the APF Gauteng is the biggest of the three APFs that exist in South Africa. The Cape Town APF is a smaller and less significant organisation that was formed with the assistance of SAMWU in 2001. It is not related to the APF in Gauteng. In addition there is another much smaller body in Nelspruit that shares the name. Activists in that city established it to link up with struggles against water privatisation, but the organisation seems to have become dormant in recent years.

2. In 2004 Appolis was expelled by CEPPWAWU for presenting a demand by workers in his region for a COSATU-wide 'workers' referendum' on the Tripartite Alliance in view of the ANC's embrace of neo-liberal policies.

3. McKinley argues that the APF can only talk of a 'support base' as it does not use the card-carrying membership model.

4. Towards the end of 2005 some of the community organisations in the APF came together under the leadership of Trevor Ngwane and formed the Operation Khanyisa Movement to contest the March 2006 elections.

5. This is shown by the report of a recent survey of COSATU members conducted by researchers at the Sociology of Work Unit (SWOP) and the Human Sciences Research Council (HSRC) at the beginning of 2004.

References

APF Gauteng. 2003. 'Celebrate May Day, Celebrate the 30 Years of the Durban Strikes'. May Day pamphlet.

———. 2004a. 'Organisational Report of the APF for the Year 2003'. http://www.apf.org.za/.

———. 2004b. 'Platform on National Elections'. *Khanya: A Journal for Activists* 5.

———. n.d. Pamphlet.

Appolis, J. 2002. 'The Political Significance of WSSD'. *Khanya: A Journal for Activists* 2.

———. 2003. Talk to Second-Year Sociology Students. University of the Witwatersrand, 16 September.

———. 2004. 'Social Movements: Where are we now?'. *Khanya: A Journal for Activists* 5.

Beckman, B. 1998. 'The Liberation of Civil Society: Neo-Liberal Ideology and Political Theory in an African Context'. In M. Mohanty and P.N. Mukherji (eds), *People's Rights: Social Movements and the State in the Third World*. New Delhi/Thousand Oaks/London: Sage.

Benjamin, N. 2004. 'The APF and the 2004 Elections'. *Khanya: A Journal for Activists* 5.

Buhlungu, S. 2003. 'COSATU's Alliance with the ANC'. *New Agenda* 10.

———. 2004. 'The Building of the Democratic Tradition in the Post-1973 Unions in South Africa'. *Democratization* 11 (3).

Cooper, F. 1996. *Decolonization and African Society: The Labor Question in French and British Africa.* Cambridge: Cambridge University Press.

COSATU. 1996. 'A Draft Programme for the Alliance'. Unpublished discussion paper, November.

———. 2002. 'Political Discussion Document'. http://www.cosatu.org.za/docs/2002/finalcec.htm.

Desai, A. 2002. *We are the Poors: Community Struggles in Post-Apartheid South Africa.* New York: Monthly Review Press.

Drakeford, M. 1997. *Social Movements and their Supporters: The Green Shirts in England.* London: Macmillan.

Garner, R. 1996. *Contemporary Movements and Ideologies.* New York: McGraw-Hill.

Haffajee, F. 2004. 'Fact, Fiction and the New Left'. *Mail and Guardian* 11–17 June.

Hamilton, W. 2002. 'The Challenges Facing the Working Class in South Africa'. *Khanya: A Journal for Activists* 2.

ILRIG. 1998. *An Alternative View of Globalisation.* Woodstock: ILRIG.

Mantashe, G. and T. Ngwane. 2004. 'Mind the Gap: A Debate between Gwede Mantashe and Trevor Ngwane'. *Debate* 10.

McDonald, D. 2002. 'The Theory and Practice of Cost Recovery in South Africa'. In D. McDonald and J. Pape (eds), *Cost Recovery and the Crisis of Service Delivery.* Cape Town/London/New York: HSRC/Zed Books.

Mngxitama, A. 2004. 'Race and Resistance in Post-Apartheid South Africa: Towards a Progressive Race Narrative'. Paper presented at the Race, Racism and Empire Conference, York University, Toronto, Canada, 29 April – 1 May.

Murillo, M.V. 2001. *Labor Unions, Partisan Coalitions, and Market Reforms in Latin America.* Cambridge: Cambridge University Press.

Ngwane, T. 2003. 'Sparks in the Township'. *New Left Review* 22.

Polanyi, K. 1957 [1944]. *The Great Transformation: The Political and Economic Origins of our Time.* Boston: Beacon.

Sachs, M. 2003. '"We Don't Want the Fucking Vote": Social Movements and Demagogues in South Africa's Young Democracy'. *South African Labour Bulletin* 27 (6).

Wainwright, H. 2003. *Reclaim the State: Experiments in Popular Democracy.* London/New York: Verso.

Interviews

Appolis, John. Chairperson of APF, 05.05.04.

Hlatshwayo, Mondli. APF Activist, Johannesburg, 27.05.04.

Lehulere, Oupa. Programme Co-ordinator at Khanya College, 19.05.04.

Madisha, Willie. President of COSATU, 14.10.03.

Magwaza, Virginia. Member of SECC and APF Activist, 15.10.04.

Mashishi, Petrus. President of the SAMWU, 19.05.04.

Mashota, Tebogo. Chairperson of the SECC, 13.10.04.

McKinley, Dale. Media and Information Officer of APF, 13.10.04.

Ngcukana, Cunningham. Former General Secretary of NACTU, 14.08.04.

5

The Concerned Citizens Forum

A Fight Within a Fight

Peter Dwyer

ALTHOUGH IT WAS launched in July 2001 and has featured prominently in the news, comparatively little is known about the Durban-based Concerned Citizens Forum (CCF) except for the account by Desai (2002). Desai shows how 'the poors' have been forced to defend themselves against the worst and immediate excesses of the government's Growth, Employment and Redistribution (GEAR) policy that has resulted in evictions and disconnection from water and electricity. As such their actions are understood as a 'local' response to 'globalisation'. Globalisation is understood as a historically specific political and socio-economic phenomenon expressed, largely, through the implementation of neo-liberal policies that most decision-makers worldwide accept as a means of solving global (and national) 'economic crises'. This includes fiscal discipline, public expenditure priorities, trade liberalisation, foreign direct investment, privatisation and deregulation (see Callinicos 2003).

This chapter reveals a loose association of individuals and organisations that bring together disparate and autonomous community-based organisations initially drawn together by the commonality of, what Meszaros (1971: 33) has called, the 'elementary imperatives of survival'. Yet they are further united by what they bring to the CCF: an array of shared living experiences, identities, loyalties, symbols and resources that they draw on, and continually create and exchange, as a source of mobilisation and campaigning.

While the term 'the poors' sought to capture this messy amalgam of people, it underplays an organisation differentiated by uneven experience, age, gender, 'culture' and 'realpolitik'. This cocktail of people, ideas and experiences does not lend itself to simple classifications. Participants of the CCF cannot be straightforwardly categorised as having a single, coherent political consciousness or identity in opposition to 'neo-liberalism' and 'globalisation'.[1]

Some participants believe that the loose and *ad hoc* form that the CCF has taken so far has contributed to the lull in organised public activities of the group since December 2002. Others see the loose form as a virtue, as the organisation can be quickly mobilised as and when the need arises, with the component groups then returning to the 'hum-drum' of 'ordinary' life. Yet for some, the CCF is moribund, and for others it no longer exists as internal differences over the organisational, strategic and tactical future of the CCF tests people's resolve to maintain unity.

Through in-depth interviews and participant observation, this chapter seeks to identify who and what the CCF is, where it is located, why and how it developed and how it operates and mobilises. Broadly, what are the organisation's forms of resource mobilisation and framing strategies and repertoires of contention? What transpires is that the very mechanisms of the political opportunity, framing and resource mobilisation processes that were once harnessed and facilitated the emergence of the CCF, have transformed into challenges that threaten its survival. These can be conceptualised as issues of identity (what type of organisation is the CCF, what image does it want to project and how?); of organisational form (does the CCF need a permanent structure?); and political agenda (what does it stand for?).

Theorising Action

In discussing the rise of popular movements in the twentieth century, Barker (1995) notes that a common thread is the organic development of a series of fundamental questions. Broadly, are our demands fitting, or should we change them? What form of organisation is needed? Can we trust those that claim to represent us? How should we handle division in our ranks? What do we want to say, what is to be hoped and what feared, what is to be thought, what is to be done?

These are similar to the theoretical issues that have concerned social movement scholars for over 30 years (see Della Porta and Diani 2003; Maheu 1995). As social movement theory evolved (see McAdam, McCarthy and Zald 1999), theorists of the political opportunities and political process school of research (see McAdam 1982; Tilly 1978) became more interested in understanding how social movements came into being and how they operated. They focused on collective activities, their organisational structures, leadership, social bases and culture, and framing strategies or consensus building.

Other classic studies of social movements direct our attention to the ways in which people 'construct', and change, the social world, and so analysis should centre on the individual actor-agency. In the *Making of the English Working Class* (1986), Thompson argues that we orientate our analysis towards actors and what is most subjective in their behaviours towards experiences. So taking into account individual, as well as collective, subjectivity, we are looking at the 'social processes' whereby actors arise, express themselves, and change.

The turn to the study of 'subjectivity' in development and social theories (see, for example, Long and Van der Ploeg 1994) often detaches agency from the complexities of the dynamics of the social relationships in which it is exercised, and so loses meaning and analytical precision. The result is a tendency towards an uncritical celebration of 'popular culture', 'the community' and the invocation of a quasi-mythical belief in all forms of discourse and action 'from below' (Brass 1995; Eagleton 2003) – reproducing the voluntarism and idealism that characterises much of this work.[2] One consequence is to eschew openly ideological debate, politics and political organisation, thus disarming participants from making normative statements that may enable them to begin to answer some of the questions posed by Barker and grappled with by social movement theorists and activists more generally.

One problem in social (movement) theory is that the social relations (structure) in which people mobilise (agency) are often set apart as 'binary opposites' (see Sibeon 1999) with the individual or social group often counterposed to structural analysis. Yet, this dichotomy between structure and agency is challenged by Giddens (1984, 1993), who argues that structures (variously referred to as social context or 'systems') influence people's agency but that they only continue to exist in so far as they are sustained by people's repeated actions.

While structure appears to be negative, a constraint on agency, we need not confine it as such. For example, Betts (1986) and Giddens (1993) argue that structural relationships can 'enable' agency. Accordingly an exclusive focus on either structure or agency misses 'the real relationship of structure and action, the structural conditioning of action and the effects of action on structure'

(Abrams 1982: 7). It is the intricacies of their intimate relationship that can help us better comprehend how organisations and people develop.

Consequently, social change is not a 'thing' that just happens or 'history without a subject' (Althusser 1972); it is a process, expressed and worked through by individual agency more often in collective organisation in specific historical and changing conditions that are subjectively interpreted. The CCF then, can be understood as open-ended activity in which participants reflect (both as individuals, leadership and as a group), develop and review their activity in the immediacy ('the transition') in which they operate.

Globalising the Local and Localising the Global

The emergence of the CCF needs to be understood against the background of the relatively slow economic growth of the last twenty years (globally and nationally what Brenner [1988] has called an 'economic crisis'), and the frustrated aspirations of those people who have to live with the contradictory outcomes of ANC government policies that are framed by a form of home-grown neo-liberalism (see Bond 2000; Marais 1998).

Walton and Seddon link an earlier wave of 'successful collective action' to the impact of similar processes: 'It is the crisis and the process of reconstruction of global capitalism that began in the late 1960s and early 1970s that has generated the economic policies of liberalization and austerity that have themselves given rise to the upsurge of popular protest across the developing world . . .' (1994: 22).

As mediators of economic and social development, governments take 'reactive-avoidance' measures (Habermas 1976) that shift the economic crisis into the political system. It is within this historical framework that popular protests are generated. Noting the continuing instability and crisis-prone nature of global capitalism, Dwyer and Seddon (2002) argue that the popular protest characteristic of the period from the mid-1970s to the late 1980s has not been extinguished. Indeed, it has continued throughout the 1990s and into the new millennium, and can be understood as 'a new wave' of popular protest.

In South Africa, the unfolding of liberal democracy since 1994 has taken place in a period in which neo-liberal economic policies have been accepted by the ANC leadership as the best way to solve the socio-economic legacy of apartheid, and has unwittingly provided a new structure of opportunity for collective mobilisation. The transition has generated expectations and rights-based claims that have placed demands on a broader array of actors and institutions. It is within this framework, the interdependent relationships between the global, national and local nexus, together with the expectations generated during the liberation struggle and the ANC promises of 'a better life for all', that we must situate the development of the CCF.

Anatomy of an Organisation: How the CCF Developed

The immediate story of the CCF begins with the formation in Durban in 1999 of a 'loose alliance', called the Concerned Citizens Group (CCG), that included the prominent sociologist and biographer of Nelson Mandela, Professor Fatima Meer, and other well-known members of the Durban Indian community. Prompted by the ANC, they started a campaign to encourage Indian people not to vote for the historically 'white' parties (the New National Party and Democratic Party) in the second general election in June 1999 (Desai 2002).

As a result of the enduring poverty in the area, they encountered a reluctance to vote for the ANC. A survey of 504 families in the Westcliff and Bayview areas of Chatsworth revealed that 75 per cent lived below the poverty line, 58 per cent were unemployed and 42 per cent dependent on welfare grants (Fatima Meer quoted in *Natal Mercury* 17 February 1999). The CCG evolved into a *de facto* human rights group campaigning against housing evictions, water cut-offs and demands for rent by the local municipality. This transformation helped revive 'flatdwellers' associations' in parts of Chatsworth (Desai 2002). In September 1999, the CCG took up the case of ten families in the Bayview and Westcliff areas about to be evicted by the council for rent arrears.

In early 2000, several people had been conducting research about water and electricity provision in KwaMashu, Umlazi, Hammarsdale, Wentworth and Chatsworth townships. Noticing a spate of evictions and the resistance this generated, they wanted to ensure that such community protests had 'an autonomous and independent identity outside of the [ANC-led] Alliance' (Interview, Anonymous, 15.07.03) and began forging connections between people across townships.

Arising from meetings of ten or so people who, one source says, had 'a lot of tentativeness' about organising, some residents were convinced that through combining legal and direct action they could prevent evictions. This generated its own publicity, seemingly spread on the 'community grapevine', and meetings got bigger, enabling them to mount more substantial challenges to the municipality.

During the course of 2000-01 different community groups across Durban began to strike up relations based on a perceived common set of problems that hinged around the provision of and inability to pay for basic services. One participant from Chatsworth describes how, having been taken to meetings with other community-based representatives in other townships, they '. . . realised that it was not just us, but there was every other community across Durban and KwaZulu-Natal that was facing that problem' [of 'social injustice'] (Interview, Anonymous, 18.06.03).

While it is difficult to pinpoint seminal moments that create and cement an organisational identity, several participants highlighted the usefulness of the regular Saturday meetings at Natal Technikon and the University of Natal during 2001. This was when participants from a range of community groups came together with students, academics and other staff, mainly from the University of Durban-Westville, to make banners, discuss actions and show political videos.

As they sat and painted banners, laughing, working together, swapping anecdotes and stories, a CCF camaraderie developed. One participant recalls how he was part of something bigger: '. . . by meeting those people what came to my mind is that I am not alone in this thing' (Interview, Anonymous, 10.08.03a).

Here we can begin to see how those in the CCF, through collective action, planned meetings and workshops, began to identify with the CCF as their organisation, an organisation that became a co-ordinating body linking groups who share common experiences.

The Composition of the CCF

The most commonly used terms to characterise the CCF by participants were a 'loose coalition', 'a network' and 'a network of organisations'. People were never referred to as 'members'. While it is possible to identify CCF affiliate groups, this 'looseness' makes a quantification of CCF participants very difficult as there are no membership lists, and no 'official' records of the numbers of people attending various mobilisations and meetings. Most participants were hesitant to put a figure on the size of the CCF. Mobilisations have ranged from several hundred in Chatsworth, 5 000 drawn from several townships and at best 20 000 outside the United Nations World Conference Against Racism in August 2001.

As there are no membership-type or political conditions placed on participation, numbers ebbed and flowed depending on the particular issue, event and resources available.

Nevertheless, what can be identified is that initially a core of city-based activists, who had access to resources, such as computers, telephones and finance, acted as central organisers, initiators and transmitters of information between groups and individuals.[3] Several identified themselves as 'petit bourgeois', as did one or two other participants, but most others referred to them as 'city-based comrades'.

This group acts as a co-ordinating network and draws around it peripheries, contacts and connections, affiliates and sympathisers through mobilising, providing and pooling resources. This enables the group to facilitate and synchronise meetings, arrange transport and pass on information, thereby connecting different groups for a march, a meeting in another community or an event elsewhere in the country.

While the CCF has a very small number of lower middle-class adherents (academics and other professionals), it is underpinned by what can be conceptualised as working-class people (largely unemployed, but not all). As such, in interviews, meetings, rallies and informal discussions, participants commonly referred to themselves and others like them in Durban and across the country as 'the oppressed', 'the deserving', 'the poor' and 'the poorest of the poor'.

If most participants in the CCF are unemployed, this mirrors experiences from other poor countries in which similar people have historically been at the forefront of popular protests and 'food riots'. Often a mixture of urbanisation, neo-liberal austerity policies and a history of forms of prior collective organisation make for an 'explosive cocktail'.[4] It is, therefore, unsurprising that such people make up the social base of the CCF.

Families, Women and the CCF

From interacting with participants, it is evident that more than an organisational network is involved in mobilising, campaigning and reliving events. This includes contacts between neighbours, friends, family, school friends and workmates who learn about issues and impending protests, and talk, debate, gossip and argue about this, and encourage each other to participate or not. For example, one participant was introduced to the CCF by her brother and another by a shop steward he met at the Workers' College.

Across Africa, the household economy has long been a crucial backbone of the political economy and Desai (2002) notes how the family unit (and extended family) became central to the CCF. One participant says that what excited him about the CCF was seeing 'families in struggle, families in motion' and how 'fractured families' could take part in direct actions (Interview, Anonymous, 15.07.03). The role of the family has been noted in earlier social movements. For example, Charlton (1997: 68) notes how the Chartists movement in nineteenth-century England '. . . was a family and community organisation in which "everybody" participated'.

While women are not the majority in the city-based core, they play a prominent role in participating organisations. It is unsurprising that CCF protests and meetings are dominated by older women, given that women have long been the main care-givers and providers in households, providing food and dealing with bills. A cursory glance at newspaper photographs and videos taken from marches and confrontations with the police shows how women were prepared to physically confront and ridicule authorities if need be.

Several youth from Hammarsdale talk of how it was a revelation to see women playing a prominent role. Although one youth lamented '. . . where I am living, women, they don't have chance to do things . . .' (Interview, Anonymous, 10.08.03b), alerting us to the unevenness of women's participation across different groups and townships.[5]

Identity, Ideology and Mobilisation

In his studies of eighteenth-century England, Thompson (1986) identifies a set of processes and relationships that he terms 'class struggle without class'. Within the collective and customary practices of the poor, Thompson identified forms of resistance to their rulers and exploiters which rested on the antagonisms inherent in developing capitalism in that period, but which the poor had not yet learned to conceptualise in 'class' terms.

This is not to say that CCF participants understand their issues and actions as 'class struggle' – although it is clear they have an intuitive grasp that 'something is up'. But what Desai (2002) shows, is that the daily struggle to survive is more pressing and it is this defensive basis upon which people initially mobilise, encourage and identify with each other.

In this way, if participants think of themselves as being in the CCF, or at least if they think of themselves as belonging together, then essentially they do.

Although most participants are often mobilised around specific issues, several participants subsequently come to identify more broadly with other people working on, what they understand as being, related issues. As such, identity is related to 'ideology', though this can be embryonic rather than elaborate.[6]

This would suggest that the general relationship between ideology, identity and mobilisation in the CCF is that identity is one aspect of ideology. Necessarily, participants have a range of, sometimes contradictory, understandings of how their environment works, the causes underlying the issue they are seeking to tackle, how they can take action to resolve that issue and who they can call on for support, etc.

These are not always shared understandings, but for the CCF to operate practically there has to be some kind of dialogue between participants and groups, and this dialogue can broadly be understood as 'ideology'. In this dialogue, the questions noted at the start of this chapter are ones that participants attempt to answer (for example, when deciding who to try to mobilise). Yet this does not exist in isolation from other problems mentioned above, which arise from the practical situation of participants.

In practice, these concepts overlap. However, they have certain points that characterise them. Identity is related to the questions 'Who am I?' (individual identity), 'Who are we?' (collective identity) and 'How do others see us?' (public identity). Objectives are related to questions such as 'What are our goals?' (generally strategically, and tactically). Ideology binds these aspects together with a coherent worldview that explains how the world is collectively represented.

Who are We and Who are They?
'The community' was an initial mobilising referent and has a strong resonance within and around the CCF. However, some participants had no illusion that this meant everyone in a township is 'in the same boat'. As one argued, 'No, we are not all one, we are rich and we are poor . . . rich people were not involved, rich people . . . oppress, they are the people who collect the rent, they are the landlords . . . ' (Interview, Anonymous, 24.06.03a).

Charlton (1997) argues that written and spoken language can be of use in understanding the motivation and intention of participants in social movements, provided we show the context in which it is used. In this way, we can see how social class location helps frame the experiences and ideas (positive and negative) that people bring to the CCF and the language they use to articulate them.

Many participants recognise there is a divide between the rich and the poor and one tells how, 'I started understanding this class dynamic and now I am fully into this whole class thing and everywhere I go that is always the thing I think of' (Interview, Anonymous, 24.06.03a). For one or two participants it is based around a notion that 'we are fighting against capitalism' (Interview, Anonymous, 10.08.03a).

Although some participants did not specify what class interests the CCF represents, it is not unreasonable to assume that the majority of people mobilised by the CCF understand that their experiences and identity are defined by the problems they have in contradistinction to others. For example, one participant tells how the CCF deals with '. . . problems in the community, people are unemployed, people don't have water, people don't have electricity . . .' (Interview, Anonymous, 13.09.03). From this, it is self-evident that for participants, those who are employed (but not part of the working-poor) are not the same as them.

A study of press releases reveals that at a collective level the CCF identified both the local municipality and national government as the cause of their problems. They identify the eThekwini Municipality 'Unicity' councillors of all parties as part of the problem, linking them to the rich or elite. In one press statement they say how councillors' children '. . . move seamlessly from Model C schools into expensive Universities and then into jobs-for-pals' (Concerned Citizens Forum 2002a). A press release from the Mpumalanga Concerned Group talks of '. . . our new oppressors – the privatisers, the elite, the sell-outs, the ANC' (Mpumalanga Concerned Citizens Group 2002).

Appeals for moral and political superiority have referred to anti-apartheid struggles. For example, Des D'Sa, chair of Wentworth Development Forum, talks of how 'we who have suffered in the past are going to suffer again' (cited in Horner 2002). In one instance Brandon Pillay, chair of Bayview Flats Residents' Association, notes how former ANC activists have betrayed their principles while getting good jobs in local government, and the irony of how those who once fought forced removals '. . . are now sitting in their air conditioned offices and giving out execution orders to relocate the poor' (cited in Naidoo 2002). While invoking past injustices, they also draw on current legal rights to protest. For example, Zelda Norris of the Tenants Association of Sydenham Heights (TASH) complains that the eThekwini Municipality '. . . is

victimising us for knowing our rights, just as the apartheid city managers did'
(Indy Media South Africa 2002).

Given the 'loose' organisational and political formation of the CCF, it is not
surprising that participants have differing social and political ideas and analyses.
Slogans can be shared, but ideologies may still differ, and we should be careful
not to mechanically read off from slogans on demonstrations that this means
participants are imbued with a particular shared ideology or 'consciousness'.
For example, despite several workshops, some participants from the KwaMashu
Activist Forum told how people from KwaMashu who had protested against
the World Economic Forum and the New Partnership for Africa's Development
(NEPAD) in June 2002, did not know what they meant.

Some CCF participants draw inspiration from movements elsewhere. The
declaration of the Durban Social Forum (see Desai 2002) makes explicit reference
to the protest outside the G8 summit in Genoa, Italy, in July 2001. Several
participants refer to videos about similar protests against the World Bank in
Prague in October 2000. At other times, they have referred to the Zapatistas in
Mexico, the poor in Thailand and Nigeria (Concerned Citizens Forum 2002b).
However, there is little evidence beyond the city-based participants and a handful
of prominent activists in affiliate groups who clearly understand what such
references allude to.

In all, while drawing on a range of, often contradictory histories, discourses
and symbols, these people identify common cause with each other largely
through shared experiences. In this way, a perceived failure of delivery that
does not match people's expectations provides the potential basis for activism.

Strategy and Tactics

Tarrow (2003) notes that 30 years of social movement research has shown that
grievances alone are insufficient for explaining what produces collective action.
This suggests that the ways in which participants fuse resources and political
opportunities is crucial. That is, it is not 'political opportunities' or 'resource
mobilisation' that 'do this' or 'don't do that'. For these organisations to have
an impact, opportunities must be recognised, seized and given a physical
expression. This is what Barker, Johnson and Lavalette (2001) mean by politics
and 'leadership'.[7] This practical, and inherently political, social and
communicative task is neglected and under-theorised in social movement theory.

When Tarrow (1994) notes how social movements are still in the process of forming when they appear publicly, it is a reminder that the participants are still 'working things out'. What the evolution of the CCF shows is that opportunities must be linked with processes of grievance attribution, thus motivating people to take action and form coalitions.

This means people becoming active while drawing on and constructing existing and newly created 'repertoires of contention' in a creative manner. The CCF has shown variety and flexibility in its tactics that have differed over time and space (and resulted in intense debates and disagreements), with some participants making a virtue of and celebrating tactical contradictions.

There are no hard and fast rules that govern the strategy and tactics of the CCF. Desai (2002: 79) notes how debates took place about whether to participate or not in local elections in December 2000, and how the CCF agreed to do this while keeping up extra-parliamentary forms of action. Such tactical flexibility is captured when one participant tells how 'one day the CCF in one area could be voting . . . and in another area maybe five kilometres away this very same CCF was campaigning vigorously against the vote in Bayview' (Interview, Anonymous, 15.07.03).

Leadership

While a focus on 'leaders' or 'leaderships' is important (especially in relation to the debates about internal democracy and transparency), the tendency to concentrate on what leaders say or do is in danger of reducing organisations to the question of 'leadership'. This can contribute to the simplification of an organisation or movement to a leader or leaders, so exaggerating their importance and influence.

However, Anthony Marx discusses how 'activist elites' played a different role in the process of 'interpreting, debating, and implementing responses to changes' in the course of the South African liberation struggle (1992: 255). As one participant makes clear, not everyone in the CCF has the same role: 'there are people who do the job of writing memorandums, planning a march, working for funds but our job is putting people into buses' (Interview, Anonymous, 24.06.03a).

Desai notes how a 'powerful leadership began to emerge' in some areas of Chatsworth and that they relied upon 'the grounding they had received as shop stewards in the union movement of the 1980s' (2002: 44). Once the CCF and the individuals it comprised began practically to engage in defensive and other struggles, questions about organisation and leadership took on an immediate and organic meaning.

We know that a particular group of people played a pivotal role in co-ordinating initiatives and eventually the formation of the CCF. One participant describes the leadership as 'a group of city-based people who are not part of other community-based organisations who do meet up and interact in a social or political way' (Interview, Anonymous, 24.06.03a). Together with Fatima Meer, this core group included several others with previous political activism during apartheid and some trade union organising experience, people such as, but not exclusive to, Heinrich Bohmke, Ashwin Desai, Joe Guy and Mandla Sishi, and who provided pivotal links in the chain that was initially forged between different townships groups.

Participants differentiated between different leaderships. For example, there is both a 'leadership' in their own community organisation and a CCF 'leadership'. The latter is often made up of, as one participant put it, 'city-based comrades', who constitute 'an informal leadership'. From the participants interviewed to people attending rallies and protests, a certain respect for many of those in the city-based leadership was evident. 'Those are the real people who do the graft [work], that stand behind the organisation' (Interview, Anonymous, 24.06.03a). The relationship was not too different from the type of relationship Bonnin describes between workers and shop stewards, in which she notes, 'the membership regards them as knowledgeable in the "ways of the material world" ' (1999: 53). These, then, are the different 'layers' of collective and individual agency that drive the CCF.

Nevertheless, differences over who is, and what constitutes, leadership are prevalent at different levels. These differences occur within constituent groups, notably Hammarsdale and Wentworth, between a constituent group such as Mount Moriah Residents and the CCF's city-based comrades and leadership. One city-based participant identifying himself as part of 'the leadership' acknowledges that 'inside the city-based people I can understand there being gripes because our approach [was sometimes] . . . decided very much in an undemocratic fashion . . .' (Interview, Anonymous, 15.07.03).

This was not due to some inherent 'will to power', but was an unintended outcome of the practical and sometimes urgent necessity to react. As he put it, '. . . somebody had to take the initiative . . . and giving orders to a certain extent' (Interview, Anonymous, 15.07.03). For some, the way in which this was done caused tensions. One participant based in a township group complained how 'the problem was between us . . . we were fighting each other, the leadership in the CCF . . . ' (10.08.03b), elaborating how some people in his township began to think that the CCF had become 'like private property' of a very small number of city-based participants.

One participant perhaps best sums up the debates around leadership in so far as he believes 'people are not against leaders. They are against leaders that have no connection with their will. We want people to lead us but we do not want them to impose that leadership on us, we want us to impose our will upon them' (Interview, Anonymous, 26.07.03a). As such, accountability is about creating a mechanism of checks and balances, not stifling action or decisions.

These characteristics of leadership in the CCF challenge the common assumption in much of the new social movement theory that the organisational structures and leaderships of such organisations are segmented and have a multiplicity of leaders with multiple links between different cells forming a loosely bound network.

Contesting Organisation

I noted how most participants understand the CCF as a 'loose coalition'. This common acceptance of the organisational form and structure, and in some respects strategy and tactics, is deceptive, for this was a highly contentious issue. One city-based participant mentions how '. . . there was a big debate about structure, do we want structure? So in that debate things were discussed very explicitly . . . It turned out they didn't end up forming any structure. There was an attempt in one meeting, but by the next meeting it had been half forgotten' (Interview, Anonymous, 23.06.03).

Others seemed to have naturalised what is contested, so, for example, the formation of the CCF was described as follows: 'We didn't want a chairperson or a secretary or whatever . . . and we still didn't see the need to have a structured committee . . . ' (Interview, Anonymous, 18.06.03). Several participants noted how the loose way of operating had a practical benefit in that it did not make component groups and individuals subject to particular organisational forms and pressures, thus making mobilising easier.

Nonetheless, people's means of contention requires adequate means of mobilisation and communication and this, organically, raises the issue of organisation. Certainly, Desai recognises the role of organisation in describing several of the existing community-based groups that became associated with the CCF; he notes how they '. . . functioned formally, met regularly, and painstakingly took mandates from public meetings' (2002: 77).

Some of these activists developed politically in the late 1970s and 1980s, when the independent trade unions were being built upon participative, not representative, democracy that required much self-sacrifice, discipline and accountability. Consequently, many participants take accountability seriously and this experience has engendered a culture of democracy (even if it was not always practised) inside working-class organisations. Therefore, the debate about organisational structure is not 'imposed' from outside or by those with an alleged 'political agenda', as some city-based participants complained – it emerges automatically.

What form an organisation takes is crucial, for while a particular framing process may encourage mobilisation, as people seek to organise and act, the potential for framing is conditional upon participants' access to mobilising structures. Without sustained mobilisation and organisation, in social isolation people can fall back into blaming themselves or scapegoating others for their problems. In tough times, characterised by poverty, fear and powerlessness, an organisation can provide a port, a compass bearing during a storm.

Additionally, it can provide the means through which people can meet to clarify ideas and share experiences collectively. Participants also need others to 'run things by' and swap advice (socially, politically and culturally). For example, when the eThekwini Municipality announced in late 2003 that it was writing off some debts, it caused much confusion.

A forum for and the facilitation of debate therefore seems important to people, and also important for the well-being of the organisation. In discussing differences over organisational form and strategy in the 'anti-capitalist' movement in Europe today, one leading UK-based activist notes that from his involvement in social movements in the 1960s and 1970s in different parts of the world '. . . I learned that it makes an enormous difference what decisions the movement makes, how you fight and what you say . . . The way you learn what is right and what is wrong in any situation is by arguing it out amongst yourselves . . . That is why in every great political movement in history, the air has been alive with arguments on every street corner. Arguing isn't sectarian. Sectarianism is refusing to act together because you haven't won the argument' (Neale 2002: 16).

New Ways of Doing

Given the differences that exist between CCF participants, an important question that emerged early on in the research was whether the CCF or individuals are (or are capable of) devising new strategies suited to the nature of their evolving struggle in a post-apartheid government.

All the participants interviewed highlighted how being in the CCF is an enjoyable and creative experience. Several older participants contrasted the fun of involvement with the CCF with dour moments and long-winded speeches that they felt characterised their previous political experiences in the liberation movement.

One participant believes the CCF is at least beginning to experiment with forms of meetings and events. For example, he tells how during one campaign '. . . not one person was allowed to tune [speak] for more than five minutes and we had an hour of speeches which is usually taken up by one drone . . .' (Interview, Anonymous, 15.07.03). Another relives how '. . . what excited me about these things, was that it was a different kind of politics. There was excitement, a vibrancy and life and I had walked away from all those involvements because there was something soul destroying [in the ANC]' (Interview, Anonymous, 24.06.03b).

All of the youth interviewed recall how they enjoyed a 'Youth Camp' that was held before a march in May 2002. About 50 youth attended and one organiser tells how the intention was to move away from the 'normal' way of doing politics by 'focusing on the idea of human interaction', the 'politics of friendship' and 'stereotyped ways of interacting' (Interview, Anonymous, 24.06.03b). With a big pot of curry 'people congregated in different groups and discussed, we lit a big fire, painted banners . . . and basically had a big party . . .' (Interview, Anonymous, 24.06.03b).

Engaging the State: The Demanding Nature of the CCF

The CCF has been criticised by the ruling party and others for not engaging with the state in a constructive manner. Yet, by invoking constitutional rights and presenting court cases, they have made use of the political spaces opened up since 1994, thus contributing to the establishment of liberal democracy.

To berate movements for not having ideological clarity is to misunderstand the history and nature of social movements. While there may be no clear definition or coherent purpose or vision in the beginning of the 'life cycle' of such groups, a definition of purpose (practically, a political programme) arises over time. This can be internally generated amongst participants with other groups and peers nationally and for some leading participants internationally.

The CCF also engages with the state by placing public demands on government officials. For example, they demanded the implementation of a 'R1 000 per month income grant for all those who have no income'. They also called for 'an end to privatisation and the implementation of economic policies that are people-centred. This means the scrapping of the disastrous Gear policy'. Building upon the links the CCF made with the Palestinian Solidarity Campaign at the WCAR, they have demanded that 'in solidarity with the people of Palestine . . . the city of Durban break off all economic, trade, consular, sporting and cultural ties with the state of Israel' (Concerned Citizens Forum 2002a).

It is sometimes said that 'all politics are local', and in one sense the experiences of the CCF would confirm this. However, the CCF, and others, should consider experiences of social movements from elsewhere. In a study of informal movements in Iran, Asef Bayat concludes by questioning the impact of the social weight, or lack thereof, that informal and community-based groups, on their own, can bring to bear upon the state and capital. Bayat notes how many of the people that these type of organisations are composed of '. . . lack the institutional capacity to exert pressure, since they lack an organizational power of disruption' – disruption in the sense of 'the withdrawal of crucial contribution on which others depend' that provides an important resource for wielding power over others (1998: 9).

Consequently, he argues that for all their developments, 'it was the state that posed the major challenge to the street politics throughout the 1980s' (Bayat 1998: 164). Post-structuralist and discursive analysis aside, to ignore the uneven circulation of power is to ignore '. . . that like it or not the [national] state does matter' (Bayat 1998: 164), functionaries of which continue to be central political players.

A Fight Within a Fight

Participation in the CCF is inherently an intuitive process in which participants try to reconcile their individual and social-collective experiences. Often this is done through a dialogue with others and is articulated as discussions around practical tasks. Conceptually it is linked to the 'who are we, who are they and what can we do about it?' type of questions noted earlier. What this ultimately represents is an argument about social change with people who share common frustrations, ambitions and social interests.

Accordingly, the struggle itself becomes a 'fight within a fight', about the meaning and direction of their struggles. This intense ideological debate has been a feature of all forms of popular movement, including the liberation movement against apartheid (see, for example, Marx 1992).

Barker (1995) notes that at every stage in the evolution of popular movements 'a war of tendencies proceeds' between and within different organisations and individuals. Without some method through which people can come together regularly as a CCF collective in order to debate, discuss and socially and morally support each other, the danger exists that participants can react by becoming demoralised, dropping out and turning on each other.[8]

Conclusion

The experiences of the people in the CCF remind us that, contrary to what some writers suggest, history is not without a subject, and demonstrate that agency does not exist in a bubble. But neither are people puppets; they have, linked to structural relationships, 'interests' to defend, and collective action most often refers to such interests that can be cultural, religious, economic and socio-political. Interests that, however 'spontaneous' they may once have been, become enmeshed in, and adapted by, other strategies and interactions, i.e. a radical anti-neoliberal populism espoused by leading participants. However, these are neither activists drilled with ideology nor passive victims of 'power', but part of collective action undertaken – 'given a try'.

Conceptually, the CCF can be understood as a negotiated, relational, dialogical form of collective organisation that is continually constructed and reconstructed as part of an ongoing interaction between those it comprises and those it seeks to challenge. Far from being fixed, its precise conceptual and practical boundaries are open to reshaping, challenges and changes. Like all collective forms of political organisation it is in and of itself an arena of ideological struggle, and this has given rise to differences within the organisation.

While spontaneity is a necessary basis for a successful challenge to the government's polices, the experiences of the CCF suggest it is insufficient and this is reflected in the lack of generalised and sustained activity since late 2002. Della Porta and Diani (2003) note how similar organisations are commonly characterised by periods of intense activity followed by a lull. What then becomes crucial, is that in the periods of abeyance, activities should be directed towards inner reflection, intellectual development and thinking through strategy and tactics.

This should involve as many people as possible. If not, it is possible that some of the problems raised in this research are likely to become obstacles to the CCF's further development. Challenges that one participant summed up as, '. . . it is one thing that we are fighting, we have to understand how are we fighting, who are we fighting . . .' (Interview, Anonymous, 10.08.03b).

In discussing the future of the CCF, one participant recalls how an old anti-apartheid activist warned of the dangers of the CCF becoming a 'popcorn organisation that just pops up every time there is an issue' (Interview, Anonymous, 18.06.03). However, while the socio-economic crisis in South Africa continues, there will always be fertile ground in which organisations like the CCF will be able to sow and nurture a larger community-based organisation in Durban – if they get it right.

Touraine urges social movements to recognise that 'it is not enough simply to denounce the order; one must show that it is not all-powerful, one must rediscover the spring hidden beneath the cement, the word beneath the silence, the questioning beneath the ideology' (1985: 55). In a small way, this is what the CCF, amongst other things, started to do. But the past is not always a guide to the future, and whether a larger and more sustainable organisation can be consolidated in Durban will partly depend on the lessons learnt by, and learning lessons from, CCF participants.

Notes

1. The CCF is not a membership-based organisation and so people will be referred to as 'participants'.
2. Desai (2002) and Desai and Pithouse (2003) replicate elements of this. However, the let-up in activity of many of these organisations seems to have induced more sober reflection (see McKinley and Naidoo 2004).
3. Several participants note how this group is not politically homogeneous and comes from and is influenced by ANC, socialist, Marxist, Black Consciousness, anarchist and autonomist ideas.
4. As Miliband (1979: 29) notes such (class) conflict 'includes all manifestations of social life, and is an economic, cultural/ideological, social and political phenomenon'. However, this does not mean that apparent social classes or individuals will understand the essential conflict in class terms – as class struggle. Neither may individuals who comprise a specific class feel antagonism towards members of other classes. As will become clear, people may or may not be partly or wholly aware of their own

struggle and not how they are linked locally, nationally or internationally to those of others (De Ste Croix 1981).

5.   Of course sexism still exists within the CCF. Yet in moments of struggle, socially constructed divisions begin to be broken down through acts of solidarity, engendering mutual respect. This is not an automatic process and several participants thought non-sexism could potentially be sustained by systematic political discussion and education. For a contrary example of this in post-1994 South Africa, see Pointer (2004).

6.   Ideology is used here in its broadest sense to understand the ideas people hold that are usually related to their social situation, and not in a narrower sense as prescribed political thought (see Harris 1971).

7.   Understood as '. . . a set of doubly "intellectual" and practical "directive" or "organizing" activities and consists essentially both in thinking about what movements can and should do, and in urging the conclusion of that thinking on others' (Barker, Johnson and Lavalette 2001: 5). In this type of activity – intellectual and directive – argument and persuasion is not confined to an elite in a group, but more in the Gramscian sense that potentially includes all participants (see Gramsci 1998).

8.   For example, what were essentially political differences could be rationalised 'racially'. Several participants from Hammarsdale told how some people started saying that resources donated to the CCF was being taken to Chatsworth because the CCF was now an 'Indian organisation'. Although this is not to say that race is not an issue in the CCF.

References

Abrams, P. 1982. *Historical Sociology*. Shepton Mallet: Open Books.

Althusser, L. 1972. *Politics and History: Montesquieu, Rousseau, Hegel and Marx*. London: New Left Books.

Barker, C. 1995. '"The Muck of Ages": Reflections on Proletarian Self-Emancipation'. *Studies in Marxism* 2.

Barker, C., A. Johnson and M. Lavalette (eds). 2001. *Leadership and Social Movements*. Manchester: Manchester University Press.

Bayat, A. 1998. *Street Politics: Poor People's Movements in Iran*. Cairo: The American University in Cairo Press.

Betts, K. 1986. 'The Conditions of Action, Power, and the Problem of Interests'. *The Sociological Review* 34 (1).

Bond, P. 2000. *Elite Transition: From Apartheid to Neoliberalism in South Africa*. London: Pluto Press.

Bonnin, D. 1999. '"We went to Arm Ourselves at the Field of Suffering": Traditions, Experiences and Grassroots Intellectuals in the Making of Class'. *Labour, Capital and Society* 32 (1) April.

Brass, T. 1995. 'Old Conservatism in "New" Clothes'. *The Journal of Peasant Studies* 22 (3).

Brenner, R. 1998. *World Economic Turbulence*. London: Verso.

Callinicos, A. 2003. *An Anti Capitalist Manifesto*. Cambridge: Polity Press.

Charlton, J. 1997. *The Chartists: The First National Workers' Movement*. London: Pluto Press.

Concerned Citizens Forum. 2002a. 'Concerned Citizens Forum Press Statement', Durban. http://sa.indymedia.org/news/2002/05/1214.php.

———. 2002b. 'Concerned Citizens Forum Press Statement', Durban. http://www.queensu.ca/msp/pages/In_The_News/2002/April/ccf.htm.

De Ste Croix, G.E.M. 1981. *The Class Struggle in the Ancient Greek World: From the Archaic Age to the Arab Conquests*. London: Duckworth.

Della Porta, D. and M. Diani. 2003. *Social Movements: An Introduction*. Oxford: Blackwell.

Desai, A. 2002. *We are the Poors: Community Struggles in Post-Apartheid South Africa*. New York: Monthly Review Press.

Desai, A. and R. Pithouse. 2003. *'But We Were Thousands': Dispossession, Resistance, Repossession and Repression in Mandela Park*. Centre for Civil Society Research Report No. 9. Durban: University of Natal.

Dwyer, P. and D. Seddon. 2002. 'The New Wave? A Global Perspective on Popular Protest'. Paper presented at the 8th International Conference on Alternative Futures and Popular Protest, 2–4 April, Manchester Metropolitan University.

Eagleton, T. 2003. *After Theory*. London: Allen Lane.

Giddens, A. 1984. *The Constitution of Society*. Cambridge: Polity Press.

———. 1993. *New Rules of Sociological Method*. Cambridge: Polity Press.

Gramsci, A. 1998. *Selections from Prison Notebooks*. London: Lawrence and Wishart.

Habermas, J. 1976. *The Theory of Communicative Action. Volume 2*. Cambridge: Cambridge University Press.

Harris, N. 1971. *Beliefs in Society: The Problem of Ideology*. Harmondsworth: Penguin.

Horner, B. 2002. 'Anti-Eviction Group get National Allies'. *Sunday Times* 15 December.

Indy Media South Africa. 2002. 'Communities to Plan Mass Rolling Action Against ANC's Forced Removal Plan'. Press statement, 10 December. http:.//southafrica.indymedia.org/news/2002/12/2701.php.

Long, N. and J.D. van der Ploeg. 1994. 'Heterogenity, Actor and Structure: Towards a Reconstitution of the Concept of Structure'. In D. Booth (ed.), *Rethinking Social Development: Theory, Research and Practice*. Harlow: Longman Scientific and Technical.

Maheu, L. (ed.). 1995. *Social Movements and Social Classes: The Future of Collective Action*. London: Sage.

Marais, H. 1998. *South Africa: Limits to Change: The Political Economy of Transition*. London: Zed Books.

Marx, A. 1992. *Lessons of Struggle: South African Internal Opposition, 1960–1990*. New York: Oxford University Press.

McAdam, D. 1982. *Political Process and the Development of Black Insurgency, 1930–1970*. Chicago: University of Chicago Press.

McAdam, D.J., D. McCarthy and M.N. Zald (eds). 1999. *Comparative Perspectives on Social Movements*. Cambridge: Cambridge University Press.

McKinley, D. and P. Naidoo. 2004. 'New Social Movements in South Africa: A Story in Creation'. *Development Update: Mobilising for Change: The Rise of New Social Movements in South Africa* 5 (2). Johannesburg: Interfund.

Meszaros, I. 1971. *The Necessity for Social Control*. Isaac Deutscher Memorial Lecture. London: The Merlin Press.

Miliband, R. 1979. *Marxism and Politics*. Oxford: Oxford University Press.

Mpumalanga Concerned Citizens Group. 2002. 'Message from Mpumalanga Concerned Citizens Group'. http://www.queensu.ca/msp/pages/In_The_News/2002/April/mcg.htm.Mpumalanga Concerned Citizens 2002.

Naidoo, S. 2002. '"We Will Not be Removed": Chatsworth Rents-Arrears Tenants Vow to Resist Council Relocation Plan'. *Sunday Times* 1 December.

Neale, J. 2002. *You Are G8, We Are 6 Billion: The Truth behind The Genoa Protests*. London: Vision Paperbacks.

Pokwana, V. 2002. 'Now the New Left Rises to Fight On'. *City Press* 25 May.

Sibeon, R. 1999. 'Agency, Structure, and Social Chance as Cross-Disciplinary Concepts'. *Politics* 19 (3).

Tarrow, S. 1994. *Power in Movement: Social Movements, Collective Action and Politics*. Cambridge: Cambridge University Press.

———. 2003. ' "Global" Movements, Complex Internationalism, and North-South Inequality'. Paper presented to the Workshop on Contentious Politics, Columbia University, October, and to the Seminar on Inequality and Social Policy, John F. Kennedy School, Harvard University, 17 November.

Tilly, C. 1978. *From Mobilization to Revolution*. New York: Random House.

Thompson, E.P. 1986. *The Making of the English Working Class*. Harmondsworth: Penguin.

Touraine, A. 1985. 'An Introduction to the Study of Social Movements'. *Social Research* 52 (4).

Walton, J. and D. Seddon. 1994. *Free Markets and Food Riots: The Politics of Global Adjustment*. Oxford: Blackwell Publishers.

Interviews

Anonymous. CCF Participant, 18.06.03.
Anonymous. CCF Participant, 23.06.03.
Anonymous. CCF Participant, 24.06.03a.
Anonymous. CCF Participant, 24.06.03b.
Anonymous. CCF Participant, 15.07.03.
Anonymous. CCF Participant, 26.07.03a.
Anonymous. CCF Participant, 26.07.03b.
Anonymous. CCF Participant, 10.08.03a.
Anonymous. CCF Participant, 10.08.03b.
Anonymous. CCF Participant, 13 09.03.

6

Building Unity in Diversity

Social Movement Activism in the Western Cape Anti-Eviction Campaign

Sophie Oldfield and Kristian Stokke

FORMED IN FEBRUARY 2001, the Western Cape Anti-Eviction Campaign is a movement of community organisations from poor, marginalised areas of Cape Town. Campaign activists and organisations share threats and experiences of evictions and water disconnections, discontent with state policies of cost recovery on public services, and dissatisfaction with local political representation (Leitch 2003). An important oppositional voice in local politics in Cape Town, they have joined together to resist disconnections and evictions as well as to intervene in city policies pertaining to housing and public services. The experiential and political unity that has built the Campaign overlies real diversity. Activists and organisations operate in diverse conditions, work from different histories of struggle and relationships with the state, and ground their activism in often-divergent politics. The strength of the Campaign derives from its common community-based identity. Yet, real tension exists between the diversity of community issues, organisations and strategies and the unity required to fight for socio-economic rights and against state policies and actions. Recent experiences highlight that only by accepting its diversity can the Campaign's unity be built.

This chapter analyses the building of the Campaign's 'unity in diversity'. After a brief discussion of public service delivery and cost-recovery policies, we examine the centrality of the Campaign's identity as a community-based movement and the inherent diversity embedded in this identity. We explore the ways in which local contexts shape diverse political practices, while also coalescing as particular modes and repertoires of protest in the Campaign. We also examine the dynamics in which Campaign leadership has emerged and attempted to negotiate and build from its diverse base. We then turn to legal and research initiatives that have brought activists and organisations together in strategic and creative ways. The analysis is concluded with a brief comment on the political significance of the Campaign.

The research has been conducted as a partnership with the Campaign's Community Research Group. While this collaboration is part of a broader agenda of breaking the boundaries between university- and community-based research and researchers, it also facilitated access and richer relationships that were critical to our analysis. With emphasis on in-depth interviews and focus groups with Campaign activists, the research methodology was designed to explore the history and dynamics of the various organisations and areas that are part of the Campaign. Two case studies were also conducted to focus on legal strategies and research capacity building through the development of the Legal Co-ordinating Committee (LCC) and the Community Research Group (CRG) respectively.

Public Service Delivery and Cost-Recovery Policies

In the same way that housing and public services were rallying points for civic struggles against apartheid (Bozzoli 2004; Seekings 2000), they are also contentious issues for new social movements. In the post-apartheid context, South Africa's adoption of liberal democracy and economic neo-liberalism frame social movement struggles for social justice (Desai 2002; Ngwane 2003). Social movements such as the Campaign politicise constitutional rights to housing and basic services, challenging the post-apartheid state's commitment to social justice and substantive democracy. One of the most visible expressions of the tension between substantive democracy and neo-liberalism in South Africa is the tendency for the state to introduce market principles and actors to provide housing and deliver services (Millstein, Oldfield and Stokke 2003; McDonald and Pape 2002; Stokke and Oldfield 2004). The degree to which these trends can be understood as outright privatisation is contested,[1] but there has been an ongoing transition from a statist delivery model to a model based on public/private partnership, in which 'the state acts as a service "ensurer" rather than a service "provider" . . . and municipal services are "run more like a business", with financial cost recovery becoming the most important measure of performance' (McDonald and Smith 2002: 1). Although there have been important achievements with major expansion of housing and service infrastructure since 1994, this impressive record is undermined by increasingly aggressive cost-recovery policies by local governments who are largely dependent on locally generated revenue.

In the Cape Town context, the city has sought to recover arrears on rates and service bills, with city policies stating, for instance, that:

> Action will be taken against those who do not pay – the Council will not hesitate to cut off services and take legal action where necessary. Residents who do not pay will be without electricity or water and will have to pay the additional costs of reconnection fees, lawyers' fees and legal costs. They could ultimately have their houses sold (if they are ratepayers) or be evicted (if they are tenants in a Council house) (City of Cape Town in Xali 2002: 110).

The implementation of this policy has been piecemeal, however, fluctuating with changing political party control of the municipality. Once the ANC gained control of the municipal government, it made some concessions for renters in state housing and for households in arrears.[2] Nonetheless, poor households face an affordability crisis due to high unemployment levels and the real difficulties of eking out livelihoods in the post-apartheid period. Families unable to meet agreements on arrear payments face evictions, disconnections of water and electricity and repossessions of furniture in lieu of rental payment. Consequently, some residents live without water and electricity, others even homes; many illegally reconnect themselves to services, and organise against cost-recovery policies in their neighbourhoods and across the city in movements such as the Campaign (Desai and Pithouse 2003; Smith and Hanson 2003).

Collective Identity Amidst Diverse Contexts

The logic of Campaign organising and politics is based on its collective identity as a community-based movement. This identity constitutes a source of strength, grounding the Campaign in dynamic grassroots struggles. The former chairperson of the Campaign, who is also a critical force in its present direction, explains this identity:

> We made it clear from the start that when people come into the
> Campaign they come in as a member of a community . . . Issues of the
> community are primary and come first. We look at their interests first
> before we think about anything else . . . That is the fundamental
> difference [between us and other movements]: we are constituted by
> community organisations and we deliberately confined the Campaign
> to that. I think that gave it [the Campaign] a different character . . . I
> think it's a process that happened that also allowed the emergence of a
> community leadership. It allowed that kind of strength to be established
> at a community level despite all the problems and confusion sometimes
> (Interview, Brown, 27.02.04).

At the same time, however, the Campaign's community-driven character also
generates organisational and resource challenges that yield fragmentation and
intense organisational politics.

A diversity of community environments frames the organisations and the
daily issues activists organise around. The Campaign grew initially in areas of
state-built rental housing, particularly Tafelsig in Mitchells Plain, Valhalla Park
and Elsies River. Built in the 1970s and 1980s, flats and maisonettes in these
areas were designated for families formerly classified as coloured. Ranging from
one-bedroom to three-bedroom structures, units that were designed for single
families are now homes for multiple generations due to insufficient state-built
housing and lack of economic means to enter into market-based rental or
ownership contracts. Much of the employment that sustained families in these
working-class coloured areas – textile and food-processing factories – has been
lost with factory closures in the 1990s (Workers World News 2000 in Xali 2002:
114). Thus arrears for rentals and water, and, in some instances, electricity,
continue to accrue, generating intense insecurity for residents and antagonism
from the municipality. Residents frequently face furniture repossessions to
compensate for accounts in arrears, and evictions as well.

Different forms of apartheid-period 'hire-purchase' homeownership
schemes, where residents are both tenants of council and homeowners, were
built across coloured group areas in the 1980s and 1990s (for example, in St
Montague Village, Lavender Hill and Lentegeur). Families moved into these
housing schemes towards the end of the apartheid period when the state was
trying to move out of a landlord role with responsibility for administration and

maintenance. Administrative confusion reigns in these areas, raising questions about rental payments, access to government subsidies for converting renters to homeowners, and issues of administrative justice where departments have not maintained accurate records or where administrative duties have shifted between various state institutions over the past two decades.

Homeowners dominate some areas of the Campaign, for instance Mandela Park in Khayelitsha, an area whose struggle has come to symbolise the Campaign recently. Housing in these areas was built in the late 1980s and early 1990s by private developers in partnership with the apartheid state and banks. Residents moved directly from informal settlements into bonded homes with obligatory monthly bond payments. Now approximately 90 per cent of the families in Mandela Park have fallen into arrear problems (McKune 2002). Banks holding bonds in the area have turned to Servcon, a joint venture between the Department of Housing and the Banking Council, to take over low-income bank-owned properties that are over three months in arrears and offering 'special rehabilitation programmes' that often involve 'right sizing' and relocation to a 'RDP' state-subsidy house elsewhere. The bank-owned house is then sold on the private market, thus enabling the bank to recoup its bond costs. This process has met with strident resistance in Mandela Park and in other parts of the city facing similar problems.

Some organisations in the Campaign organise in informal settlements and new neighbourhoods where post-1996 subsidy-built housing has been constructed by the state, such as Delft South and Philippi. The poor quality of housing, inability to pay water bills and the future threat of evictions due to non-payment of rates are the issues that have catalysed Campaign activities in these areas.

Plurality of Political Strategies
Organisations in the Campaign employ a wide range of political practices, from legal battles to mass 'informal' reconnections of services and territorial control over neighbourhoods. Strategies grow from heterogeneous local contexts and logics, but are also articulated and mediated by citywide and regional processes and debates. In this section we draw on a selection of organisations to demonstrate the ways in which local context and political practice define multiple positions along a continuum that spans engagement with and opposition to the state.

Some organisations in the Campaign engage with the state, its institutions, officials, politicians and its structures of governance on a daily basis. Activists in these contexts stress the imperative to engage. An Athlone civic activist, for example, argues:

> The difference is, and that is part of the things that I preach with the other comrades, get organised. You must know that we started off as concerned people and when we approached council politicians they said you people are only concerned you are not recognised. I think that is a little bit of the difference. Like I said, get organised, register yourself, get a constitution. That's a first good step. Politics has changed today in South Africa. You know, when we were in the struggle, we were heard on the streets. But what I have noticed being an activist with the Anti-Eviction coming out of Athlone, to be heard today you've got to sit with these bastards in the boardroom. Sorry to say it. You've got to sit with them in the boardroom because we've got boardroom politics now here in South Africa (Interview, Anonymous, 06.02).

Registration as a community organisation with the city is not an unusual choice but it does shape and reflect an organisation's strategies.

In stark contrast, engagement comes with explicit constraints and great costs in other cases. In a neighbourhood in the Philippi area, opposition to government policy on water cut-offs is read as opposition to the ANC. Two activists explain the logic and strategy of mobilising against water cut-offs in this context:

> We [the youth] tried to form our own organisations in regard to social and environmental issues. Through these issues we can attack government but in a polite, indirect way. If you confront them directly about politics they won't listen. But by talking about environmental or social issues, you can address community issues (Interview, Anonymous, 04.06.02).

Organising against government policy is read as anti-ANC by local leaders and therefore as radical and disruptive. They continue to explain:

You can't say you object to the water policy, for instance. You will get marked; you will run the risk of being eliminated. Rather you keep your cover. People fear being killed . . . If you organise, mobilise other people, you are at risk of being killed, they see you as opposition . . . So we are a group here, not an organisation, that way we look neutral (Interview, Anonymous, 04.06.02).

Anecdotal evidence suggests that people in power in the area have vested interests in local government contracts, such as the installation of water and electricity services and the building of state-subsidised houses. Threats to policies connected to service and infrastructure delivery are interpreted therefore as challenges to these interests and more broadly to ANC-led governance in the area.

The Philippi and Athlone cases indicate that activism is defined in local contexts and through particular sets of relationships between organisations and a range of state institutions and officials. This can be further illustrated by two brief case studies in Valhalla Park and Mandela Park.

The Valhalla Park United Civic Front provides a useful case to examine the ways in which community activists and organisations engage with state officials and institutions and also, simultaneously, oppose it through overt and covert actions. The Civic has made significant gains by working within the system while also working outside of state-accepted norms of behaviour. Mixing engaging in the system and acting in protest reflects the organisation's strategic choices and hard-won experiences over the past two decades.

The Civic is characterised by persistent engagement with officials in the police and the health and housing departments. By building up relationships with local officials over a long period of time, Civic leaders have found ways in which to make them more responsive. In the case of the police, for instance, leaders' personal connections and direct contact provide an intermediary between residents and the local police station. Relationships with the police are also nurtured through participation in the Community Policing Forum. A similar personal relationship has developed with the local head of the Housing Office, who, unlike officials in many poor parts of Cape Town, has allowed unemployed residents unable to pay rentals to apply for indigent status to relieve them of some of the burden of their bills. Although Civic leaders engage with officials, they do not depend on these types of relationships to resist evictions or to improve conditions in the neighbourhood.

A creative combination of engagement and opposition has generated a series of successes for the community. Residents and Civic activists are vigilant about council activities in the area. If residents see a council vehicle enter the neighbourhood, they alert the Civic leaders. Residents and activists then respond immediately to ensure that council does not cut off water or electricity without negotiating with the Civic structures. Their persistence and insistence that council must consult the Civic has paid off from their perspective as the council rarely enters the area without consultation.

Personal experience of evictions drives many leaders to continue to work hard to protect and support neighbours and the community. Leaders play multiple roles, but they are also supported by a structure of other community leaders operating at the street level. A weekly meeting is held every Thursday night where street leaders and the executive committee report back to residents on progress on issues. It is in these forums that decisions are taken on appropriate responses and strategies – in particular when to work in the system and when to disrupt and challenge it. Although leaders of the Civic continue to pursue goals through working with council officials and politicians, in general they have little faith in the system. Two executive committee members conclude:

> Council don't listen to us if we go through the right channels. They don't listen. They make as if they listen if you go through the right channels. They don't take notice of us. But, if we do what we do, then immediately they respond . . . If they take too long, then we do our own thing (Interview, Anonymous, 14.08.03).

The United Civic Front's latest victory is their most significant. 'Homeless' Valhalla Park residents occupied state-owned land in the neighbourhood to make the city council move towards providing more housing in the area. When the council applied for a court interdict to remove the families and also implicated the Civic in the so-called illegal land invasion, the United Civic Front filed a counter claim in the high court to demand their constitutional right to emergency housing. The judgement in favour of the residents of the informal settlement and the Civic has the potential to impact on the city's legal obligations in providing services for informal settlement, not only in Cape Town but also regionally.

Whereas the Valhalla Park United Civic Front has successfully combined political engagement and mass mobilisation, the anti-eviction campaigns in Tafelsig and Mandela Park have gradually entered into a strategy of collective resistance and a confrontational relationship with local government, the banking sector and the police (Desai and Pithouse 2003; Legassick 2004).

The cornerstone of the Mandela Park Anti-Eviction Campaign (MPAEC) has been the weekly community meeting, with large numbers of residents attending. The community meetings discuss the problems facing the community and make decisions about strategies and activities. Campaign activists also report back to the community about their communication with banks, councillors and state institutions. The MPAEC has sought an active dialogue with the banks and the Provincial Minister of Housing, inviting them to community meetings but refusing to send delegates to meetings outside the community. The campaign has raised collective demands regarding the sub-standard quality of the houses, ownership of the land, housing subsidies and the handling of outstanding debts. These demands have not been addressed in any meaningful way by the relevant state institutions. Instead, activists have been met with what they see as attempts at diffusing the issues and confusing the activists, as they are told to take their housing complaints to the developers, their economic problems to Servcon, and their land demands to politicians. All the invited banks, Servcon and the Provincial Minister of Housing have failed to meet with the campaign in the community.

The explicit policy of the MPAEC is to build alliances with those who support them in their struggle, but not spend time on talks that can take away the focus from the collective struggle. So far, no councillors, political parties, trade unions or non-governmental organisations (NGOs) have taken up this supportive role on terms that are acceptable to the community. This lack of meaningful political engagement, combined with the actual practices and future threats of evictions, have made the MPAEC resort to various forms of public protest, such as public demonstrations and occupations at banks and political institutions. The community has mobilised against evictions and repossessions of property and has also put evicted families back into their homes. These various actions have been met with increasingly harsh measures, including a court interdict on behalf of the banks against community leaders, arrests and lengthy periods of incarceration of activists, and increased use of police violence during evictions and repossession of property.

In general terms, the MPAEC has experienced a criminalisation of the campaign and its leaders. Community members and activists are spending time and energy in court and trying to raise funds for bail and lawyers. Despite a constant lack of funds, both the Tafelsig and the Mandela Park campaigns insist on maintaining their autonomy with regard to all NGOs. A community activist explains this position:

> We don't accept money from anybody for a simple reason: we don't want them to direct us. We are on the ground; we will direct our struggle. So we don't want NGOs to rule us or to act on our behalf, because they don't have our interests at heart. They have their own interests at heart. We understand that and I always make it clear that the NGOs get paid to be in the struggle, – we don't. We are forced to be in the struggle because of our circumstances at home (Interview, Anonymous, 05.02).

With limited economic resources, organisational fragmentation in the absence of a co-ordinating ideological movement and no political allies, the collective resistance in Mandela Park and Tafelsig faces the danger of becoming 'isolated militant particularisms, unable to function in the face of sustained repression' (Desai and Pithouse 2003: 23).

These experiences from different communities demonstrate unity in facing common problems, but also diversity of contexts and strategies. Most groups seek to engage council and other relevant stakeholders. However, the experiences of accessibility are diverse. The modes of protest and traditions of organising vary considerably across former coloured and African group areas as well as among organisations within neighbourhoods and sections of the city. Consequently, the present repertoire of protest ranges from strategies that are compatible with the rules and procedures of the formal political system (for example, community meetings, petitions, negotiations and legal demonstrations) to practices that are more confrontational and unlawful (for example, illegal reconnections, occupations of houses, forceful blocking of evictions and sit-ins). Many of the organisations combine diverse kinds of protests and only employ the more radical tactics to solve problems and to resist when negotiations and legal demonstrations fail to yield acceptable outcomes. At a Campaign scale, the diverse community organisations under its ambit produce a complex mixture of political strategy and ideology that is both a strength and identity of the Campaign as well as a source, at times, of intense confrontation and contestation.

The Politics of Organisation and Leadership

The Campaign faces a formidable challenge to merge diverse local issues and political practices into a coherent and effective citywide organisation. It needs to encompass and to include groups from across the city with different ideologies, traditions of protest, expectations of leadership and organisation with few resources and in a context where crises (from evictions to arrests) arise frequently. The ideological, geographical and racial differentiation that characterises community organisations within the Campaign, however, is not an absolute obstacle to the development of political strategy and practice at a Campaign scale. Instead it has provided at times an impetus for innovation where organisations learn from each other and generate more effective local and citywide strategies and networks. Reflecting on the relationship between neighbourhood work and the Campaign, the former chairperson observes:

> Many [community workers] started seeing themselves as being activists within the campaign more on the Western Cape level instead of where they were in the past in their own geographical area. And so they started to organise – go out to other areas and help people and assist, pamphleteering and stuff like that. They started to work at that level and I think that was a qualitative growth, people weren't confined to their residential, geographical area anymore in terms of their organisation. It [activism in the Campaign] opened up the space for people now to go over geographical borders and limits (Interview, Brown, 27.02.04).

The Campaign came into existence as a response to the scale and violence of state-led evictions; in particular activists in affected communities formed a steering committee to organise a march against evictions in the centre of Cape Town. The march publicised the existence of the Campaign, alerting people facing evictions in poor areas across the city. Although the Campaign grew with the momentum of publicity, and as a result of the work of activists and the Uni-City's implementation of its threats of evictions, the steering committee ceased to function due to practical organisational constraints. Nevertheless, it was evident that the Campaign in embryonic form filled a political and organisational vacuum. An activist recalls the first march:

> We marched to Peter Marais [then the city mayor]. This was the first
> time the communities came together on the streets and marched to the
> city centre . . . that was the first indication that there was a basis to
> organise people and to take things forward. People realised that they
> have to work outside of the official structures or the traditional structures.
> I think it was partly that link and the memory of the 1980s . . . and the
> UDF [United Democratic Front] style of organising. There was also
> another factor: there was this vacuum; there was nothing to take up
> mass mobilisation and local issues (Interview, Brown, 27.02.04).

After the first march, a loose group of activists with connections from the 1980s
started to meet and discuss the possible formation of a network, something
creative to challenge the state and move beyond traditional ways of organising.
A variety of meetings occurred in 2001, but it proved difficult to co-ordinate
local activism and form an organisational structure.

In 2002 the need to establish accountability in order to deal with finances
and ensure representation once again raised the issue of the formation of a
more formal Campaign, which then became the subject of debate. The issues
of structure and leadership were hotly contested. Debates highlighted divisions
in ideology and personality, but also in the direction that the Campaign should
take. For instance, some argued: 'To proceed in legal and policy challenges – to
challenge the state seriously – requires the Campaign to constitute itself formally
and legally as a body.' Others argued the counterpoint: 'By establishing ourselves
legally and publicly, we make ourselves a target and we diminish our strength,
which is the Campaign's informality and flexibility and our less visible power
across the city' (Campaign meeting June 2002). Despite some dissension, in
mid-2002 a constitution was drafted, and an executive committee was formed
with an elected chairperson, treasurer and secretary.

The executive committee operated in the 2002–03 period, establishing three
units: the LCC, the CRG, and a media unit (the latter was later disbanded).
However, the executive committee found it difficult to function: some leaders
were arrested; others were on the run from the police; and the committee had
no budget and resources. Frequently, even the costs of bringing members
together for meetings were prohibitive:

A number of people stopped functioning because they were unable to and others because they were arrested or restricted from attending meetings. So once again you had three individuals who had to take responsibility for co-ordinating the structure . . . The lack of opportunity to really deal with these issues – the chance to really talk things through – that was very much absent and problematic. The nature of the Campaign and its lack of a resource base also emerged [as an issue]. These things bedevilled the Exco to a large extent (Interview, Brown, 27.02.04).

The holding of regional councils and annual general meetings (AGMs) – prescribed as requirements by the Campaign's constitution – also proved extremely difficult. The AGM that was finally organised at the end of 2003 showed that there was no consensus on the way forward. Elections could not be held and members were unwilling to postpone them while maintaining the executive committee. At the same time serious tensions over financial accountability arose. With increasing numbers of arrests for serious criminal charges, the Campaign also needed to come up with large amounts of bail monies and lawyers' fees. In this complex, highly contested context, the executive committee disbanded and some activists left the Campaign. The dissolution of the formal structures of the Campaign can be read as a result of a combination of resource issues, the problem of differential ideologies and strategy, and a failure in managing representation from the diverse communities constituting the Campaign.

Nevertheless, despite leadership and organisational problems, the Campaign has not ceased to exist. Unable to hold elections, the decision-making process has been devolved to the community level, the place in which it originated in 2001. To revitalise itself, the Campaign has dealt systematically with the conflicts that led to the splintering of the executive committee in 2003. Activists have been called to account for the conflicts, particularly for financial transactions in 2003–04. The process facilitated making the issues underpinning the conflict transparent. Since this difficult process of review and accounting was completed, in 2005 the Campaign held strategic planning sessions as well as continued discussions on structure and leadership at a community-organisation level.

Unifying Campaign Activism Through Legal Struggle and Research

Despite a vacuum in its structures and leadership, the Campaign has not disintegrated. Several important initiatives have functioned to bring activists and organisations together to continue to protect families against evictions and cut-offs and to build the Campaign's potential in the future. The following discussion focuses on attempts to build unity and challenge policy through legal means and community research.

Legal Struggles

Arrests and cases of police brutality in Tafelsig and Lavender Hill in late 2000 were the initial sparks that fuelled the development of the Campaign. Since then a string of arrests of activists has peppered the Campaign's existence. The starting point for the Campaign's engagement in legal struggles has been defensive, a response to the criminalisation of activism through summonses, interdicts and arrests. The most publicised instances have been criminal cases lodged against activists in Mandela Park, and against Max Ntanyana in particular. Bail has been refused at times and has, when granted, included far-reaching apartheid-like conditions (Desai and Pithouse 2003; Legassick 2004). Criminal and common law proceedings have also targeted residents, activists and organisations in Vrygrond in 2000, in Tafelsig and in St Montague Village in 2001–02, and in Valhalla Park in 2002–03.

Legal defence is costly and the process of generating bail funds and payment of lawyer fees has consumed immense amounts of energy and frequently caused internal friction in and between community organisations and the Campaign. In this situation, the LCC has been established as the Campaign's systematic response, under the leadership of Ashraf Cassiem and with assistance from Michael Murphy, a lawyer frequently representing Campaign members and families facing evictions. Murphy recalls the context for the LCC:

> Every single day there would be another case . . . Every case involved experts giving evidence . . . it was just impossible to manage. I said to Ashraf then: look you guys must make up your minds. If we don't go the legal route, I agree but then stop phoning me . . . The alternative is that we have to find a way to use the law to help . . . If you looked at the courts, like Goodwood or Kuils River, so many people are being evicted everyday. It [the court] is being used as a debt collection system: just queues and queues of people and all that would happen is that, if they had a lawyer then they would negotiate their date to leave [the house].

More often than not they never had a lawyer – or the lawyer would never arrive – and they [families] were being evicted hand over fist. The very bulk of it gave me the idea for our sole aim to delay and frustrate, to clog the courts up . . . So I tried to show them [LCC activists] how to delay and frustrate in ridiculous ways (Interview, Murphy, 21.06.04).

To set up the LCC, Murphy ran a five-month course on court procedures, legal arguments, and loopholes through which activists could represent families facing evictions. People who want to be represented by the LCC officially join the Campaign for the Recognition of the Fundamental Right to a Home, which substantiates the LCC's access to magistrate and high courts. The LCC initially facilitates the postponement of the case so that it will be heard in court, rather than negotiated outside of the magistrates' court. The LCC then submits affidavits that deny the grounds of the eviction according to rights protected by other laws and the constitution. The affidavits force the evicting parties (banks or the state) to prove all contextual issues in court. This obligation increases the costs and time of the eviction process, while also allowing the LCC to challenge evictions as arbitrary and the claim that there are no other options. The LCC's goal is therefore threefold: to stop the rubber-stamping of eviction orders in magistrates' courts; to ensure that cases are being heard in court; and to generate a court record on the arbitrary and inequitable nature of evictions as a basis for opposing them in the constitutional court. Cassiem recounts some of his court experiences to explain the intimidating context but also the power of the LCC to disrupt the legal process:

In the court the magistrate asked: but *who are you?* They belittle you; make you feel like a nothing. I say: I am here to represent a poor family, to save these people from being evicted . . . Our goal is to tell these stories, to get these stories on the court record. Just by standing up there, I am a spanner in the works. In the high court, I stood up in my Landless People's Movement T-shirt. We're not there to win. We know we'll lose (in most cases). So I laugh at the process – I laugh at them, they don't know how to deal with that . . . In the high court you're not allowed to speak until you're recognised by the judge. To be recognised by the judge, to even be heard, you have to speak; you have to be rude and loud so they know that you are there. One time the judge towered over me and shouted: *Who are you? What are you doing here?* I just talked until he stopped and saw that he must let me talk. So I talked really loud and really fast. The process is intimidating and lawyers, magistrates and judges intend to intimidate us (Interview, Cassiem, 10.05.04).

The LCC process is demanding for the activists. In mid-2004 they had 40 cases with more families arriving every day. Officials at magistrates' courts and even lawyers in private practice have advised families to turn to the LCC for help. Once they take on a case, the responsibility is immense. Although LCC intervention buys time for families facing evictions, the process of building a constitutional court case requires resources and professional legal practitioners, as well as policy intervention and political debate that questions not only the legality or constitutionality of evictions but their humanity and morality as well.

The LCC's activities constitute an important element of the Campaign's legal struggle but at present they do not directly challenge policy. Another case, in Valhalla Park, has challenged the City of Cape Town's housing policy through strategic use of the legal system. The Valhalla Park United Civic Front (UCF) won a landmark case in July 2003 in which the high court rejected the City of Cape Town's application to evict and remove the 7de Laan informal settlement in Valhalla Park and also ruled that the city is responsible for giving the residents permanent tenure in the area and to provide services (High Court of South Africa, City of Cape Town vs. Neville Rudolph and Forty Nine Others, Judgement Case 8970/01). The city's application argued that the continued existence of the informal settlement on city land zoned as a park was a land invasion that set a dangerous precedent:

There is a potential, if the situation is not restored, of massive invasions in numerous other areas particularly where invasions are driven by organisations using people as pawns in the process. United Front Civic [sic] Organisation's role in causing the park to be occupied cannot be ignored. Further invasions may have devastating consequences for proper town planning, health laws and management thereof and the maintenance of law and order (Case 8970/01 2003: 21).

The Legal Resource Centre responded on behalf of the Valhalla Park UCF with a counter-application that argued that the city had failed to deliver on its constitutional obligation to provide housing to families in desperate, immediate need for shelter. The city disputed that the families were in desperate need or that their need was any different from other families on the housing waiting list. The presiding judge ruled in favour of the Valhalla Park UCF and explicitly addressed what he calls the city's 'denial' of their constitutional and statutory obligations with regards to housing:

> In light of these facts, and the circumstances under which these people have been living, it is astonishing to find that Applicant's [City of Cape Town] Head of Housing makes the assertion that none of the Respondents are 'persons in crisis' as contemplated in *Grootboom*. This statement is indicative of a state of denial on Applicant's part and a failure to recognise and acknowledge that there is, in fact, any category of persons to which it has any obligation beyond the obligation to put them on the waiting-list for housing in the medium to long term, because they are people 'with no access to land, no roof over their heads, and who were living in intolerable conditions or crisis situations'. It is in my view, precisely the same failure as was held, in *Grootboom*, to constitute a breach of the Constitution (Case 8970/01 2003: 44–5).

Judge Selikowitz ruled that the city must provide emergency services and that the residents have the right to stay on the land where they have squatted. Although the city has not yet met the judge's ruling, the Valhalla Park UCF and the Campaign consider the case a qualified victory.

The Campaign's legal experiences are mixed. In disputes, the city seems quite prepared to take activists and organisations to court, which forces the Campaign to engage in time-consuming and costly legal struggles. Even when cases have been won, the possibilities for appeals and continued delays are large. At the same time, legal cases are a form of struggle that state officials take seriously and where there is a potential for progressive policy changes.

Linking Activism and Research to Challenge Policy

The Campaign has also initiated a number of research initiatives, such as the CRG, which supports research by activists on the issues that drive community organisations and the Campaign. The CRG works on two premises: first, that research is critical to substantiate and shape activism in order to challenge policy;

and, second, that activists research in their existing activities but often lack resources and skills to make it strategically useful. Reflecting the general dialectic between unity and diversity in the Campaign, the CRG has changed its focus from working on one joint project in 2003 to supporting a range of projects in particular community organisations in 2004. The CRG experiences demonstrate the potential to support activism in four ways: first, through building local organisations; second, by affirming activists' identities and experiences; third, by substantiating claims in order to challenge policies effectively; and, fourth, by facilitating sharing and learning between activists and organisations and thus building unity.

Activists have found that research on relevant issues has helped them to build their local organisations. In Valhalla Park, for instance, research on families living in backyards has helped to link activists with residents. In this case, the research has involved a door-to-door survey to document the numbers of families living in backyards and the conditions that they negotiate. One participant describes how this research process has deepened their understanding of the community:

> We thought we knew what was going on in our area but we found out that there are actually many things that we didn't know. Now, we feel like we really know what's going on in people's lives and that people are suffering. We found out also that people don't know their rights. They really don't. For many it's not necessary that they go through what they are going through. It's because they don't know their rights (CRG Research Launch, Valhalla Park United Civic Front, 24.09.04).

Other activists articulate the research process in a personal way. In the Silvertown Anti-Eviction Campaign's project to document the effects of arrears on different groups such as pensioners, single parents and the unemployed, an activist has found recognition and affirmation of his own struggles. He testifies:

> The stories I wrote are all true; they happened to me. There's no lies in them . . . The reason I wrote these stories is because this is how it happened to me. I thought I was the only one . . . now I know other people have the same problems. There's comradeship in that (CRG Research Launch, Silvertown Anti-Eviction Campaign, 24.09.04).

His organisation plans to use the in-depth interviews and life histories to produce a booklet for the community to open up discussion about arrears and the immense stresses they generate in families. This booklet will accompany a document on city policies that affect Silvertown residents directly and their corresponding rights.

The Lentegeur Community Forum has compiled an array of documents and personal experiences to support their claim that their housing bills are too high and that many residents should already own their houses. It is premature to draw a direct relationship between such research and policy challenges, but one activist articulates the potential power of the documentation produced through their project:

> In order to speak out we need the proof to speak to officials. We have that proof here [in the document]. We have that proof in our community . . . The research did wonders. If we didn't have the research, I would never have compiled my facts into this book . . . This is a true document . . . Everybody can look at it and see our issues. *'Fear not when the people are near.'* The only thing is first *do* your research so you can back yourself up (CRG Research Launch, Lentegeur Community Forum, 24.09.04).

The CRG project has proved a forum through which activists can operate at a Campaign scale. This space has been especially important in a situation where Campaign structures are in flux and not fully operational. CRG workshops and meetings have facilitated a sharing of experiences, strategies and support. At the same time, the 2003 and 2004 projects have enabled the CRG's own organisational development and articulation of its agenda to locate ownership of research within the Campaign rather than with externally-based researchers and institutions. The CRG represents an initiative through which Campaign organisations use research to support activism, to develop research capacity, and to contribute to the Campaign's activism in proactive ways.

The Political Significance of the Campaign

The Western Cape Anti-Eviction Campaign has emerged from local everyday experiences of municipal cost-recovery policies with consequent evictions, disconnections and state repression. The local nature of these mobilising issues, combined with the ideological, geographical and racial differentiation that characterises the community organisations, make the activism within the Campaign highly localised and diverse. While the parallel experiences and demands across the city provide a basis for unity, the actual diversity produces fragmenting and often conflicting tendencies that challenge attempts to generate organisational coherence. Thus, the Campaign has so far been localised and issue-based with limited capacity to merge diverse issues and effectively challenge policy-making processes. However, the absence of a well-functioning organisation with extensive capacity to utilise the political opportunity structures of the liberal democratic state should not be used to write off the Campaign as little more than a set of particularistic struggles. As fragmented and under-resourced as it is, the presence of the Campaign nevertheless poses a systemic challenge at a symbolic level as it questions the government's continued commitment to the working poor and their everyday struggles.

In simplified terms, the South African political field is marked by a competition over the right to be the legitimate representatives of 'poor people in struggle'. On the one hand there are the hegemonic forces of the Tripartite Alliance and its civil society affiliates, with extensive symbolic capital rooted in and maintained through representations of the anti-apartheid struggle and post-apartheid political achievements. On the other hand there are the new social movements that mobilise communities in a continued struggle for socio-economic justice and substantive democracy. The struggle over meaning between the 'old' and 'new' movements revolves around shared reference points, as both claim to be the legitimate representatives of poor people that struggle for social justice. This congruence creates a political space for constructive collaboration as well as political contestation. Whereas the government alliance relies on extensive objectified political capital, the power of movements such as the Campaign originates in their ability to mobilise communities for public acts of resistance and to speak on behalf of the working poor. This symbolic capital holds the potential of being transformed into institutionalised political power through political negotiations or future electoral contestation. The development of counter-hegemonic discourses and consciousness regarding people, their rights and public resistance contributes to an alternative 'common sense' and to political contestation and uncertainty in socio-economic policy-making. The Campaign's participation in this post-apartheid struggle over meaning is a source of internal unity and political influence, even in a situation of organisational weakness and fragmentation.

Acknowledgements

Although we take full responsibility for the analysis in this report, we thank activists in the Campaign who have generously given their time for interviews and discussions with us. We also thank the Network on Contextual Politics and Development at the University of Oslo, Norway, as well as the project organisers for research funding.

Notes

1. The most recent expression of this debate is found in the letters and commentaries in the *Mail and Guardian* following Ferial Haffajee's 'Fact, Fiction and the New Left' where she argues that privatisation is exaggerated in the South African case and illustrates the ways in which social movements try 'to make South Africa a node on the map of anti-globalisation resistance' (*Mail and Guardian* 18–24 June 2004). A series of replies contested her argument, including interventions from the Social Movements Indaba, academics and activists Fatima Meer and Patrick Bond, and Roger Ronnie, general secretary of the South African Municipal Workers' Union (*Mail and Guardian* 25 June – 1 July 2004; 2–9 July 2004).
2. From 1 April 2004 rental arrears accumulated before July 1997 have been written off and the city will match R1 for every R1 repayment on arrears accrued between July 1997 and June 2002 (*Cape Times* March 2004).

References

Bozzoli, B. 2004. *Theatres of Struggle and the End of Apartheid.* Johannesburg: Witwatersrand University Press.

Desai, A. 2002. *We are the Poors: Community Struggles in Post-Apartheid South Africa.* New York: Monthly Review Press.

Desai, A. and R. Pithouse. 2003. *'But We Were Thousands': Dispossession, Resistance, Repossession and Repression in Mandela Park.* Centre for Civil Society Research Report No. 9. Durban: University of Natal.

Judgment in the High Court of South Africa (Cape of Good Hope Provincial Division) in the matter between: The City of Cape Town and Neville Rudolph and Forty Nine Others, Case 8970/01. 7 July 2003. 1–55. Judge Selikowitz.

Legassick, M. 2004. 'Direct Action in South Africa: Militant Community Struggles for Housing against Post-Apartheid capitalism'. *Labour's Militant Voice: Building a Socialist Alternative to the Dictatorship of Big Business* 12 (spring/summer): 8–9.

Leitch, R. 2003. Campaign Notes. Cape Town: Community Research Group, Western Cape Anti-Eviction Campaign.

McDonald, D. and J. Pape (eds). 2002. *Cost Recovery and the Crisis of Service Delivery in South Africa.* Cape Town: HSRC Press.

McDonald, D. and L. Smith. 2002. 'Privatizing Cape Town: Service Delivery and Policy Reforms since 1996'. Occasional Papers No. 7. Cape Town: Municipal Services Project.

McKune, K. 2002. 'The Pursuit of Justice and Equity: The Case of Evictions in Mandela Park, Khayelitsha'. Masters thesis, Department of Geography, Royal Holloway, University of London.

Millstein, M., S. Oldfield and K. Stokke. 2003. 'uTshani BuyaKhuluma – The Grass Speaks: The Political Space and Capacity of the South African Homeless People's Federation'. *Geoforum* 34: 457–68.

Ngwane, T. 2003. 'Sparks in the Township'. *New Left Review* 22: 37–56.

Seekings, J. 2000. *The UDF: A History of the United Democratic Front in South Africa, 1983–1991*. Cape Town: David Philip.

Smith, L. and S. Hanson. 2003. 'Access to Water for the Urban Poor in Cape Town: Where Equity Meets Cost Recovery'. *Urban Studies* 40 (8): 1517–48.

Stokke, K. and S. Oldfield. 2004. 'Social Movements, Socio-Economic Rights and Substantial Democracy in South Africa'. In J. Harriss, K. Stokke and O. Törnquist (eds), *Politicising Democracy: The New Local Politics of Democratisation in Developing Countries*. London: Palgrave Macmillan.

Xali, M. 2002. ' "They are Killing us Alive": A Case Study of the Impact of Cost Recovery on Service Provision in Makhaza Section, Khayelitsha'. In D. McDonald and J. Pape (eds), *Cost Recovery and the Crisis of Service Delivery in South Africa*. Cape Town: HSRC Press.

Interviews

Anonymous. Community Activist, 06.02.

Anonymous. Community Activist, 04.06.02.

Anonymous. Community Activist, 14.08.03.

Anonymous. Community Activist, 05.02.

Brown, Faizel. Ex-Chairperson, Western Cape Anti-Eviction Campaign, 27.02.04.

Cassiem, Ashraf. Legal Co-ordinating Committee, Western Cape Anti-Eviction Campaign, 10.05.04.

Murphy, Michael. Lawyer. 21.06.04.

Community Research Group (CRG) Research Launch, Panel Presentations:

Lentegeur Community Forum, 24.09.04.

Silvertown Anti-Eviction Campaign, 24.09.04.

Valhalla Park United Civic Front, 24.09.04.

7

The Landless People's Movement and the Failure of Post-Apartheid Land Reform

Stephen Greenberg[1]

IN 2001, REPRESENTATIVES of landless formations from around South Africa came together to form a national umbrella to take their struggles forward in a united way. The resultant Landless People's Movement (LPM) has arisen in a context of the negative effects of years of belt-tightening fiscal policies on the poor and marginalised majority of the country, following the adoption of the neo-liberal Growth, Employment and Redistribution (GEAR) macro-economic strategy in 1996. Despite the historically significant process of political democratisation, marked by the first universal democratic elections in South Africa in 1994, economic restructuring has favoured the owners of economic power over those without. The ANC provides the political leadership for an alliance that groups large-scale capital with the organised working class to pursue seemingly common interests based on a developmental platform. The resulting corporatist arrangement, exemplified by the tripartite National Economic Development and Labour Council (NEDLAC), ties a redistributive project to capitalist economic growth based on an export-led strategy. While the inward-looking apartheid economic institutions and regulations are dismantled in favour of outward-looking institutions and regulations that facilitated globally competitive economic activity, social policies are designed to play a welfarist role to ameliorate the fallout of economic restructuring. This is coupled with the marketisation of social services, where potential citizens entitled to social services are transformed into customers (clients or consumers) who have to pay for these services.

In rural and urban areas alike, the most marginalised under apartheid bear a heavy burden in post-apartheid economic restructuring. Farm dwellers and labour tenants face mass retrenchments and evictions as landowners are exposed to global competition and reorganise their product mixes and workforces. Residents of informal settlements in and around major conurbations find that investment-friendly government policies are raising the value of the land they live on but do not have legal access to, greatly increasing their tenure insecurity as owners speculate and clear the land for future development. Political channels to deal with this are closed as residents remain disorganised; it is said the ruling party imposes its control over channels for public participation, and local planning and development objectives are increasingly skewed towards the interests of the capitalist economy (Greenberg 2004).

Globally the shift away from government-led redistributive land reform to land market reform in the 1980s (Riad El-Ghonemy 1999: 1) resulted in a 'willing-seller, willing-buyer' model of land redistribution supported and implemented by the World Bank. It sparked renewed global struggles around land, in which the Brazilian landless workers' movement (Movimento dos Trabhaladores Rurais Sem Terra, MST) has been the most influential. In southern Africa the issue of land dispossession also rose to prominence following the Zimbabwean government's sudden shift from a 'willing-seller, willing-buyer' model of land reform to a policy of large-scale expropriations in 2000. This context saw the rise of a number of grassroots movements that are politically independent of the ruling Alliance and organise in opposition to the government's macro-economic policies and its negative effects. A loose alliance has developed between the landless movement and these other formations in their common antagonism to evictions and forced removals, water and electricity cut-offs and failure to deliver on promises to redistribute land.

Responding to Exclusion: Mobilising the Landless

[I]t is a struggle in the dark. In each of these groups, the original movement is deviated by the necessities of expression and action, by the objective limitation of the field of instruments (theoretical and practical), by the survival of outdated significations and the ambiguity of new significations (Sartre 1968: 123).

The majority of the South African population is landless, in the sense that they do not have ownership of, or legally secure access to, land in their own name. In most cases, whether urban or rural, the majority are living on land that legally belongs to someone else. Their tenure rights are insecure and constantly open to threat, be it from the state or private landowners. From this perspective, not only farm workers and their dependents are landless, but also workers in the formal economy, informal workers and domestic workers who rent residential property or live in informal settlements, and the millions who reside in communal areas where land is owned and controlled by the state and traditional authorities. The strength of the workers' movement from the early 1970s in particular and the unifying ideology of black nationalism in the struggle against racial oppression overshadowed the more deeply entrenched processes of capitalist development that underpinned land dispossession as they unfolded concretely in South Africa. Land dispossession was viewed through the lenses of racial policies and lack of political democracy.

Under apartheid, the struggle for land was subsumed under a broader struggle for political rights and for unprejudiced participation in the economy. Land demand was not articulated in and of itself, but rather as a symbol of the lack of political democracy and the racism of the apartheid regime. Continuing tenure insecurity in the post-apartheid era, with limited protection of tenure rights on land not legally owned by occupiers in both rural and urban areas and limited redistribution of legal ownership, has exposed the limits of the processes of political democratisation and formal deracialisation. The landless movement has emerged in this space to begin constructing an identity around landlessness. This has been done on the basis of reformulating demands that have existed for decades around the issue of land – access to basic services; freedom of movement and freedom to choose to stay in one place; participation by people in decisions affecting their own lives. This reformulation can be seen as the construction of a demand for land, but the deeper content goes beyond land. As Gillian Hart (2002) puts it, the landless movement is grappling with one dimension of the failure of the political class in the post-apartheid era to address ongoing poverty and inequality.

Not all members of the movement are landless in the sense of having no land at all in their own names. African commercial farmers are represented in the movement at all levels. Relatively wealthy labour tenants, with access to tracts of land and owning substantial cattle herds, work side by side with very poor tenants in the movement. This suggests that the formulation of the identity of 'landless' has as much to do with issues of redress and justice, the experience of dispossession, and inadequate access to land for productive purposes as it does with issues of insecure tenure or total lack of access to productive land. This points to the reality of the landless movement as a popular movement without a clearly defined class base, reflecting the formulation of a growing demand for access to and ownership of land across classes. The movement is a mix of different class and social forces that the hegemonic bloc has been incapable of entirely absorbing into its own project.

NGOs and the Formation of the Landless Movement
It is impossible to separate the formation of the LPM from the non-governmental organisations (NGOs), and in particular the National Land Committee (NLC) and its affiliates. Following political democratisation in 1994, NGOs tried to construct a rural movement of one type or another from above. The interpretation of the meaning and form of a movement remained a point of contestation. Reasons for supporting the formation of a movement varied from a desire by activists working in the NGOs to support an independent and radical grassroots movement of the landless, to a technocratic calculation that a national grassroots organisation aligned with a national NGO structure would have more influence in policy-making circles.

One of the first national efforts was the Rural Development Initiative (RDI), a temporary coalition of NGOs and community-based organisations (CBOs) with a broad-based rural character. The RDI was closely aligned to the dominant developmental project, although in places an emerging critique of macro-economic constraints and the failures of delivery were evident. For example, in the section on rural economic development, the Rural People's Charter that came out of the RDI noted that 'budget cuts for social services and infrastructure are having a negative socio-economic effect on rural communities' and 'many of the causes of poverty are the result of the private sector's interests in short-term profits at the expense of longer-term social goals'. On land, there was a demand that 'unused or underutilised land be transferred to the landless for productive use' (RDI 1999). The artificial, top-down character of the RDI, resting as it did on passive communities led by professional NGOs, led to its immediate collapse once funding dried up.

In 2001 the debate around social movements in the rural NGOs heated up and became more practical in the context of the rise of independent community movements struggling against privatisation, service cut-offs and evictions in the main urban areas, with an overtly antagonistic stance towards government. While many individuals working in the rural NGO networks had come to the point where they saw the potential value of a mobilised grassroots movement in legitimising and supporting demands for redistribution and delivery, the majority were not in favour of an anti-government stance.

The central role of the NGOs in forming the landless movement is highlighted by the significance of two United Nations events that took place in South Africa at the start of the new millennium. In 2001, the World Conference Against Racism (WCAR) in Durban permitted the NGOs to raise resources to facilitate a gathering of the community groups they had been working with. The resultant Landless People's Assembly set the stage for the launch of the Landless People's Movement. The WCAR also provided the space and opportunity for resource mobilisation for the first joint national action of the new independent community movements under the banner of the Durban Social Forum (Naidoo 2002).

The movement launched at the WCAR in 2001 was formed around two different types of grassroots mobilisation. On the one hand, there were groups organised through the NGOs (primarily NLC affiliates) to participate in government land reform programmes. For example, there are restitution forums, communal property associations, farm worker forums, land rights forums and so on. In all cases there has been an interaction with government, whether at the political or administrative level, to expedite the return or redistribution of land. In many cases, a key reason for dissatisfaction is that promises made by government officials in these meetings are not kept. In this light, frustration and a radicalisation of demands often stems from political and administrative dishonesty rather than from a thoroughgoing critique of the land reform programme itself.

On the other hand, the other type of mobilisation that formed the base of the LPM is spontaneous[2] organisation to resist encroachment on existing land access. In the informal settlements, especially around Gauteng, the LPM spread rapidly by coming to the defence of residents who were faced with the immediate threat of forced removal in 2001 and 2002. As one member of the LPM in Eikenhof informal settlement in southern Gauteng put it: 'The LPM came to our rescue. We called the LPM at the time when the Red Ants were firing live bullets at our comrades. They came here. A person who helps you when you're in danger is a person who really cares about you' (Interview, Koithing, 03.09.03).

In 2002, the United Nations' World Summit on Sustainable Development (WSSD) in Johannesburg provided another opportunity for the NGOs to raise resources to bring the constituent parts of the movement together for the second Landless People's Assembly. On the outskirts of Soweto, more than 5 000 delegates from around the country participated in a week of meetings and discussions. The week culminated in a 25 000-strong march, together with other social movements and international organisations, against the neo-liberal hijacking of sustainable development for its own agenda through the WSSD. The WCAR and WSSD were formative in structuring the trajectory of the movement, and in materialising connections with other like-minded movements both nationally and globally. Important global links were formed with the MST and La Via Campesina, the international peasant movement. The extent and impact of the LPM's involvement would have been significantly less without the donor resources and the facilitation of the NLC.

The very success of the WSSD mobilisation, where resources were captured for a radical expression of land demand, brought to a head simmering tensions between different political trajectories. The fundamental lines of division related to the question of the attitude the movement should adopt towards government. Some NGOs and a portion of the movement sought a continuation of a relationship of critical engagement. This was understood to mean that the movement would continue pursuing claims for restitution and redistribution of land within the government's official land reform framework. The challenge here would be to exert enough pressure to convince the government that obstacles and blockages to land reform should be removed. The assumption underlying this approach was and is that government would like to see large-scale land redistribution but bureaucratic inertia and various incapacities stand in the way. On the other hand, a sizeable portion of the movement was convinced that a more antagonistic relationship with government was necessary. In their view, government has the capacity to carry out the substantial and rapid transfer of land to the landless but has opted for a different political and economic path. Pressure, therefore, needs to be applied to shift the government from its political and economic trajectories through mass collective action. Failing that – or parallel to it – redistribution from below through mass occupations would be necessary to ensure the transfer of land.

The political fallout included a split in the NLC as uncritically developmentalist NGOs left the network on the one side, and activists were marginalised and pushed out of the network on the other. In this way, the NLC re-stabilised itself as a smaller 'moderate' centre focused on continuing a critical engagement with the government's land reform programme. The affiliates that split to the right adopted an uncritical engagement with the state's programme, while the expelled activists sought the elaboration of a mass-based alternative to the government's programme.

Inside the movement, the LPM cobbled together a compromise national leadership structure to try to hold the different factions together and avoid an internal split. This was partially successful at the level of the national council, but not without its own political costs. The withdrawal of resources for a radical project facilitated a slump in nationally co-ordinated actions. This exacerbated a widening gap between the national leadership on the one hand and provincial and grassroots leadership on the other, a tendency institutionalised in the composition of the compromise national structure. The compromise national structure included delegated representatives of active grassroots structures sitting alongside individuals with limited, if any, organisational base. The compromise structure resulted in a disengagement between national leadership and provincial and grassroots leadership in some provinces. On the ground, the LPM was pulled in different directions depending on the dominant approach adopted by the affiliate on which a specific section of the LPM relied for resources and support. Highly dependent on the NLC's provincial affiliates, most of the LPM's grassroots formations were under pressure to align with the position of 'their' NGO or face isolation and a choking of the resource supply.

On the basis of these splitting and controlling tactics, the NLC and its affiliates attempted, with quite some success, to smother the radical potential of the grassroots landless movement, and to reassert their control over the political direction and programme of grassroots mobilisations (or lack thereof) around landlessness. Despite this, elements of the movement remained steadfast in trying to elaborate an independent vision and programme of action that could present an alternative to the government's land reform programme and ensure the actual redistribution of land on a mass scale. However, these attempts occurred in the context of an almost absolute lack of resources or institutional support.

Although the movement at a national level took a decision to formalise membership through the issuing of membership cards, this process only occurred unevenly and was essentially halted as political tensions exploded after the WSSD. As the situation stands, formal membership does not represent the active membership of the movement. And given the broad base of potential support for the movement, its aim and reach respectively is likely to appeal to, and extend well beyond, the active membership.

Structure versus Spontaneity in the Movement

The LPM has a constitution that details a formal structure including a national council, provincial councils and branch structures. The national council is structured around provincial representatives. Most members of the council do not have secure access to land, although there are some with land but who need or want more. Labour tenants, farm workers, residents of informal settlements and rural towns, restitution claimants and small-scale commercial farmers are represented on the national structure. Formal branch structures with paid-up membership exist in very few places. Without these basic organisational building blocks, mandate and accountability are impossible, thus blunting internal democracy.

At a general level, the LPM is structured at the top and mainly unstructured at the bottom. In the case of the NGO-related grassroots formations (i.e. not the groups that initially connected with the LPM through their own spontaneous struggles), there is some structure on the ground. There are some provincial structures, mostly with limited formal accountability to the grassroots. The movement is thus a hybrid between a party-like, hierarchical organisational structure and an agglomeration of grassroots struggles, the latter sometimes spontaneous and at other times facilitated by the formal structures of the movement.

It may be that attempts to provide a tightly defined structure for the movement all the way up to the national level were premature, primarily emerging as a result of the historical experiences and ideological frameworks of activists and development workers involved with the movement. There are differences of opinion inside the movement and amongst activists working with it about the extent to which the movement should be structured. On the one hand are those who believe that structure is a requirement for a programmatic approach. On the other hand, there are those who believe that the imposition of structure creates artificial hierarchies that become sites of struggle for control over the movement separated from support to actual grassroots struggles. Too much structure can lead to tactical and strategic inflexibility, but too little structure can cause disintegration of the movement and an inability to break out of localised struggles in a sustained way.

Jean-Paul Sartre describes the process through which a group of atomised individuals form a collective with a common purpose, but this usually disintegrates or becomes ossified once the immediate purpose has been achieved. First, atomised, 'serialised' individuals operate in conditions of separation, social impotence, numerical equivalence, pseudoreciprocity, unity in exteriority and passive activity – the abdication of praxis in favour of inertial 'occurrences' (Flynn 1984: 95–6). Serial relations bind human beings in passivity and make the future appear as destiny.

The formation of a group that acts with common purpose negates the practico-inert. The LPM emerged in Gauteng when previously atomised individuals responded to the perceived immediate threat of forced removals by forming a conscious association to defend one another. More broadly speaking, the coalescence of a group of people around the identity of landlessness reveals the immediate threat to survival experienced as a result of a lack of secure access to land. Individual need is felt as common need, and each individual projects herself or himself 'in the internal unification of a common integration, towards objectives which it produces in common' (Sartre 1976: 115). This is the phase of acting with others in the immediate present. The inter-relationship between theory and action – praxis – that characterises the group in these conditions mediates the relations between the human beings in the group. The reciprocity and collective praxis that emerge from the fused group show the individuals involved in the group their freedom manifested in reality, the 'sudden resurrection of freedom' (Sartre 1976: 401).

When the immediate danger that shook serial individuals into relations of 'true reciprocity' through the group recedes, the praxis that mediated the group dissolves in the 'reintroduction of serial otherness into interpersonal relations' (Flynn 1984: 119). If the group does not entirely break up, the dissolution of praxis may be accompanied by an institutionalisation of the relations between individuals who remain in the group. The organised group tends to harden into hierarchical strata; self-preservation of the organisation becomes the overriding concern; the group (the 'mediating Third') crystallises into an insuperable Other; and some inside the group emerge as 'more equal than others' (Flynn 1984: 119). Instead of co-sovereignty in the group, individuals construe themselves through the Other 'as an inorganic tool by means of which action is realised' (Sartre 1976: 599). Human beings are no longer agents but objects again. And so it is with the participants in the LPM's initial defence against forced removals. Many have lapsed back into individualised serial relations, while some remain structured into institutional forms that also serialise relations through hierarchies, based on organisational forms that emerged in a different context. This process is part of the ebb and flow of struggle.

The decline in popular participation after the initial fusion has brought to the fore politics based on 'the historical emphasis on the role of leadership and cadres as those endowed of translating the unruly politics of the crowd into a sense of strategic and political purpose' in words used in a slightly different context by Franco Barchiesi (2004: 5). The externalised, or formalised, practice characterising the hierarchical institution results from 'the mechanical application to new processes of forms derived from a previous process' (Vazquez 1977: 211). The disintegration of group praxis has left behind an institutional shell that may or may not be capable of renewing social relations based on reciprocity and mediated by praxis. Difficult as these questions may be to answer in theory or practice, the very fact that the existence of the movements poses such questions as practical exigencies suggests the germination of an alternative collective activity that attempts to surpass the limitations evident in previous struggles for human freedom, whether socialist or national liberation.

Class, Race and Gender Dynamics in the Movement
Class
As already described above, NGOs played a central role in the formation of the LPM. This has significantly coloured the form and content of the movement. The professionalisation of the NGO stratum, especially from the early 1990s in parallel with the shifting political terrain from 'resistance to reconstruction', led to the dissipation of activist relationships with the grassroots and the rise of a technocratic developmental approach in the NGOs. The emphasis was placed on measurable outputs, financial management and procedure. Technical expertise and management skills rose in prominence and shaped the way NGO workers interacted with the grassroots. Grassroots formations were marginalised as NGOs took on the task of designing and lobbying for policy positions.

In the light of control over access to resources and networks, there is a danger of patronage relationships developing between well-networked individuals working with the movement and individuals inside the movement. Those – usually middle-class individuals – with access to global and regional contacts have immense power in shaping the image of the movement, and thereby of channelling the direction of resources. This is particularly dangerous when the grassroots movement, like the LPM, relies almost solely on external funding for its survival (in its present form) and is highly dependent on a small group of people in facilitating global links.

Class dynamics are not only pertinent to the relationship between middle-class activists providing support from outside the movement and members of the movement. The class basis of the programmes and activities carried out by the movement has not been clarified. This is largely because of the multi-class character of the demands for land access and redistribution. It is also because the class conflicts that are likely to emerge once the movement has succeeded in accessing land remain for the future.

In the rural areas, struggles by labour tenants to retain and extend access to land remain largely undifferentiated. The diverging trajectories of struggles by relatively wealthy labour tenants to become commercial farmers in their own right, compared to struggles by the poorest labour tenants without any land access or any livestock under their command to secure tenure have not yet emerged as practical challenges for the movement. However, wealthier tenants are more vocal, and men dominate this stratum. This could have implications for the types of redistribution that the movement supports.

In the informal settlements of the peri-urban areas, similar quasi-class conflicts lurk just beneath the surface. In one settlement in southern Gauteng, the local state has attempted to drive a wedge between residents by offering the 'formal' residents (who nevertheless still live in informal housing) the opportunity for tenure security, a formal house and services at a nearby site, in exchange for an agreement that backyard dwellers be removed 'from shack to shack' to a distant and inconvenient site (Interview, Anonymous, 03.09.03). Depending on how the LPM formulates common demands to overcome this division or, failing that, which group the movement aligns itself with can have fundamental implications for the class character of the movement in the future. The chosen trajectory is heavily dependent on local leadership, the character of the movement's base in the settlement, and the links between the settlement and other sections of the movement.

Race

Forced land dispossession took place on the basis of race. It is not surprising, therefore, that the movement is overwhelmingly black in composition and there is a strong race consciousness in the movement. There is a close relationship between white privilege and access to resources that form the basis for dependency relationships, reinforcing the apartheid legacy. In principle, the movement has adopted a position of anti-racism in its constitution. However, this does not reveal the diversity of opinion in the movement with regard to race and racial identity. Africanism, Black Consciousness and the non-racial tradition of the Congress movement all command support.

Systematic discussion about the relationship between race and landlessness has been limited to sporadic political education workshops in parts of the country, and has occasionally been placed on the agenda at national and some provincial council meetings. While it appears that there is value to creating fora where issues of race (amongst other topics) can be discussed at a theoretical level, there is a tendency for such discussions to become abstracted from practical activities. The relationship between racial oppression and land dispossession, and the consequent ways that the ongoing struggle against racial oppression and its legacy are carried out in the particular struggle for access to and redistribution of land, is dynamic and can only be determined through praxis.

Gender

In the process of struggling for secure access to land, women are forced to confront a patriarchal power structure. Women participate in a movement that becomes antagonistic to government and its programmes because channels and solutions are not available to them in their struggle for survival. But the movement is a product of the society it emerges from, and women often remain oppressed by the norms, relations and expectations of the past. At all levels of the movement, there has been very little or no discussion of gender in relation to the work and struggles of the movement (see, for example, Cross and Hornby 2002: 124–7 on the KwaZulu-Natal Tenure Security Co-ordinating Committee, a key affiliate of the LPM). Patriarchy and outright sexism, the lack of space for women to articulate their own specific demands around land, the tendency for political discussions to be held at times and places where it is more difficult for women to participate, all contribute to skewing the movement's ideas and activities in favour of the interests of men in the movement.

Women inside the movement, especially longstanding political activists, are prepared to take up this struggle. There is a strand inside the movement that takes gender equality seriously and seeks to build this into the work and structures of the movement. The failure of the majority of NGO staff to work directly with the movement on a day-to-day level has meant that interventions on gender equality in the movement have been limited to rote workshops that do not engage with the real practices of the movement – an institutional serial relationship based on passivity. There is a push from some quarters inside the movement to establish a women's caucus. These have been stalled through lack of resources, but there is enough impetus to make this a likely possibility in future.

Strategic and Tactical Orientation
Land Demand and Post-Apartheid Hegemony
The LPM operates both inside and outside the hegemonic framework. This is partly conscious and partly by default. Inside the hegemonic framework, the LPM's demands are constructed around the development agenda, on the terrain defined by dominant power. Key demands emanating from the movement are around the pace and scope of land redistribution, but with a critique of government programmes mainly limited to method and not principle. For example, criticism of the 'willing-seller, willing-buyer' model is premised more on its inability to redistribute land as promised, than on a critique of the land market and private ownership that underpin the model. At the same time, as frustration with limited redistribution gathers pace, it intensifies contradictions and opens the space for a more radical critique of the programme as a whole within the post-apartheid political economy.

Meaningful participation in official decision-making processes is also important to members of the movement. While members accept that the formal structures of participation in public life are acceptable in theory, in practice citizens who are not members of the ruling party are not able to enter these structures or participate in formal channels. Yet the movement as a whole persists in its demand for formal consultations, indicating that it has not abandoned formal participation. This occurs at local or provincial level – such as the demand for Gauteng premier Mbhazima Shilowa to sit down and negotiate with the provincial LPM structure, or the Wakkerstroom labour tenants' demands for Land Affairs to sit with it to map out a plan for transfer of farms in the area. It also occurs at national level, for example through the unrelenting call for a National Land Summit to discuss the failures of the land reform programme and to design a way forward.

Demands are thus both for democratisation – in particular, effective participation – and a redistributive agenda. Both of these can be considered within the hegemonic discourse of development, i.e. they do not necessarily question or threaten the capitalist underpinnings of the developmental project. However, hegemonic power seeks to control the expression of these demands and capture them within a framework that serves or balances the various interests of the hegemonic bloc. Therefore, although the demands may be legitimate even from the point of view of the hegemonic project, the methods used to make demands or their practical realisation may push the demander into opposition to the dominant powers.

As with the other new community movements, mass mobilisation is the basis of the LPM's legitimacy. But even mass mobilisation does not automatically put the movement outside the hegemonic discourse. Indeed, mass mobilisation fits snugly within the hegemonic framework – so long as it is within the confines of the law or strategies approved by the Congress Alliance. That is why it's possible for the South African Communist Party (SACP) recently, or the Congress of South African Trade Unions (COSATU) more generally, to call for and engage in mass mobilisations. Given the location of these formations in the hegemonic bloc, mass mobilisation has as its political goal the management or reduction of contradictions in the bloc. A defining feature of the LPM and other new community movements is that mass mobilisation serves to intensify contradictions in the hegemonic bloc and its ideological framework. This is partly through strategic choice, but also through the various responses of the dominant bloc, and especially of the state, to these mobilisations.

On the basis of a common antagonism to the ill effects of the government's macro-economic strategies on the poor and marginalised, as well as the focus on mass activity as the primary method for challenging these strategies, the LPM has entered into a loose alliance with other movements sharing this broad approach. Grouped under the Social Movements Indaba (SMI), but also on the basis of bilateral solidarity and interactions, the LPM stands allied with the Anti-Privatisation Forum (APF), the Concerned Citizens Forum (CCF) in KwaZulu-Natal and the Western Cape Anti-Eviction Campaign (AEC). Although interaction is somewhat sporadic at times, due to resource constraints and political disagreements, these movements have all worked with one another on the theoretical, political and practical levels.

The LPM has adopted a number of controversial tactics and campaigns to highlight its demands for a radical redistribution of land and secure tenure. Most notable of these is the movement's support for Zimbabwean president Robert Mugabe's land expropriation programme and its own land occupations campaign. Prior to the WSSD in 2002, the LPM requested Mugabe to come to speak to its members in South Africa. Says Maureen Mnisi, Gauteng chair:

> What I can say on the issue of Zimbabwe, I recommend what Mugabe was doing to take back the land as the president. There was always this pressure from people that they need the land and the farmers are occupying a lot of land compared to the Africans. And the President believed, he knows that the land belongs to the people, and he took back the land and gave it to the owners, meaning the people who are supposed to get the land. I recommend Mugabe as a president to do that (Interview, Mnisi, 21.11.03).

Many in the movement view Mugabe's disregard for the conventions and niceties of liberal democracy as resistance to neo-colonialism. A burning sense of injustice and a desire for a decisive remedy from those in political power are at least as important considerations for support of Mugabe as is the tactical value of supporting the state-led land expropriations in Zimbabwe.

Land occupations have been identified as part of the repertoire of actions the movement is willing to carry out. Mass occupations are not uncommon in the history of the land struggle in South Africa. In urban areas, the intense demand for housing has resulted in regular mass land occupations. Many, if not most, of the informal settlements around the major urban areas are the direct result of illegal occupations in the past. This has been the form of urbanisation in South Africa, shaped by displaced urbanisation and the migrant labour system. In rural areas, there are a number of recorded occupations by groups who have claimed land through the restitution process but have not received any satisfactory redress. Mass occupations of vacant or abandoned rural land are also fairly widespread. Labour tenant occupations on functioning commercial farms are far less common, because of the much greater potential for violent opposition from landowners (see Steyn 2002: 3–4 and Appendix A for a list of known or threatened rural occupations). The LPM's threat is driven by a deep frustration with engagement with the state's land reform programme that has failed to deliver. In some cases, community groups have waited for seven years or more without tangible progress in resolving land claims or in transferring land.

At present, the movement lacks the political or organisational strength to co-ordinate and sustain such actions. But the idea of mass occupations remains a popular expression of frustration and desire for rapid redistribution of land. According to Jabu Dladla, an LPM organiser in Mpumalanga, 'People here are ready to occupy. They have been calling on the leadership to do this, but we have been delaying because we suspect people won't be strong enough to stand against farmers and the police' (Interview, Dladla, 18.10.03). By targeting un- or under-used land and abandoned farms, the movement indicates its willingness, at least in the initial phases, to accommodate landowners and commercial agriculture, but also to take into account its own strength. A sterner challenge arises from the call for expropriation or occupation of farms owned by abusive farmers. This begins to question the role of super-exploited farm labour in constructing the commercial agricultural sector and makes demands for reparations that transcend the official land reform and human rights agendas.

State and Hegemonic Bloc Responses to Rising Land Demand

The emergence of the LPM, in tandem with the unfolding land expropriation process in Zimbabwe, has raised the profile of land dispossession in the public mind in South Africa. The state has responded with a mixture of reform and repression, while other elements of the hegemonic bloc have become more vocal about their opinions on land redistribution. Following the initial and much publicised rise of the LPM, both the SACP and COSATU have made public statements calling for the speedier and more effective implementation of the official land reform programme. Just prior to the national elections in 2004, SACP general secretary Blade Nzimande indicated that the SACP's Red October campaign would be broadened to include a focus on acceleration of land and agrarian transformation (SAPA 2004: 3). Mirroring the LPM's call for a land summit to discuss the land reform programme and to plot a way forward, COSATU affiliate the Food and Allied Workers' Union (FAWU) called on government to convene a land summit to seek ways of promoting subsistence farming and increase the pace of land reform (Petros 2003: 4). After calling for a 'drastic review' of land reform procedures, saying the 'willing-seller, willing-buyer' approach was not working, COSATU general secretary Zwelinzima Vavi said: 'In 2014, we will be 20 years into (our) democracy and if we . . . have not redistributed the land by then, we will find ourselves in a Zimbabwean situation' (Mboyane 2004: 1). The motivations for these pronouncements may vary from a political strategy to absorb land demands into the ambit of the Alliance, or they may be a genuine attempt to provide greater support to the struggles of the landless (whether inside or outside the LPM). However, this sudden emphasis on land redistribution cannot be separated from the rise of the LPM, and at the very least indicates the broad appeal of its basic demands.

Business leaders and their associated media and political spokespersons have also felt the need to make a call for the implementation of the government's land reform programme. The largest national farmers' union, Agri-SA, has worked closely with government to design a plan for commercial agriculture that incorporates land reform as a component (NDA 2001). The editor of the influential *Business Day*, after calling for the improvement of the efficiency of the land reform programme, opined that 'meaningful progress demands a . . . social compact between commercial farmers and the rural poor' and that formalisation of this process 'is the only practical route to long-term sustainability in South African agriculture' (*Business Day* 18 May 2004: 10). A survey by research group Markinor in 2004 found that 75 per cent of white farmers canvassed felt land reform was inevitable, while 54 per cent were willing to sell their land to advance the process (Reuters 2004: 3).

To date, government has tended to be more responsive to the calls of capital and business than to the ANC's own Alliance partners or the LPM. The 'willing-seller, willing-buyer' model remains non-negotiable, and the 2004 Medium Term Expenditure Framework keeps the entire budget of the Department of Land Affairs (DLA) at below 0.6 per cent of total national expenditure up to the fiscal year 2006/07 (Department of Finance 2004: 825). The share of the DLA budget going to land redistribution was actually forecast to drop, while the emphasis is placed on finalising the restitution programme (Department of Finance 2004: 829). In line with the equity-type black economic empowerment model characterising redistribution under Thabo Mbeki's reign, the land and agriculture ministry also began the process of constructing an empowerment charter that would see greater black ownership in agri-business throughout the value chain (Nair 2004: 4). A number of large-scale black empowerment deals, notably in the sugar and wine sectors[3], were sealed at around this time to give weight to the focus on racial ownership patterns in large-scale enterprises.

These partial shifts on the ideological terrain, which reveal a growing pressure to acknowledge the legitimacy of land demand and a tacit recognition of a 'landless' identity, have been accompanied by state repression. In the lead-up to the WSSD in particular, the movement was required to respond to a heightening of evictions and the use of state force against its membership. In April 2002 farm workers and labour tenants marching in the rural town of Ermelo were arrested by police for an 'illegal gathering'. Charges were later dropped. In the week before the WSSD, residents of informal settlements around Johannesburg marched to demand a moratorium on evictions and to be included in development planning in their areas. Police forcibly dispersed them, arresting 72 and detaining them for three days. Charges were later dropped. In 2003, seven LPM youth members were arrested on false murder charges and were kept in jail for three months before their trial, at which the charges were dropped.

The reliance by the state on coercive responses to the LPM indicates a perceived threat to its power. The case of the LPM's No Land, No Vote campaign is revealing. In numeric terms, the LPM posed little or no threat to the state in its mobilisations in the months leading up to the elections on 14 April 2004. An attempt to hold a small gathering in Tembelihle in Gauteng on election day was met with high levels of police aggression, the jailing of protestors and the intimidation and torture of LPM members in police custody overnight (Hooper-Box 2004; Hofstätter 2004). This violent response suggests a vulnerability to the criticisms highlighted by the campaign, in particular the abysmal record of land redistribution ten years after democratisation, the rise in forced removals and evictions, and the failure of parliamentary democracy to design an acceptable process for resolving (rather than managing) long-standing social problems. As Barchiesi (2004: 24) points out, by 'bringing to the fore the demands of constituencies historically marginalised within nationalist discourse, like the landless', the LPM has directly challenged the ANC's construct of 'the nation', and has opened up new areas for political contestation.

Law defines the boundaries of the hegemonic project or, in the words of Poulantzas (1978: 83), 'law is a constitutive element of the politico-social field'. Outside the hegemonic framework, the movement and its constituents are increasingly forced into a situation where they can see no option but to embark on illegal actions. A key example is popular sentiment in favour of mass land occupations. This illegality – or the threat of illegality – drives the movement into opposition to the hegemonic discourse and framework. Illegality brings people into confrontation with seemingly given social relations, and exposes these relations as nothing more than constructed relations between human beings, maintained by atomised passivity and obedience.

Conclusion

The LPM is a product of a combination of the ravages of a capitalist system on the poorest and most marginalised sections of the population, and the resultant resistance to this system. The movement would not have emerged but for the active synthesis of the lessons of history by a mass of people constantly struggling to break free of serial relations and their desire to forge relations of true reciprocity through collective praxis. Institutions and organisational forms are never free of the past, and this forces an iterative process on the challenge to inequality and injustice, always partially hampered by inadequate or inappropriate forms of organisation and action. The LPM and allied movements are engaging in this historical process against overwhelming odds. A new capitalist hegemony has entrenched itself in post-apartheid South Africa, and the process of overcoming this will involve long, difficult and painstaking work to rebuild popular struggle against capitalist exploitation and the attendant expressions of racial, gender and other forms of oppression and exclusion that are constantly reproduced by it. Despite flaws and divisions, tactical and strategic mistakes and a constant pressure on individuals to fall back into isolated seriality, the movements have infused new life into political and social action that was fast becoming institutionalised and closed.

Notes

1. This research was based on a participatory action research methodology. The key principles of this method are that research should play a direct role in building independent grassroots organisation, and that the subjects of the research drive the research agenda. The research must be a useful contribution to consolidating and carrying forward the independent programme of the subject organisation, i.e. knowledge is generated for purposes of action (Babbie et al. 2001: 314). The research process was driven by participant observation, which translated into active engagement with the structures of the movement at branch, provincial and national levels. A research team conducted around 140 semi-structured interviews with movement members and activists at all these levels, but mainly at branch level. Less formal and ongoing dialogue with movement members and supporting activists from around the country supplemented these interviews throughout the period of research.

I wish to acknowledge the great value and contribution to this chapter of ongoing discussions and debates with activists and members of the Landless People's Movement. In particular Ann Eveleth, Samantha Hargreaves and Andile Mngxitama have provided plenty of food for thought in the ongoing struggle to build a strong, independent and radical movement of the landless. Thanks also to Jabu Dladla, Zakes Hlatshwayo, Peter Jacobs, Ricardo Jacobs, Nosicelo James, Thabo Manyathi, Sylvia Ngwenya, Shamim Meer, Maureen Mnisi, Fana Mthethwa, Phillip Phosa, Sphamandla Tshabalala, Zeph Tshabalala, Bongani Xezwi and countless other members and supporters of the movement for sharing their knowledge, insights and experience with me. What I say here is interpreted through my own subjectivity.

2. To use the term 'spontaneous' is not to deny the presence of pre-existing networks, formations or structures, but rather to suggest that these did not play a leading role – in their existing forms and on the basis of their already-constituted ideological frameworks – in generating or organising the new struggles.

3. See N. Jenvey, 'Illovo hives off Gledhow mill, land for R335m', *Business Day* 15 May 2004: 13; Bloomberg, 'KWV advances 55c after Phetogo deal', *Business Day* 11 June 2004: 13.

References

Babbie, E., J. Mouton, P. Vorster and B. Prozesky. 2001. *The Practice of Social Research*. Cape Town: Oxford University Press.

Barchiesi, F. 2004. 'Classes, Multitudes and the Politics of Community Movements in Post-Apartheid South Africa'. Paper presented at the How Class Works Conference, 10–12 June. State University of New York.

Cross, C. and D. Hornby. 2002. 'Opportunities and Obstacles to Women's Land Access in South Africa'. Research report for the Promoting Women's Access to Land Programme. Pretoria/Johannesburg: Department of Land Affairs/National Land Committee.

Department of Finance. 2004. 'National Budget 2004 Vote 30: Land Affairs'. www.polity.org.za/pdf/LandAffairs.pdf.

Flynn, T. 1984. *Sartre and Marxist Existentialism*. Chicago: University of Chicago Press.

Greenberg, S. 2004. *Post-Apartheid Development, Landlessness and the Reproduction of Exclusion in South Africa*. Centre for Civil Society Research Report No. 17. Durban: University of KwaZulu-Natal.

Hart, G. 2002. 'Linking Land, Labour and Livelihood Strategies'. *South African Labour Bulletin* 26 (6).

Hofstätter, S. 2004. 'Police Tortured Us, Claim LPM Members'. *This Day* 28 April: 3.

Hooper-Box, C. 2004. 'Soweto Police "tortured us on election day"'. *Sunday Independent* 2 May: 4.

Mboyane, S. 2004. 'Vavi Warns on Land Grabs if Targets are Missed'. *Business Day* 28 May: 1.

Naidoo, P. 2002. 'From WCAR to WSSD: The United Nations, Globalisation and Neoliberalism'. *Khanya* 1 (August).

Nair, K-V. 2004. 'Didiza Sows Seeds of Charter for Agriculture Sector'. *Business Day* 9 June: 4.

National Department of Agriculture (NDA). 2001. 'The Strategic Plan for South African Agriculture'. www.nda.agric.za/Sectorplan/sectorplan.htm.

Petros, N. 2003. 'Union Calls for Speedy Land Reform'. *Business Day* 21 November: 4.

Poulantzas, N. 1978. *State, Power, Socialism*. London: Verso.

Reuters. 2004. 'White Farmers Accept Land Reform – Study'. *Business Day* 8 June: 3.

Riad El-Ghonemy, M. 1999. 'The Political Economy of Market-Based Land Reform'. UN Research Institute for Social Development Discussion Paper No. 104, June. Geneva: UN Research Institute for Social Development.

Rural Development Initiative (RDI). 1999. 'Rural People's Charter'. Adopted at the RDI Convention, 23–25 April, Bloemfontein.

SAPA. 2004. 'SACP Strives for "landslide victory" for Ally ANC'. *Business Day* 16 February: 3.

Sartre, J-P. 1968. *Search for a Method.* Translated by Hazel Barnes. New York: Vintage.

———. 1976. *Critique of Dialectical Reason.* Translated by Alan Sheridan-Smith. London: New Left Books.

Steyn, L. 2002. 'Review of Land Occupations in South Africa'. Report prepared for Africa Groups of Sweden.

Vazquez, A. 1977. *The Philosophy of Praxis.* Translated by Mike Gonzalez. London: The Merlin Press.

Interviews

Anonymous. Community Activist, 03.09.03.

Dladla, Jabu. LPM Mpumalanga Interim Council Member, 18.10.03.

Koithing, Isaac Sello. Community Activist, 03.09.03.

Mnisi, Maureen. LPM Gauteng Chairperson, 21.11.03.

8

The Homeless People's Alliance

Purposive Creation and Ambiguated Realities

Firoz Khan and Edgar Pieterse

Today's social movements are seen as playing a central role in producing the world in which we live, its social structures and practices, its meanings and cultural orientations, its possibilities for change. Social movements emerged out of the crisis of modernity; they oriented themselves towards the constitution of new orders, and embody a new understanding of politics and social life itself. They result in the formation of novel collective identities which foster social and cultural forms of relating and solidarity as a response to the crises of meanings and economies that the world faces today (Escobar 1992: 396).

THE CRISES OF meanings and economies are most visibly evident in the proliferation of slums in most parts of the developing world (Davis 2004). Slums attest simultaneously to the capricious effects of a globalised system of uneven development and the ingenuity of subaltern classes to make meaning, livelihood and life under any conditions. This ingenuity is increasingly being tapped by a multi-national network of urban social movements that seek to empower their members and, through painstaking organisation, increase their 'political footprint' in the political economy of cities.

In South Africa, the Homeless People's Alliance (HPA) is a prime example of this worldwide category of social movements that resonates closely with the conceptual lens of Arturo Escobar above. Relative to other social movements in South Africa, the HPA (comprising the Homeless People's Federation [a CBO], People's Dialogue [an NGO] and uTshani Fund [community-managed revolving loan fund]) is unique. It was established inside the transitional moment from apartheid to political freedom, but consciously defined itself outside of the dominant imagination of the anti-apartheid movement. Furthermore, with the birth of democracy in 1994, the HPA defined itself in complex relation to the state: neither too close nor too far, but rather on its own terms. This confidence was born out of a philosophical commitment to remain rooted in the everyday realities of its members, while ensuring their empowerment in dealing more effectively with their social reproductive challenges, especially housing. The HPA is also unique in terms of phenomenal growth during its first decade of existence.

What is particularly fascinating about this movement – 'based on trust, saving systems and lateral learning' (Development Works 2003: 28) – and its partners across the world, is that despite its grassroots preoccupation and rejection of the official development horizon and outputs, it ends up exercising a profound influence over the state and its urban development ambitions and programmes. Thus, by the late 1990s the South African state mainstreamed the substantial components of the community mobilisation methodologies of the HPA – the People's Housing Process (PHP) – into government policy. This opened the door for the HPA to become a key political actor in development policy debates about effective urban poverty reduction. The shift did, however, introduce a new challenge: being equally effective at engaging the state and maintaining the core grassroots values and identity of the movement.

In this chapter, we trace the evolution, ideological framework, organisational praxis and developmental impact of the HPA. Considerable space is devoted to the ideology and identity of the movement, which is anchored in deep democracy.[1] However, this only makes sense if located in the over-arching political transition from apartheid to political democracy. Across these two sections, the unique approach of the HPA to the state is explored, best characterised as a politics of 'bargaining at the top, pressure from below'. The state is not seen as a body to be 'taken over' and turned into an 'instrument of drastic social change' (Farhi 2003: 37).

Analysing the genesis, rise, restructuring and consolidation of the HPA from a civil association to a civil/political movement – i.e. from concentrating solely on community mobilisation to gradually combining community work with political engagement with state actors at different scales (Millstein, Oldfield and Stokke 2003) – is no small undertaking. The internal and external relational dynamics are dense and complex, entailing multi-pronged strategies of localisation – a place-based localised strategy for the defence of livelihoods – and a shifting political strategy linking identity, territory and culture at different scales spanning the globe (adapted from Escobar 2001: 163).[2] Our central concern – spanning the period 1991 to mid-2004 – is to elucidate the confluence of forces that enabled this social movement to eschew emergent (post-apartheid) official discourses about 'appropriate' community development processes in the shelter sector, and, more interestingly, the (selective) appropriation of elements of the HPA's approach into official praxis. We further highlight the emerging, contradictory consequences of the HPA's seeming 'victory' in the hegemonic elevation of its ideology and praxis.

Locating the HPA in the Transition

During the past decade, many scholars have analysed the compromise-ridden nature of the political settlement that made the 1994 democratic elections possible (see Bond 2000; Habib 1998; Jenkins 2002; Marais 1998). It is agreed that a key factor in the nature of the transition was the ability of the anti-apartheid movement to weld together a diversity of concerns into a 'united front against the regime' (Greenstein 2003: 29). The elevation of the need for unity and the resulting relegation/subordination of local concerns and interests to the background – ostensibly until the larger question of political transition was settled – (un)wittingly spawned a political culture wherein the space for dissenting interests and values was restricted. Consequently, the space for a radically pro-poor, post-apartheid order was very limited indeed. Moreover, in the transition process there was clearly an active and/or *de facto* demobilisation of grassroots structures that was pivotal in weakening the apartheid regime to the point of negotiations (Pieterse 2003).

The dynamics of political power at local level further diminished hopes of the new dispensation being radically pro-poor. At ground level, petit bourgeois elements were (and still are) often in control of the party machinery, development forums and civic bodies. This local political elite was under 'no pressure to extend their socio-political reach to their poorest neighbours' (residents of informal settlements, backyard shacks and hostel dwellers), who were dissuaded from active participation in local politics (Everatt 1999: 27). So while the ANC committed itself to delivery to the poor, local reality remained one of 'shutting out the poor' (Everatt 1999: 25), compounded by the fact that the ANC did not have (and still does not have) a 'public language to deal with the[se] intense local power struggles' (Jensen 2001: 107, 118). In this context, the HPA, which explicitly set out to mobilise the poor, was initially viewed by both the ANC and civics as a 'threat'. The HPA skilfully defused tensions through working on a settlement-by-settlement basis, assuaging fears and building trust by underscoring its non-political orientation.

In part by default, in part by design and in part through structural configurations, most civil society organisations that purported to service the needs of the poor tended to marginalise the most vulnerable segments of society from township political life and development processes. Most urban development non-governmental organisations (NGOs) involved in addressing the shelter needs of low-income communities worked through male-dominated local civics, failing to 'represent equally' those living in townships. The poorest households, women and squatters, were under-represented and effectively excluded from these development interventions. Secondly, most NGOs and civics focused on ensuring improved housing provision or that capital markets better served low-income communities, rather than strengthening the political capacity of the urban poor to define, articulate and champion their own needs and projects (Bolnick and Mitlin 1999). By inserting itself into this vacuum, the HPA has become one of the most effective social movements of the urban poor.

Ideology of the HPA and its Identity

The HPA is founded on a most critical reading of South Africa's political economy and the practices of the liberation movement. The key ideologues of the HPA – most notably those in People's Dialogue – were of the view that the 'state and market act in ways that are universally against the interests of the poor' and that it would be 'horribly naïve' (Anon.(a) n.d.: 1) to believe that a new government – notwithstanding their 'genuine interest in addressing the needs of its largest constituencies' (uTshani Buyakhuluma publication n.d. cited in Tweedie 2003: 5) – would mediate national resource struggles in ways that discontinue benefiting dominant social classes. Less subtly, they charged that the 'needs and problems of the urban poor were not going to be a priority for the new government' (Baumann and Bolnick 2001: 106).

The ideologues were also 'explicitly uncomfortable with the politics of the liberation movement' (even in the early years of the struggle) and 'contemporary anti-communist ideas of "open society"'. They were not convinced that the creation of an 'open society' – enshrining autonomy and citizen equality – was a 'necessary and sufficient guarantee' for the realisation of the rights of the poor (uTshani Buyakhuluma publication n.d. cited in Tweedie 2003: 5). Not only was this related to deep scepticism of government's (past and present) commitment to the poor, but also its shallow understanding of poverty, often constructed as 'strictly an apartheid derivative', which effectively 'underplayed or ignored' the 'full extent of the current problems facing the poor in South Africa' (Anon.(b) n.d.: 1).

During the period of political liberalisation in the early 1990s, the ANC and the South African National Civic Organisation (SANCO) made explicit commitments to urban development as a vehicle to mobilise the urban poor. It was a time of high expectations and 'generous promises from politicians'. According to the ideologues, a 'top-down "delivery" process' was envisaged wherein the 'triumphant liberation movement would solve all the problems of the dispossessed'. They argued that the poor, for the ANC, were '*objects* of "development"' (Baumann and Bolnick 2001: 109; original emphasis).

Yet, they realised the futility of directly confronting a state that commands unprecedented levels of support and legitimacy, even through wielding an apparatus of power 'designed to be regulatory and not developmental' and governing a society that remains 'deeply authoritarian and controlled by a very aggressive and organised private sector' (Anon.(a) n.d.: 3). They reckoned that pragmatic rather than confrontational engagement would yield more fruitful outcomes for the urban poor. Pragmatic engagement entailed securing working relationships with formal market institutions and the state to maximise the access of the poor to legal entitlements; in this case, the housing subsidy.

For the HPA, enhancing access to legal entitlements pivots on the construction of new pro-poor relational fields of politics, a prerequisite being that the poor have a 'truly self-organised presence in the political sphere' (People's Dialogue 2000: 42). The HPA thus sought to initiate a 'grassroots, non-hierarchical process to reclaim the latent collective power of the poor', drawing on their collective knowledge and capacities to address their needs. The creation of a 'self-conscious movement of the poor, aware of its needs, socio-political situation and with collective capacities' – posited the ideologues – would empower them to become 'creative agents', '*subjects* of their own progress' versus *objects* to be acted upon (Baumann and Bolnick 2001: 106, 109).

Mobilisation Ideology in Form and Practice
Building the capacities and capabilities of the urban poor constituted the main
thrust of the HPA's work in the first three years of its existence (1991–94). Its
priority was to become a 'rallying point for the urban poor, an institution in
which the poor and homeless people could find a safe passage to decent and
affordable shelter' (People's Dialogue 1996).

To achieve this, a 'space'/site was created for poor men and women of
slums – regardless of their political persuasion – to share their experiences and
strengthen their positions. The 'space'/site – a 1991 housing conference for
slum and shack dweller organisations – was configured to enable the poor to
'learn from each other through dialogue among themselves about what does
and doesn't work' (Wilson and Lowery 2003: 51). Critically, the middle-class
activists (key ideologues) who created the space believed that 'whatever emerged
from the dialogue' conducted in that space 'belonged to the participants and
was therefore the only possible outcome' (Wilson and Lowery 2003: 51). The
conference was a success and the seeds of the Federation were planted.

Around this time, the NGO People's Dialogue on Land and Shelter was
formed, with a key ideologue and creator of the 1991 space, Joel Bolnick, serving
as director. People's Dialogue had very humble beginnings and, despite its
powerful reach and impact, it still remains a small NGO, with a staff-to-CBO
ratio of approximately 1:5 000 (BRCS 2002: 4, 12). Dialogue supports and
facilitates the efforts of poor people, instead of delivering professional solutions
through interfacing between formal institutions and the poor; assists in
designing strategies that members learn and practice; and works with external
agencies to create space for people's organisations. The communities themselves
assume responsibility for organising and networking.

From its inception to January 2002, the Federation grew to comprise a
network of autonomous community-based organisations (CBOs) (1 100 savings
schemes), with 100 000 members, 85 per cent of whom are women, in receipt
of monthly incomes below R1 000.[3] The Federation has a flat leadership
structure, with a core group of nine national leaders and teams based in regional
Federation centres that fulfil key learning and administrative roles. The
Federation also maintains regionally pooled savings funds financed by
contributions from local savings collectives (BRCS 2002: 12).

Whereas Federation members demonstrated incredible energy, initiative
and skill, they lacked sufficient material resources to meaningfully transform

their living and shelter conditions. In 1993, the HPA decided to establish a finance scheme to secure, consolidate and deliver funds on a collective basis to the Federation-affiliated savings schemes (see Baumann and Bolnick 2001 for a full discussion of the fund). After an unhurried period of capacity building – including a major conference on housing finance in June 1994 – uTshani began operations in January 1995.

Initially housed as a financial institution within Dialogue, uTshani Fund is the asset builder and asset manager of the Federation. It is a community-managed revolving loan fund capitalised (initially) by foreign donors and government grants. The fund is the primary partner of the Federation in its land, infrastructure, housing and economic development activities and shares joint responsibility with Dialogue to partner the Federation in its savings activities.

The institutional architecture of the HPA is deliberatively designed to support an unambiguously people-led, people-centred and people-controlled development strategy, termed in the literature as asset-based community development (ABCD) (see Mathie and Cunningham 2003). This approach is about fostering transformative, self-reliant and self-replicable social development practices modelled around: asset mobilisation; asset mapping; community-based problem solving; and 'progressive scaling' up of activities as outside external institutions are called upon to invest in community-devised and locally-driven development initiatives. Key practices or rituals to give effect to this strategy include: enumeration and mapping; surveying; house modelling and savings schemes establishment; exchange visits between settlements and internationally; precedent setting; and claim making.

In contrast to mainstream claim-making practices, the HPA's strategy in its engagement with the state is underpinned by the belief that official programmes 'need to be redesigned and redeveloped by the poor' so that they 'work for them', followed by negotiation with the state to obtain support for the implementation of their 'solution' (People's Dialogue 1996: 21). The solutions championed aim to strengthen long-term capacity and capability building through three linked change processes: asset building (mobilising social capital through federating, networking and exchanges, savings and loan activities); developing a knowledge of community priorities and needs and how best to meet them, and accumulating and mobilising resources to test the efficacy and sustainability of the solution (via enumeration, community planning and house design exercises, supported by exchange visits); and, engaging the state to support the solution engineered by the poor, without strangling the 'life out of their organisations' (People's Dialogue 1996: 21; People's Dialogue 2000).

A key outcome of these processes of capacity-capability enhancement is for the poor to lead by example wherein communities pioneer and develop their own solution and demonstrate its practical viability before engaging the state in an effort to transform official programmes. Significant here is not pitting the solution proposed by the poor against the state programme or lobbying directly for policy change. Rather, the approach is to seek 'shifts' in the institutional arrangements that determine the way policy translates into action. The 'attendant shifts in the institutional framework, if they are of some magnitude, will be bound to have a direct impact on policy' (People's Dialogue 1996: 21). Joel Bolnick captured the spirit of this form of engagement most eloquently: 'Don't confront authority head on. Instead of storming the citadel, infiltrate it . . . Play judo with the state – use its own weight to roll it over' (Interview, 07.04.04).

Consequently, the modalities of state engagement are extremely sophisticated. It involves straddling diverse spatial scales and territorial-administrative jurisdictions; criss-crossing the political and official divide; deal making with progressive and conservative political parties; and, playing off one level of government against another. This strategic practice arises from multi-scalar organisation building interventions (local/regional/national/ international exchanges and affiliation to Shack/Slum Dwellers International[4]) whose roots are anchored in communities.

'Federating' of community-based organisations at city, provincial and national scales is the first step. Once federations are active, negotiation with government officials commences around the priorities of the poor, and the solutions devised by them. Significant in HPA's multi-scalar practice are the contributions of the international donor community. The flexibility of donor funding facilitates innovation, which is needed to ensure effective utilisation of government funds (Development Works 2003). Donor funding also creates the multi-national language and legitimacy for HPA interventions.

The superior track record of this ABCD approach is most visible in the HPA's widely celebrated housing delivery strategy. While the state was finalising its supply side, state-facilitated and private-sector-driven housing programme (in a forum that excluded the homeless poor and their organisations), the HPA used a combination of uTshani Fund loans (capitalised at that stage by European donors) and savings from collectives to build homes that were larger, cheaper and of better quality in comparison to those delivered via the state-developer partnership route.

The HPA model became increasingly attractive to government. Following the promotion of the model as sustainable at the Habitat II Conference in 1996, global funders[5] provided direct support for the adoption of a housing approach based on self-help construction through the formation of a People's Housing Partnership Trust within the Department of Housing in 1998. The purpose of the Trust was the 'institutional capacitation and empowerment at the provincial and local spheres of government and among NGOs to support the people's process' (Huchzermeyer 2001: 322).

In May 1998, the Ministry of Housing introduced a version of the People's Housing Process (henceforth referred to as the official PHP [OPHP]) as a means of accessing that portion of the capital subsidy allocated to the top structure. Government placed considerable emphasis on community/beneficiary contribution to the process of house construction (sweat equity). Thus, the OPHP approach is ostensibly about people building their own houses utilising subsidised materials, with government extending the necessary infrastructure (Huchzermeyer 2001: 323). For the HPA and many progressive development practitioners, the adoption of PHP by the state is trumpeted as an important victory for those committed to people-centred development (Wilson and Lowery 2003: 54).

Vicissitudes of Mainstreaming

Government's appropriation of the HPA model – with considerable adaptation – has become a significant pillar of the official housing programme. The OPHP facilitates incremental housing delivery by scaling up participatory processes, relying on self-help processes, communities' resources and empowerment. To strengthen community initiatives, the programme liaises with grassroots groupings located in slums. It sets up housing support centres to stimulate and assist self-help community efforts by passing on information; identifying and channelling subsidies; providing technical advice; and, developing co-operative arrangements to purchase building/construction material (Miraftab 2003). From the very beginning, though, serious concerns were registered about the efficacy and viability of the OPHP approach within a broader policy framework that remains stubbornly wedded to neo-liberal, macro-economic precepts, modernist planning orientations and the technocratic projections of the state (Rust 2002).

From the HPA's perspective, the state has adopted the PHP in a partial manner. The emphasis of government policy is on the rapid delivery of products/outputs, while the HPA's PHP approach is more concerned with process, building social capital, skills formation and beneficiary empowerment. The emphasis on outputs restricts claim making to 'projects', wherein the poor become bound to development 'solutions' defined and designed by others. The project-based model has a short-term logic of investment, accounting, reporting and assessment. 'Slow learning and cumulative change' are not easily reconciled with the 'temporal logic of projects' (Appadurai 2002: 30). For this reason, the OPHP is equated with financial cost reduction and individualism, rather than collective beneficiary planning, decision-making and more productive housing delivery (Development Works 2003; BRCS 2003).

The PHP is presently being re-emphasised by the Department of Housing as a 'way of helping the public housing programme' (Rust 2002: 14) cope with the departure of the private sector from the low-income housing sector and capacity constraints of government. The rediscovery of the PHP recognises that with regard to the poorest households it is extremely difficult to combine the quantitative objective of mass private-sector delivery with the requirement of a minimum house size of reasonable quality, conforming to national standards, and delivered at a reasonable pace. The state views the PHP as a delivery mode that reduces costs, enhances quality of output, leverages beneficiary resources, speeds up land release, and prevents alienation of housing benefit (resale of new houses) below the value of input costs.

In pursuit of these objectives, the local state is increasingly tightening its control over the PHP through dominating all or most roles and choices, such as choice of the support organisation, house design and building material suppliers, leaving only sweat equity to beneficiaries. OPHP delivery regimes on the ground presently violate (at worst) and/or are clearly at odds with almost every aspect of national PHP policy and regulations (see BRCS 2003: 51–3 for a full discussion).

The impulse to tighten control derives from the fundamentally contradictory motivational frameworks in terms of what citizens want from the housing programme and state priorities. The state, on the one hand, privileges loss avoidance and risk minimisation in the application of the subsidy resource.

This undermines indigenous and evolutionary processes of home building as pursued by communities and households (Rust 2002: 14). The state perceives subsidised housing as a communal 'capital' asset that outlives immediate housing beneficiaries and is reluctant to work with/through community-based organisations and NGOs. Beneficiaries, on the other hand, prioritise choice and flexibility in subsidy deployment because this allows them to produce better homes as immediately useful items to themselves. They prioritise quality over quantity and prefer working through CBOs and NGOs to protect their interests (BRCS 2003: i)

The inability of the state to productively negotiate the differences in programmatic thrusts and motivational frameworks is borne out by a poor PHP delivery record. Less than 3 per cent of subsidised houses built since 1994 to 2003 can be called PHP products (BRCS 2003: 2). Complicating matters further is the finding of a comprehensive review of the PHP that 'the requisite policy, implementation, and institutional infrastructure remain weak, contradictory, underdeveloped, and systematically biased against it [the PHP]' (BRCS 2002: 7).

Tensions, Contradictions and Challenges

The vicissitudes of mainstreaming are not simply confined to the subversion or corruption of a people-engineered housing process. Far more damaging to the ideology, identity and praxis of the HPA was the state not honouring its commitment in the 'partnership' arrangement to support the people-driven housing delivery strategy. Problematic internal relational dynamics and the state not fulfilling citizens' constitutionally enshrined rights to the housing subsidy precipitated major crises for the HPA, which it attempted to address through a restructuring exercise in 2001–02.

Initially in 1995–96, the HPA used uTshani Fund loans in selected communities to pilot its shelter approach,[6] with a view to attracting government support, both through housing subsidies and equity injections. This strategy was possible because the fund's equity was derived from grants, and it was authorised to extend bridging finance to members before subsidies were secured. From 1997–2000, the HPA used the uTshani Agreement[7] with the national Department of Housing that permitted it to access subsidies directly from government. The fund could either provide bridging loans before accessing subsidies and then claim the money back from government or disburse subsidies up-front to members for housing construction.

The HPA's success in the construction of large, high-quality houses with uTshani loans coupled to the rapidity of loan release – indeed the people's process moves considerably faster than the delivery of state funds (Baumann and Mitlin 2002) – encouraged explosive growth in Federation membership. New groups expected to benefit from the fund, and numerous Federation leaders began promoting this entitlement (the loan), rather than daily savings as an avenue to build the movement. This was a radical shift away from an emphasis on savings as the cornerstone of community mobilisation. The deposit to access the loan (5 per cent/R500) came to be viewed as a way of purchasing the loan, and members who would otherwise save more in the collectives quickly accumulated R500 to access the R10 000 loan at a repayment rate of R120 per month. While the cost of building materials increased due to inflation, the subsidy amount remained static. The loans were therefore insufficient for the HPA to construct houses that earlier members had built. Although the ritualised processes of mobilisation continued, it was difficult for the HPA to shift members' consciousness from the dream of large homes (in line with changing material resource constraints), thus fuelling a tendency for members to 'overbuild' – laying out large foundations for houses that could not be consolidated with the available finances. This produced 'unfinished homes', placing pressure on the fund to release further finance to protect the HPA's reputation (and ensure uninterrupted access to subsidies) thereby pushing members further into debt[8] and increasing overall 'systemic risk'.[9] Additionally, the incentive to promise large homes contributed to the tendency to recruit better-off members who could top up their loan funds and subsidies with non-Federation savings. In a nutshell, the HPA and its members – through the financial-institutional innovation of uTshani – became over-focused on the 'golden egg' of housing to the 'detriment of the underlying social mobilisation, via daily savings, that constitutes the proverbial "goose"' (BRCS 2001: 54–6).

The centralised nature of the fund's financial management and decision-making produced another series of dilemmas. Risks associated with uTshani's bridging loan strategy were transferred to People's Dialogue and the Federation leadership, with local leaders shielded from having to make difficult decisions around resource allocation. Although some Federation leaders and members were aware of financial sustainability problems, they tended to see their role as expanding membership to access more subsidies and capital, compromising further the fund's viability.

The sustainability of the fund was, however, most severely compromised by the slow release of state subsidies. Not all provinces accepted the uTshani Agreement and PHP approach. Even where adopted, there was no guarantee that provincial officials would approve HPA subsidy applications. Even when approved, subsidy release was more often than not delayed or undelivered due to a combination of bureaucratic inertia, differing provincial policies and local government reluctance or inability to engage with community development processes. The core of the problem was, and still is, the HPA believes, the capital subsidy system that is 'simply not designed to seek out, identify, and take advantage of functional grassroots channels through which state housing resources can flow to produce adequate shelter for those who don't have it' (Baumann and Bolnick 2001: 108). For the HPA, the subsidy system – which is supposedly an entitlement under law, based on the constitution – is as good as 'not there in practice' for the majority of Federation members, which accounted for the fund's present crisis. On a more sinister level, if a household builds its own house – through a diversity of non-official funding sources rather than waiting for a subsidy – it is classified as housed and therefore ineligible for further assistance. In other words, perversely, the initiative of the poor effectively disqualifies them from the subsidy (Rust 2002: 14).

Without the housing subsidy, the HPA would 'never have considered uTshani Fund lending on the size and scale it has actually undertaken: sustainable, large, long term loans to the poorest of the poor for complete housing is wishful thinking and certainly not the business of the Alliance' (BRCS 2001: 76). With the subsidy 'not there' in practice, the fund was in an increasingly tenuous situation as the *de facto* creditor to a large group of the poorest South Africans, who could not be expected to repay substantial housing loans and who did not believe that this was what they had agreed to do. Yet, in reality the state, not the Federation (notwithstanding declining loan repayments), was the fund's largest debtor. In early 2004, government owed R54 million in subsidy money to the HPA (Interview, Van Rensberg, 29.04.04).

People's Dialogue attempted on numerous occasions to limit the loans to R6 000, but Federation leaders under pressure from members found this unacceptable and refused to implement the policy. It was argued that limiting access to the R10 000 loan would '"kill the Federation" – compelling support for the view that mobilisation around uTshani Fund resources had replaced mobilisation around better allocation of state resources' (BRCS 2001: 56). By late 2000, the overall rate of repayment to the fund was so low that the HPA leadership was left with little choice but to suspend lending and embarked on a process of re-evaluation and restructuring. Since 2001, the focus shifted to accessing subsidies up-front. The fund began concentrating on helping the Federation to identify land and acquire development rights; secure subsidies to retire bridging loans and/or fund new projects; manage, co-manage and support projects; and provide support for income generation (BRCS 2002: 22).[10]

This predicament was shaped by the long-run tendency to transform the fund from a communal resource of the Federation into an 'avatar of the subsidy entitlement itself' (Baumann and Bolnick 2001: 112). The expectation that the fund would deliver an entitlement was incompatible with a financial system based on a revolving fund model. Clearly, in a situation of rapid membership expansion, weak savings records, low repayment rates, and the non-delivery of subsidies, funds simply did not revolve sufficiently to meet ongoing expectations of the membership. In turn, this impacted negatively on the capacity for collective action around deepening access to subsidies, wherein the latter came to be seen as a means to an end; i.e. an 'entry point for mobilisation, rather than organisational goals in themselves' (People's Dialogue 2000: 25).

Conceptual Intimations[11]

For a social movement – whose main aim is *reclaiming the democratic right and power of the poor to choose* – engaging a popular state around policy through established institutional mechanisms and channels is unlikely to yield the desired outcomes. The attainment of an alternative activist development approach calls forth a very different form of politics aimed at transforming the existing institutional architecture and tilting the balance of power in favour of the poor. Central to this project is a radical deconstruction of the 'frame of existing politics'; i.e. technical practices, forms of knowledge and institutions (Barry 2002).

The HPA realised that particular ways of thinking about society and social change are engraved in the organisation of officially sanctioned participatory spaces, and that every space has etched into it the traces of its 'generative past'. In this context, the HPA chose not to 'insert' the urban poor into a pre-defined (liberalising, compacted/corporatist political) space, but sought to develop their capacities/capabilities to negotiate with the powerful. The enhancement of people's capabilities to claim their entitlements and their right to shape the contours of the shelter production regime (its organisation, functioning and output) – apart from being broadly in line with the ABCD approach versus the supply-driven, technocratic deficit models of development – witnessed the HPA initiate and create new spaces/sites for citizens to act '*without* (both outside, and in the absence of [the state]) and *on* it' (Cornwall 2002: 20; original emphasis). These chosen spaces – created by participants themselves – constitute 'sites of radical possibility' (Cornwall 2002: 17), where those who are excluded find a place and a voice to defend their interests and champion their own development path.

The site constructed is a relatively durable institutionalised space from which citizens/communities practice self-provisioning of credit to satisfy needs; participate in networks that go beyond the boundaries of the nation-state (exchanges); and engage in governance by influencing public policy through advocacy and modelling alternatives (precedent setting). As such, they also contain sites wherein citizens and their intermediary organisations '*assume* some of the *functions* of *government*' (Cornwall 2002: 20, 21, 17; emphasis added). Although these sites are relatively autonomous from the state, the HPA's sites are connected to government both directly and indirectly in different aspects of shelter provision.

Despite considerable strides registered by the HPA in articulating, championing and operationalising a people-led, people-centred and people-controlled development approach, it does so in an era of disjunctive democratisation[12] and the dominance of supply-side citizenship.[13] Here our research raises questions about the extent to which the HPA's development praxis and mobilisation strategies constitute not so much a challenge to the 'frame of existing politics' but rather a potential reproduction of it. Our contention is that the HPA possibly reproduces liberal or authoritarian 'rationalities of rule' wherein the core rituals regularise the conduct of the social and economic life of the urban poor through the 'creation of locales, entities and persons able to operate a regulated autonomy' (Rose and Miller 1992: 173).

The HPA's Alternative to the Mainstream Model: Ambiguated Realities

The core 'rituals' of the HPA – echoing those of the state – include enumeration and mapping,[14] surveying and house modelling, as well as exchanges for lateral learning. Savings, the main instrument the Federation uses for mobilisation, is variously described as the 'cement that binds people together', the 'goose that lays the golden egg', and 'the means that creates space for the poor to identify, understand and articulate their own priorities'. Savings are fundamental to the Federation's strategy of mobilising the urban poor through their own resources, experience and capacities in order to transform relations between their members and state institutions. For the president of the Indian National Slum Dweller's Federation, daily savings is the bedrock of every activity of the Federation. When the president and others in the HPA speak of savings, they see it as a 'moral discipline' (in his words, it is like 'breathing'), which builds a certain kind of political fortitude and spiritual discipline (cited in Appadurai 2004: 11–12). In another vein, savings could also be potentially viewed as a criterion for localised (HPA-based) citizenship.

The combination of self-enumeration, self-regulation and the notion of savings as 'spiritual' or 'moral' discipline – the foundations of a potentially exclusionary citizenship[15] – could arguably be seen as a form of 'auto-governmentality'. While those in the HPA would prefer to see it as a method to fashion and dictate their own social and political legibility (rather than having one imposed on them by the state – an exercise in counter-governmentality), the combination is 'truly insidious in its capillary reach' (Appadurai 2002: 36). If governmentality is accepted to mean the complex array of techniques – programmes, procedures, strategies and tactics – employed by non-state agencies and state institutions to shape the conduct of individuals and populations; if governmentality extends from political government right through to forms of self-regulation – namely 'technologies of self';[16] if governmentality (in its present guise) centres on social responsibilisation – a matter of personal provision and self-empowerment (Lemke 2001), then some serious questions need to be asked about the nature and content of the HPA's contestation of the 'frame of existing politics'.

Globally, neo-liberalism is linked to a 'wider range of political subjects than is typical of orthodox liberalism' and tends to 'promote "community" (or a plurality of self-organising communities) as a flanking, compensatory mechanism for the inadequacies of the market mechanism' (Jessop 2002: 455). The invocation of 'community' as a means of fostering civic responsibility is an essential tenet of (social democratic) Third Way politics (Flint 2003: 615). Although many disastrous consequences can flow from this type of social engineering, others point to examples of communities that are able to take advantage of new opportunities provided for citizens to claim and retain the rights and entitlements of state and global citizenship threatened by pervasive market forces. Against this backdrop, it is argued, civil society can play an important role – 'humanising capitalism' (Edwards 1999 cited in Mathie and Cunningham 2003: 9) through nurturing social and economic assets existing in the poorest communities and then advocating for a range of interventions to ameliorate poverty. In this instance, ABCD is said to occupy the 'middle ground where the logic of competition meets, and mixes with, the logic of co-operation', 'activating the social capital required for community-driven initiatives, for collaborative partnerships with external institutions, and for claiming the rights and entitlements of citizenship' (Edwards 1999 cited in Mathie and Cunningham 2003: 9). Through this humanisation of capitalism, civil society can supposedly generate 'the less tangible assets that enable people to bargain, negotiate and advance their interests' (Edwards 1999 cited in Mathie and Cunningham 2003: 9), ultimately leading to self-belief, self-esteem and self-actualisation. Thus when one reads about the developmental impact of the Alliance's programmes on the psychological fabric of its members; i.e. I can, I care; We can, We care (Wilson and Lowery 2003: 62), coupled with the statements about the humanisation of capitalism, the question arises as to whether it is not perhaps an endorsement, even if unintentional, of a neo-liberal rationality; i.e. the congruence achieved between a 'responsible and moral individual and economic rational actor' (Lemke 2001: 201).

In short, there is perhaps an idealisation of self-help/ABCD by the HPA that allows the state to shift responsibilities for adequate shelter provision on to poor communities. The HPA's non-confrontational 'politics of patience' blunts, and even discourages,[17] (potential) resistance and opposition, and the technologies of self-governance or remaking of self serve as the legitimating psycho-social handmaiden – the technology assists, facilitates, supports and enables the state's unilateral downsizing of its shelter policy. This is indeed not such a far-fetched idea especially given the enthusiastic (re-)embrace of the PHP in the recent re-jigging of the national shelter programme (Khan 2004).

The motivations for a 'renewed' people-centred housing strategy arise primarily from private sector withdrawal from the subsidised housing sector coupled with government's capacity constraints. This leaves the state with little option but to turn to beneficiaries as the main source of delivery. In the revamped policy, the PHP model does not require a cash contribution, which is (un)wittingly pushing provincial and municipal housing authorities to opt for the PHP route. In the state's imagination, the PHP is coming to be seen as no more than sweat equity applied to a state-driven housing delivery programme, whose subsidy programme increasingly shows signs of upward redistribution; i.e. serviced sites and PHP for the poor, while others who can pay the R2 479 contribution and more – as a condition to access the housing subsidy – will access better quality housing in possibly less peripheral locations.[18] On the other hand, the renewed emphasis by the state on the PHP is partly to arrest the selling and abandonment of RDP homes by beneficiaries by requiring them to invest sweat equity in the hope that this will generate a sense of ownership and 'responsible' asset management.

Although there are very profound and fundamental differences between the state's PHP programme and those of the HPA, the mechanics of the self-help housing appropriation by the state – given the earlier comments on auto-govermentality – are still to be coherently thought through by the HPA. Indeed, the very essence of liberal government, governance and governmentality is about drawing on the processes, modes of regulation, values and expectations that are located in civil society. In other words, liberal governments' model interventions on the forms of regulation, expectations and values that are already in operation in civil society. It is in this sly and subtle colonisation of civil society that state ambitions achieve a quiet but effective hegemony. This involves a three-layered folding process: the unfolding of the formally political sphere into civil society (linkages, partnerships and networking – i.e. the uTshani Agreement); an enfolding of the regulations of civil society into the political domain (entrepreneurialism, self-provisioning of credit, consumerism); and a refolding of the real or ideal values and conduct of civil society onto the political (supply-side citizenship, sweat equity/R2 479 contribution, deregulation, workfarism) (Dean 2002: 45).

This line of argument raises a difficult question: what is the complicity of the HPA in the content and operationalisation of the state's PHP in light of the unfolding, enfolding and refolding processes just described? Clearly, the HPA should have focused some energy on exploring the 'optical frame' of the state when it crafted its PHP policy, which was partly fashioned and moulded on the HPA approach. This, in our view, is a critically urgent need in the HPA's ongoing struggle to optimise the terms of trade between recognition and redistribution and its engagement with the PHP, now and in the future.

Conclusion

Social movements essentially represent a social-cultural practice rooted in everyday struggles for survival and 'space' in urban areas, increasingly marked by the limited reach of the state. Inside these spaces, in many cities of the developing world, poor citizens are mobilising in creative ways to claim, define, map, regulate and populate territories in terms of a grassroots imaginary and practice of social solidarity. In South Africa, the HPA has been at the forefront of these dynamic processes. We have sketched the impressive genesis of this social movement, its emergent identity, adaptiveness in a context of dramatic political change and, most importantly, its marked reflexivity. At the heart of the chapter is an episode that deals with a crisis of legitimacy and effectiveness that the movement faced in the early part of the current decade. Through its tumultuous efforts to understand and respond to this crisis, we aimed to provide an insight into the durability of the movement's core identity, the calibre of its leadership, and its vision of empowerment of its members – the urban poor left behind by the terms of the compacted transition process. The crisis, for us at least, also raises important conceptual questions about the veracity of the movement's ideology – mutual-help and social solidarity – when it was appropriated by the state to legitimate its own efforts to renew and refurbish its failing housing policy, but with dubious consequences. In this unresolved moment, our snapshot freezes time and leaves it to the reader to form a perspective on the significance of the HPA for furthering a politics of redistribution and democratisation.

Notes

1. Defined as people directing their own development initiatives and organisations through 'active internal debate' and a 'commitment to transparency and inclusion'; the poor engaging key actors in the state and local administrations; and, individuals and communities who 'achieve solidarity and are empowered through horizontal connections' to other individuals and groups (Wilson and Lowery 2003: 51).
2. Unpacking the complexity and density of the relational dynamics is rendered more complicated by a post-apartheid transformation project that combines – in varying amounts and varying over time – *democratic developmentalism* and *developmental democratisation*. The state is on one day a friend of the poor; on the next a foe; and, on another day both friend and foe. It is this dynamic that we wrestled with in this chapter focusing on the HPA's genesis to consolidation; i.e. from 1991 to mid-2004.
3. Rose Molokane estimated that in April 2004 around 2 500 savings groups existed with over 800 000 people having directly and indirectly benefited from it (Interview, 13.05.04).

4. Shack/Slum Dwellers International (SDI), a global network of poor people's organisations from eleven countries of the South, comprises Federations of community organisations that are linked to NGOs and groupings of professionals who support Federation initiatives. Unlike other transnational citizen networks, the locus of power lies in communities themselves rather than in intermediary NGOs at national and international levels. This is partly because the SDI and its counterparts were not set up to influence global policy-making or lobby international financial institutions (though these roles are increasing). Rather, their aim is to promote practical solidarity, mutual support and the exchange of information about strategies and concrete alternatives among their members (Edwards 2001).
5. The United Nations Commission for Human Settlements (UNCHS) and the United Nations Development Programme (UNDP) – co-convenors of the Habitat II Conference – and the United States Agency for International Development.
6. Using funds from European donors, lending for housing construction through group-based finance commenced in April 1995 and over 700 housing loans were distributed (Bolnick and Mitlin 1999: 227).
7. In 1995, the National Housing Board approved an agreement with the fund – uTshani Agreement – that recognised the latter as a legitimate conduit for subsidies to Federation members (Anon.(a) n.d).
8. Taking loans to finish homes and progressively undermining their already limited ability to repay loans.
9. Not surprisingly, the number of homes delivered through the PHP route is contested. BRCS (2003) reports that 12 000 homes were delivered using the subsidy, member's savings, bridging loans and other resources. In the interview with Molokane (13.05.04), she estimated that 14 000 home were delivered. In a proposal to the City of Cape Town, motivating a partnership between the City and the HPA around enumeration, it is stated that between 1995 and 2000, the Federation constructed over 15 000 houses in all provinces (Homeless People's Federation and People's Dialogue 2004).
10. As of 2003, the fund had a portfolio of approximately R65 million, the bulk of which accounted by its loan book, financed nearly 9 500 houses (BRCS 2003: 13).
11. We employ the present tense in this part of the chapter as the deconstruction of the underlying philosophy and associated practices (rituals) are not bound to the period under discussion (from 1991 to mid-2004). Instead, the problems identified with the HPA's philosophy and rituals – cross-referenced to liberal or authoritarian 'rationalities of rule' – remain relevant today.
12. Disjunctive democratisation refers to systematic violation of human rights and institutionalised exclusion in elected constitutional-liberal regimes (see Holston 2002; Kabeer 2002 for a full discussion).
13. Supply-side citizenship denotes and elevates personal autonomy, self-reliance, social initiative based on the ability to pay, equality of opportunity, volunteerism, workfarism, no rights without responsibility, etc. (see De Beus and Koelble 2001).
14. This type of inscription – making people write things down and count them – is itself, argues Rose and Miller (1992: 187), a kind of government of them, inciting individuals to construe their lives according to such norms. Through these mechanisms, authorities can register and act on those distant from them in the pursuit of various objectives without encroaching on their 'freedom' and 'autonomy'. These mechanisms assume considerable importance in modern modes of government.
15. The possibility of unintentional selection in the recruitment of Federation membership is an area to be investigated by the HPA (Huchzermeyer 2001: 315).
16. Within liberal regimes, governmental objectives are secured not through direct intervention in people's lives, but through 'realignment' of subjects' identities and by implicating self-regulation

within governmental aims. Processes of liberal government therefore focus on technologies of the self as governance attempts to shape subjects' conduct around a moral discourse of 'responsible behaviour'. These technologies represent governance at a distance, rather than a reduction in government. While subjects are constituted as active and autonomous agents, their freedom is regulated through implicating subjects in deeper and wider relations of power (see Flint 2003: 612–14). The savings collectives of the HPA can be read as communities that are responsible for their own self-regulation and well-being.

17. The political practices of the HPA which emphasises negotiation, compromise and accommodation are being questioned by some members:

> The poor got amazing patience. Sometimes I don't have patience and I think it is rubbing off on them. But I don't know where the people get this patience from. I don't know where . . . Sometimes I sit in a meeting and I look at these people, and I think: 'They are twice my age and they still have no house and they still come to save.' And I am thinking: 'Are you people really relying on me to pull this one off?' When your metro is not interested in meeting, neither with me nor you; and sometimes you find that militant group that wants to march, and I am saying, listen guys: 'I am not going to stop you. If you want to go and march, go and march.' I can't. Because that is not the Federation's style to have public demonstrations. Because they are always told that they are an exclusive group, they don't do such things; they don't invade land, they don't toyi-toyi, they don't evict people. You know they [HPA] got invasion on their land. On their own land! And they don't want to [evict] the people, because it is not their value. They don't invade land, they don't evict, they don't toyi-toyi. They are slowly becoming very militant . . . They are talking to others (Interview, Van Rensberg, 29.04.04).

18. It needs to be pointed out that the housing policy is being incrementally refined.

References

Anonymous (a). n.d. 'Housing and the Urban Poor'. http://www.dialogue.org.za/Documents/ Outside%20Docs/ (accessed 18 July 2004).

——— (b). n.d. 'SA Homeless People's Federation and People's Dialogue: An Alliance at the Cutting Edge'. http://www.dialogue.org.za/pd/Four%20Way%20Street%202000.htm (accessed 11 August 2003).

Appadurai, A. 2002. 'Deep Democracy: Urban Governmentality and the Horizon of Politics'. *Public Culture* 14 (1): 21–47.

———. 2004. 'The Capacity to Aspire: Culture and the Terms of Recognition'. In V. Rao and M. Walton (eds), *Culture and Public Action*. Standford: Stanford University Press.

Barry, A. 2002. 'The Anti-Political Economy'. *Economy and Society* 31 (2): 268–84.

Baumann, T. and J. Bolnick. 2001. 'Out of the Frying Pan into the Fire: The Limits of Loan Finance in a Capital Subsidy Context'. *Environment and Urbanisation* 13 (2): 103–15.

Bauman, T. and D. Mitlin. 2002. 'The South African Homeless Federation: Investing in the Poor'. Paper presented at Rural and Urban Development Conference, Rietvleidam, History Workshop and National Land Committee.

Bay Research and Consultancy Services (BRCS). 2001. 'The South Alliance'. Report prepared for the Homeless International, Cape Town.

———. 2002. 'Delivering the Housing Subsidy in a People's Housing Process Context: Challenges, Experiences and Options'. Cape Town.

———. 2003. 'The People's Housing Process in South Africa: Review for the People's Housing Partnership Trust'. Cape Town.

Bolnick, J. and D. Mitlin. 1999. 'Housing Finance and Empowerment in South Africa'. In K. Datta and G.A. Jones (eds), *Housing and Finance in Developing Countries*. London: Routledge.

Bond, P. 2000. *Elite Transition: From Apartheid to Neoliberalism in South Africa*. Pietermaritzburg: University of Natal Press.

Cornwall, A. 2002. 'Making Spaces, Changing Places: Situating Participation in Development'. IDS Working Paper 170, October, Institute of Development Studies, Sussex.

Davis, M. 2004. 'Planet of Slums'. *New Left Review* 26 (March–April): 1–23.

Dean, M. 2002. 'Liberal Government and Authoritarianism'. *Economy and Society* 31 (1): 37–61.

De Beus, J. and T. Koelble. 2001. 'The Third Way Diffusion and Social Democracy: Western Europe and South Africa Compared'. *Politikon* 28 (2): 181–94.

Development Works. 2002. 'Cities Alliance Project on a Pro-Poor Slum Upgrading Framework for South Africa for Submission to the Cities Alliance/United Nations Centre for Human Settlements'. Working report prepared by Development Works for People's Dialogue, Johannesburg.

———. 2003. 'Cities Alliance Project on a Pro-Poor Slum Upgrading Framework for South Africa for Submission to the Cities Alliance/United Nations Centre for Human Settlements'. Final report prepared by Development Works for People's Dialogue, Johannesburg.

Edwards, M. 2001. 'Global Civil Society and Community Exchanges: A Different Form of Movement'. *Environment and Urbanisation* 13 (2) October: 145–9.

Escobar, A. 1992. 'Culture, Practice and Politics: Anthropology and the Study of Social Movements'. *Critique of Anthropology* 12 (4): 394–432.

———. 2001. 'Culture Sits in Places: Reflections on Globalism and Subaltern Strategies of Localization'. *Political Geography* 20: 139–74.

Everatt, D. 1999. 'Yet Another Transition? Urbanization, Class Formation and the End of the National Liberation Struggle in South Africa'. Woodrow Wilson Centre for Comparative Urban Studies Occasional Paper Series 24, Washington D.C.

Farhi, F. 2003. 'The Democratic Turn: New Ways of Understanding Revolution'. In J. Foran (ed.), *The Future of Revolutions: Rethinking Radical Change in the Age of Globalization*. London and New York: Zed Books.

Flint, J. 2003. 'Housing and Ethnopolitics: Constructing Identities of Active Consumption and Responsible Community'. *Economy and Society* 32 (3): 611–29.

Greenstein, R. 2003. 'State, Civil Society and the Reconfiguration of Power in Post-Apartheid South Africa'. Paper presented at WISER Seminar, 28 August, University of the Witwatersrand, Johannesburg.

Habib, A. 1998. 'Structural Constraints, Resources and Decision-Making: A Study of South Africa's Transition to Democracy'. PhD thesis, Department of Politics, City University of New York.

Holston, J. 2002. 'Urban Citizenship and Globalisation'. In A.J. Scott (ed.), *Global City-Regions: Trends, Theory, Policy*. Oxford: Oxford University Press.

Homeless People's Federation and People's Dialogue. 2004. 'Submission to the City of Cape Town for Enumeration and Surveying'. Unpublished document available from People's Dialogue.

Huchzermeyer, M. 2001. 'Housing for the Poor: Negotiated Housing Policy in South Africa'. *Habitat International* 25: 303–31.

Jenkins, P. 2002. 'The Role of Civil Society in Housing Policy Development: Some Lessons from Southern Africa'. In S. Romaya and C. Rakodi (eds), *Building Sustainable Urban Settlements: Approaches and Case Studies in the Developing World*. London: ITDG Publishing.

Jensen, S. 2001. 'The Battlefield and the Prize: ANC's Bid to Reform the South African State'. In T.B. Hansen and F. Stepputat (eds), *States of Imagination: Ethnographic Explorations of the Postcolonial State*. Duke and London: Duke University Press.

Jessop, B. 2002. 'Liberalism, Neoliberalism, and Urban Governance: A State-Theoretical Perspective'. *Antipode* 34 (1): 452–72.

Kabeer, N. 2002. 'Citizenship, Affiliation and Exclusion: Perspectives from the South'. *IDS Bulletin: Making Rights Real: Exploring Citizenship, Participation and Accountability* 33 (2): 12–23.

Khan, F. 2004. 'The City and its Future? The Eternal Question'. *Development Update* 5 (1): 5–52.

Lemke, T. 2001. '"The Birth of Bio-Politics": Michel Foucault's Lecture at the College de France on Neoliberal Governmentality'. *Economy and Society* 30 (2): 190–207.

Marais, H. 1998. *South Africa: Limits to Change: The Political Economy of Transformation*. Cape Town: University of Cape Town Press.

Mathie, A. and G. Cunninghan. 2003. 'Who is Driving Development? Reflections on the Transformative Potential of Asset-Based Community Development'. Paper delivered at the conference 'Participation: From Tyranny to Transformation', 27–28 February, University of Manchester.

Millstein, M., S. Oldfield and K. Stokke. 2003. 'uTshani BuyaKhuluma – The Grass Speaks: The Political Space and Capacity of the South African Homeless People's Federation'. *Geoforum* 34: 457–68.

Miraftab, F. 2003. 'The Perils of Participatory Discourse: Housing Policy in Postapartheid South Africa'. *Journal of Planning Education and Research* 22: 226–39.

Nederveen Pieterse, J. 2000. 'After Post-Development'. *Third World Quarterly* 21 (2): 175–91.

People's Dialogue. 1996. 'What are those Bastards up to Now? A Review of the Interactions between the South African Homeless People's Federation/People Dialogue Alliance and the South African Government of National Unity'. http://www.dialogue.org.za/pd/bastards.htm.

———. 2000. 'The Age of Cities and Organisations of the Urban Poor'. Unpublished document available from F. Khan and E. Pieterse.

Homeless People's Federation. 2004. 'Community-Led Enumeration of the N2 Corridor Settlements'. Proposal to the City of Cape Town. South African Homeless People's Federation/People's Dialogue.

Pieterse, E. 2003. 'Rhythms, Patterning and Articulations of Social Formations in South Africa'. *Development Update* 4 (3): 101–36.

Rose, N. and P. Miller. 1992. 'Political Power beyond the State: Problematics of Government'. *British Journal of Sociology* 43 (2) June: 172–205.

Rust, K. 2002. 'No Short-Cuts: Implementing the South African Housing Policy'. Paper prepared for the Institute for Housing of South Africa.

Tweedie, D. 2003. 'People's Dialogue and the South African Homeless People's Federation'. http://www.audacity.org/IH-03-11-2003.htm (accessed 27 April 2004).

Wilson, P.A. and C. Lowery. 2003. 'Building Deep Democracy: The Story of a Grassroots Learning Organization in South Africa'. *Planning Forum* 9 (Spring): 47–64.

Interviews

Bolnick, Joel. Co-ordinator of Urban Resources Centre and Co-ordinator of Shack Dweller's International, 07.04.04.

Molokane, Rose. General Secretary of Inland Provinces (Homeless People's Federation) and Co-ordinator of Shack Dweller's International, 13.05.04.

Van Rensberg, Sandra. uTshani Fund Co-ordinator for Gauteng, North West and Mpumalanga, 29.04.04.

9

Elusive Boundaries

SANCO, the ANC and the Post-Apartheid South African State

Elke Zuern

The APF (Anti-Privatisation Forum) is . . . calling on all organisations and movements of the poor to reject cooption . . . and to expose SANCO as a front for the ANC government's control and containment of the emerging and ever-growing militant anti-capitalist struggles of the poor (McKinley 2003).

We (SANCO) were successful (in) convincing the leadership of the ANC to a point where they realised that an independent, critical voice is actually to the benefit of government, that once you have collapsing civil society, our democracy will be in danger, that the possibilities of developing a monster, developing anarchy, in some cases is very likely if you do not have a vibrant civil society (Interview, Hlongwane, 09.06.04).

ANALYSES OF SOCIAL movements and civil society most often begin with the assumption that these actors and mobilisations are largely independent of the state. Social movements by definition are first and foremost understood to constitute some form of 'collective challenge' (Tarrow 1994: 3–4) that necessarily entails conflict with existing organisational, political or cultural structures and norms (Touraine 1985: 750). Much of the literature on social movements therefore focuses on mobilisations that directly or indirectly challenge the state (see, for example, Desai 2002; Mamdani and Wamba-dia-Wamba 1985; McAdam,

McCarthy and Zald 1996; Tilly 1985) by employing 'non institutional channels' (Jelin 1986 quoted in Escobar and Alvarez 1992: 15) of action. The broader category of civil society, while clearly comprising actors who fall along a wide range of positions from challenging to supporting the state or larger social or economic structures (Fatton 1995; Foley and Edwards 1996; Ndegwa 1996), is commonly defined as a sphere autonomous of the state (see, example, Cohen and Arato 1992: ix; Habib and Kotze 2002; Habib 2003). In practice, however, both social movements and civil society actors are never so neatly distinct.

The tendency to clearly delineate civil society and social movements from the state may be useful as a simple analytic model, yet it works to cloud more precise understandings of the very porous boundaries between these constructs. In his discussion of what he defined as the elusive boundary between state and society, Mitchell argued that 'this elusiveness should not be overcome by sharper definitions, but explored as a clue to the state's nature' (1991: 77). This lesson is equally apt for any discussion of civil society and social movements. Goldstone has underlined the problem of assuming that social movements must by definition be 'challengers' to the state arguing, in a similar vein to Mitchell, that 'there is only a fuzzy permeable boundary between institutionalised and non-institutionalised politics' (Goldstone 2003: 2). In the study of social movements, while the state's importance is underlined in the creation of political opportunities and constraints, it is rarely treated as an actor intimately connected to many social movements themselves.[1]

The general tendency, in drawing boundaries with the state or governing party, as demonstrated by the quotations above, is to assert that an actor is either critical or co-opted, either 'in' or 'out'. This creates a simple dichotomy distinguishing those organisations independent of the state from those effectively controlled by it. These frameworks draw upon the experiences of societal actors under non-democratic states, ranging from the former communist states of Eastern Europe to apartheid South Africa. In these struggles, popular organisations were forced to work outside of institutionalised channels denied to them and overwhelmingly worked in clear opposition to the government, the regime and often the state. Formally democratic states, by contrast, are by definition understood to offer a wider range of not only civil and political rights but also greater institutionalised opportunities for making claims and voicing demands. It should therefore be at least theoretically possible for movements working within such democratic states to employ both institutional and extra-institutional tactics, to both challenge and co-operate with the state. Whether or not such approaches are successful constitutes a separate question.

States, particularly those with democratic regimes, do not simply repress or accept movements (Goldstone 2003: 13; Cunningham 2003; Luders 2003), but rather engage in a much more sophisticated set of interactions with various movement actors, tolerating and undermining, encouraging, and stifling; similarly, movements do not simply challenge the state, but often prod, promote, bait and bargain.[2] In post-apartheid South Africa, two self-defined movement organisations stand out for innovative approaches in their interactions with the state. While the case study of the Treatment Action Campaign (TAC) suggests the potential benefits for movement actors to employ institutional mechanisms and to, at times, co-operate with the state (see Chapter 2, this volume), the case study of the South African National Civic Organisation (SANCO) suggests the difficulties and contradictions of such interactions and its very mixed impact upon the very people named as its constituents. SANCO, in particular, presents an example of extraordinarily fuzzy boundaries between state and non-state actors. The complex interactions between SANCO, the ruling ANC and the state shed light not only on SANCO as an organisational model but much more importantly upon the nature of political opportunities and constraints for popular actors in South Africa's new democracy.

The South African National Civic Organisation – A Model

Despite many dire predictions (Hlongwane 1997; *Mail and Guardian* 4 February 2003; Makura 1999; Seekings 1996), significant and repeated internal crises, shifting relations with external actors, and various hotly contested debates concerning its role in a democratic South Africa, SANCO maintains a significant though weak presence as a national body with local branches in South Africa today. As a national organisation, SANCO is the product of local civics, community-based organisations, first formed in Port Elizabeth and Soweto in the late 1970s to protest and attempt to improve township living conditions. By the mid-1980s, civics stood as powerful community actors in the majority of urban townships across South Africa and increasingly worked within the broad camp of Charterist organisations that supported the ANC. After the formal end of apartheid in 1994, civics experienced a sharp decline, but did not disappear.

SANCO's continued existence should not be understood to imply that it has lived up to its aim to organise and mobilise South Africans in defence of 'people-centered, people-driven' development. Its persistence as an organisational form does, however, challenge observers to look beyond a static understanding of the formal political opportunities and constraints presented by a new democracy to the dynamic and evolving relationships between state and civil society actors (McAdam, Tarrow and Tilly 2001).

SANCO's national body today claims 4 300 branches in 56 regions, and a potential membership of 6.3 million[3] (Interview, Hlongwane, 09.06.04), but does not have the resources to support these broadly contested claims. There is no single portrait of SANCO that can fully represent the diversity, multiplicity and contradictions of the larger organisation and its local branches. On the one hand, SANCO is presented as a body of horizontal local associations, the ideal of civil society, thriving in local communities where residents come to civic leaders as their advocates *vis-à-vis* local government, parastatals or private actors (Heller and Ntlokonkulu 2001). This is a picture of vibrant grassroots democracy within local branches. On the other hand, SANCO is also described as a vertical, hierarchical organisation in which institutional structures constrain the aspirations of lower-level community actors (Zuern 2001). This is a national organisation in crisis, bankrupt, riven by scandal, and weakened by its alliance with the ANC. From this perspective, SANCO's national structure serves to undermine true participatory processes. Both of these interpretations offer important insights into the functioning and challenges faced by SANCO. Added to this, is a third view, offered by some SANCO leaders, that SANCO is a potentially vibrant and massive social movement, but also a 'sleeping giant' (Interview, Mngomezulu, 14.01.04).

SANCO's 'strength', whether defined by members, branches, meetings or other criteria, is not, however, the most significant aspect of the organisation for an understanding of South Africa's democracy today. It is SANCO's organisational model, and its elusive boundaries with the state, that provide the most interesting insights into the opportunities and constraints offered by the new system. SANCO's model is exceptionally broad. It defines itself as a tiered, unitary civic organisation, comprised of national, provincial, regional and local branches. Though this seems to be a model better suited to a political party than a grassroots association, SANCO leaders have historically supported this structure in an effort to enable SANCO to speak with a single voice at the national level. SANCO's national leadership is closely allied with the ANC and currently two of its six office bearers also hold ANC positions in national government.[4] At the local level, many SANCO leaders are also ward councillors and the majority hold some position working in or with local government, ranging from elected representatives to community liaisons. Though the nature of the relationship between the ANC and SANCO has changed over time, SANCO's self-definition has, since its founding, been closely tied to the question of its relationship with the ANC. Similarly, SANCO's successes and failures have been closely tied to its ability to position itself *vis-à-vis* the ruling party.[5]

By 1997, just five years after its launch, SANCO was in a visible state of crisis. SANCO's president, Mlungisi Hlongwane, admitted the organisation's difficulties at the national conference: 'Let us at the forefront admit that the sweeping political changes were too revolutionary in their pace that we were caught with our pens down. We have not come to grips with post-liberation politics' (Hlongwane 1997: 2). While the national leadership of SANCO initially described its difficulties as a product of insufficient resources, as time went by, it increasingly also pointed to the uncertain and difficult role that SANCO sought to play as an ally to the state and the ruling political party, while simultaneously asserting its independence (Zuern 2002). This has perhaps been most visible in struggles over the contradictory roles of its leadership.

Since 1994, SANCO has lost many of its good leaders to government. This led the National General Council to reverse its earlier policy and to allow individuals to remain in their leadership positions in SANCO while also accepting government roles. Mlungisi Hlongwane[6] argued that the decision to allow SANCO leaders to hold public office was one of practical considerations rather than abstract, theoretical, academic debates (*New Nation* 20 March 1997: 20). SANCO simply could not afford to lose these leaders in the short term. The problem, however, would be the longer-term impact that the 'wearing of two hats' by much of SANCO's leadership would have on the organisation. A regional SANCO leader commented: 'How will a SANCO leader, who also holds the position of councillor, conduct himself if he is called on to lead a march of residents against the local authority? Who will he lead the march against – himself?' (*New Nation* 28 February 1997: 33). Another regional leader admitted: 'As a former leader of SANCO, now an ANC leader in government, you don't account to SANCO; you account to the ANC and report to SANCO. You report to SANCO what is happening, but cannot be held responsible for actions by SANCO' (Interview, Sandi, 05.08.97). SANCO leaders who accepted positions in the ANC, whether or not they maintained their positions in SANCO, could not effectively represent SANCO's interests when and if they went against those of the ANC or the government.

Leaders at all levels of the SANCO structures also complained that ANC leaders often attempted to give them instructions and that ANC officials felt they had the right to veto SANCO programmes. Conflicts between SANCO and ANC members were, however, most common at the level of local government. When civic branches criticised the work of local government in general or ANC councillors in particular, local ANC leaders often responded defensively and even aggressively. A February 1997 summit between SANCO and the ANC noted the 'widespread tensions between structures of the ANC and SANCO, especially at a local level' and the negative impact this had upon the 'delivery and development' of infrastructural and economic upliftment projects (SANCO 1997: Annexure C: 16). Concerns in many townships about the level of support that civics gave to the ANC also led to tensions. This was slightly ironic since the overwhelming majority of civic leaders vowed to vote for the ANC and also campaign for the ANC despite their periodic criticism of the party and some of its members. A final popular complaint among civic leaders in numerous townships was that they felt that they did a good deal of local work for which the ANC would later take credit.

Adding to its difficulties, SANCO was desperately short of resources. While many local civic structures had received donor funding prior to the 1994 elections, such funding quickly dried up. By 1996, SANCO national had also lost its last significant external donor support, leading the national office to cut its remaining two administrative staff members after six others had left earlier in the year (*Mail and Guardian* 20 December 1996). The unitary structure of SANCO also fuelled tensions between the various levels by effectively making each level of SANCO responsible to the next higher level rather than the one below. The constitutional clauses granting decision-making powers to national bodies were top among the 'frustrating' aspects of the organisation's new constitution for local civic leaders. It is possible that local civics would have acceded to this power structure with considerably less complaint if they felt that they received something in return, but given the dire financial state of the national office, local civics gained few resources from their affiliation to SANCO.

Given these difficulties, local structures within SANCO often found much to complain about. Those that complained the loudest tended to be some of the strongest structures prior to the formation of SANCO and those who had the least of their former leaders represented at the highest levels of SANCO; these were primarily the civics in South Africa's commercial heartland, Gauteng. It was here in 1997, that a combination of suspensions and resignations of a number of popular leaders severely fractured the civic. The debates within SANCO's ranks concerning each of these long-time civic leaders were both public and vicious. Local and national newspapers reported on the battles and were increasingly critical of SANCO's approach and questioned its organisational strength. SANCO's response to the defections from its ranks did not help its public image. Its leaders frequently characterised the moves made by individual leaders away from SANCO as moves away from the ANC. Such accusations only increased the public perception of SANCO as not only an ANC ally but also an ANC lackey. In 1998, Gauteng SANCO dissidents, Mzwanele Mayekiso, Ali Tleane and Maynard Menu among others, launched a new federal civic structure, the National Association of Residents and Civic Organisations (Narco).

SANCO's difficulties were not, however, limited to Gauteng. In late 1997, the leadership of the Transkei region of SANCO broke away from the national body citing SANCO's ties to the ANC as a major concern (Lodge 1999: 90). In early 1998, the Northern Cape region also considered breaking away from SANCO (Gumede 1998). In 1999, a number of SANCO regions in the Eastern Cape passed a vote of no-confidence in their Provincial Executive Committee; the regions also agreed to oust all SANCO executives who simultaneously held political posts (*Daily Dispatch* 18 May 1999). These events, similar to those in the Gauteng Province that led to the formation of Narco, were quite dramatic. In less dramatic fashion, a number of local civic structures increasingly distanced themselves from SANCO and returned to the earlier strength of the civics, their localised nature and the autonomous development of responses to local issues.

Reassessing SANCO's Role

In a 1999 SANCO discussion document, which was subsequently excerpted in the ANC's publication, *Umrabulo* (7, 1999), SANCO's leaders tabled a number of options for SANCO's future. The five options reflected longstanding discussions and competing ideals of interaction with the state: become a political party; remain a watchdog; maintain its current confused state; transition to a development agency; or become a revolutionary social movement.[7] Of these, two alternatives led to the greatest debates: SANCO as a political party and SANCO as a social movement. The first suggested that SANCO should formally contest local government elections. At the time, this option was most strongly supported by local SANCO activists who were frustrated with their ANC councillors.

While this proposal was not endorsed by SANCO at its national conference and SANCO national again pledged its support for the ANC in the 2000 local government elections, the Eastern Cape region of SANCO defied this directive and vowed to only endorse individual candidates (SANCO PEDU 2000). The president of SANCO, clearly rattled, threatened that an intervention from the national office might become necessary if there was no change in approach, but the regional leaders were undaunted, arguing that they could not let SANCO's affiliation to the ANC undermine their local responsibilities (Interview, Tofile, 22.01.01). Penrose Ntlonti, a regional SANCO executive member, argued that SANCO would support independent candidates because it needed to be accountable to its constituents (quoted in *Daily Dispatch* 8 July 2000); he later admitted that SANCO was also frustrated that some of its candidates had been dropped from local election lists (*Financial Mail* 29 September 2000: 39). One Eastern Cape civic leader, who was quite concerned as to the possible repercussions of their challenge to the ANC, argued that unquestioning support for the ANC significantly threatened the civic's continued existence. 'We find in SANCO that the more we stick within the Alliance, the more we became dictatorial to our people' (Interview, Anonymous 1, 2001).

Both the authors of the SANCO discussion document and the Eastern Cape supporters of independent candidates overestimated local support for SANCO candidates who challenged the ANC. None of the Port Elizabeth candidates won local office. This failure at the polls demonstrated the continued overwhelming electoral support for the ANC despite considerable discontent with local government performance and the failings of numerous ANC councillors (Zuern 2002). A local SANCO supporter in the Port Elizabeth region voiced his frustration at the results: 'People still see the ANC as the only agent to change their lives; they don't see that their lives are in their hands' (Interview, Anonymous 2, 2001). National leaders of SANCO employed this lack of success at the polls to underline their pronouncements that SANCO would not and should not become a political party.

Despite these arguments, concern, particularly within the ANC, that SANCO might reconsider clearly remain. In Hlongwane's address to the ANC at its 2002 national conference he stressed once again that SANCO would not become a political party, noting: 'SANCO would have no relevance if its intention is to compete with the ANC'[8] (SAPA, 18 December 2002). While the national leadership of SANCO remains committed to this promise, local SANCO leaders continue to stress the need to keep their options open, depending upon local government performance in the run-up to the 2005 local elections.

Despite the contrasting models offered for SANCO, the existing organisational structure demonstrated remarkable resilience and an idealised understanding of this model continued to receive considerable support.[9] This ideal was best represented in the final option presented in the SANCO discussion document: SANCO as a revolutionary social movement. This option was clearly favoured by a number of SANCO leaders including its president and reflected the theme of the 1997 conference.

> SANCO is an independent and autonomous organ of civil society, implementing its resolutions, guided by its mass base and informed by its historical mandate. It is confrontational and champions the cause of the historically marginalised. It does not digress from the National Democratic Revolution (quoted in *Umrabulo* 7 1999).

Interestingly, this option concluded by challenging the two-hats policy in place since 1997, clearly arguing that a social movement needed to be more independent of the state in order to be effective.

Mlungisi Hlongwane's victory in the presidential contest at SANCO's third national conference and the eventual collapse of the alternative models, seemed to suggest that SANCO would follow the final option and transform itself into a truly revolutionary social movement. The conference's resolutions and Hlongwane's statements, however, already demonstrated that SANCO would not pursue the distinct path laid out in the discussion document. The conference did not change SANCO's policy allowing dual leadership roles in SANCO and government. Instead, Hlongwane, in his addresses to the conference, noted the need for SANCO to strengthen its relationship with the ANC, but now as an equal partner in the Alliance. President Mbeki, who also addressed the conference, underlined the civic's role as a partner to government, arguing that 'SANCO should help the local government in delivering services' (SAPA 21 April 2001, 22 April 2001).

SANCO as a Revolutionary Social Movement?

In 2000 and 2001, SANCO did, however, engage in a number of actions that directly challenged the core principles of the government's macro-economic policy. In May 2000, for example, SANCO, along with COSATU and other organisations, protested Johannesburg's Igoli 2002 plan (SAPA 18 May 2000). In 2001, SANCO joined COSATU's two-day stayaway to protest privatisation (SAPA 31 August 2001). The ANC was clearly frustrated by SANCO's support for the growing anti-privatisation movement, championed not only by COSATU but also by new bodies such as the Anti-Privatisation Forum (APF), which ANC leaders had collectively branded as 'ultra left'. This led to rumours that the ANC's National Executive Committee would support Moses Mayekiso's new civic, the Congress for South African Non-Racial Civic Organisations Movement (Cosancom), which was still receiving considerable attention at this time (*Mail and Guardian* 28 September 2001).

Between the 2001 and the 2002 COSATU anti-privatisation strikes, SANCO's national leaders reconsidered their support for COSATU's actions and their more publicly critical stance *vis-à-vis* government polices. SANCO leaders underlined that their first priority was in helping poor communities and that this concern importantly included the efficient delivery of basic services. Second, they argued that they were concerned by what they saw as the conflictual relationship between COSATU and the ANC, which SANCO leaders defined as increasingly unproductive (Interview, Williams, 04.06.04). It is quite clear that given this situation, SANCO's leaders felt pressed to choose a side in the polarising debate. When COSATU launched its next anti-privatisation strike in 2002, SANCO pulled out at the last minute. Though the circumstances of this pull-out have been hotly debated, SANCO leaders have offered a clear rationale for their actions. Mlungisi Hlongwane argued:

> The tone had changed . . . because we started realising that the issues that COSATU were [sic] advancing were beginning to be much more broader than just fighting against privatisation, but it was beginning to question the leadership of the African National Congress in the Alliance (Interview, Hlongwane, 09.06.04).

SANCO national had both strategic and substantive reasons for withdrawing its support. In direct contrast to new movements such as the APF, the Soweto

Electricity Crisis Committee (SECC) and the Anti-Eviction Campaign (AEC), which directly challenged not only forceful state-supported or state-led actions such as service cuts and home evictions but also the very policies of the state, SANCO leaders endorsed the state's cost-recovery model of development. SANCO also strategically supported the ANC's call for unity to further the National Democratic Revolution. SANCO leaders argued that the best way to bring greater benefits and services to the people would be to support government programmes rather than to engage in what they defined as ideologically motivated debates.

SANCO's strategic decision, while creating some confusion and provoking sporadic resistance in local areas, did pay off in terms of the national structure's formal relationship with the ANC. While some local SANCO leaders defied SANCO's call, which they first heard on Radio 702, to withdraw their support for the anti-privatisation strike,[10] ANC leaders were clearly pleased by SANCO's support. In November, SANCO strengthened its ties to the ANC and further weakened already elusive boundaries by electing two senior ANC members to SANCO's senior leadership. The Minister of Public Enterprises, Jeff Radebe[11] (recently ousted from the South African Communist Party's central committee), joined the National Executive Committee and Susan Shabangu, the Deputy Minister of Minerals and Energy, became SANCO's treasurer (*Mail and Guardian* 29 November 2002). At the ANC's national conference in December, President Mbeki importantly called on the ANC to expand the Tripartite Alliance to a quad alliance that would include SANCO as a full member (*Financial Mail* 20 December 2002).[12] As the ANC sought to revive its branches and its connection to township residents in the wake of growing discontent and the rise of new social movements challenging the government, it was clearly reaching out to SANCO for help. In the run-up to the next elections, the ANC sought SANCO's support for door-to-door community campaigns in return for greater acknowledgement of SANCO's role as an Alliance partner.

Expanding Political Opportunities

During the first decade of democratic rule, SANCO experienced a sharp decline as a national civic structure; it suffered multiple public crises and many of its former local branches simply ceased to operate and those that continued to exist were often dormant until a local crisis occurred. In this state of affairs, SANCO's claim to represent masses of community residents across the country was often greeted with strong scepticism if not outright disbelief. SANCO's greatest success toward the end of the decade was in its renewed ability to exploit its relationship with the ANC in order to maintain itself as a presence in South African political debates despite its pressing weaknesses as a national structure. SANCO could not realistically claim the breadth of support that it hoped for, but it could finesse its position between the ANC and the local communities where it did still have effective and popular local leaders.

SANCO's greatest public coup concerned electricity arrears in Soweto. Since 1994, service delivery had clearly posed one of the biggest challenges to friendly but critical relations between community activists and ANC local government representatives. While local civic responses varied from community to community, SANCO's overall policy supported the logic of credit control measures even where this meant widespread electricity disconnections and the installation of waterflow restrictors.[13] As residents became increasingly desperate and angry, groups such as the SECC that took a more radical approach, gained in popularity. SANCO's response to this challenge was to leverage its position by threatening mass action in an attempt to upstage the SECC[14], while simultaneously presenting itself as a credible negotiating partner with Eskom. In 2002, SANCO participated in negotiations with Eskom and government representatives which led to an agreement that residents with faulty meters would pay a flat fee of R120 per month until their meter was fixed (SAPA 26 April 2002). In local areas such as Zola, civic leaders strategically drew attention to these agreements to work to convince community residents that SANCO rather than the SECC would find a solution to their problems (Interview, Monnakgotla, 15.07.02). SANCO effectively sought to assert itself as the primary broker between township residents and state actors.

SANCO's greatest triumph, however, came in May 2003. Eskom and the Ministry of Public Enterprises (headed by Jeff Radebe, a recent member of SANCO's NEC), along with the Human Rights Commission and SANCO, came to an agreement to write off R1.39 billion in Johannesburg arrears. While this write-off was clearly in response to the great impact that groups such as the SECC and APF had on government policy, SANCO rather than the SECC or APF was included in the negotiations as a public representative and therefore given at least formal credit for the write-off. A supporter of the SECC and APF campaigns wrote: 'All but moribund 12 months ago, SANCO has suddenly come to life with resources and influence from political heavyweights in national

government, determined, it would seem, to counter the growing influence –
and anti-neoliberalism – of SECC and the AFP' (McDonald 2003).

A SANCO leader summed up SANCO's strategy regarding the challenges it
faced from groups such as the SECC and the ways in which it employed its
relationship with government:

> Credit goes to SANCO . . . As a civic movement we grab those people
> that support Trevor (Ngwane), look at their issues and actually change
> them. We can strategise . . . Let the credit come to SANCO, and then
> SANCO will take the credit back to government. It is quite a nice ballgame
> . . . Whilst now we confront, they deliver, the credit goes to SANCO, you
> take the credit back to government. You call a mass meeting, address
> the people, and say government has delivered . . . That is how you deal
> with it; you actually strategically try to isolate them (SECC and others)
> (Interview, Anonymous 4, 2004).

SANCO therefore presented itself to local communities as a problem solver that
could employ its relationship with the government to address residents' concerns.
This argument, however, deliberately ignores the role that the SECC had played.
Without pressure from the SECC and massive non-payment, Eskom would never
have offered such a large write-off. In contrast, in Tshwane, where SANCO
leaders participated in a series of negotiations with the metropolitan government
council and where no group such as the SECC had engaged in large mobilisations
prior to negotiations, the council refused SANCO's request to write off
outstanding arrears, arguing that effective credit control measures were already
in place (SAPA 12 May 2003).

The Case of Tshwane
SANCO's success on the question of electricity arrears in Tshwane was therefore
limited by its relatively non-confrontational approach, but Tshwane's greater
vibrancy as a local SANCO region was a result of an interesting diversity of
seemingly contradictory tactics. Tshwane serves as an interesting case study of a
SANCO region as it is both active and remains connected to the higher level
structures of SANCO; it is therefore an excellent example of both the strengths
and limitations of the SANCO model of co-operation with the state and the
ruling party where it works effectively. In the region, SANCO leaders offer formal

support to a number of government policies endorsed by SANCO national but bitterly contested by many new social movements. These policies include the contentious credit control procedures from services to housing. SANCO leaders supported, even endorsed, the cutting of electricity, but also argued for lifeline tariffs which would give all residents access to a minimal amount of water and all paying consumers a small amount of electricity for free (Interviews, Qhakaza, 15.01.04; Tshabalala, 17.01.04). SANCO branches also work with banks to try to help people to get loans, but are then asked by the banks for a quid pro quo. One local civic leader commented: 'The banks are honest with us, to say: "We want to help, if you can assist in those who owe us, we will also assist you in those who need loans." It puts us in a difficult position, but you see we must sit down and see what we can come up with' (Interview, Katumele, 11.06.04).

When asked to point to one of their most vibrant regions, national and provincial level leaders of SANCO frequently mentioned Tshwane and argued that one of the reasons for Tshwane's success has been the quality of its leadership (Interviews, Matila, 15.01.04; Mdakane, 16.01.04; Mngomezulu, 14.01.04). Many of Tshwane's leaders seem to be so successful because they have become quite adept at managing the contradictions of their role as SANCO leaders in alliance with the ANC *vis-à-vis* their role as representatives of poor communities. While functioning SANCO structures throughout Gauteng put aside their SANCO work to campaign for the ANC in the 2004 national and provincial elections, Tshwane stood out as the only SANCO region in Gauteng to openly campaign for the ANC in the 2000 local government elections (Heller and Ntlokonkulu 2001: 39). Local SANCO leaders argue that their support for the ANC at the local level was a simple product of their ability to place a rather large number of SANCO leaders and supporters on the ANC lists, but even with this potential support, SANCO leaders found that they needed to continuously demonstrate their support in order to press their concerns to local councillors (Interviews, Katumele, 11.06.04; Makahanya, 11.06.04; Mgidi, 11.06.04; Qhakaza, 15.01.04).

Though SANCO as an organisation always stressed negotiations over protest, with mass protests only as a last resort, local SANCO leaders repeatedly argued that it was necessary to demonstrate their capacity for protest and even the potential to cause 'damage' to draw attention to their concerns:

I believed in our branches in SANCO actually creating damage so that the ANC can run to us and say 'comrade'. The ANC will keep despising you if you are not acting . . . That's why we go there and stop the project completely. And then the leadership would come to me or government would call me and say 'look your people on the ground are actually stopping the project' and I say 'why? why are they stopping the project?' 'No we don't know, they are arrogant.' . . . I say, 'No, they have a reason. Arrange a meeting, and then we will come and speak formally, but by the time I come to you I will have met my (people) on the ground, and I will be coming to you with concrete reasons why they stopped the project.' . . . And I know, I know, I was part of stopping that project, but I will behave innocently as if I don't know. But I already know the reason (Interview, Anonymous 5, 2004).

SANCO leaders openly acknowledged that their actions contradicted SANCO policies, but noted that this was simply the most effective way of bringing about change.

And therefore whilst we were supporting as leaders, but we will treat it very sensitively, because we know that we want to achieve certain things, but it is also wrong. And therefore, we will distance ourselves, not necessarily distance ourselves from the leaders (in the community), but we will distance ourselves from the act. To say that we condemn that act . . . When you are a leader and you have followers, they wouldn't necessarily do things like those without informing you. They would actually want your approval . . . And you wouldn't say to them: 'Look, invade the land.' You would just say to them: 'Comrade, you are a leader. Do what has to be done. Take a decision and implement.' . . . We can't just distance from you, we can distance from the act that you are doing, if it is illegal, but we won't distance ourselves from you (Interview, Anonymous 5, 2004).

SANCO leaders therefore navigated a careful line of supporting popular community demands while presenting themselves as viable and reliable negotiators with local government authorities. This brokerage role allowed SANCO to exploit its local position as well as its alliance with the ANC. In this case, what was often seen as an impediment was turned into a strength by a careful shifting of the rules of the game. Here, SANCO could potentially capture the power of a locally-based social movement by encouraging protest and then harness that influence by employing its politically connected national institutional structure.

These contradictions do, however, become even more difficult to navigate when SANCO leaders work for local government authorities in some capacity. While such contradictions are almost impossible to exploit when SANCO leaders are also local councillors, individuals working in other positions in local government can, at times, employ their access to press civic concerns. A local SANCO leader in this position explained his trepidation in honestly representing SANCO in a meeting with the local authority who was also his boss:

> (My chairperson in SANCO) gave the introductory remarks and said: 'Now I am going to let (my deputy) speak on behalf of local issues.' The (government official) is my boss; he is my boss . . . Before I could speak, I had a sip of water, because I didn't know how I could respond. Then I started to put the positions, 'These are the things; this is what is happening . . .' Then the (government official) responded, he said: 'You have highly, highly disappointed me.' That I don't behave like other officials. I did not even tip him to say that SANCO was coming. I didn't even tell him so that he can prepare himself. And then he pointed to some comrades who were with SANCO somewhere, he said: 'See these guys when they see anything on the ground they rush to me . . . So these guys are talking to me, but you don't report to me.' And I said: 'You see, (sir), you are right, I am your employee, but in SANCO I am your boss, because I am . . . here to represent that organisation.' . . . From there I felt bad, but I was not representing myself, I was representing the organisation (Interview, Anonymous 6, 2004).

The individual who stood up to present these grievances admirably demonstrated his dedication to SANCO's ideals and risked his primary employment by doing so. Such interventions can potentially build upon and support local mobilisation to bring residents' concerns to local authorities, both on the street and in council chambers. This represents an ideal model for SANCO's role as an agent of participatory processes of democracy and development, but as the local official's response clearly indicates, this is clearly not the norm in SANCO-ANC relations.

Between Co-option and Defiance

SANCO defines itself today as a revolutionary social movement seeking to promote 'people-driven and people-centered development'. SANCO leaders argue that they have opened doors for greater participation in public debates by engaging government within established institutional structures and convincing the ANC of the importance of SANCO as an alliance partner (Interview, Williams, 02.06.04, 04.06.04). This naturally leads to the question, asked by many, as to whether SANCO has simply been co-opted by or sought to be co-opted by the ANC. SANCO's president replies:

> Our call that we needed to be recognised as a fully fledged member of the Alliance, it was purely based on ensuring that our voice is not a voice of a distant step-child screaming outside hoping to be heard when policies were being made inside the Alliance, inside the African National Congress. If people call that co-option, it is fine (Interview, Hlongwane, 09.06.04).

Local and national SANCO leaders consistently argue that SANCO does not seek to draw attention to itself through the media and that it seeks to bring about change through negotiation. This clearly clouds the question of co-option, because SANCO leaders will argue that their interests in general correspond to those of the ANC government. It is therefore difficult to demonstrate recent instances in which SANCO as a national body has affected changes in government policy.

One SANCO officer, a well-known Tshwane leader who is now the organising secretary for SANCO Gauteng, argued that SANCO's overall role is to ease relations between township residents and the government.

> SANCO is a cushion, on both sides . . . It works both ways. It is a cushion on the government side, but it is also a cushion on the people's side. Then it actually eases tensions, because anything that happens, we do not say: 'Look, do as you wish.' We are saying: 'We are negotiating' (Interview, Qhakaza, 15.01.04).

SANCO clearly plays this brokerage role. It has positioned itself as an intermediary between communities and local government authorities. It has offered its support to the ANC to help the party campaign in national, provincial as well as local government elections; it has offered its position in local communities to inform people of government policies and programmes. How well it plays this role and whether or not in doing so it represents the interests of the majority of local residents completely depends upon the actions of local SANCO leaders. Tshwane's success was a result of the dedication of its leaders and their ability to work within the given context. Where local leaders can effectively manage the contradictions they face, they can potentially help both government and poor communities. Where, as is often the case, SANCO structures are weak or non-existent and local SANCO leaders are seen as too closely allied with government, or are government leaders themselves, frustrated communities have increasingly organised alternative movements to more directly challenge the state.

The last five years have been quite clearly marked by the rise of new, radical social movements rather than the revitalisation of SANCO as a mass-based, revolutionary actor. Though SANCO national has made considerable strides in encouraging ANC leaders to publicly acknowledge and praise the role of SANCO, there is little evidence that SANCO has been able to act as a full member of the Alliance, except in implementing election campaigns preceding national and provincial elections. While SANCO has succeeded in muting talk within some quarters of the ANC of turning SANCO branches into ANC branches, SANCO has failed to follow the course of the revolutionary social movement that it set out for itself. In areas such as Tshwane, local SANCO branches are quite vibrant and leaders are engaged in an impressive schedule of meetings to discuss local concerns and the most effective means of addressing them, but even here, local leaders admit significant difficulties in signing up members and relaunching branches.

Continuities and Contradictions

Many analysts and political actors who expected or called for SANCO's demise following South Africa's formal transition to a democratic state, argued that the changing context and the new political opportunities and constraints it offered worked against a civil society organisation as broad as SANCO. SANCO's model, many argued, was only viable in a non-democratic state in which truly oppositional political parties were banned and government sought to repress rather than represent the majority of the population. In this earlier context, a broad range of civics offered local residents the opportunity not only to meet and discuss local concerns but also to stand clearly outside of the state and pressure the regime to address local and national demands. With the legalisation of banned opposition parties and the advent of a democratic state, the institutions of the state were now meant to take over many of the roles that the civics had performed, thereby blurring the boundaries between civic and state functions and making the civics redundant. This static understanding of political opportunity and interpretation of civil society as necessarily oppositional fatally simplified the complex interactions between state and civil society actors.

These arguments also failed to recognise the severe challenges faced by the new local authorities after 1994 and the ways in which these challenges were to affect citizen-government relations. Local and national government simply could not meet the overwhelming material needs of poor communities from housing and services to jobs and security. Local government authorities were under-resourced and far too frequently failed to adequately represent, let alone meet, the basic concerns of their constituents. The increasing material deprivation and the dearth of locally-based popular representation that followed the formal transition of power, provided a space for local SANCO branches to continue to operate; it also provided an opportunity for a new breed of social movement that would stand to the left of SANCO and put far greater pressure on the state to meet popular demands than SANCO was able or willing to do. This combination of the state's lack of local capacity and the growth of these new radical movements, offered SANCO an opportunity to navigate the gap by employing the potential influence of its remaining local branches and its association with the ANC government.

Clearly, the space for SANCO is limited. It is frequently caught between its challenge to and its support for the ANC, but what political opportunity theorists missed, were the possibilities for SANCO to build upon the discontinuities within its own structures and the wider political system to navigate the elusive boundaries of state-civil society interactions. SANCO's continued ability to employ the local contradictions of democratic rule under a dominant political party do not, however, imply that it successfully empowers the poor and marginalised. While SANCO's local support rests upon its representation of community needs, its national level support (from the ANC) seems to rest upon its ability to effectively contain community demands. As a result, SANCO's overall impact upon redistribution and democratisation is mixed. While it may rhetorically champion popular representation at the local level, the structure of the national organisation channels and co-opts such representation. In this way, SANCO clearly assists the ANC in pursuing its goals for the development of a new South Africa and to represent those who endorse its policies. Its continued existence will therefore remain closely tied to the successes and, more importantly, shortcomings, of the ANC government.

The case of SANCO also importantly demonstrates that boundaries may not only be porous and elusive but also contextual. In one setting, SANCO leaders call upon their role as 'outsiders', non-state and local community actors to challenge government policies, forcefully if necessary; in another setting, they assert their close connection to the state and the ruling political party to negotiate, offer support and seek patronage. The brokerage role that SANCO leaders in Tshwane successfully play involves both the construction and the continued transgression of boundaries between SANCO and state and party offices. SANCO leaders threaten, distance, demand and concede, while state officials offer carrots and sticks. By approaching SANCO's leaders as brokers standing between community demands, more radical social movements, and the state, the dynamics of politics and the constraining structures of power become much more apparent. Such an analysis may not provide easy answers, and it does serve to make definitional questions much more complicated. It also, however, provides an approach that captures the porous and changing nature of boundaries that are so often taken for granted and may provide a better grasp of the political opportunities and constraints facing those who wish to make claims against the state.

Notes

1. Goldstone's 2003 edited volume offers an important exception to this general tendency. Unfortunately, while presenting a number of interesting case studies, the volume does not effectively bring the insights of these case studies together to theorise patterns or forms of social movement and state interactions.
2. In her investigation of student protest in the United States, Van Dyke has demonstrated that the mere presence of allies within the state does not simply make protest less likely (2003: 240).
3. ANC conference delegates were reportedly 'stunned' by Mlungisi Hlongwane's announcement to the 2002 conference that SANCO had six million members (*Sunday Times* 22 December 2002).
4. Ruth Bhengu is the deputy president of SANCO and the ANC provincial and local government committee chair. Susan Shabangu is the treasurer of SANCO and the deputy minister of minerals and energy.
5. For a more detailed account of SANCO's historical evolution see Zuern (2000, 2004).

6. SANCO asked its third president to give up his position as a local government leader in the Vaal to return to SANCO full time; he did (*New Nation* 28 February 1997: 33).

7. A final option, not mentioned in the SANCO discussion document but in the article following it in *Umrabulo* 7, offered an ANC position that SANCO had failed as a membership-based national civic organisation and should fold into a new type of ANC branch (Makura 1999). This suggestion angered many SANCO supporters and was not considered as a valid option within SANCO.

8. In a further attempt to calm any ANC concerns, Hlongwane also pledged that SANCO would not accept any expelled ANC members into its ranks. 'SANCO also has a warning to all opportunists. SANCO has closed its door to all people who were expelled from the ANC and who have jumped to SANCO' (SAPA 18 December 2002).

9. In 2001, after a rather bitter presidential election, Moses Mayekiso was defeated by the standing president and resigned to form a new national civic structure, the Congress for South African Non-Racial Civic Organisations Movement (Cosancom). While Mayekiso championed a more independent and a federal rather than unitary structure (Interview, Mayekiso, 13.01.04), he launched a national, broad-based civic structure remarkably similar to SANCO. His new structure echoed the structure of Narco, created by the Gauteng dissidents, who also emphasised the necessity for political independence and federalism. Importantly, neither group of dissidents sought to radically change the SANCO model, only to revise it. Both new organisations failed to develop an effective national structure.

10. One local SANCO leader was pressed to the head of his local march: 'The president announced, of SANCO, to say no one must take part in these demonstrations of anti-privatisation. You remember? Now, being a member of the . . . Union . . . and affiliated to COSATU, I went to a march of COSATU. When I arrived there, a lot of comrades were saying: "Yeah, come, come, come." You know, I was wearing a COSATU cap and knowing that I am the (leader) of SANCO and the president announced that we should not take part, they insisted that I must be in the forefront. I must lead the march so that the president can see that you are violating' (Interview, Anonymous 3, Gauteng, 2004).

11. After the 2004 elections, Jeff Radebe became the Minister of Transport.

12. This echoed SANCO President Hlongwane's call at SANCO's 2001 conference, cited above, that SANCO become an 'equal' partner in the Alliance.

13. One civic leader in the Vaal summed up SANCO's general approach: 'We need to protect (the consumer) as SANCO, but you protect a consumer who is obedient' (Interview, Lehoko, 09.06.04).

14. In June 2001, for example, just days ahead of a planned SECC march, SANCO also threatened mass action (SAPA 7 June 2001).

References

Cohen, J. and A. Arato. 1992. *Civil Society and Political Theory*. Cambridge, MA: MIT Press.

Cunningham, D. 2003. 'State versus Social Movement: FBI Counterintelligence Against the New Left'. In J. Goldstone (ed.), *States, Parties and Social Movements*. Cambridge and New York: Cambridge University Press.

Desai, A. 2002. *We Are the Poors: Community Struggles in Post-Apartheid South Africa*. New York: Monthly Review Press.

Escobar, A. and S. Alvarez (eds). 1992. *The Making of Social Movements in Latin America: Identity, Strategy and Democracy*. Boulder: Westview Press.

Fatton, R. Jr. 1995. 'Africa in the Age of Democratization: The Civic Limitations of Civil Society'. *African Studies Review* 38.

Foley, M.W. and B. Edwards. 1996. 'The Paradox of Civil Society'. *Journal of Democracy* 7 (3).

Goldstone, J. 2003. 'Introduction: Bridging Institutionalized and Noninstitutionalized Politics'. In J. Goldstone (ed.), *States, Parties and Social Movements*. Cambridge and New York: Cambridge University Press.

Gumede, W. 1998. 'Implosion on Main Street.' *Siyaya*.

Habib, A. 2003. 'State-Civil Society Relations in Post-Apartheid South Africa'. In J. Daniels, A. Habib and R. Southall (eds), *State of the Nation 2003–2004*. Pretoria: HSRC.

Habib, A. and H. Kotze. 2002. 'Civil Society, Governance and Development in an Era of Globalisation'. In O. Edigheji and G. Mhone (eds), *Governance in the New South Africa*, Cape Town: University of Cape Town Press.

Heller, P. and L. Ntlokonkulu. 2001. 'A Civic Movement, or a Movement of Civics? The South African National Civic Organization (SANCO) in the Post-Apartheid Period'. Centre for Policy Studies Research Report No. 84.

Hlongwane, M. 1997. 'Building a Revolutionary Social Movement to Conquer Challenges of the 21st Century'. Presidential Address, SANCO 2nd National Conference, 16–20 April.

Lodge, T. 1999. *South African Politics Since 1994*. Cape Town and Johannesburg: David Philip.

Luders, J. 2003. 'Countermovements, the State, and the Intensity of Racial Contention in the American South'. In J. Goldstone (ed.), *States, Parties and Social Movements*. Cambridge and New York: Cambridge University Press.

Makura, D. 1999. 'The MDM, Civil Society and Social Transformation: The Challenges of Building a Popular Movement for Transformation'. *Umrabulo* 7.

Mamdani, M. and E. Wamba-dia-Wamba (eds). 1985. *African Studies in Social Movements and Democracy*. Dakar: CODESRIA.

McAdam, D., J. McCarthy and M. Zald (eds). 1996. *Comparative Perspectives on Social Movements*. New York: Cambridge University Press.

McAdam, D., S. Tarrow and C. Tilly. 2001. *Dynamics of Contention*. New York: Cambridge University Press.

McDonald, D. 2003. 'More Carrot, Less Stick'. *Mail and Guardian* 26 May.

McKinley, D. 2003. 'ANC's "consensus" '. Znet, Africa 21 July.

Mitchell, T. 1991. 'The Limits of the State: Beyond Statist Approaches and their Critics'. *American Political Science Review* 85 (1).

Ndegwa, S.N. 1996. *The Two Faces of Civil Society: NGOs and Politics in Africa*. Connecticut: Kumarian Press.

Seekings, J. 1996. 'The Decline of South Africa's Civic Organizations, 1990–1996'. *Critical Sociology* 22 (3).

South African National Civic Organisation (SANCO). 1997. 'Secretary's Report'.

South African National Civic Organisation, Port Elizabeth, Despatch and Uitenhage (SANCO PEDU). 2000. 'Memorandum to SANCO National and Provincial Offices'. 14 July.

Tarrow, S. 1994. *Power in Movement: Social Movements, Collective Action and Politics*. New York: Cambridge Press.

Tilly, C. 1985. 'Models and Realities of Popular Collective Action'. *Social Research* 52 (4).

Touraine, A. 1985. 'An Introduction to the Study of Social Movements'. *Social Research* 52 (4).

Van Dyke, N. 2003. 'Protest Cycles and Party Politics: The Effects of Elite Allies and Antagonists of Student Protest in the United States, 1930–1990'. In J. Goldstone (ed.), *States, Parties and Social Movements*. Cambridge and New York: Cambridge University Press.

Zuern, E. 2000. 'Democracy from the Grassroots? Civic Participation and the Decline of Participatory Democracy in South Africa's Transformation Process'. PhD dissertation, Columbia University.

——. 2001. 'South Africa's Civics in Transition: Agents of Change or Structures of Constraint?' *Politikon: South African Journal of Political Studies* 28 (1).

——. 2002. 'Fighting for Democracy: Popular Organizations and Post-Apartheid Government in South Africa'. *African Studies Review* 45 (1).

——. 2004. 'Continuity in Contradiction: The Prospects for a National Civic Movement in a Democratic State: SANCO and the ANC in Post-Apartheid South Africa'. A case study for the UKZN project entitled 'Globalisation, Marginalisation and New Social Movements in Post-Apartheid South Africa'.

Interviews

Anonymous 1. Port Elizabeth, 2001.

Anonymous 2. Port Elizabeth, 2001.

Anonymous 3. Gauteng, 2004.

Anonymous 4. Gauteng, 2004.

Anonymous 5. Tshwane, 2004.

Anonymous 6. Tshwane, 2004.

Hlongwane, Mlungisi. President of SANCO, 09.06.04.

Katumele, Jan. Co-ordinator, SANCO Mamelodi West, 11.06.04.

Lehoko, White. Vaal Regional Secretary, SANCO, 09.06.04.

Makahanya, Jack. Co-ordinator, SANCO Mamelodi West, 11.06.04.

Matila, Toenka. Secretary, SANCO Gauteng, 15.01.04.

Mayekiso, Moses. Managing Director, SANCO Investment Holdings until 2001, 13.01.04.

Mdakane, Richard. Chairperson, SANCO Gauteng, 16.01.04.

Mgidi, Julius. Chair Ward 29, SANCO Soshanguve, 11.06.04.

Mngomezulu, Linda. National Secretary, SANCO, 14.01.04.

Monnakgotla, Sugar. Zola Ward Councillor, Soweto, 2002, 15.07.02.

Qhakaza, Lucas. Organising Secretary, SANCO Gauteng, 15.01.04.

Sandi, Dan. Chairperson of the Western Region, Eastern Cape, 1997, SANCO, 05.08.97.

Tofile, Mike. Sub-Region President, 2001, SANCO Port Elizabeth, 22.01.01.

Tshabalala, Jabulani. Regional Secretary, SANCO Tshwane, 17.01.04.

Williams, Donovan. National Executive Committee Member, SANCO, 02.06.04 and 04.06.04.

10

Connecting the Red, Brown and Green

The Environmental Justice Movement in South Africa

Jacklyn Cock

ON A HOT SATURDAY morning in the summer of 2003 about 80 people crowded into a small garage on the outskirts of Vanderbijlpark. Packed closely together on wooden benches and sitting on the concrete floor, they seemed to represent our 'rainbow nation', including black workers and white small holders from the surrounding area. Despite the fresh green of the willow trees and the blue sky, it was impossible to ignore the grey slag dump dominating the skyline, or the smell and clouds of smoke belching from the Iscor plant a few kilometres away.

The occasion was a meeting of the Steel Valley Crisis Committee (SVCC), a group formed in 2002 to indict Iscor for its pollution of the air and water of the area that had resulted in loss of livelihoods, and serious health problems ranging from kidney disease to cancer for 450 people. Everyone listened intently as the legal team explained what the legal processes would involve. The meeting seemed like a vindication of the truimphalist claims sometimes made about the contemporary environmental movement; an illustration of the capacity of environmental issues to overcome ethnic, racial and class divisions and unite various 'particularistic identities' in a common cause. This chapter, however, questions this conclusion, demonstrating the inadequacy of this depiction as an accurate reflection of developments in South African environmental struggles.

The central research question this chapter addresses is whether there is a single, coherent environmental movement that is mobilising under the comprehensive banner of *environmental justice* and whether the Environmental Justice Networking Forum (EJNF) is its organisational expression. Answering this question involved site visits, focus groups, participant observation, interviews with 30 key informants selected for their expertise on environmental activism and a literature review of primary and secondary sources.

The chapter argues that there is no single, collective actor that constitutes the environmental movement in South Africa and no master 'frame' of environmentalism encoded in any blueprint. The environmental movement has no coherent centre and no tidy margins; it is an inchoate sum of multiple, diverse, uncoordinated struggles and organisations. It is argued, however, that a nascent environmental justice movement is emerging that has the capacity for mass mobilisation. This is best described as a web-like universe made up of highly interconnected networks clustered around a few key nodes or hubs, namely EJNF, Groundwork and Earthlife Africa. It is characterised by a radical decentralisation of authority, with no governing body, official ideology or mandated leaders, minimal hierarchy and horizontal forms of organising.

This embryonic environmental justice movement is bridging ecological and social justice issues in that it puts the needs and rights of the poor, the excluded and the marginalised at the centre of its concerns. It is located at the confluence of three of South Africa's greatest challenges: the struggle against racism, the struggle against poverty and inequality and the struggle to protect the environment, as the natural resource base on which all economic activity depends. The movement is stratified in a complex layering involving national networks, non-governmental organisations (NGOs) and local grassroots groups. Within this multiplicity of organisational forms, the vitality of the movement flows from the bottom up, being driven by the unemployed and lower working class, 'the poors' (Desai 2002). This social base is distinctively different from the middle-class composition of the mainstream environmental movement that focuses on the 'green' issues of curbing species loss and habitat destruction.

The Environmental Movement

Some of the most exciting forms of new social activism in post-apartheid South Africa are focused on 'brown' or urban environmental issues. As McDonald writes, 'The lack of basic services like sewage and sanitation for millions of urban South Africans is arguably the most pressing environmental justice problem in the country today' (2002: 10). Several informants stressed the interconnection between brown and green issues. For example, 'You can't separate brown and green issues; they complement each other. The environment is not only about brown issues. The conservation and welfare of animals is important' (Interview, Mentoor, 2003). Nevertheless the broad environmental movement in South Africa is extremely fragmented.

This fragmentation revolves around a fault-line that divides the movement into two main streams: those organised around the discourse of sustainable development, and those organised around the discourse of environmental justice. Both of these are powerful discursive strategies. The discourse of sustainable development is an advance on earlier protectionist models of environmentalism in that it is concerned with human needs, but is generally marked by technicist, pragmatic and reformist attempts to bring environmental externalities into the marketplace through ecological modernisation. The concept has been extensively criticised for the vagueness that has enabled it to be incorporated into neo-liberal approaches (Bond 2002; Sachs 1999). It can also mean that environmentalism is voided of political content and can 'be defined as a public concern with environmental deterioration – a concern, not necessarily the object of a social struggle, a cause without conflict' (Acselrad 2002: 18).

Two South African environmental NGOs are the organisational expressions of this approach, the Endangered Wildlife Trust (EWT) and the Wildlife and Environment Society of Southern Africa (WESSA). Both are socially shallow with a mainly white, middle-class support base and are predominantly concerned with preserving biodiversity. The discourse of environmental justice provides a radical alternative, questioning the market's ability to bring about social or environmental sustainability. It asks the question 'What is morally correct?' instead of 'What is legally, scientifically, and pragmatically possible?' The difference between the two approaches can be illustrated by the different responses to corporate power on the part of EWT and a key, environmental justice organisation, Groundwork. While EWT relies on corporate sponsorship, Groundwork has developed a critical approach demanding corporate accountability. It is one of the key environmental justice organisations that have brought about a reconfiguration of the discourse on environmentalism.

Environmental Justice: A Reconfiguration of the Discourse on Environmentalism

During the apartheid regime, environmentalism operated effectively as a conservation strategy that neglected social needs (Beinart and Coates 1995; Kahn 1990; Mittelman 1998). The notion of environmental justice represents an important shift away from this traditional authoritarian concept of environ-mentalism, which was mainly concerned with the conservation of threatened plants, animals and wilderness areas, to include urban, health, labour and development issues (Cock 1991). It is linked to social justice as 'an all-encompassing notion that affirms the use value of life, all forms of life, against the interests of wealth, power and technology' (Castells 1997: 132).

This concept of environmental justice as a mobilising force emerged in the US in the last 40 years, in opposition to practices that were classified as environ-mental racism. This is defined as 'any policy, practice or directive that differentially affects or disadvantages (whether intentionally or unintentionally) individuals, groups or communities based on race or color' (Bullard 2002: 16). Several informants stressed the relevance of the concept in post-apartheid South Africa.

In this context the concept of environmental justice potentially provides an organising tool for mobilising multiple, diverse communities into political action on a variety of rights and claims. Some of these rights have a constitutional grounding as the Bill of Rights Section 24 states that 'everyone has the right to an environment that is not harmful to their health or well being'. The core of the notion of environmental justice as a powerful mobilising force lies in this notion of rights – rights of access to natural resources and to decision-making. The notion of rights is used to legitimise demands and claims. The counter-hegemonic potential lies in the challenge to power relations that this notion of rights implies.

While the concept of environmental justice emerged from the US, there are important differences in the South African adaptation of the concept. Here the focus is on total change driven by majority rather than minority interests, and includes class issues, whereas in the US it is class-blind, focusing exclusively on environmental racism. Also the movement here frequently addresses the root causes of environmental degradation – processes such as privatisation and deregulation – whereas the US focus is on symptoms. In the South African context, environmental justice means social transformation directed to meeting basic human needs and rights. It is the central idea in a grassroots movement that is fuelled by the growing contradiction between the discourse of rights and the experience of unmet needs.

A few key nodes or hubs provide organisational resources to this nascent environmental justice movement. The following three organisations operate at different levels and show how this movement is growing in terms of geographic spread, political reach and social cohesiveness.

Key Nodes of the Environmental Justice Movement
The Environmental Justice Networking Forum

This is potentially the organisational expression of a coherent, comprehensive environmental justice movement in South Africa. It describes itself as a 'democratic network, a shared resource, a forum which seeks to advance the interrelatedness of social, economic, environmental and political issues to reverse and prevent environmental injustices affecting the poor and the working class' (Interview, Madihlapa, 2003). It aims to achieve this through two broad inter-connected programmes – environmental governance and community campaigns – which focus on mining and ecological debt, energy, food security and waste. It is a nationwide umbrella alliance of over 400 participating organisations (POs) characterised by an ideological and social diversity. An example is Soweto's Mountain of Hope (SOMOH). Founded by the former EJNF Gauteng co-ordinator, Mandla Mentoor, in 2001, this project is transforming the rocky Tshiawelo koppie in Soweto, which was a feared crime and litter-ridden space into a green project as a continuation of the 80s peace-park movement. This is a concrete expression of the linkages between environmental and social justice issues that EJNF emphasises. 'Social justice and environmental justice go together, they are interlinked . . . The framing of issues doesn't matter that much . . .' (Interview, Madihlapa, 2003).

EJNF was initiated at a conference hosted by Earthlife Africa in 1992. From the outset there was a clear and strong commitment to social transformation through an expanded conception of environmental justice that was directed towards meeting basic human needs. To signal a decisive break with the dominant, narrow, authoritarian conservationism, the pioneer founder Chris Albertyn promoted a very inclusive understanding of the environment (Albertyn 1995).

Over the ten years of its existence, EJNF has changed a great deal. In its pioneering phase, the period 1994–98, the emphasis was on policy formulation in close collaboration with the state. Since then, the focus has shifted to grassroots campaigning, its ideology has become increasingly racialised and, as a key component of the Social Movements Indaba, relations with the ANC and the post-apartheid state have become increasingly confrontational.

Overall, by naming the experiences of the poor and the marginalised and drawing out from those experiences the connections between power, development, rights and social and environmental justice, EJNF has contributed to the reconfiguration of the discourse on environmentalism in South Africa. It is building the social infrastructure for a strong environmental justice movement in the country in collaboration with other key organisations such as Groundwork.

Groundwork

The second node in the embryonic environmental justice movement in South Africa is Groundwork, a non-profit, environmental justice service and development organisation. It was founded in 1999 by three ex-EJNF activists to improve the quality of life of vulnerable people in southern Africa. It has four main projects focusing on air quality, healthcare waste and incineration, industrial landfills and corporate accountability. The organisation makes no claims to speak on behalf of others; nor does it claim to represent the environmental justice movement. 'We are not defining the agenda, we don't want to control it, we're trying to participate in it' (Interview, Peek, 2003). It provides crucial support to about twelve different communities and a number of community-based organisations, including the South Durban Community Environmental Alliance (SDCEA) led by Desmond D'Sa, which it helped to establish.

Groundwork has redirected the Department of Environmental Affairs and Tourism's strategy for pollution control; has gained publicity for community issues; provided community access to decision-makers; and combines science and policy work with action. However, the director believes that 'the crucial task is to take the environmental debate into the social movements, that's where the energy is' (Interview, Peek, 2003).

Earthlife Africa

Another key node in the environmental justice movement is one of EJNF's participating organisations, Earthlife Africa (ELA). This is a loose, nationwide alliance of volunteer activists, grouped into local branches. It is a flat, non-hierarchical, decentralised organisation, which one member described as 'democratic to the point of inertia' (Interview, Anonymous, 2003). It produces and distributes a newsletter, and has monthly meetings of five different action groups: toxics, nuclear, zero waste, animal action and climate change report.

The organisation is known for its very imaginative tactics. For example, in the 1998 campaign against air pollution in Johannesburg three prominent sculptures were decorated with gas masks. The organisation disseminates information on issues such as climate change, genetic engineering and nuclear energy.

A key project is the Sustainable Energy and Climate Change Partnership (SECCP). The project aims to link renewable energy and energy efficiency to advocacy around climate change, with a view to influencing relevant development policies. Earthlife's anti-nuclear campaign demonstrates its capacity to reach down into grassroots communities, particularly those living in the vicinity of Pelindaba such as Attridgeville and Diepsloot as well as up into policy work such as making parliamentary submissions and attending public hearings on the Draft Radioactive Waste Bill. Strategies include producing a popular book, meeting with the national nuclear regulator, mobilising health professionals to undertake an epidemiological study of communities living near Pelindaba, court action, as well as demonstrations, arguing that the environmental impact assessment was flawed. The campaign is working with EJNF to create an anti-nuclear alliance and is making 'strong efforts to involve the trade unions, particularly COSATU and NUM' (Interview, Phalane, 2003).

Along with EJNF, ELA played a crucial role in several iconic moments that helped to generate a reconfiguration of the discourse on environmentalism in South Africa. One such moment was the exposure of pollution by Thor Chemicals, a corporation that imported toxic waste into South Africa. ELA worked closely with the Legal Resources Centre, the Chemical Workers' Industrial Union, affected workers and local communities. The case illustrates the importance of alliances between environmentalists and organised labour and, according to Barnett (2003), was the crucial turning point in the re-framing and 'browning' of environmentalism in South Africa.

The Chloorkop campaign against the siting of a toxic waste dump in Chloorkop between 1993 and 1996 was another watershed event. The lead organisation was the EJNF affiliate, ELA, and involved the establishment of a broad coalition, which included the Tembisa branch of the ANC, the Pan-Africanist Congress (PAC), the Transport and General Workers' Union, the Democratic Party as well as the Afrikaner Weerstandsbeweging (AWB) (Phadu 1997). According to a participant, 'the Chloorkop campaign was a rainbow group organised against environmental injustice' (Interview, Sugre, 2003). The

ANC branch in Tembisa played a very active role, which illustrates how established organisations may be a source of resources facilitating movement emergence. The South African Youth Congress played a major role in the third iconic moment, the Mafefe asbestos exposure of the devastating health impacts of asbestos mining on the village, and was part of a struggle that 'combined research with advocacy and grassroots mobilisation' (Interview, Felix, 2003).

These three iconic 'moments' provided the impetus to a growing grassroots environmental justice movement in South Africa driven mainly by EJNF and ELA. The 1998 EJNF poverty hearings were particularly important in this process as the impact of environmental degradation on poor communities was highlighted. Also significant was the leadership of visionary individuals such as Chris Albertyn, Bobby Peek, Mandla Mentoor and Thabo Madihlapa. They frame(d) the issue of environmental justice in ways that resonate with people's needs and experience.

These three organisations are most effectively promoting environmental justice in South Africa. However, this focus on the three organisations as nodes or hubs should not imply a highly centralised picture. The environmental justice movement in South Africa is untidy with many loose ends and rough edges. As one key informant said, 'There are lots of pockets of good environmental stuff going on' (Interview, Anonymous, 2003).

Other Significant Environmental Justice Organisations

While it is argued that EJNF, ELA and Groundwork are the key nodes in the environmental justice movement, other significant organisations are the Environmental Monitoring Group (EMG) and the Group for Environmental Monitoring (GEM). New coalitions are forming in response to issues such as genetically modified foods, and the water and energy caucuses are particularly significant.

The actions of both the water and energy caucuses demonstrate how the re-ordering of the political opportunity structure since 1994 in South Africa has created space for previously excluded groups to contribute to policy formulation, to make claims through the courts, and to mobilise. The post-apartheid constitution provides the framework for a rights-based approach to social mobilisation. But the context is one of increasing deprivation and degradation. The contradiction between the discourse of rights and the experience of unmet needs is the main source of growth of the environmental justice movement.

The emphasis on 'rights' in the post-apartheid dispensation, linked to vast areas of unsatisfied social needs that are increasing with the privatisation of basic services and the use of cost-recovery mechanisms, provides the main impetus for the movement.

The growth of such popular organisations outside the established framework of political representation has often evoked a hostile response from the post-apartheid state. A striking characteristic of the state response to various forms of recent social activism has been criminalisation in the form of arrests and the use of force expressed in teargas, rubber bullets, live ammunition and stun grenades, as well as mockery and abuse. The state has clearly embarked on a political propaganda campaign that portrays these new social movements and their activists as the 'ultra left', as 'criminals' and 'anarchists'. This is the context in which mobilisation around environmental issues is increasing and engaging a wide repertoire of strategies and tactics.

Characteristics of the Environmental Justice Movement

The environmental justice movement is a realm of dynamic and complex interactions, but it is possible to point to the following characteristics: it is stratified with a complex layering ranging from national networks to NGOs to communities at the local level. The movement is increasingly organising around key nodes. Organisations such as EJNF, ELA and Groundwork are providing a social infrastructure for environmental justice. It is characterised by what Escobar (2004) terms 'meshworks', meaning flexible, non-hierarchical, decentralised, horizontal networks and forms of organising with no governing body, official ideology, blueprints or mandated leaders.

The environmental justice movement is a loose network; like the global justice movement it involves new forms of organising, new alliances and presents a contrast to the traditional membership-based bureaucratic and hierarchical means of organising in civil society. Its power is not expressed in quantitative terms like numbers of members but in its potential capacity for mass mobilisation. For this reason one informant argued that the new social movements require new kinds of analysis that focus on patterns of interaction and social mobilisation rather than rely on numbers.

There is a pluralist conception of power. Networking is the dominant relational form and in a decentralised social network there is no centre of power. The decentralised network structure of the environmental justice movement enhances its democratic nature. There is no elected body that makes decisions on behalf of multitudes of others without consultation. It is a dense space of thick, interconnected networks that links organisations, individuals and resources around diverse strategies and tactics including policy advocacy, legal demands and claims, in addition to direct, popular mobilisation. These strategies are often (but not invariably) interconnected. For example, all of the new social movements are using the language of new rights to both mobilise and seek enforcement through the courts. Many initiatives are counter-hegemonic, which implies an alternative world that challenges the legitimacy of the current social order.

It operates at multi-levels, local, national and global. As a movement it is embedded in multiple 'militant particularisms' (Harvey 1997); it uses grassroots needs as the point of mobilisation; the focus is on daily realities, on survivalist issues of direct relevance. While the emphasis is on the local, grassroots groupings are finding new ways to combine local activism with horizontal, global networking.

Leadership

Leadership depends on a handful of charismatic leaders who are 'bridging individuals'. They operate in local, national and global social spaces and bridge issues and organisations. Some key informants were highly critical of the current leadership of the new social movements, and specifically of Trevor Ngwane because of his hostility to the ANC. 'The new social movements are driven by activists who are confrontationist – they don't build organisations with membership structures. There's no accountability' (Interview, Anonymous, 2003).

Others stressed the role of leadership in connecting immediate needs to a broader, alternative vision, as illustrated by Trevor Ngwane talking about the links between daily local concerns and global capital: 'In Soweto its electricity. In another area, it is water . . . But you have to build a vision . . . electricity cuts are the result of privatization. Privatization is the result of GEAR. GEAR reflects the demands of global capital . . . connecting with what touches people on a daily basis, in a direct fashion, is the way to move history forward' (Ngwane 2003: 56). This is a good example of passionate 'framing work', providing frames that justify and dignify collective action, shaping grievances into broader claims.

Social Base

A key question concerns the social base of the environmental justice movement. Does it articulate the needs, demands and aspirations of subordinate groups? What are the social characteristics of the participants? It has been claimed that environmental issues can be a catalyst for very broad civil society mobilisation, in that they have a 'supra-classist dimension' (Acselrad 2002: 20). This 'rainbowism' was articulated by Nelson Mandela in 1995 when he referred to how 'environmental concerns can unite South Africans going beyond economic and political barriers' (cited by McDonald 1998: 76). Despite the expectations of the SVCC, very few current struggles involve socially inclusive, multi-racial coalitions. All environmental issues have a class pertinence and the differences between the social base of the old and new environmental struggles is significant. This is a new moment in the history of environmentalism in South Africa. The environmental concerns of the past – preservation and conservation – driven by a largely white, middle-class constituency, are being supplanted by new struggles with a different social base.

All informants agreed that 'the poors' (the unemployed and lower working class) were the most relevant political force in the environmental justice movement. 'It is the poors who have opposed the water and electricity cut-offs and evictions' (Desai 2002: 3). The movement is giving them voice in the sense that it provides a means of expressing their interests and values and of translating these into policy. Many of the activists in these grassroots environmental justice initiatives are young people and women. The female activist role often stems from traditional women's socialisation to be the administrators of household consumption. In this capacity they are the shock absorbers of environmental degradation. It is women who struggle with the dust from a defunct gold mine in Kagiso and so constitute the driving force in the Kagiso Environmental Awareness Forum, which is campaigning for the rehabilitation of the Tailings dam. It is women who have to walk further and struggle harder to obtain access to clean water, so the largest social category attending mass meetings called by the Coalition Against Water Privatisation are older women, 'the grannies'.

The Nature of Social Bonds

The nature of social bonds varies. Some of the organisations and the loose-knit networks that constitute the environmental justice movement involve high levels of social cohesion and solidarity. Several informants described ELA as marked by durable relations of trust and co-operation. The social relations among members of the Coalition Against Water Privatisation are marked by concern and practical action to support participants arrested in protest actions. Other examples of these social groupings acting as an informal resource pool include providing shelter for those evicted and help with disconnections of water and electricity. All of these organisations are an important source of resources. People with limited resources cannot sustain contentious collective action. Several informants stressed that the collapse of the SVCC was partly due to a lack of organisational resources. But overall the nature of the social bonds established between participants in environmental justice struggles are very different. In the case of the SVCC, as will be demonstrated below, they were transient, perfunctory, friable and short lived, involving no long-term commitments and obligations. In the case of participants in actions like those around the World Summit on Sustainable Development (WSSD), they could best be described as what Bauman calls 'carnival bonds' rooted in intense, public displays (2001: 72). Generally, the environmental justice movement contains pockets of strong personal relations, collective identities, thick social networks marked by a social cohesiveness, what Tarrow terms 'embedded networks, rather then "contingent alliances" which are short term and instrumental' (2003: 19). For many activists social interactions have a depth and intensity that contrast with the thin, atomised identities of citizen and consumer. In this sense, the movement is disseminating new images of solidarity and connectedness.

A Bridging of Social and Environmental Issues

While there is no master frame of 'environmentalism', the movement is bridging ecological and social justice issues – in this sense there are strong connections being forged between the 'red', the 'green' and the 'brown'. As Harvey writes, 'the movement for environmental justice twins ecological with social justice goals in quite unique ways' (1997: 387). He stresses the links between the environmental justice movement and the broader movements that have been termed 'the environmentalism of the poor'. This means that the environmental justice movement is very inclusive and in this sense is 'virtually boundary less' as Foreman writes of the movement in the US (1998: 12).

The movement has the potential to address root causes. According to an activist, 'environmental justice is able to bring together all of these different issues to create one movement that can really address what actually causes all of these phenomena to happen and gets to the root of the problems' (cited by Di Chiro 1998: 124). For many 'the root of the problem' is the privatisation and cost-recovery policies that constitute the foundation of neo-liberalism. The Anti-Privatisation Forum (APF) is a significant example of what Ruiters has argued for, 'a deeper approach to environmental justice', which involves 'a focus on the production . . . of injustices' (2001: 112). As McDonald states, all the evidence shows that 'privatization worsens access to core services for the urban poor and ultimately exacerbates environmental degradation' (2002: 296).

Strategies and Tactics

All the decentralised networks that comprise the environmental justice movement engage in a variety of struggle activities. These include strikes, litigation and court applications, advocacy, negotiation, boycotts, organised marches, public petitions, use of media, Internet connections and demonstrations. Particularly significant here is the use of strategies that emphasise constitutional rights as a way of countering hegemonic practices. These rights strategies may strengthen marginalised communities trying to leverage the state to access resources.

Not all of these tactics are 'new', which points to the importance of not exaggerating the distinctiveness and 'newness' of movements such as the environmental justice movement. Not only is there a degree of continuity in the repertoire of tactics and strategies, there is also some transference of leadership from the old to the new struggles. Trevor Ngwane, for example, was both a prominent anti-apartheid activist as well as being central to the APF and the Soweto Electricity Crisis Committee (SECC). There has not been a total rupture with the past because of strong traditions of social movement unionism that linked struggles in the workplace to the community issues.

Some of these forms of social activism among poor and vulnerable communities are new in the sense that they involve new targets (corporations and multi-national institutions rather than states), a global terrain, innovative connections between issues (such as militarisation and environmental damage) and novel forms of horizontal organising that connect people and information through the Internet. These new patterns of social mobilisation go beyond political parties, trade unions and NGOs; they represent a new type of populist politics. But the crucial question is whether these are largely ephemeral, and incapable of establishing a sustained, durable presence. Or could they move beyond the confines of 'militant particularisms', and generate a broader, transformative politics that involves a deepening of democracy?

Tactics are often extremely innovative, such as the 'toxic tours' organised by the SDCEA in South Durban, and the Greenwash Academy Awards, a.k.a. Green Oscars, targeting infamous corporate environmental abusers organised by Groundwork at the WSSD in 2002. Direct action has involved the reconnection of electricity and water and is sometimes dramatic.

For example, in 2002 a total of 52 municipal workers' union members were arrested after emptying buckets of shit outside the municipal offices. This echoes a protest that took place in 1993 when a group of women in Ivory Park, furious at the suspension of sanitation services in the township, protested by marching to the administration offices with 140 buckets full of shit from overflowing toilets and hurled the contents of the buckets at local authority officials (Bhagowat 1993). This protest illustrates what Arjun Appadurai (2002) has called 'the politics of shit', meaning struggles around the most basic of human needs. The phrase seems particular significant at this moment when the Igoli 2002 privatisation plan has been renamed 'E. coli. 2002' for a good reason: excrement from the pit latrines of Johannesburg's slums regularly pollutes upmarket Sandton's borehole water supplies (Bond 2002). Some of these recent protests have involved women's use of their sexuality. For example, in 1996 a group of women from Orange Farm, protesting about water cut-offs, marched to the municipal offices with a memorandum and some of the women undressed. In 1999 women from Orange Farm initiated the closing off of the Golden Highway by blocking the flow of traffic.

Another strategy is to provide expert engagement in policy processes. Examples are Groundwork's submissions on the Air Quality Bill, or ELA's comments on the Draft Radioactive Waste Bill. This policy engagement does not only involve expert reports in the conventional sense. It also involves the recognition of local, indigenous knowledge and experiential evidence. For example, in November 2002 Groundwork facilitated an active member of the Sasolburg Environmental Committee to travel to Cape Town from Zamdela to address the Minerals and Energy Portfolio Committee in parliament.

All the networks that comprise the environmental justice movement use the Internet to co-ordinate their activity and give visibility to their issues. They also produce publications such as EJNF's quarterly publication *The Networker*, the ELA newsletter and Groundwork's series of annual reports. These publications are an important vehicle by which the environmental justice movement is able to amplify grassroots voices, experiences and participation in policy formulation. This is also achieved through critical research, especially when it builds capacity in grassroots communities. The research on Orange Farm undertaken by the Coalition Against Water Privatisation involved training some 60 members of that community. Groundwork has emphasised the development of community air monitoring programmes in selected communities affected by industrial pollution. And as will be demonstrated below in the case of the SVCC the emphasis on litigation displaced collective mobilisation. This is in stark contrast to the other case study, the Coalition against Water Privatisation, where litigation was only one tactic in a wide repertoire of struggle.

The main mobilisation strategy is to reframe needs as rights. 'We take what people experience as needs and re-formulate them as rights to mobilise around' (Interview, Madihlapa, 2003). This reframing clearly relates to the new political opportunities presented by the Bill of Rights in the post-apartheid constitution.

Litigation to claim these rights is one of the main strategies used by various components of the movement. Many legal challenges have recently been brought by civil society against industries for environmental health damages. For example, damage claims have been made by asbestos workers, vanadium workers, ex-workers of Thor Chemicals and the Steel Valley community. However, the case of Steel Valley demonstrates the limitations of litigation. As Ruiters claims, 'litigation occurs after the event, and the high costs of litigation and the expertise required to engage effectively in the legal system discourage environmental activism' (2001: 102). Furthermore, it does not address class injustices, which are central to the growing global mobilisation for environmental justice.

Local and Global Alliances

The networks that make up the environmental justice movement are all locally embedded, but globally connected. For instance, in its campaign against the siting of a hazardous waste incinerator in Sasolburg, the Sasolburg Environmental Committee got support from the Global Anti-Incinerator

Alliance, based in the Phillippines. In its campaign against Mondi's plans to build a boiler in South Durban, the SDCEA threatened to launch an international boycott of Mondi Paper products and claimed to have the support of 189 organisations in 55 different countries.

So, do these localised, but globally connected organisations present a new 'vision of how the global and the local can become reciprocal instruments in the deepening of democracy'? (Appadurai 2002: 25). Appadurai argues that 'transnational advocacy networks' (TANs) provide 'new horizontal modes for articulating the deep democratic politics of the local' and 'create forms of knowledge transfer and social mobilization . . . on behalf of the poor that can be characterized as "grassroots globalization" or . . . "globalization from below"' (2002: 272).

For this grassroots globalisation, the World Social Forum (WSF) is an important social space. According to one informant, what defines new social movements as different and distinctive from other political forms is that they are aware that they are part of a global justice movement. The WSF is widely understood to be at the core of this. About 100 000 people from 100 different countries attended the fourth WSF in 2004, and all indications are that it is likely to grow further. However, connections to global civil society are somewhat thin at the grassroots.

The environmental justice and other new social movements also have to confront the important strategic question of their relationship to the mass-based organisations of COSATU and the ANC. Do they link up with labour? Several informants expressed a scepticism about existing trade unions and political parties, though all stressed that the relations between the labour and environmental justice movements should be strengthened as the corporate plunder of non-renewable resources is growing. Environmental organisations could be invaluable allies to worker organisations in opposing capitalism. However, while there may be shared goals, as in COSATU's and the South African Municipal Workers' Union's (SAMWU's) opposition to the privatisation of water, the strategies of the labour and environmental justice movements are very different.

As stated above, this specific struggle is driven by older women. These 'grannies' are the most vulnerable, powerless social category. They are ill equipped to move beyond particularistic struggles and confront the systemic patterns and causes of environmental injustice. What such a confrontation involves may be illustrated by a case study that demonstrates the difficulties in challenging the powerful corporate interests that are at the forefront of both environmental and social injustice.

Case Study: Water

The case study focuses on water, a natural resource that is a basic need, framed as a right by the post-apartheid constitution. Access to clean water is threatened by two processes: *pollution* and *privatisation*. The case study focuses on two organisational responses to this threat: the SVCC, which is mobilising against the pollution of the groundwater by Iscor, and the Coalition Against Water Privatisation, which is mobilising against the installation of pre-paid water meters that are having devastating health and social impacts on poor communities.

Access to Water: The Coalition Against Water Privatisation

Formed in 2003, this organisation, of which EJNF is a member, illustrates what Greenstein (2003) terms the 'legal-activist' route to social mobilisation. The Coalition uses a rights discourse to challenge the state's commitment to cost recovery in basic service delivery. The challenge involves litigation and direct action, as a means for grassroots mobilisation. The main demand is for the decommodification of water, which makes this a Polanyian-type struggle (those defined by the need to oppose commodification in the market) as opposed to a Marxist-type struggle defined by exploitation in production (Burawoy 2003).

The Coalition is extending its international linkages, and an international solidarity campaign is growing around the world as water is being privatised. Once understood as a commonly held resource, to be managed by communities and states for the public good, it is now being redefined as a commodity to be managed by market forces. Solidarity is a strong theme in the Coalition and involves support of comrades charged in court, through, for example, providing legal aid and raising bail money for the 'water warriors'. In this respect it acts as an important source of resources that deepens strong social bonds. Sometimes this solidarity extends to assisting impoverished households with illegal connections.

Some violent confrontation has resulted. The post-apartheid state's response to coalition activities has largely been criminalisation, leading one activist to say, 'It is not easy to stand up for your rights today' (Interview, Kensani, 2004).

Ironically, the language of rights is also used by Johannesburg Water, which links this to an appeal to modernity. It tries to sell the pre-payment system as a modern, post-apartheid development enabling consumers to exercise choice.

The main participants in mass activities are older women, and this clearly results from their role as administrators of household consumption. For some of them, the water issue is about survival. Several residents interviewed in Orange Farm maintained that 'we can cope with pre-paid electricity meters, because we can use other sources like coal stoves and primuses for cooking but we can't cope without water' (Interview, Motumi, 2003). Another said, 'we don't want things for free; we are loyal to our government, but the problem is affordability' (Interview, Daniels, 2003). For others the issue is embedded in the wider struggle against neo-liberalism. For all participants, mobilisation is about transforming needs into rights. This differs significantly in the second case, which focused almost exclusively on a legal strategy, and which became disempowering.

The Steel Valley Crisis Committee

The SVCC emerged in 2002 from action to indict Iscor for their pollution of the groundwater of the Vanderbijlpark area, which has resulted in loss of livelihoods, and serious health problems ranging from kidney disease to cancer involving 450 people. Initially it appeared to illustrate the capacity of environmental issues to overcome the racial and class divisions between victims such as the Matsepo and Cock families and unite their 'particularistic identities' in a common cause.

Strike Matsepo cashed in his pension to buy a smallholding in the area and has lived there since 1993 but has now lost most of his livestock due to contaminated water. He says, 'It used to be a good place, but my twenty-six cows have died, five sheep and six goats, three tortoises, one pig, three dogs and four cats (Interview, Matsepo, 2003). Mr Matsepo himself is sick and his sister who lived with him has just died. He asserts, angrily, 'My sister would be alive now without Iscor' (Interview, Matsepo, 2004). Strike Matsepo's sister had high levels of cadmium in her blood and scientific evidence has confirmed the presence of a number of other dangerous and carcinogenic substances in the groundwater.

The Cock family lived for fourteen years on a smallholding on the edge of the unlined Iscor canal carrying water to the dams. Mrs Cock states, 'We were a farming family and had goats, sheep, ducks, horses, geese, but they all died. Many animals were born malformed. We left when the whole family got sick, skin growths, emphysema and cancer. My one daughter has been diagnosed with three types of cancer. The doctors relate these cancers to the canal water. As a youngster she played in it and we drank it. The Iscor water has made all my children and my grandchildren sick' (Interview, Cock, 2003).

The SVCC was formed to mobilise the community and co-ordinate efforts to engage Iscor, the courts and the government to deal with the pollution crisis. Actions included a protest march to Iscor in 2001, picketing action at the WSSD conference and litigation. But this had no effect in changing the company's practices or in getting compensation. And pollution of groundwater continues.

The SVCC is an example of a failed struggle against environmental injustice. The main reasons for this failure are the power of Iscor and the SVCC's reliance on a legalism that displaced social mobilisation. The collapse of the SVCC is part of the social disintegration of the entire Steel Valley community. This was previously 'a strong community' with social infrastructure in the form of shops, schools, churches and bus services, which have all now collapsed. Mr Matsepo was part of the 2002 protest, but, he says, 'there is nothing happening now. The people who organised the protests are no longer here. There is no money for travel in buses. We are waiting for the people to unite again. We are now ruined and hopeless' (Interview, Matsepo, 2004).

Conclusion

These two struggles illustrate a number of themes: both involve legal strategies but the differences between the two demonstrate thin and deep levels of mobilisation. In the case of the SVCC, the major flaw was a legalism that was disconnected from mass action. Secondly, the organisations demonstrate how environmental justice is embodied in many contemporary struggles, but they are not necessarily labelled as environmental justice struggles. Neither the pollution nor the privatisation of water was framed as an environmental justice issue. Both struggles were framed in terms of health and economic issue. The discourse is that of impacts on health or livelihoods due to the lack of access to clean water, either because of pollution or privatisation. Both struggles are rooted in the growing contradiction between the discourse of rights and unmet needs in post-apartheid South Africa.

Both struggles illustrate globalisation from above and from below. Globalisation from above is evident in the international linkages of the corporations involved. In June 2004 the Competition Tribunal approved the takeover of Iscor by global steel giant LNM, which operates in 22 countries and had expected revenues of more than US$15 billion in 2004. The company installing the pre-paid water meters, Johannesburg Water, is linked to Suez, one of the ten 'global water lords' (Barlow and Clarke 2002: 109–12). The corporate interests in both cases used the law to suppress resistance. For example, there was court action and gagging orders against both the Iscor litigants and the Phiri resisters. However, while the Phiri protestors' actions were framed in heroic terms, as those of water warriors, the Iscor litigants largely became depressed and demoralised. Both local struggles against powerful corporate interests attempted to link with international organisations, and in this sense they illustrate grassroots globalisation or globalisation from below.

Clearly the Coalition and the SVCC are part of significant new patterns of grassroots mobilisation that are emerging in post-apartheid South Africa, which involve a mix of 'red' (social justice), 'brown' and 'green' issues. The anger and energy of these struggles generally comes from the crises experienced by poor, vulnerable communities without access to jobs, housing, land, clean water and sanitation. In this context it is unclear whether the notion of environmental justice could provide a platform to address these issues; a master frame with a unifying potential, a source of shared claims, demands and goals.

Perspectives on the capacity of EJNF varied, but most informants agreed that it was potentially the 'carrier' of a strong environmental justice movement in South Africa. This is increasingly connected to a global justice movement that, according to Naomi Klein, is marked by 'two activist solitudes'. 'On the one hand, international activists fighting issues which are not connected to people's daily experience', and on the other hand, 'thousands of community-based organisations fighting daily struggles for survival' (Klein 2002: 245). This conception parallels what Castells has described as two forces in the 'back alleys of society': 'alternative electronic networks' and 'grassrooted networks of communal resistance' (Castells 1997: 362). This is where he has 'sensed the embryos of a new society' (1997: 362). In South Africa these two different kinds of networks are merging and providing powerful models of resistance to corporate globalisation. This could be part of the 'sea change from Marxian to Polanyian struggles' that Burawoy (2003) has pointed to; part of a Polanyian second movement in civil society that could have great potential.

Such a movement is crucial. Corporations are driving the process of globalisation, which is widening inequalities throughout the world, and are doing so through the increasing commodification of natural resources. A focus on the role of corporations illustrates how environmental and social justice issues are indivisible. While the trajectory of the SVCC exploded any romantic notion of a 'rainbow coalition', this chapter has argued that EJNF and other organisations constitute key nodes in a environmental justice movement that is growing in terms of geographic spread, analytical depth, political impact and social cohesiveness.

References

Acselrad, H. 2002. 'Environmentalism and Environmental Conflicts in Brazil'. Unpublished paper.

Albertyn, C. 1995. 'Towards Sustainable Reconstruction'. *Environmental Justice Networker* 1.

Appadurai, A. 2002. 'Grassroots Globalization and the Research Imagination'. In J. Vincent (ed.), *The Anthropology of Politics*. London: Blackwell.

Barlow, M. and T. Clark. 2002. *Blue Gold: The Fight to Stop the Corporate Theft of the World's Water*. New York: The Free Press.

Barnett, C. 2003. 'Media Transformation and New Practices of Citizenship: The Example of Environmental Activism in Post-Apartheid Durban'. *Transformation* 51: 1–24.

Bauman, Z. 2001. *Community: Seeking Safety in an Insecure World*. Cambridge: Polity.

Bhagowat, C. 1993. 'Dung-Ho Women Pelt Local Officials'. *The Star* 18 March.

Beinart, W. and P. Coates. 1995. *Environment and History: The Taming of Nature in the USA and South Africa*. London: Routledge.

Bond, P. 2002. *Unsustainable South Africa. Environment, Development and Social Protest*. Pietermaritzburg: University of Natal Press.

Bullard, R. 2002. *Confronting Environmental Racism*. Boston: South End Press.

Burawoy, M. 2003. 'For a Sociological Marxism: The Complimentary Convergence of Antonio Gramsci and Karl Polanyi'. *Politics and Society* 13 (1): 1–69.

Castells, M. 1997. *The Power of Identity*. London: Blackwell.

Cock, J. 1991. 'Going Green at the Grassroots'. In J. Cock and E. Koch (eds), *Going Green: People, Politics and the Environment*. Cape Town: Oxford University Press.

Desai, A. 2002. *We are the Poors: Community Struggles in Post-Apartheid South Africa*. New York: Monthly Review Press.

Di Chiro, G. 1998. 'Nature as Community: The Convergence of Environment and Social Justice'. In M. Goldman (ed.), *Privatizing Nature*. New Brunswick: Rutgers University Press.

Escobar, A. 2004. 'Post Capitalist Cultures'. In J. Sen, A. Anand, A. Escobar and P. Waterman (eds), *Challenging Empires*. New Delhi: The Viveka Foundation.

Foreman, C. 1998. *The Promise and Perils of Environmental Justice*. Washington: Brookings Institute Press.

Greenstein, R. 2003. *State, Civil Society and the Reconfiguration of Power in Post-Apartheid South Africa*. Centre for Civil Society Research Report No 8. Durban: University of KwaZulu-Natal.

Harvey, D. 1997. *Justice, Nature and the Geography of Difference*. London: Blackwell.

Khan, F. 1990. 'Involvement of the Masses in Environmental Politics'. *Veld and Flora* 21: 36–8.

Klein, N. 2002. 'Reclaiming the Commons'. *New Left Review* May: 81–9.

McDonald, D. 1998. 'Three Steps Forward, Two Steps Back: Ideology and Urban Ecology in South Africa'. *Review of African Political Economy* 75: 73–88.

———. (ed.). 2002. *Environmental Justice in South Africa*. Cape Town: University of Cape Town Press.

Mittelman, J. 1998. 'Globalisation and Environmental Resistance Politics'. *Third World Quarterly* 19 (5): 847–72.

Ngwane, T. 2003. 'Revolt against the ANC'. *New Left Review* 22: 37–58.

Phadu, T. 1997. 'Chloorkop Toxic Waste Dump'. *Environmental Justice Networker* 12: 14–17.

Polanyi, K. 1957. *The Great Transformation*. Boston: Beacon Press.

Ruiters, G. 2001. 'Environmental Racism and Justice in South African's transition'. *Politikon* 28 (1): 95–103.

Sachs, W. 1999. 'Sustainable Development and the Crisis of Nature'. In F. Fisher and A. Hajer (eds), *Living with Nature*. Oxford: Oxford University Press.

Tarrow, S. 2003. 'Global Movements, Complex Internationalism and North-South Inequality'. Paper delivered at the Workshop on Contentious Politics, Columbia University.

Interviews

For reasons of confidentiality five informants are cited as anonymous.

Black, Vanessa. Director of The Greenhouse, 2003.

Cock, Joey. Member of the Steel Valley Crisis Committee, 2003.

Daniels, P. Orange Farm Resident, 2003.

Felix, Marianne. Occupational Health Worker, 2003.

Fig, David. Environmental Activist, 2003.

Hallowes, David. Environmental Activist, 2003.

Kensani, E. Phiri Resident, 2004.

Koch, Eddie. Environmental Activist, 2003.

Lakhani, Muni. Earthlife Zero Waste Campaign Co-ordinator, 2003.

Mabilitsa, Zac. EJNF Office Bearer, 2003.

Madihlapa, Thabo, Director of EJNF, 2003.

Matsepo, Strike. Member of the Steel Valley Crisis Committee, 2003, 2004.

Marnewick, Daniel. EWT, 2003.

Mentoor, Mandla. Director of the Soweto Mountain of Hope, 2003.

McDonald, David. Municipal Services Project Director, 2003.

Mokoena, Mwike. Member of the Steel Valley Crisis Committee, 2003.

Mokoena, Samson. Chairperson of the Steel Valley Crisis Committee, 2003.

Motumi, E. Orange Farm Resident, 2003.

Ntoapane, Caroline. Sasolburg Environmental Committee Member, 2003.

Peek, Bobby. Director of Groundwork, 2003.

Phalane, Mashile. Earthlife Nuclear Campaign Co-ordinator, 2003.

Sugre, Anne. Director of Eco-City, 2003.

Victor, Margie. Advocate, 2003.

Worthington, Richard. Earthlife Gauteng Co-ordinator, 2003.

Van Zyl, André. EWT, 2004.

11

Reconstructing a Social Movement in an Era of Globalisation

A Case Study of COSATU

Adam Habib and Imraan Valodia

A SOCIAL PHENOMENON rarely emerges without giving birth to its nemesis. This is no more true of capitalism at the dawn of the nineteenth century than it is of globalisation at the end of the twentieth. Just as capitalism gave birth to the industrial worker, so globalisation has given birth to the international social movements. Of course, this did not occur in a single event at a particular moment as is intimated in the foregoing phrase. Capitalism, like globalisation, evolved over decades and centuries, and their nemeses too emerged sporadically, and in spurts through the centuries. But as much as the nineteenth century was the era of capitalism and the industrial worker, so the end of the twentieth and beginning of the twenty-first is that of globalisation and international social movements.

International, it must be noted, does not mean transnational. While the latter stresses the geographical character of the movement, the fact that the movement is located in multiple national sites, the former speaks to its perspective, its recognition that the globe is interconnected and that struggle has to be conducted on an international plane. It is this latter characteristic which essentially defines the contemporary global social movements. Again, this epoch does not hold monopoly over such an international perspective. There have been movements over the millennia that also operated beyond national contexts.[1] But never in history have so many movements, on so many issues, in so many countries, conducted struggle on a global plane.[2] Moreover, even those with a distinct national focus have constructed alliances, and drawn support from agencies across national boundaries. Social movements have become truly internationalised in this epoch.

This chapter focuses on a South African social movement, the Congress of South African Trade Unions (COSATU), in the era of globalisation. COSATU is an interesting case study for three reasons. First, unlike many of the other social movements under study in this volume, COSATU predates the democratic transition. Indeed it was one of the more important constituent elements of the anti-apartheid social movement to which the new South Africa owes its birth (Murray 1994; Adler and Webster 1995). Unlike other social organisations of the pre-1994 era, COSATU has survived as an organisation and remained politically relevant. Indeed, its story of strategic calculations and miscalculations, organisational decline and renewal, is an important case in any study on social movements in South Africa's democracy, for not only has the organisation undergone enormous changes in the last decade, but its pre-1990 origins enable a comparative reflection to be made. Second, COSATU, at just under two million members, is the largest social organisation in the country. Its influence is enormous, with other movements either emulating or distinguishing themselves from it. This capacity to act as a model or an example to avoid suggests that it is perhaps the single most defining element in the social movement universe in South Africa.

Finally, COSATU, unlike other social movements in this volume, operates within what in sociological jargon is known as the arena of production. Because of this characteristic some scholars, particularly those associated with the 'New Social Movement' intellectual tradition (Touraine 1988; Escobar and Alvarez 1992), would prefer to define it out of the social movement universe. But this is clearly inappropriate. Not only does COSATU meet all the defining characteristics of a social movement (Desai and Habib 1994), but a cursory historical overview of the union federation would indicate that in its case the arenas of production and reproduction cannot be conceptualised in rigid terms. After all, this federation was explicitly involved in political and social struggles in both the apartheid and post-apartheid periods. As a result, a number of scholars have referred to COSATU as a typical example and exponent of what is known as social movement unionism (Webster 1988; Seidman 1994).

This chapter begins with a historical overview of the federation's birth and genesis, followed by an analysis of the changing character of its constituency and personnel in the 1990s. It then investigates the particular set of problems spawned by globalisation and the democratic transition, the solutions COSATU advocated and the strategies it adopted to address them. These solutions and strategies are contrasted with those of other social movements in order to subject them to critical scrutiny, and to determine their appropriateness for a democratised and globalised political environment. Finally, some reflection is undertaken on the strategic paths currently confronting COSATU, and the one it is likely to embark on in the foreseeable future.

The Formation of COSATU

The 'Durban Moment' (Webster 1993) in 1973, when over 100 000 workers in the city downed tools to demand higher wages, was a historic moment in working-class resistance in South Africa.[3] COSATU, and one of its antecedents, the Federation of South African Trade Unions (FOSATU), emerged out of these strikes. The period between the banning of the ANC and the South African Communist Party (SACP) and the effective crippling of the South African Congress of Trade Unions (SACTU) in the early 1960s and the 1973 strikes, represented an era of relative industrial peace in which all forms of resistance to apartheid were crushed. The initial focus of activity for the trade unions emerging out of the 1973 strikes was the rebuilding of a trade union movement and fighting for formal recognition by the state and employers. A new federation of 'progressive' unions, FOSATU, was formed in April 1979, with some 20 000 workers represented in 12 industrial unions (Baskin 1991: 25).

From their inception, the new trade unions had to define their role within the wider struggle against apartheid in South Africa. FOSATU emphasised the importance of worker control, institutionalised through branch executive committees with delegates from every factory. The federation's leadership argued the need for working-class autonomy from other social and class interests. At the Congress of 1982, when FOSATU's membership stood at over 100 000 (Baskin 1991: 25), Joe Foster, the federation's general secretary, concluded his address with the following warning:

> It is, therefore, essential that workers must strive to build their own powerful and effective organisation even whilst they are part of the wider popular struggle. This organisation is necessary to protect worker interests and to ensure that the popular movement is not hijacked by

elements who will in the end have no option but to turn against their
workers supporters (quoted in Plaut 2003: 305).

Nevertheless, despite the seeming reluctance of the federation's national
leadership, FOSATU unions were quickly drawn into building alliances with
community organisations and involvement with them in consumer boycotts.[4]

Another form of trade union organisation, the so-called 'community
unions', emerged in the late 1970s, mainly in the Eastern Cape. These unions
differed from their FOSATU counterparts, arguing that it was impossible to
separate struggles on the shopfloor from the wider struggle against apartheid.
As a result, they aligned themselves closely with community civics and their
leadership often played important roles in both organisational arenas. The
community unions affiliated to the United Democratic Front (UDF), which was
launched in 1983, and had close relationships with the ANC in exile, primarily
through the then exiled leadership of SACTU. The membership of these
community unions grew dramatically at first, with, for example, the South
African Allied Workers' Union having a membership of 15 000 within a year
of its inception (Baskin 1991: 28). Yet these rapid membership gains quickly
eroded without the strong shopfloor structures advocated and pioneered by
FOSATU.

In the Johannesburg area, a range of new unions, strongly influenced by
the Black Consciousness movement, emerged, and subsequently gathered
together under the auspices of the Council of Unions in South Africa (CUSA),
formed in 1980 with 9 affiliates and a membership of 30 000 (Baskin 1991:
30). In contrast to both FOSATU and the community unions who professed a
non-racial ideology, the CUSA unions, influenced by the Black Consciousness
tradition, argued for black leadership of the unions. One of their key initiatives
was the organisation of mineworkers through the National Union of
Mineworkers (NUM), which would later become the most prominent affiliate
of COSATU.

A critical political development at the time was the appointment of the
Wiehahn Commission, in May 1977, to examine the apartheid labour market
and its laws, and advise government in terms of reform. Somewhat surprisingly,
the Commission report, released in May 1979, recommended recognition of
the right of African workers to form and belong to trade unions. Wiehahn
argued that African workers had a moral right to organise and form trade

unions. But the Commission's intention was also to control the emerging black trade union movement and prevent it from linking up with the political movement against apartheid. This was to be done through proposed legislation outlawing formal links between trade unions and political groups. The reforms aimed to incorporate the unions into the formal labour market institutions, while ruthlessly repressing those that chose not to register.

The Wiehahn reforms posed a dilemma for the emerging unions: register and submit to formal controls or resist and lose the rights to bargain and face state repression. The FOSATU unions, arguing that a gap had opened which should be exploited, decided to register. Though recognising some of the dangers of incorporation into the apartheid labour relations system, the federation was not too concerned about control by the state. As Alec Erwin, then a leading official of FOSATU argued, 'they could not control us because they did not understand us' (Friedman 1987: 162). The community unions, on the other hand, vehemently opposed registration, arguing against incorporation into the apartheid state's systems of control. This 'registration debate' was to be a key factor dividing the emerging black trade union movement, and, together with the aforementioned differences in political strategy, served to keep the unions apart until the early 1980s when unity talks[5] led to the formation of COSATU.

COSATU was formed in November 1985, with 33 affiliates representing 460 000 workers (Baskin 1991: 53). Its formation symbolised the coming together of two separate ideological strands within the labour movement: workerism and a particular variant of nationalism. The organisational and political principles of the new federation included, among others, the establishment of shopfloor organisation and the election of shop stewards, non-racialism and worker independence from political organisations (Baskin 1991). From its inception, however, COSATU linked workers' struggles more openly to those in the wider community. The opening speech of the inaugural congress outlined COSATU's position in this regard:

> As trade unions we have always thought that our main area of activity was on the shop floor – the struggle against the bosses. But we have always recognised that industrial issues are political . . . The struggle of workers on the shop floor cannot be separated from the wider struggle for liberation . . . When we do plunge into political activity, we must make sure that the unions under COSATU have a strong shop floor base not only to take on the employers but the state as well (SALB 1986: 45).

The political tensions that divided the union movement until the formation of COSATU continued inside the new federation and often manifested itself in the debate between 'workerists', who argued for independence from the then banned ANC, and the 'populists', who argued for a closer alignment with the political struggle in South Africa under the leadership of the nationalist movement. COSATU did not adopt a political policy at its launch, instead referring the matter to the first Central Executive Committee (CEC) of the federation. The policy subsequently adopted at the CEC was a compromise, reflecting the deep political divisions within the federation. It articulated a political role for COSATU in alliance with other political organisations, but remained ambiguous about who the federation should be aligned to, and how such alliances would be formed (Baskin 1991: 92). The political tensions inside COSATU became evident when Jay Naidoo, the federation's first general secretary, met officials of the ANC and SACTU in Harare in January 1986. A number of unionists expressed their dissatisfaction, arguing that Naidoo had not been mandated to meet the ANC and that there had been no discussion about the visit within COSATU structures. Some unionists even argued that the visit marked the beginning of the 'takeover of the trade union movement by populism' (quoted in Baskin 1991: 74). Although the political divide between 'workerists' and 'populists' continued to define the ideological schism within COSATU, in practice the federation moved ever closer to the UDF and ANC. A meeting between senior COSATU officials and the ANC in March 1986 declared that:

> . . . lasting solutions (to the crisis in South Africa) can only emerge from the national liberation movement, headed by the ANC and the entire democratic forces of our country of which COSATU is an important and integral part (SALB 1986: 29).

In the course of the next three years, COSATU adopted the Freedom Charter and moved closer to the UDF, participating in a number of stayaways called by the civic movement. Nevertheless, it needs to be stressed that this move towards a closer relationship with the ANC was not uncontested as 'workerist' unions continued to have significant influence within the federation.

After its launch, COSATU grew rapidly. In its first 18 months the federation's paid-up membership grew from approximately 460 000 to about 769 000. This membership was consolidated into 12 industrial unions by the 1987 Congress, rationalised down from 33 affiliates at the federation's launch (SALB 1987: 57). NUM and the National Union of Metalworkers of South Africa (NUMSA) represented the majority of COSATU workers. In time, COSATU came to be the most organised element of the working class in South Africa.

In its early years, despite phenomenal increases in its membership, and a number of significant victories both on the shopfloor and beyond, COSATU had to fight for its survival in the face of a repressive onslaught from the apartheid state. This manifested itself in the declaration of the State of Emergency in 1986, the subsequent banning of the UDF and the imposition of restrictions on COSATU in 1987. Nevertheless, despite labouring under restrictions, COSATU kept the 'mass-democratic movement's torch alive', while the ANC and UDF were banned (Baskin 1991: 450). The federation itself only avoided being banned because of its shopfloor strength. Its programme during this time focused on shopfloor struggles. In 1987 the Living Wage Campaign was launched, with centralised bargaining forming one of the key demands. In 1988 a COSATU special congress was called to consider the banning and restriction of organisations and to develop a response to the new Labour Bill, which attempted to roll back the gains made by unions. The conference resolved to convene a broad anti-apartheid front to challenge the state's repressive tactics. This strategy was re-endorsed at the following year's congress. COSATU led a number of mass stayaways – against municipal elections, and the proposed new Labour Relations Act (LRA). These campaigns culminated in the withdrawal of the 1988 LRA amendments by employers and the state. This success was largely the result of COSATU's ability to mobilise and engage in mass action (Baskin 1991: 450).

Two critical developments, one in the economy and the other in the political arena, shaped the character and political strategy of COSATU in the 1990s. Economic slowdown combined with a structural decline in key industries led to massive industrial and company restructuring, which had a profound impact on COSATU. The unbanning of the ANC and the subsequent democratisation of South Africa facilitated a decisive shift from the politics of resistance to structural reforms, which also significantly shaped COSATU's political programme. Given the importance of both developments for the evolution of COSATU, a detailed examination of these processes and their impact on the federation is warranted.

Economic Liberalisation, Developments in the Labour Market, and their Organisational Consequences

After a boom in the gold price in the early 1980s, economic growth rates in South Africa began to decline rapidly. Output in the mining and manufacturing sectors of the economy, from which COSATU drew the most significant part of its membership, and which throughout the 1960s and 1970s had been the key drivers of economic growth, dramatically contracted (see Gelb 1991). Confronted with an economic crisis, the apartheid state began a process of trade liberalisation by 1987. Thus, even before the political transition, COSATU unions were having to face up to a process of deep-seated economic restructuring as South African mining and manufacturing linked up to the global economy. Retrenchments were widespread, and COSATU affiliates were increasingly drawn into negotiations about firm restructuring.

This process of economic integration continued, and indeed gained further momentum when the ANC came to power. Perceiving the economy as one in terminal decline, the ANC sought to reinvent a national economic growth path through export-led industrialisation, which the ANC argued necessitated further trade liberalisation. Even prior to taking power, the ANC, and indeed even the trade union movement, was party to South Africa's offer to the General Agreement on Tariffs and Trade (GATT) in 1992, whereby the country undertook to significantly reform its tariff structure. This was ratified upon South Africa's accession to the World Trade Organisation (WTO). On assuming power, the ANC government announced trade liberalisation programmes for two important industries – motor vehicles and clothing and textiles – which exceeded the requirements of the GATT undertakings. Liberalisation of the financial sector, through legislation allowing foreign banks and security dealers to operate in South Africa, facilitated a rapid financial integration of the economy, and significantly increased inflows and outflows of capital (see Gelb 2003). Allied to this, the fiscally conservative macro-economic stance adopted by the government was premised on achieving credibility in international markets. At the national level, the effect of import liberalisation was accentuated by the introduction of more stringent competition policy. The combined effect of these initiatives was the rapid transformation of the national economy.

These developments within the economy, and in economic policy, have had a significant impact on the character and operations of COSATU. A number of trends are evident. First, COSATU's initial massive growth in membership was stemmed. This is primarily the result of the failure of the economy to produce new jobs and attract new entrants into the labour market. Table 11.1, which shows employment data for the national economy over the period 1997–2001 using the various October Household Surveys (OHS) and the more recent Labour Force Surveys (LFS), demonstrates that although total employment has fluctuated significantly, employment in the formal non-agriculture segment of the economy has remained relatively stable over this period. It is only the informal sector that has witnessed a growth in employment. The ranks of the unemployed have increased over this period from 2.4 million to over 4.5 million workers.

Second, COSATU's traditional membership, largely drawn from the ranks of the unskilled and semi-skilled workers, has borne the brunt of the economic restructuring. Table 11.2, which indicates the skills composition of the various sectors of the economy from 1985 to 2002, demonstrates a dramatic fall in the employment index for unskilled workers in almost all sectors, and a rapid increase in the indices of skilled and especially high-skilled workers. It also shows that, over this period, there has been a fundamental restructuring of the workforce to the disadvantage of COSATU's traditional support base.

Table 11.1:   Labour market trends in the formal and informal economy, 1997–2001.

	OHS 1997	OHS 1998	OHS 1999	LFS Feb 2000	LFS Sep 2000	LFS Feb 2001	LFS Sep 2001
Formal	6 405 953	6 527 120	6 812 647	6 677 923	6 841 877	6 678 219	6 872 924
Commercial agriculture	495 530	726 249	804 034	756 984	666 940	698 879	665 941
Subsistence agriculture	163 422	202 290	286 856	1 508 264	964 837	653 428	358 983
Informal	965 669	1 077 017	1 573 986	1 820 350	1 933 675	2 665 227	1 873 136
Domestic work	992 341	749 303	798 524	1 001 108	999 438	914 478	915 831
Unspecified	70 986	107 966	92 905	115 106	305 797	227 013	146 000
Total employed	9 093 901	9 389 946	10 368 951	11 879 734	11 712 565	11 837 244	10 832 816
Unemployed	2 450 738	3 162 662	3 157 605	4 333 104	4 082 248	4 240 034	4 525 309

Source: Own calculations from OHS and LFS

Table 11.2: Employment indices by skill category and sector, 1985–2002 (1985=100).

Sector	Semi-/Unskilled			Skilled			Highly Skilled		
	1985	1995	2002	1985	1995	2002	1985	1995	2002
Agriculture	100	91	77	100	121	130	100	197	284
Mining	100	78	52	100	96	77	100	145	127
Manufacturing	100	90	76	100	104	97	100	145	145
Utilities	100	59	47	100	79	84	100	173	227
Construction	100	86	51	100	83	50	100	98	68
Trade	100	82	80	100	103	111	100	117	140
Transport	100	62	43	100	66	51	100	117	120
Financial services	100	94	105	100	123	131	100	165	196
Government & community	100	87	99	100	126	125	100	128	125

Source: Gelb 2003: 21

Third, and as a result of the aforementioned labour market developments, the membership base of COSATU changed dramatically. Since its inception in 1985, the federation had been dominated by the large industrial unions in the metal and mining industries. The crisis in these two sectors, and the ANC government's economic policies, have resulted in a structural transformation of the workforce, which has undermined the traditional support base of COSATU. As indicated earlier, Table 11.1 demonstrates that the formal sector has been unable to create new job opportunities. Only the services sector of the formal economy, in industries such as finance and banking, has been able to register some employment growth, although this has been more than deflected by the numbers of jobs lost in the manufacturing and mining sectors. There has also been an increased feminisation of the workforce (Casale and Posel 2002). Collectively, these trends have significantly undermined COSATU's traditional powerbase, represented in unions such ase NUM and NUMSA. These trends are reflected in the new membership profile of COSATU, shown in Table 11.3. While there has been significant recruitment in the public sector and so-called new unions, their primary and manufacturing sector counterparts have registered a dramatic drop in membership. These changes in the membership profile of COSATU have changed the character and programme of the federation. COSATU now represents a somewhat more established and institutionalised segment of

Table 11.3: Profile of COSATU membership.

Union	1997	1999	2003
CAWU	31 606	31 606	
CEPPWAWU	104 422	89 000	67 162
CWU	40 000	40 398	29 320
FAWU	139 810	100 000	85 069
DENOSA			72 000
MUSA			700
NEHAWU	162 530	231 825	234 607
NUM	310 596	251 954	299 509
NUMSA	220 000	220 000	174 212
PAWE			365
POPCRU	44 999	59 145	75 937
SAAPAWU		29 000	21 966
SACCAWU	102 234	102 234	107 533
SACTWU	150 000	127 000	110 216
SADNU			8 680
SADTU	146 000	210 509	214 865
SAFPU			198
SAMA			4 224
SAMWU	108 738	11 6524	114 127
SAPSA	14 318	14 318	144 127
SATAWU	90 150	100 438	79 325
SASBO	70 377	62 544	58 656
TOTAL	**1.6 m**	**1.7 m**	**1.8 m**

Source: Authors' adaptation of various COSATU Congress reports

the waged workers, while the majority of the unemployed and those surviving in the informal economy remain outside of the formal union movement.

The changes in the economy, and their consequences for the labour market, have dramatically impacted on COSATU's membership. But, there have also been important changes in the organisational culture of the federation. The political transition, and in particular, the movement of COSATU officials into parliament as ANC representatives has taken a heavy toll on the federation and on its affiliates. Ironically, some within COSATU have argued that this has had positive spin-offs in that its leadership is now much more representative of the working class. Neil Coleman, COSATU's parliamentary officer, notes:

> I think the leadership of COSATU has come of age . . . Look at the Central Executive Committee now, it's basically made up of worker leaders who have come through the ranks. Take someone like Zweli [Zwelinzima Vavi – the COSATU general secretary]. He was a mineworker and a . . . shop steward on the mine. If you look at the leadership core in the manufacturing unions and in the public sector unions, they have all come through the ranks over a long period of time. As a result they have a greater sense of cohesion. If you think back to the early executives, it was really dominated by a few people. Now one gets a sense of an interactive engagement from a number of levels. The regions of COSATU are much more dynamic and assertive. Whereas before they almost had observer status in the executives and were scared to speak, now they play a much more assertive role. They reflect the provincial and local structures of the federation . . . Without judging the previous comrades, I have discovered we have a much better leadership now, much more coherent, and that's emerged out of a whole long process (Interview, Coleman, 08.03.04).

But the transformation within COSATU has also had organisational costs. As Sakhela Buhlungu (2003) has argued, the political transition and COSATU's engagement in formal institutions have depoliticised the trade union movement, and forced it to operate like a normal social institution. This has resulted in COSATU's activities shifting away from marginalised communities. It has also led to a professionalisation of its officials. Buhlungu argues that 'there has been (a) change to the dress code, to the cars which officials drive, and in general, the social circles in which they move' (2003: 188). His overall conclusion is that the union federation is a very different institutional animal from the 'social movement' union that represented marginalised communities in the 1980s.

Many of the federation's officials would recognise much of what Buhlungu describes (Interviews, Moni, 20.05.04; Coleman, 08.03.04; Bodipe, 20.05.04; Ehrenreich, 08.03.04). But most would argue that he goes too far in his conclusion when he suggests that COSATU is now dislocated from its original base. The concerns of marginalised working-class communities, they maintain, still informs the federation's agenda. Moreover, they insist that these communities have experienced a net gain in their circumstances, in particular through how COSATU managed the economic and political challenges of the 1990s. As Oupa Bodipe, the then strategic manager in the federation's secretariat, argues:

> The establishment of institutions of social dialogue . . . such as NEDLAC and the parliamentary processes . . . were a huge gain for workers. I mean, even with GEAR you still had a commitment . . . to providing the social wage which was important to our members, who you will find have to spend a lot of money on transport, education and housing. The fact that the state was providing this was quite important for our constituency, which was low-paid working-class communities. Of course . . . the working class had to pay certain costs in terms of growth and employment. The strong push for cost-recovery policies undermine . . . the universal access to basic services. But I think so far the benefits have sort of outweighed the costs (Interview, Bodipe, 20.05.04).

Many others would of course contest Bodipe's conclusion.[6] Perhaps the effectiveness of COSATU's management of the political and economic challenges spawned by the period is best assessed by examining its ability to improve the lives of its members. Table 11.4, which shows the distribution of GDP between profits (returns to capital) and wages (returns to workers), provides an economy-wide indicator for determining how successful COSATU has been at shifting resources to the advantage of its members. Although not conclusive, the table does demonstrate that the wage share of national output has been falling rapidly

Table 11.4: Profit and wage share of output as a percentage of GDP at factor cost.

	1985	1990	1995	2000	2002
Wages (employees' remuneration)	57.1	57.2	55.8	53.9	51.4
Profits (gross operating surplus)	42.9	42.8	44.2	46.1	48.6

Source: *South African Reserve Bank, Quarterly Bulletins, various issues, quoted in Gelb 2003: 21*

throughout the transition while the profit component has been increasing. The only conclusion that can be derived from this fact is that relative to capital, labour's gains have been limited in this transition. However, it is important to note that workers have made gains through government expenditure with some of the evidence pointing toward social spending via the fiscus having substantially reduced inequalities (see Van der Berg 2001).

How did this come to pass? What was COSATU's strategic orientation in managing the challenges of this transition? And, what were the consequences? It is to these questions that we now address our attention.

The Rise and Decline of Social Movement Unionism

South Africa's democratic transition, like most of the Third Wave of democracies (Huntington 1991), has been characterised by two distinct transitional processes, political democratisation and economic liberalisation. The goal of the former is representative government. The latter has as its aim the integration of South Africa into the global economy. Both processes, of course, pose dilemmas and raise challenges, many of which have been defined above. COSATU, its leadership and officials were refreshingly aware of the dilemmas spawned by this Janus-faced transition from very early on in the 1990s. And through the first few years of the negotiations period, they groped their way to a new strategic vision that the federation's September Commission formally labelled social unionism (COSATU 1997). The term was, of course, borrowed from the writings of a number of labour sociologists loosely associated with the federation, who since the mid-1990s toyed with terms such as strategic, social and social movement unionism to describe what was by then the new path that COSATU had begun to tread (Webster 1988; Von Holdt 1992; Webster and Von Holdt 1992).

There are important conceptual differences between these terms, particularly within the industrial sociology discipline. Social movement unionism is defined in this academic tradition as 'a highly mobilised form of unionism which emerges in opposition to authoritarian regimes and repressive workplaces' (Von Holdt 2002: 285). This concept is often used to explain COSATU's involvement in the wider anti-apartheid struggle and its close relationship with the UDF. Strategic unionism, however, refers to a form of trade unionism that seeks to strategically influence economic and social policy by participating in forums where these policies are formulated. The objective is to influence policies to the advantage of workers and other marginalised communities. Strategic unionism emerged in South Africa during the early 1990s, when COSATU began to engage in economic policy discussions in the National Economic Forum (NEF) (see Joffe et al. 1995).

In the post-apartheid period, COSATU continued this form of engagement, and indeed even increased its role substantially in institutions such as the National Economic Development and Labour Council (NEDLAC). This engagement of COSATU has been described by the union federation's leadership as social unionism. The term, officially introduced by the September Commission, describes the federation's unionism as:

> social in the sense that it is concerned with broad social and political issues, as well as the immediate concerns of its members. It aims to be a social force for transformation. Its goal is democracy and socialism. Its influence on society is based on its organised power, its capacity to mobilise, its socioeconomic programme and policies and its participation in political and social alliances. It is committed to workers control and democracy, and to maintaining its character as a movement. It is proactive and effective. It is able to negotiate and monitor complex agreements with government and employers. It is able to make important contributions to national economic and social development (COSATU 1997).

While recognising the importance of these conceptual differences in certain academic traditions, it is not necessary for them to be highlighted for the purposes of this chapter. After all, the focus of this study is on the political evolution of COSATU, and how this informed its practice and engagement in the democratic era. As a result, this chapter holds the view that COSATU's adoption, through the September Commission, of 'social unionism', is consistent with and informed by its early practices of social movement and strategic unionism.

The September Commission had as its mandate the determination of a strategic orientation for COSATU. Confronted with the economic and political challenges of the transition, the federation's leadership established the Commission to inform them on organisational renewal and strategic political alliances. The Commission premised its reflections on three scenario-building exercises. Scenario one was defined as involving no economic growth, the abandonment of the Reconstruction and Development Programme (RDP) by the ANC, high levels of political instability, and increasing industrial strife. Economic growth and modest delivery distinguished scenario two. In this option, racial divisions continue, but the black middle class is empowered. Scenario three was defined by massive growth and development with significant job creation and delivery as per the RDP. Unions were imagined in this option as engaging in joint decision-making.

The Commission viewed a combination of the second and third scenarios as most likely and argued for a programme of social unionism to increase the trade union movement's influence on the political and socio-economic outcomes of the transition. In the words of the Commission, social unionism is

> the strategy which will enable COSATU to . . . proactively contest the transition . . . The aim is to harness the organised power of COSATU, its capacity to mobilise, its socio-economic programmes and policies and its participation in political and social alliances to make important contributions to national, economic and social development (COSATU 1997).

It was hoped through this strategic orientation to increase the influence of the working class so that labour can move to 'co-owning the transformation project' (COSATU 1997).

The social unionism strategic vision had its roots in three related but distinct reflective exercises. First, there was the attempt by a number of senior unionists and some labour sociologists to legitimise COSATU's increasing involvement in tripartite forums that also involved representatives of both the business community and the state.[7] The exercise began with two public interventions in the *South African Labour Bulletin* (SALB) by Geoff Schreiner and Adrienne Bird who theorised the federation's participation in tripartite forums as an example of a social contract, and suggested that this should not only be continued, but also intensified under a new democratic government (Schreiner 1991; Bird and Schreiner 1992). Their intervention spawned a debate both within and outside the labour movement that was to go on for years (Godongwana 1992; Webster and Keet 1992; Callinicos 1992; Baskin 1993; Desai and Habib 1994) and that eventually culminated in COSATU's adoption of most of their original recommendations and its participation in corporatist institutions.

Second, there was the initiative of a number of economists associated with the Economic Trends Group (ETG) and the Industrial Strategy Project (ISP) who were contracted on behalf of COSATU to investigate an alternative, more labour-friendly industrialisation strategy. Their research also generated a fair amount of controversy since their recommendations were premised on the view that South Africa's economic growth depended significantly upon whether or not the country became internationally competitive in its manufacturing sector. Their formal recommendations included industrial beneficiation, the creation and development of South Africa's manufacturing exports, and ultimately South Africa's integration into the global economy (Gelb 1991; Joffe et al. 1995). Finally, and ironically, the least controversy was generated by COSATU's decision to enter into a strategic alliance with the ANC for the 1994 elections. To be fair, the controversy in this regard had taken place some years earlier, when COSATU entered an alliance with the UDF. In any case, COSATU's electoral pact with the ANC came with preconditions, which the federation codified in a reconstruction accord, commonly known as the RDP that the ANC adopted as its electoral platform (ANC 1994).[8]

These three initiatives then, or at least their recommendations, served as the basis of what eventually came to be known as social unionism. Social unionism is thus defined by three elements. First, it involves a corporatist strategy with the labour movement participating in tripartite forums and entering into social pacts with the state and the business community. Second, it involves an assumption that integration into the global economy is inevitable, the realisation of maximalist outcomes is not realisable, and that a strategic economic compromise between capital and labour is necessary. Such a compromise would involve, in Adler and Webster's words, a '"bargained liberalisation": liberalisation, because the changes involve opening up to the global economy; bargained, because agreements are subject to the institutionally structured interplay of societal interests'. 'Bargained liberalisation', in their view, 'may provide workers and marginalised social strata with an opportunity to engage the state and capital over the form and pace of adjustment, allowing the extension of some measure of social regulation to those whose livelihoods are threatened by economic restructuring' (Webster and Adler 1999: 351). Finally, social unionism requires COSATU to politically align itself with the ANC. Such an alliance is legitimised through the conceptual banner of the national democratic revolution, implying that the immediate outcome is a democracy essentially defined by a combination of a representative political system and a Keynesian-type economic strategy.

Social unionism's highpoint is without doubt the period between 1994 and 1996. Labour recorded significant successes in these years. NEDLAC was established in February 1995, and the LRA, which greatly enhanced organised workers' bargaining position, was agreed to by the social partners, subsequently passed in the national legislature, and promulgated by the president (Habib 1997; Marais 2001). A raft of other legislation, such as the Skills Development Act, which benefited workers in a variety of ways, also originated in this period even though they were only passed in subsequent years. And the final draft of the constitution that was promulgated in 1996 addressed many of the concerns raised by labour and enshrined socio-economic rights, even if these were restricted by the limitation clause.[9] For a while it did seem as if South Africa was going to defy the odds and that social unionism would, without question, succeed.

But this was not to last. The symbolic turning point came with the emergence of the Growth, Employment and Redistribution (GEAR) strategy. GEAR violated all three of the central tenets of social unionism. It bypassed the corporatist structures and was imposed by cabinet without any discussion with the social partners (Adam, Moodley and Slabbert 1997; Bond 2000; Marais 2001; Alexander 2002). Even President Mandela acknowledged this in his speech at COSATU's sixth congress, saying '. . . It was unfortunate that here in GEAR we did not have sufficient consultation with other members of the alliance. In fact even the ANC learnt of GEAR when it was almost complete . . . We ignored those who put us in power . . .' (Mandela 1997). Its economic strategy violated the compromise ethos described by Adler and Webster (1995, 1999) as the hallmark of social unionism. And, finally, its passage suggested that the tripartite balance was not an effective mechanism to ensure COSATU's influence on the ANC. Indeed, the passage of GEAR suggested that COSATU's influence was waning.

If there remained any doubt of this, this was put to rest with what in effect was Thabo Mbeki's 'State and Social Tranformation' document. This document, released in 1996, explicitly identified the high government debt, the mobility of capital, and a changing global environment as inhibiting features that limited the abilities of the government to implement democratic transformation on its own. On this basis, Mbeki argued that the ANC needed to transcend its previous antipathy to the business community, abandon its wish for '. . . the total defeat and suppression of the national and class forces responsible for . . . apartheid', and focus on the establishment of a democratic state that would involve 'a dialectical relationship with private capital as a social partner for development and social progress' (ANC 1996: 22). This call for a strategic alliance between the state and capital was a milestone, because it signalled a significant departure from the ANC's traditional approach to alliances, which tended to prioritise labour and other marginalised sectors within the black population.

The consequences of this were dramatic. COSATU's relationship with the ANC deteriorated badly from 1996 and the trade union federation has since embarked on a series of high-profile public stayaways against one or other aspect of government policy. Person days lost in this period increased from 650 000 in 1997 to 1.25 million in 2001 (Andrew Levy and Associates quoted in Devey, Valodia and Velia 2004). These public protests outraged the ANC leadership who on a number of occasions explicitly challenged COSATU to leave the Tripartite Alliance.[10] Increasingly left-leaning activists within the ANC have also been pressurised to publicly tow the leadership's line, a process that graphically culminated in the public humiliation of Jeremy Cronin by some members of the ANC's National Executive Committee (NEC) in 2002.[11]

The heady optimism of social unionism advocates also dissipated so that their assessments on the prospects for unions and workers became more sober and realistic as the Mandela presidency came to its end. This is most evident when comparing Adler and Webster's two interventions on labour and democracy in South Africa. The first, written in 1994 and published in 1995, is largely an actor-based theory of the transition that prioritises agency over structure, even though they deny this, and demonstrates the central role played by COSATU on the transition and its evolution. Their central message was that '. . . the South African transition may constitute the first significant challenge to the predictions of orthodox transition theory, (which suggested) . . . that the democracy resulting from the transition process is conservative economically and socially' (Adler and Webster 1995: 100), if COSATU continued to adopt the strategy of radical reform whose constituent elements involve among others, participation in corporatist forums, seconding COSATU leaders as ANC MP's to national and regional parliaments, and participation in the formulation of the RDP. Their second intervention written in 1998 and published in 1999, was theoretically and conceptually more nuanced, recognising the conditioning effects of structures on actors, and comparatively more relevant for it reflected on the experiences of both the developed and developing worlds.[12] Although the message was similar, that class compromise was still possible, they tended to be less sanguine about its realisability and more aware of the structural conditioning effects on the ANC to abandon the interests of workers and marginalised communities in favour of an 'elite compromise'. The article still betrays an exaggerated assessment of the capacities of the labour movement, which is reflected in their conclusion that South Africa is in the throes of a class stalemate (Webster and Adler 1999). But their intervention suggests that social movement advocates have graduated to a more sober assessment of the prospects for a worker-friendly political dispensation.

The other noteworthy consequence of the crisis of social unionism was that it emboldened the marginalised activists and critics of the mid-1990s. Now mainly located in the arena of reproduction, these activists, many of whom were in the leadership of the new social movements, regained their confidence, and even though their organisations were comparatively far smaller than the labour federation, they began to become politically assertive. More significantly, a coherent conceptual strategic alternative to social unionism emerged on the political horizon. Although social movement activists articulated the options in stark terms – revolution versus reform[13] – measured critical assessments tended to present the debate in an increasingly nuanced form. Essentially this view suggests that a human-centred development programme is dependent on the emergence of substantive uncertainty in South Africa's political system because this enables government to be held accountable to its citizenry.[14] But, as in many other Third Wave of democracies, substantive uncertainty is the missing political ingredient in South Africa. As a result, one witnessed the erosion of the significance of the vote, the one leverage held by citizens over their government. A consequence was that political and state elites tended to find in favour of corporate interests (whose leverage is investment) when the latter's interests clashed with those of economically marginalised citizens (Habib 2004). The solution advocated was the reintroduction of substantive uncertainty through an abandonment of participation in corporatist institutions and a break in the Tripartite Alliance (Desai and Habib 1994; Habib and Taylor 2001). Without such measures, these assessments held that COSATU would not be able to realise its own social democratic agenda.

COSATU thus entered the new millennium on decidedly disadvantageous terms: its strategic orientation was in disarray, its relationship with the ANC was bad and getting worse, it was increasingly confronted by assertive critics, and an organisational alternative was emerging onto the political scene. The labour federation was in need of a new strategic path.

In Search of a Strategic Path

What, then, are the strategic options that confront COSATU? Three scenarios are on the table. First, COSATU could act merely as a trade union. In this sense, it would behave in a politically neutral fashion, like the other union federations, the Federation of Unions of South Africa (FEDUSA) and the National Council of Trade Unions (NACTU). There is some support for this both within the union federation and in the ANC leadership[15] (see Seidman 1994). But it is not feasible. The COSATU leadership recognises that to behave in a politically neutral fashion would leave the federation merely reactive. As Crosby Moni, deputy president of NUM, argues:

> That is a dangerous proposition. Governments come and go. What if one day, a right wing government banned political activity. Yes . . . this would appear to make sense to . . . people who have not been banned in the 1980s . . . We had no political voice in the country, and never again shall we allow that situation to come around. Our stance is that never again shall we find ourselves in the same situation as we have been from 1960 to 1990 . . . It was 30 years of hell. Those who have never experienced it would easily come with suggestions that we must be apolitical (Interview, Moni, 20.05.04).

This view is widely held among the COSATU leadership (Vavi 2005). They recognise that the policy choices of state elites have had and will continue to have a dramatic impact on the federation's membership. As a result, they will not adopt a strategic path that will leave COSATU without any control over its own destiny.

The second strategic path is consistent with the strategy of social unionism. Its advocates essentially argue that the ANC should not be handed over to conservative or bourgeois interests. A struggle needs to be had for the soul of the ANC. Crosby Moni, again, sums up this view:

> The African National Congress is like an omnibus; it has all the tentacles inside it. When a pro-worker tendency is weak inside the African National Congress, you will see it drifting away from the workers . . . When workers have the upper hand, the ANC and unions will come closer . . . Our starting point . . . in the elections was let us do every-

thing in our power and give the ANC an overwhelming victory. They have it now. We have our claim to that because we were part . . . of telling our people to vote ANC. What we are looking . . . for now is an ANC that is friendly to workers, and which approaches worker issues with a bias (Interview, Moni, 20.05.04).

Advocates of the social unionism view also suggest that it is in the long-term interests of workers for COSATU to remain in the Alliance because this enables the federation to influence policy. Neil Coleman, for instance, suggests that government's moderate shift to the left, manifested in its retreat on privatisation, and its current focus on employment, is something that COSATU can justifiably claim credit for. He thus echoes a widely held view in the leadership when he maintains that an abandonment of the Alliance would marginalise the interests of workers in the policy process (Interview, Coleman, 08.03.04).

There is significant support for this strategy among the membership of the federation. Three surveys of COSATU shop stewards conducted over the last decade by the Sociology of Work programme at the University of the Witwatersrand demonstrate categorically that a majority of shop stewards support the Alliance and its continuation. Table 11.5, which summarises the results of the surveys, demonstrates that support for the Alliance has decreased over the last decade from 82 per cent in 1994 to 66 per cent in 2004 (see also Buhlungu 2006; Pillay 2006). Nevertheless, almost two-thirds of COSATU's membership is still in favour of the Alliance. This, then, lends credence to the leadership's

Table 11.5: **COSATU members' attitude towards the Alliance.**

	1994 (%)	1998 (%)	2004 (%)
Support Alliance	82	70	66
SACP alone	2	4	4
ANC alone	n/a	n/a	n/a
New workers' party	n/a	4	6
Non-aligned	15	14	18
Another party/ies	n/a	1	2
Do not know	n/a	4	5

Note: N/A means this question was not asked in that survey
Source: Pillay 2006

view that the Alliance can only be abandoned at great cost to the unity of the federation itself.

There are weaknesses, however, associated with this strategic path. Left-leaning critics of COSATU would argue that as a result of this strategy over the last few years, labour has experienced a net loss in benefits and influence. In particular, they would point to statistical data that suggest that unemployment has increased to 41.8 per cent of the workforce[16] (UNDP 2003), and poverty to between 45 per cent and 55 per cent of the population (Department of Social Welfare 2002; Everatt 2003). Of course, advocates of the social unionism strategy would contest this, pointing to the raft of legislation, and more recent policy changes that have benefited workers.[17] But the more serious criticism that these advocates would need to respond to is that which suggests these outcomes were systemically predictable and likely to continue so long as substantive uncertainty is not reintroduced into the political system. As Habib has argued elsewhere, 'so long as we postpone the realisation of substantive uncertainty, so long will we postpone the goals of development, poverty alleviation and egalitarianism' (*Sunday Times* 4 April 2004).

This, then, takes us to the third and final strategic option confronting COSATU, namely abandoning the Alliance and charting a political path independent of the ANC (McKinley 2001; Habib and Taylor 2001). Such a decision would, of course, fundamentally alter the political system in South Africa and plunge COSATU into uncharted territory. Advocates of this strategy suggest that this is necessary for it would reintroduce the missing element of substantive uncertainty into the political system. This, it is maintained, is necessary for political elites to take the interests of workers and ordinary citizens more seriously (Habib 2004). Critics of this view argue, to the contrary, that there are great dangers if the labour movement were to go down this path. They point to the danger that the labour movement could fracture, thereby threatening order and stability.

Jeremy Cronin, deputy general secretary of the SACP, puts it most evocatively in two separate interviews: the first being the now notorious one with Irish academic Helena Sheehan, for which he was rapped over the knuckles by the ANC leadership, and the second with Adam Habib and Imraan Valodia very soon after the ANC received its overwhelming electoral mandate in the 2004 elections. In the former interview, Cronin explicitly states, 'what people don't realise is that breaking the alliance means splitting all three organisations. You are talking of 2 million COSATU members, more than 80 percent of which are ANC members' (Cronin 2002; Southall 2003: 65). For this reason it is imperative to remain within the Alliance, not only to ensure that the ANC is not handed over to the neo-liberals, but also because it is increasingly becoming possible to win political victories as the shine of the Washington consensus policies begin to fade. This optimism carries through to the more recent interview, where once again Cronin highlights the political possibilities that arise as a result of the contemporary crisis of the global economy. He concludes: 'the strategic priority of the day in South Africa is to have a significant political majority capable of spearheading fundamental transformation' (Interview, Cronin, 21.04.04), which he maintains has the greatest likelihood of being realised through the ANC.

In any case, for now, COSATU seems to have made its decision in this regard. In the build-up to the 2004 elections, and in the aftermath of the very acrimonious relations that characterised COSATU-ANC engagements in 2001 and 2002, attempts have been made by the federation to once again repair their relationship with the ruling party. As a result, COSATU threw its political weight behind the ANC for the 2004 elections. And the results were phenomenal. The ANC garnered approximately 70 per cent of the electoral votes. But the ANC government has also reciprocated. The budgets of the last two years have announced significant increases in social expenditure, including infrastructural investment, public work programmes and social welfare, policy planks closer to what COSATU has been advocating for a number of years.[18]

But how sustainable these new policies are is anyone's guess. Critics of COSATU from the more radical social movements and some political analysts suggest that these policy options will be off the table once the 2004 elections are over.[19] COSATU leaders, on the other hand, are less cynical, suggesting that this does in part reflect a new realisation on the path of government leaders that their earlier gamble did not pay off. But COSATU is also careful to open up other strategic options. Some within the federation have argued that COSATU needs to build stronger alliances with the other social movements that are discussed in this volume. Indeed, COSATU has already embarked on joint campaigns with some social movements. Most prominent among these has been its campaigns with the Treatment Action Campaign (TAC). However, while there is evidence of a more accommodating view within COSATU to other social movements that are more openly against the ANC,[20] key strategic differences still remain. As long as COSATU remains in the Alliance it is unlikely to forge lasting strategic relationships with social movements that question the social unionism model and its relationship to the ANC. As argued by NUM general secretary, Gwede Mantashe, 'where we differ with our friends in the social movements is that we prefer to engage [the state]' (Mantashe 2003).

Whether Mantashe or his critics are right is a matter of speculation for now. What is without doubt is that should the COSATU leadership's gamble not pay off, the union federation would be all the weaker for it with adverse consequences for workers and the marginalised sectors of our society. Were it to succeed, COSATU would not only advance the interests of its members and their social allies, it would also establish a new strategic trajectory that would probably be emulated by unions across the developing world.

Notes

1. Note, for instance, the operations of the international worker and communist movements.
2. Anheier, Glasius and Kaldor demonstrate that there has been a tremendous growth in the scale of international and supranational organisations. They provide data showing that the membership density of NGOs has grown from 30 persons per million in 1990 to 43 persons per million in 2000, with membership of NGOs growing over the period from 148 501 to 255 432. See Anheier, Glasius and Kaldor (2001).
3. For an overview of the 1973 strikes, see Friedman (1987).
4. Two prominent examples of these were the Ford and Fattis and Monis strikes. For greater detail in this regard, see Baskin (1991).
5. See MacShane, Plaut and Ward (1984) and Baskin (1991) for details of the unity process.
6. The common view held among the leadership of the more radical social movements is that poor marginalised communities have experienced a net economic loss in this period. See Desai (2002); Bond (2000); and also a number of the other chapters in this edited volume.
7. This followed the successful anti-LRA campaign that resulted in a restructured tripartite National Manpower Commission (NMC) and in the establishment of the National Economic Forum (NEF).
8. For different critical reflective summaries of the RDP, see Lodge (1999); Bond (2000); Habib and Padayachee (2000); and Marais (2001).
9. A number of recent cases in the constitutional court were founded on the second-generation rights clause of the constitution. The most prominent of these are the Grootboom case involving the issue of housing in the Western Cape, and the Treatment Action Campaign's legal challenge, which focused on compelling government to roll out anti-retroviral provision for AIDS sufferers.
10. Even Mandela publicly criticised those who were critical of GEAR, and challenged them to leave the ANC if they were uncomfortable with its direction (Habib, Daniel and Southall 2003: 4).
11. For a reflective discussion of this, and its consequences for the Tripartite Alliance, see Southall (2003).

12. There is, for instance, a very useful reflection on the experiences of the Indian state, Kerala, and the lessons this may hold for democratic transitions in the South. See Webster and Adler (1999: 356–8).
13. For a summary of these views, see Pillay (2006).
14. A similar thesis is advanced on the origins of development states in Northeast and Southeast Asia in Doner, Ritchie and Slater (2005).
15. Zwelinzima Vavi, general secretary of COSATU, also indicated that there were some within government and the movement who preferred this option, although he himself was very critical of it. See Vavi (2005).
16. This is using the expanded definition of unemployment. Use of the more restrictive definition would put unemployment at 30.5 per cent (UNDP 2003).
17. See The Presidency's Ten Year Review in this regard (PCAS 2003). Also note Bodipe's argument quoted earlier in the chapter.
18. It is worth noting that Neil Coleman believes that policy is still operating within the GEAR framework:

> The essentials of the strategy remain the same. Like at the level of competitiveness, export orientation, and a restrictive expenditure policy. In terms of . . . social expenditure . . . we are back to the real spending per capita of 1995. So all we have done is to re-establish . . . lost ground (Interview, Coleman, 08.03.04).

For another reflection on the contradictions in government's current policy, see Habib (2004).
19. This was the view of Steven Friedman, articulated in the question and answer session of a presentation to the Harold Wolpe Lecture series, hosted by the Centre for Civil Society, University of Natal, in November 2003.
20. At a recent conference, COSATU invited a number of social movement activists.

References

Adam, H., K. Moodley and F. Van Zyl Slabbert. 1997. *Comrades in Business: Post-Liberation Politics in South Africa*. Cape Town: Tafelberg.

Adler, G. and E. Webster. 1995. 'The Labor Movement, Radical Reform, and Transition to Democracy in South Africa'. *Politics and Society* 23 (1): 75–106.

African National Congress (ANC). 1994. *The Reconstruction and Development Programme: A Policy Framework*. Johannesburg: Umanyano Publications.

———. 1996. 'The State and Social Transformation'. Discussion document.

Alexander, N. 2002. *An Ordinary Country: Issues in the Transition from Apartheid to Democracy in South Africa*. Pietermaritzburg: University of Natal Press.

Anheier, H., M. Glasius and M. Kaldor. 2001. 'Introducing Global Civil Society'. In H. Anheier, M. Glasius and M. Kaldor (eds), *Global Civil Society 2001*. Oxford: Oxford University Press.

Baskin, J. 1991. *Striking Back: A History of COSATU*. Johannesburg: Ravan Press.

———. 1993. 'The Trend Towards Bargained Corporatism'. *South African Labour Bulletin* 17 (3).

Bird, A. and G. Schreiner. 1992. 'COSATU at the Crossroads: Towards Tripartite Corporatism or Democratic Socialism?'. *South African Labour Bulletin* 16 (6).

Bond, P. 2000. *Elite Transition: From Apartheid to Neoliberalism in South Africa*. Pietermaritzburg: University of Natal Press.

Buhlungu, S. 2003. 'The State of Trade Unionism in Post-Apartheid South Africa'. In J. Daniel, A. Habib and R. Southall (eds), *The State of the Nation 2003-2004*. Cape Town: HSRC Press.

———. (ed.). 2006. *Trade Unions and Politics: COSATU Workers after 10 Years of Democracy*. Cape Town: HSRC Press.

Callinicos, A. 1992. *Between Apartheid and Capitalism*. London: Bookmarks.

Casale, D. and D. Posel. 2002. 'The Continued Feminisation of the Labour Force in South Africa: An Analysis of Recent Data and Trends'. *South African Journal of Economics* 70 (1): 156-84.

COSATU. 1997. 'Report of the September Commission'. http://www.cosatu.org.za/shop/shop0604.htm#September.

Cronin, J. 2002. 'An Interview with Helena Sheehan'. http://www.comms.deu.ie/sheehanh/za/cronin02.htm.

Desai, A. 2002. *We are the Poors: Community Struggles in Post-Apartheid South Africa*. New York: Monthly Review Press.

Desai, A. and A. Habib. 1994. 'Social Movements in Transitional Societies: A Case Study of the Congress of South African Trade Unions'. *South African Sociological Review* 6 (2): 68-88.

Devey, R., C. Skinner and I. Valodia. 2004. 'Definitions, Data and the Informal Economy in South Africa: A Critical Analysis'. Paper presented to the School of Development Studies Conference, 20-22 October, Durban.

Devey, R., I. Valodia and M. Velia. 2004. 'Constraints to Growth and Employment: Evidence from the Greater Durban Metropolitan Area'. School of Development Studies, University of KwaZulu-Natal.

Escobar, A. and S. Alvarez (eds). 1992. *The Making of Social Movements in Latin America: Identity, Strategy and Democracy*. Boulder: Westview Press.

Everatt, D. 2003. 'The Politics of Poverty in South Africa'. In D. Everatt and V. Maphai (eds), *The (Real) State of the Nation*. Johannesburg: Interfund.

Friedman, S. 1987. *Building Tomorrow Today: African Workers in Trade Unions, 1970-1984*. Johannesburg: Ravan Press.

Gelb, S. (ed.). 1991. *South Africa's Economic Crisis*. Cape Town: David Philip.

———. 2003. *Inequality in South Africa: Nature, Causes and Responses*. Johannesburg: The Edge Institute.

Godongwana, E. 1992. 'Social Contract: Which Way for South Africa?'. *South African Labour Bulletin* 16 (4).

Habib, A. 1997. 'From Pluralism to Corporatism: South Africa's Labor Relations in Transition'. *Politikon* 24 (1).

———. 2004. 'The Politics of Economic Policy-Making: Substantive Uncertainty, Political Leverage, and Human Development'. *Transformation* 56.

Habib, A. and V. Padayachee. 2000. 'Economic Policy and Power Relations in South Africa's Transition to Democracy'. *World Development* 28 (2).

Habib, A. and R. Taylor. 2001, 'Political Alliances and Parliamentary Opposition in Post-Apartheid South Africa'. *Democratization* 8 (1).

Habib, A., J. Daniel and R. Southall. 2003. 'Introduction: The State of the Nation 2003-2004'. In J. Daniel, A. Habib and R. Southall (eds), *The State of the Nation 2003-2004*. Cape Town: HSRC Press.

Huntington, S. 1991. *The Third Wave: Democratization in the Late Twentieth Century*. Oklahoma: University of Oklahoma Press.

Joffe, A., D. Kaplan, R. Kaplinsky and D. Lewis. 1995. *Improving Manufacturing Performance in South Africa: Report of the Industrial Strategy Project*. Cape Town: University of Cape Town Press.

Joffe, A., J. Maller and E. Webster. 1995. 'South Africa's Industrialisation: The Challenge Facing Labour'. In S. Frankel and J. Harrod (eds), *Changing Labour Relations in Industrialising Countries*. Ithaca: Cornell University Industrial and Labour Relations Press.

Lodge, T. 1999. *South African Politics Since 1994*. Cape Town: David Philip.

MacShane, D., M. Plaut and D. Ward. 1984. *Power: Black Workers, Their Unions and the Struggle for Freedom in South Africa*. Nottingham: Spokesman.

Mandela, N. 1997. Speech by President Nelson Mandela, at the Sixth National Congress of COSATU. http://www.sadtu.org.za/press/speeches/2001/16-9-1997.0.htm.

Mantashe, G. 2003. 'Trade Unions and Social Movements in SA'. *South African Labour Bulletin* 27 (6): 33-4.

Marais, H. 2001. *South Africa: Limits to Change: The Political Economy of Transition*. London: Zed Books.

McKinley, D. 2001. 'Democracy, Power and Patronage: Debate and Opposition within the African National Congress and the Tripartite Alliance since 1994'. *Democratization* 8 (1).

Murray, M. 1994. *The Revolution Deferred: The Painful Birth of Post-Apartheid South Africa*. London: Verso.

Pillay, D. 2006. 'COSATU, Alliances, and Working Class Politics'. In S. Buhlungu (ed.), *Trade Unions and Politics: COSATU Workers after 10 Years of Democracy*. Cape Town: HSRC Press.

Policy Co-ordination and Advisory Services (PCAS). 2003. 'The Presidency, Towards a Ten Year Review: Synthesis Report on Implementation of Government Programmes'. October.

Plaut, M. 2003. 'The Workers Struggle: A South African Text Revisited'. *Review of African Political Economy* 96: 305-13.

Report of the Committee of Inquiry into a Comprehensive System of Social Security for South Africa. 2002. *Transforming the Present – Protecting the Future*. Pretoria: Department of Social Development.

Schreiner, G. 1991. 'Fossils from the Past: Resurrecting and Restructuring the National Manpower Commission'. *South African Labour Bulletin* 14 (7).

———. 1994. 'Restructuring the Labour Movement after Apartheid'. *South African Labour Bulletin* 13 (2).

Seidman, G. 1994. *Manufacturing Militance: Workers' Movements in Brazil and South Africa, 1970–1985*. Berkeley: University of California Press.

South African Labour Bulletin (SALB). 1986. 'ANC-SACTU-COSATU Talks'. *South African Labour Bulletin* 11 (5): 29-31.

———. 1987. 'Jay Naidoo on COSATU: Interview with Jay Naidoo'. *South African Labour Bulletin* 12 (5): 57-66.

Southall, R. 2003. 'State of the Political Parties'. In J. Daniel, A. Habib and R. Southall (eds), *State of the Nation 2003-2004*. Cape Town: HSRC Press.

Touraine, A. 1988. *The Return of the Actor*. Minneapolis: University of Minnesota Press.

United Nations Development Program (UNDP). 2003. *South Africa Human Development Report*. Cape Town: Oxford University Press.

Van der Berg, S. 2001. 'Redistribution through the Budget: Public Expenditure Incidence in South Africa 1993-97'. *Social Dynamics* 27 (1).

Vavi, Z. 2005. 'Keynote Address of the General Secretary to the COSATU Conference to Celebrate 10 Years of Democracy'. Midrand, 5-8 March.

Von Holdt, K. 1992. 'What is the Future of Labour'. *South African Labour Bulletin* 16 (8).

———. 2002. 'Social Movement Unionism: The Case of South Africa'. *Work Employment and Society* 16 (2): 283-304.

Webster, E. 1988. 'The Rise of Social Movement Unionism: The Two Faces of the Black Trade Union Movement in South Africa'. In P. Frankel, N. Pines and M. Swilling (eds), *State, Resistance and Change in South Africa*. London: Croom Helm.

———. 1993. 'Moral Decay and Social Reconstruction: Richard Turner and Radical Reform'. *Theoria* 80/81.

Webster, E. and G. Adler. 1999. 'Towards a Class Compromise in South Africa's "Double Transition": Bargained Liberalization and the Consolidation of Democracy'. *Politics and Society* 27 (3): 347–85.

Webster, E. and D. Keet. 1992. 'National Economic Forum: Parallel to CODESA?' Interview with Sam Shilowa. *South African Labour Bulletin* 16 (3).

Webster, E. and K. von Holdt. 1992. 'Towards a Socialist Theory of Radical Reform: From Resistance to Reconstruction in the Labour Movement'. Paper delivered to the Ruth First Memorial Symposium, University of the Western Cape.

Interviews

Bodipe, Oupa. Johannesburg, 20.05.04.
Coleman, Neil. Cape Town, 08.03.04.
Cronin, Jeremy. Cape Town, 21.04.04.
Ehrenreich, Tony. Cape Town, 08.03.04.
Moni, Crosby. Johannesburg, 20.05.04.

12

Collective Action
in the Informal Economy

The Case of the
Self-Employed Women's Union, 1994–2004

Annie Devenish and Caroline Skinner

TRADITIONALLY, IN SOUTH AFRICA, trade unions were seen as the primary arena for organising the working poor. Given the national trend towards the informalisation of work, formal economy workers belonging to trade unions are becoming a smaller and smaller proportion of the workforce. The trade union movement has found it difficult to organise informal workers into the ambit of the formal trade union system. The Congress of South African Trade Unions (COSATU) claims to have become a 'social movement union' speaking on behalf of those in formal jobs, but also for unemployed and informal workers. However, partly as a result of their dissatisfaction with the formal trade union movement, informal workers have begun to organise themselves. These new informal economy unions are an interesting component of new social movements in South Africa. The type of organisation, the issues fought, the means of organisation, and the links to other social movements, differ substantially both from the traditional trade unions and from the other new social movements that have emerged in the post-apartheid period. This chapter provides an insight into this arena of social action through its focus on the Self-Employed Women's Union (SEWU).

SEWU was launched in 1994, at the time of the political transition. Its constituency was self-employed women working in the survivalist end of the economy – largely street traders and home-based workers. SEWU was formally constituted, and explicitly saw itself as a union. The union was an organisational response to marginalisation in post-apartheid South Africa, which experienced some success in empowering a group that is particularly marginalised. This chapter aims to document SEWU's approach over its ten years of existence. In the process, the similarities and differences with other movements analysed in this volume become clear and broader themes within social movement literature are referred to. The chapter starts by assessing the context from which SEWU stemmed and the context to which it responded. The emergence of SEWU, its organisational form and membership are then considered. This is partly where SEWU differed most from other social movements. It is argued that SEWU had particular success in building grassroots leadership. Attention is then turned to an issue all movements face – material resources and, more specifically, financial sustainability. SEWU's approach to building international and local alliances is also considered. The bulk of the chapter examines SEWU's activities over time, its relations with the state, its approach to skills training and its activities with respect to access to credit and savings facilities. The chapter then assesses the strengths and weaknesses of the organisation. The conclusion reflects on whether or not SEWU can be regarded as a social movement and outlines challenges that the case of SEWU poses to social movements in South Africa.

The chapter draws on key informant interviews with staff, office bearers and members operating in various branches in KwaZulu-Natal, the Eastern Cape, Mpumalanga and the Orange Free State. Primary documents such as annual reports, reports to funders, newsletters, submissions to policy processes were also collected and analysed. In August 2004, SEWU underwent an enforced liquidation as a result of a judgement against the organisation brought by people who were employed over five years ago, and has thus ceased to exist. The judgement resulted in a back-pay claim of over R500 000. Given its already stretched financial position, the union was forced to close. In late 2004, COSATU made a commitment to find a new organisational home for this constituency and by February 2005 the federation had agreed to assist in establishing a new informal economy union. This new union will draw on the experience of SEWU – it is likely to employ similar organising strategies and may well hire former SEWU staff. However, it is unlikely to organise only women.

The Context from which SEWU Stems; the Context to which SEWU Responds

SEWU emerged in the early 1990s at the time of political transition in South Africa. On the one hand, this was a time of policy dynamism. A new constitution was being formulated, women's issues were being addressed through the establishment of a variety of structures within the new state, the labour relations system was being reworked and numerous other new policies were being tabled. This opened up opportunities to influence policy processes. On the other hand, the South African government pursued a path of rapid integration into the global economy (Marias 1998; Michie and Padayachee 1997). Trade and industry policy, as Valodia (2001) argues, quickly exposed the industrial sector to international competition. This has led to employment losses in the formal sector, particularly in manufacturing, which has forced more South Africans to seek work in the informal economy. Further, there has been a process of restructuring within firms leading to the introduction of more flexible forms of work arrangements, resulting in the informalisation of work.

Worldwide there has been an increase in the numbers of people working in the informal economy, either self-employed in unregistered enterprises or as wage workers in unprotected jobs. This is part of a documented international process of the informalisation of work that is closely associated with globalisation (see, for example, Standing 1999; Chen 2001; ILO 2002). In South Africa, according to the September 2003 Labour Force Survey (LFS), 25.1 per cent of those working in South Africa operate in the informal economy. This is constituted by 1 899 000 people operating in the informal economy (which Statistics South Africa defines as those operating in unregistered firms and their employees) and 1 022 000 domestic workers (Stats SA 2004). Although the figures fluctuate, informal work is one of the few areas in post-apartheid South Africa where there has been growth in employment (Devey, Skinner and Valodia 2003a). As is the case internationally, there is a strong correlation between being poor and working in the informal economy in South Africa. According to the September 2003 LFS, 54 per cent of those working in the informal economy earn R500 or less and 92 per cent earn less than R2 500. There is also a gender and race dimension to the informal economy in South Africa. More men than women work in the informal economy, but the ratio of men to women is less than is the case for the formal economy. Within the informal economy, qualitative work indicates that women tend to be over-represented in the less lucrative tasks (see, for example, Lund, Nicholson and Skinner 2000 on street trading), and the majority of those working in the informal economy are black (Devey, Skinner and Valodia 2003a).

Although individual incomes in the informal economy tend to be extremely low, international experience demonstrates that collective action can result in significant improvements in working and living conditions of informal workers. One of the best examples of this is the Self-Employed Women's Association (SEWA) in India. SEWU is modelled on SEWA and it therefore warrants brief attention. Formed in 1972, SEWA is now the largest trade union in India with over 700 000 members. Members are both rural and urban dwellers and include home-based workers, vendors or traders, labourers and service providers and small producers (SEWA 2002: 1). As a trade union, SEWA offers its members a combination of services including organisation into trade groups, co-operatives or producer groups, collective bargaining and opportunities for members to develop local leadership abilities. SEWA has established a number of institutions to complement its trade union activities. For example, SEWA Bank provides credit, savings and insurance to members and SEWA Social Security provides health and childcare services. There have been many studies measuring the impact of different aspects of SEWA's activities (see, for example, Vaux and Lund 2003; Datta 2003). Chen, Khurana and Mirani (2004) provide the most comprehensive synthesis demonstrating that for the majority of members SEWA's interventions have increased the regularity or security of their work and improved their physical well-being. They go on to argue that over the past three decades SEWA's interventions have led to structural changes and have contributed to the mainstreaming of women's issues in development discourses and planning.

In the South African context, there has been relatively little progress in organising those in the informal economy. The informalisation of work has posed a significant challenge to the formal economy union movement. Some COSATU-affiliated unions have recently begun attempting to organise casual or informal workers in the industries in which they operate, but with the exception of the transport union the numbers of informal worker members are still very small (see Goldman 2003). At a federation level it is only recently that concrete actions have been taken. However, given high levels of retrenchments, unions are overstretched even in their traditional areas of competence, and organising those in the informal economy is particularly challenging. It requires a shift in the mindset of trade union officials (away from the position that informal workers are simply a threat to formal workers), different organising strategies (given that the employer is often absent or difficult to find) and a different set of services from what formal unions are used to supplying.

There is a group of organisations that focuses solely on organising informal workers like street trader organisations. In 1998/99 Lund and Skinner (1999) conducted a review of the structure and activities of twenty-two street trader organisations operating in five South African cities. This research indicates that trader organisations are often not formally constituted and in many cases this occurs only when crises arise. In other cases they focus on providing business services like bulk buying and in most cases they are led by men. More recent research on, for example, the trader associations operating in the centre of Johannesburg indicates that little has changed (see Thulare 2004). Further, many of the social movements that operate in residential areas where there are high concentrations of informal activity focus on basic service provision and tend not to address work-based issues. It is thus clear that organising efforts in the informal economy in the post-apartheid period have, with a few exceptions, been largely unsatisfactory.

The Emergence of SEWU, its Membership and Organisational Form
The Self-Employed Women's Union was founded by Pat Horn who has a long history of organising in the formal union movement in South Africa. She explains the origin of SEWU as follows:

> I was on a sabbatical in early '91 . . . doing research on what happens to the status of women in times of political change . . . In my literature searches I read about SEWA. In the women's committees of the unions which I'd been in, we became aware that most women who were working were not in unions because they were in the informal economy. I just assumed, like so many people do, that you could not unionise those in the informal economy. This was until I read about SEWA. SEWA made me realise that it was possible (Interview, 27.02.04).

Once Horn had drawn up a funding proposal, the Dutch funders HIVOS agreed to support the first year of SEWU's activities. SEWU was officially launched in

1994 in KwaZulu-Natal, with a number of branches in the Durban area. In 1997 SEWU launched regional branches in the Western Cape and the Eastern Cape and in 2001 in the Free State and Mpumalanga.

As outlined in their constitution SEWU membership was open to all adult women involved in 'an economic activity' and who 'earn their living by their own effort, 'without regular or salaried employment' and 'who do not employ more than three persons on a permanent basis' (SEWU 1994: 1). SEWU was thus targeting the poorer end of the informal economy. It also excluded men, which attracted some criticism from others in the labour movement. SEWU's decision to organise only women was informed by a commitment to confronting not only a patriarchal society but also the gendered nature of informal work (SEWU founder interviewed on a documentary made about SEWU in 1996).

SEWU's membership consisted predominantly of black women situated in the survivalist end of the informal economy. In a membership survey conducted in 1997, it was found that 61 per cent of the 131 members interviewed earned less than R100 a week (James 1998: 10). Members' activities can be broadly divided into home-based production, street trading and part-time domestic work. Figure 12.1 shows membership numbers from 1994 to 2003, with figures reflecting paid-up membership at the end of the given year.

It is clear from Figure 12.1 that SEWU's membership, although increasing over time, fluctuated over the years. At the beginning of 2004, however, SEWU's membership only stood at a total of 1 967 paid-up members, suggesting another recent and significant lapse in membership.

Analysis of the membership data over time indicates that there are three major inter-related membership trends over the last ten years. SEWU underwent a shift from a mainly urban to a mainly rural membership with the exception of the Western Cape, which only had urban-based members. The union also experienced a shift from a predominance of street vendors to a predominance of home-based workers. In addition, there was a significant weakening of a previously strong and concentrated SEWU membership in the Durban inner city and beachfront, which defined the movement in its early years. However, in more recent years, new points of strength were established as membership spread to other areas and provinces. These shifts had implications for the way in which SEWU chose to organise and the kind of strategies and services that it provided to its members.

SEWU's structure was informed not only by the experience of SEWA but also by Horn's union history. She notes 'in the unions we were always very strict

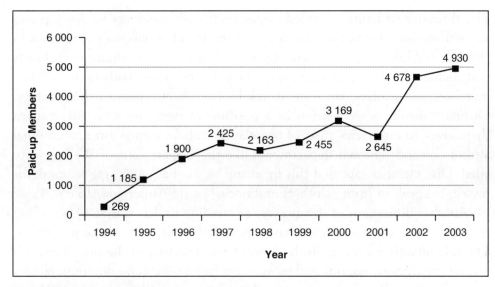

Figure 12.1: SEWU paid-up membership, 1994–2003.
Source: SEWU Annual Reports, 1994–2003

about workers controlling their organisations' (Interview, 27.02.04). SEWU was designed on the principle of direct democracy and its organisational form was similar to formal unions. Members were organised into branches and within branches members elected trade leaders, and trade leaders collectively formed trade committees. Trade committees elected two members to represent them regionally in the Regional Executive Committee (REC), which oversaw the activities of branches and regional staff. Four representatives from each REC were elected to the National Executive Committee (NEC), which was responsible for management of the union as a whole. As noted in the constitution (1994), however, the governing body of the union was the annual conference to which branches were entitled to send one delegate per twenty members. The conference was where key policy decisions were made and the national office bearers – the president, vice-president and treasurer – elected. This structure of direct democracy is very different from other organisations that organise those working in the informal economy (see, for example, Lund and Skinner 1999 on street trader organisations) as well as some other new social movements.

The SEWU constitution states that one of the union's objectives is 'to build leadership among women in the lowest strata of the wider working class' (1994: 2). The structure of direct democracy went some way to satisfying this objective.

The three-tier structure provided opportunities for members to develop and move from one level to the next. Many of the members elected to positions in SEWU would have few, if any, other opportunities to be in positions of authority and thereby develop their leadership skills. In interviews with both ordinary members and leaders, we were struck by the effectiveness of this strategy. Ordinary members were often in a position to negotiate with government themselves. In interviews, cases of negotiating with local authorities, traditional authorities and national departments like the Department of Welfare were cited. One member captured this by saying 'SEWU has taught me to speak for myself, to speak in front of others and not to be shy' (Interview, 16.03.04).

Another dimension of this process of building leaders was SEWU's staffing strategy. Most social movements have a powerful, charismatic founder member. The role of such a founder in the longer-term trajectory of the organisation is an issue many organisations and movements face. SEWU is no different. Horn's exit strategy was discussed from when the union was first launched in 1994 and she withdrew from SEWU slowly but systematically, creating a space for new leadership to emerge. Originally SEWU employed staff with formal economy union experience. In more recent times, there were increasing numbers of staff who were originally members and had worked their way up the ranks. SEWU's national general secretary started in the organisation as a home-based worker. She became a leading strategist in the organisation. She negotiated with funders and lobbied government and represented SEWU in national and international forums. SEWU's president, a trader at the traditional medicine market in inner-city Durban, is another case in point. She is a formidable negotiator. Despite there being articulate male traders in the market, she chairs the traditional medicine market committee, the main point of contact between the council and the traders and heads a new development initiative aiming to address sustainability and marketing issues in the traditional medicine industry. This ability to build grassroots leadership is a particularly striking aspect of SEWU's history.

Financial Sustainability and Relationship with Donors

Financial sustainability was an ongoing challenge for SEWU. From inception, its approach was informed by a formal union logic that to be independent, unions have to be self-sufficient. SEWU members paid a joining fee of R10 and monthly subscriptions of R8. As a result of an organiser being robbed, as well as internal corruption, a decision was taken at the 1998 annual conference to move to a system of membership fees being paid by stop order and there was a big drive to assist members to get bank accounts. The banks, however, are notorious for being unwelcoming to poorer clients. There were cases of clients having insufficient funds to pay stop orders and the bank charged a R95 penalty, leading to some members accumulating large debts (Interview, Regional Organiser, 05.03.04). This obviously had implications for sustaining membership. SEWU experienced such significant problems with the stop order system that they reintroduced collecting subscription money by hand.

Since its inception, SEWU was dependent on donor funding and it was established with funding assistance from HIVOS. From early on funds from the international trade union movement were sought. This was part of a strategy to secure the acceptance of the principle of SEWU within the trade union movement. FNV Mondiaal, the Dutch Trade Union Federation's development wing, was SEWU's longest-standing and largest donor. More recently SEWU sourced funds from elsewhere. There were changes over time with respect to negotiating power with funders. In the mid-1990s there were occasions where SEWU declined funding overtures. In more recent times, SEWU struggled to secure funding and in 2003 they retrenched half of their staff due to funding shortages.

SEWU raised funds on the proviso that they were moving towards being financially self-sustaining. Donors like FNV, although very supportive of SEWU, were clear that the organisation had to demonstrate progress to this end. In reality little progress was made. Financial sustainability is likely to be an issue for any organisation of informal economy workers and this was a critical problem for the South African Domestic Workers' Union. Financial self-sustainability depends on sustaining and increasing membership. Members' incomes are at best precarious. SEWA's approach to this is informative. Their membership fees are only 5 rupees a year and some of their institutions, such as SEWA Bank, are now self-sustaining, which has been achieved through reaching scale.

International and Local Alliances

One of the issues raised in Chapter 1 is the role of transnational advocacy networks, which may lead movement activists in one country to appeal to actors beyond their borders to bring about domestic change. SEWU developed strong international alliances that gave the organisation an international profile that could be argued as disproportionate to its size. It was affiliated to several international trade unions and developed a number of regional links with trade unions and informal economy unions in southern Africa. SEWU also had a longstanding relationship with SEWA, which for many years has been active in international forums. There are also a number of international networks that both SEWU and SEWA were and are involved in – the research and advocacy network Women in Informal Employment Globalising and Organising (WIEGO); the international alliance of home-based workers or HomeNet; and more recently the international alliance of street traders or StreetNet (which SEWU's founder was instrumental in establishing). Partly through these international networks SEWU was involved in International Labour Organisation (ILO) policy processes – most notably the process on home-based work, which resulted in the 1996 Convention on Home Based Work and the 2002 International Labour Conference on decent work in the informal economy that in turn resulted in a significant shift in thinking about the informal economy. SEWU used experience gleaned from these international links partly as an internal training and consciousness-raising exercise, and to influence and lobby local players like the trade union movement and local governments. For example, in negotiations with local government increasing reference was made to ILO policy on the informal economy.

With respect to local alliances, given that SEWU saw itself as a workers' organisation, the focus of its attention was COSATU. From the beginning the founder stressed that it was strategically necessary to position SEWU and its aims within the broader trade union movement. This was in fact critical to SEWU securing funding from the international trade union movement. COSATU head office acknowledged SEWU from the outset but ironically only at the time of SEWU's closure did national staff pay much attention to this small union. Prior to this, national SEWU staff expressed much frustration at the numerous meetings they tried to schedule with COSATU head office staff, that were either cancelled or no one arrived. SEWU, however, worked alongside COSATU in the National Economic Development and Labour Council (NEDLAC) and on initiatives like the Financial Service Sector Campaign (FSSC). Regional SEWU staff reported that they had a good working relationship with COSATU at a regional level. With the exception of the Eastern Cape, all of SEWU's regions had some contact with COSATU affiliates. Cases were cited where affiliates shared office space and equipment and assisted SEWU with workshops and membership training.

SEWU had fairly limited contact with other social movements. The national office attended meetings of the Treatment Action Campaign and the Landless People's Movement once a month (Interview, General Secretary, 01.03.04). In SEWU's regions most contact was with non-governmental organisations like the Black Sash and women's organisations such as the Women on Farms Project, Network on Violence against Women and other organisations that deal with domestic violence and rape.

Relations with the State

SEWU's relations with the state tended to be framed in terms conventionally employed by unions – collective bargaining, negotiations and lobbying. In a context of worker organising where there is often no employer, the state frequently becomes the negotiation partner. As would be the case in a traditional union setting, although largely opting for negotiation and lobbying tactics, SEWU did not shy away from more adversarial acts like marching. SEWU's negotiations/ collective bargaining and policy lobbying activities were partly what distinguish it from many other social movements. The trends over time are detailed below.

From inception to the late 1990s, a significant focus of SEWU's activities was negotiations. With the high proportion of membership being street traders, most negotiations were with local government.[1] This was a period where local governments were trying to make sense of how to deal with street traders. The apartheid state's response to traders had largely been to violently remove them. During the transition new legislation was passed allowing street traders to operate. SEWU emerged during the period of local governments trying to re-regulate trading activities. Negotiations have largely focused on street trading by-laws and provision and regulation of infrastructure – water, toilets, shelter and storage facilities – as well services such as childcare and overnight accommodation. SEWU initiated and participated in both bilateral and joint forum negotiations with the town councils of Eshowe, Stanger and Matatiele regarding the regulation and provision of facilities for street traders. For example, in 1996 in Matatiele the local town council agreed to SEWU's demands for shelters for street traders. These shelters were completed during the course of the year. When they were built a number of male waged workers applied for the use of them, but through negotiations with the council SEWU ensured that existing street traders were given preference, thus preventing the women from being pushed aside (SEWU 1996: 4). In 1997 SEWU was also able to initiate bilateral and joint forum discussions regarding regulations and facilities for street traders in central Cape Town and Mitchell's Plain.

The city where most SEWU negotiations occurred and where there was greatest success was Durban. This is partly because of the predominance of SEWU membership operating as street traders in Durban in SEWU's earlier years. In 1994 SEWU negotiated with the Durban City Council to install water supplies and temporary toilet facilitates at points identified by members. In 1995 the Durban City Council started to formulate new street trading by-laws and SEWU was represented on all the relevant committees and forums. These initial engagements led to a sustained working relationship between SEWU and local government in Durban. Between 1995 and 1998, on the streets SEWU's elected trade leaders became recognised as representatives in different areas, providing channels for greater influence on decisions affecting their work and livelihood. SEWU also established monthly bilateral negotiations with the council and was successful at getting a number of specific issues onto the council's agenda, like overnight accommodation, storage and childcare facilities (SEWU 1996: 4). Shelters were built for traders throughout the inner city and a new market for traditional medicine traders was planned and started. Although SEWU was not solely responsible for these interventions, not only did it significantly contribute to the pressure to incorporate traders into city plans, but its sustained engagement ensured that interventions were appropriate to women traders' needs. (For detailed evidence see, for example, Nesvag's [2000] analysis of the role SEWU played in the redevelopment of the traditional medicine market.)

In parallel to the negotiations and collective bargaining, SEWU placed much emphasis on influencing policy at local and national level. At a local level, SEWU's efforts experienced most success in Durban. In 2000 Durban initiated a comprehensive informal economy policy process. Two researchers who had worked closely with SEWU since 1998 were employed to assist the city in developing the policy. In the policy consultation process SEWU staff were interviewed, membership consulted and SEWU, alongside the international alliance of street trader organisations or StreetNet, gave detailed written comments on the draft. The person responsible for drafting the policy noted how the experience of the SEWU commissioned research and SEWU input in the process informed her thinking (telephone conversation, 15.07.04). The policy was adopted by the Unicity Council in 2001. This policy is looked to as an international best practice (see Chen, Jhabvala and Lund 2002).

SEWU's interventions have doubtlessly contributed to securing a progressive policy approach to the informal economy in Durban. The founder and former general secretary, reflecting on the leadership role that Durban has come to play with respect to informal economy policy, argued that SEWU could take some credit for this. Although noting that there was a 'political moment' given that the ANC had been elected into power on the basis of improving the lives of the poor, SEWU provided the city councillors and bureaucrats with some pointers as to how to do this.

> [SEWU] showed [Durban City Council] a way of dealing with the working poor . . . which was not a small business approach . . . but an approach based on ongoing negotiation. SEWU gave them a route and a direction . . . [The Council] have now provided a much bigger developed model. SEWU certainly cannot take responsibility for all of it but I think SEWU's intervention within this process has been important. I think it was coup (Interview, 27.02.04).

SEWU's early years were marked by active engagement in the post-1994 flurry of national government policy-making. SEWU's agenda was to ensure the needs of those working in the informal economy were addressed. Written submissions to a number of different national government departments were made on, among other issues, the new Labour Relations Act (LRA); small business policy; rural financial services; gender sensitive budgeting and international migration. SEWU, by its own admission, experienced mixed success. It is noted, for example, that while its submission on the LRA was 'largely ignored', in the case of its submission on small business policy 'SEWU's less radical recommendations subsequently appeared in the White Paper' (SEWU 1996).

It is clear that both policy lobbying and negotiations have been less of a focus in recent years. There are, however, fewer policy processes than there were in the mid- to late 1990s. With respect to negotiation, there have been *ad hoc* negotiations with national government departments (welfare, agriculture), but not sustained negotiation relationships. This is likely to be due to a combination of factors. SEWU's membership changed over time and to more home-based workers than street trader members. There are fewer negotiation opportunities for home-based workers. For the remaining street trader members, there is less policy dynamism as the city's approaches have become more entrenched. Finally, the complex task of negotiation and collective bargaining in an informal economy context was a particular skill and focus of the first general secretary and since her departure, there was less capacity (and perhaps passion) among staff to engage in ongoing negotiation processes.

Social movements' engagements with the state fall on a continuum between in-system collaboration and out-of-system adversarial relations. As many studies in this volume demonstrate, a clear position on either end of the spectrum is rare and most movements incorporate a mix of strategies. Similarly, SEWU falls somewhere between the two extremes, moving up and down the continuum according to various contexts. SEWU's negotiation and lobbying cannot be described as collaboration, nor does it embark exclusively on adversarial strategies.

Skills Training and Education and Training

A key focus of SEWU's activities was membership training. It has been argued elsewhere that training those working in the informal economy has fallen through a national government policy gap (Devey, Skinner and Valodia 2003b). SEWU's role in enabling its members to access training was thus particularly important. It distinguished between skills training and education and training. Skills training referred to training in skills related to a member's income-generating activities and was accessed through externally accredited trainers with members contributing to cover costs. Education and training referred to training in broader empowerment and development issues. This training was conducted internally in workshops organised by SEWU and was free to all members.

SEWU had to work alongside trainers to ensure the training was appropriate to their members' needs in terms of training times, mode of delivery and course content. For example, it was critical that courses were offered part time, did not assume that participants were literate and that thought was given to childcare issues. One of the benefits of SEWU membership was that members were offered R500 worth of skills training annually. Although SEWU offered a wide range of skills training, its strategy was to encourage members, through its subsidy structure, to acquire skills in traditionally male-dominated areas of employment that often have far greater income-generating potential. With training in traditionally female skills, such as sewing, SEWU covered 50 per cent of the costs of training and members paid the remaining 50 per cent. For traditionally male-dominated areas of employment, such as wire fence making, block making and electrical wiring, SEWU paid 80 per cent of training costs with the members covering the remaining 20 per cent. There was thus a financial incentive for women to be trained in these areas (Interview, National Education Secretary, 18.02.04).

The coverage, range of skills offered and types of skills are noteworthy. From Table 12.1 it is clear that SEWU facilitated members to attend over 2 600 courses in a wide-ranging set of skills over the eight-year period for which there is information. Further, SEWU had some success in encouraging members to train in traditionally male-dominated skills. Of the total of 2 613 courses SEWU members attended, 879 were in areas that are dominated by men. The second

Table 12.1: SEWU skills training by type and numbers of members attending, 1995–2003.

	1995	1996	1997	1998	1999	2000	2001	2002	2003	Total
Sewing	106	53	68	52	95	80	33	26	1	514
Building		20	26	17	159	108	43	47	12	432
Glue appliqué	77	62		25	84	34			2	284
Poultry farming					104	88	24	6	45	267
Business skills			7	77	4	116		17	4	225
English/ABET	43	34	35	6	32	24	30		10	214
Catering					14	32	32	39		117
Wire fencing					54	46			16	116
Fashion design		44				7	4	4	37	96
Baking					48	11		1	10	70
Arts and crafts						12	7	11	14	44
Tourism						37				37
Driving					4	7	2	13	9	35
Childcare		8		4	3	8		15	2	40
Other	7	0	14	54	13	13	4	3	14	122
Total	233	221	150	235	614	623	189	182	166	2 613

Source: SEWU Annual Reports

most frequently attended course was in building (more specifically block making) and nearly 120 members were trained in wire fencing. There is clearly a trend over time for training in these kinds of skills – compare, for example, the trends over time in sewing courses and block making courses completed.

According to SEWU's financial statements, the union spent over R380 000 on skills training in eight years for which there is information. SEWU staff noted that it was increasingly difficult to secure donor funds for training. More recently SEWU was looking for ways to access government funding, particularly from the Department of Labour, for its skills programmes. This is another example of SEWU's attempts to engage with the state to leverage services for their members.

With respect to education and training, workshops were conducted at a branch level twice a year. Recently, due to financial difficulties, this training was conducted on a less regular basis. In terms of content, the training concentrated on five broad areas: workshops on building the organisation and organisational skills like lobby and negotiating skills; business skills training covering issues such as understanding the economy, business management and marketing, as well as savings and bank account management; understanding the law; workshops about sexual harassment and domestic violence; and workshops on health issues, specifically occupational health and HIV/AIDS. In 2001 SEWU employed a national education officer specifically to design and implement suitable training and education workshops.

The positive impact of both skills training and education and training was mentioned in interviews. A SEWU member in Durban said that she decided to become a member of SEWU because 'SEWU opens your mind and teaches you how to take care of yourself as a woman' (Interview, 15.03.04). SEWU training was identified by members as giving them greater financial self-sufficiency and confidence in their households and domestic relations. A SEWU craft seller and home-based producer said 'a lot has changed in my household since I've joined SEWU. I've helped my brother to pay *lobolo* [a payment to the bride's family before marriage] and I am now preparing to build my own house in Ntuzuma and buy furniture for this house' (Interview, 15.03.04). Another member said that SEWU had made her confident and enabled her not to rely on men. 'I can now pay school fees without asking for money from other people and can buy food to support my family' (Interview, 17.03.04).

SEWU's skills training and education and training services were an important and widely accessed service. Skills training assisted a significant number of members to better establish themselves in their work and opened up new opportunities. The education and training gave members the confidence and skills to be able to negotiate with different authorities and speak out for their rights.

Access to Credit and Savings Facilities

Both the Durban and Johannesburg surveys of those working in the informal economy found that firm owners identified access to credit as the key constraint to growth (Skinner 2003; Chandra and Rajaratnam 2001). There are few service providers willing to service this group as they are seen as risky and the transaction costs are high. Commercial banks see this group as unprofitable and the Department of Trade and Industry's interventions have up till now met with little success (Skinner 2000). Where credit institutions, like the international micro-finance organisation FINCA, do accommodate those working in the informal economy they tend to use group-lending techniques. Group lending devolves the risk of default to fellow group members who are often the least able to cope with it. In previous interviews with SEWU members it was noted that, for these reasons, they disliked the group-lending techniques (Skinner 2000: 13).

In a nine-year period SEWU facilitated access to loans for nearly 600 members (calculated from SEWU annual reports). SEWU's strategy was to work with existing institutions to make them more accessible to their members. Between 1994 and 1998 SEWU negotiated and worked with a number of different institutions. Through trial and error SEWU discovered that the Land Bank Step Up loan scheme was the most appropriate for those working in the informal economy. The Land Bank offers individual loans of between R250 and R6 000 in a graduated programme that allows recipients to progressively take out larger loans once they have paid back their previous loan. SEWU used the Land Bank almost exclusively from 1999 onwards.

In interviews with members, SEWU's facilitating access to credit was identified as a critical intervention. Land Bank loans have assisted a number of SEWU members to access capital to buy stock or items of equipment essential to their business. For example, a member from the Durban beachfront branch reported how a Land Bank loan enabled her to buy beads to make the jewellery she sold

(Interview, 01.03.04). Another SEWU member from a more rural branch, involved in a sewing project, was able to buy her sewing machine (Interview, 05.03.04).

There was a tendency for SEWU members, like others working in the informal economy, to identify access to credit as a blanket cure for all their problems. Access to credit is access to debt and, if not well managed, can lead to further hardship. When a business analysis is conducted, it is often found that other interventions are required to make the enterprise successful. SEWU was well aware of this and the general secretary articulated it as follows:

> When the business is not growing it's not that the business needs a loan. It's like a headache; if you have a headache it doesn't mean that you need a painkiller. You have to think about all the causes of the headache (Interview, 12.02.04).

SEWU combined access to credit with the training described above. There was also an emphasis on savings. The international literature, informed by the experience of institutions like the SEWA bank, is placing increasing emphasis on the importance of savings (Rutherford 1999). SEWU made important interventions in this regard, by its involvement in a campaign to reform commercial banks, and through its negotiations with Post Bank.

The Financial Service Sector Campaign (FSSC) is a campaign backed by the SACP, COSATU, the ANC and a number of non-governmental organisations. The campaign aims to transform financial institutions, making them accessible to poor people. According to the FSSC co-ordinator (Interview 29.06.04), SEWU played a key role in the campaign's work. She cited the example of the problems SEWU experienced while trying to implement the debit order system as being an important empirical base that the campaign used to strengthen its arguments. The campaign has experienced considerable success, particularly with respect to criteria for first-time bank account holders and penalty payments.

In 2003 SEWU's negotiations with the Department of Communications led to the union being involved in a Savings Campaign with Post Bank and the Department of Communications, which continued into 2004. The aim of this campaign was to assist SEWU members and informal traders at large to open savings accounts with Post Bank (Interview, General Secretary, 12.02.04). SEWU negotiated with Post Bank to ensure that its savings accounts were more suitably tailored to the needs and limitations of those in the informal economy. Bank charges are significantly less than those of the commercial banks. No minimum bank balance was required and empty accounts could be kept open for three months (Interview, General Secretary, 22.06.04).

It is thus clear that SEWU both facilitated access to credit for its members and contributed to more affordable and accessible savings for informal economy workers. These services still have some limitations, in contrast to the SEWA Bank, as they are not tailor-made to the needs of women who are informal economy workers. SEWA's banking services are likely to contribute to securing loyal membership. For institutions to provide credit and savings facilities to the poor, in a financially sustainable way, they need to reach scale, i.e. have large numbers of clients. SEWU did not manage to secure enough members to consider establishing their own bank. Ironically if SEWU had established a bank, members would have been less likely to lapse but SEWU could not provide such a service precisely because of lapsed membership.

Successes and Failures

The ten-year review of SEWU's structure, activities and achievements highlights some successes and failures. In terms of successes, through negotiations SEWU secured appropriate infrastructure, especially for street trader members. SEWU's interventions strengthened its members' income-earning capabilities by developing their existing livelihood activities (business skills training, access to credit, savings facilities) and opening new opportunities by, for example, retraining (especially in traditionally male-dominated occupations like block making). There has also been a broader empowerment of members, from knowing their legal rights to knowing how to conduct a meeting. SEWU developed a new group of formidable leaders and negotiators, through training and organisational experience. At a policy level, SEWU raised the visibility of women working in the informal economy locally (especially in Durban) and to some extent nationally and internationally. By organising only women, SEWU instilled a gender consciousness in members and led to gender-informed interventions. From the perspective of the labour movement, organisationally SEWU has set a precedent. SEWU successfully organised those working in the informal economy – an extremely difficult task. SEWU was run true to its constitution – a functioning membership-controlled organisation that built the capacity of its members.

In terms of failures, despite ten years of experience, SEWU was not able to reach scale. Membership numbers were low and lapsed membership became a terminal problem. Given the context where more and more South Africans are being forced to seek work in the informal economy, it is surprising that SEWU did not have more members. We attribute the problem of lapsed membership and the lack of sustained membership growth to a variety of factors. First, there were internal problems like cases of corruption that led to membership attrition. Second, although there were policy opportunities, SEWU operated in an environment that is often unaccommodating to the informal economy. Its experience with the commercial banks in instituting the stop order system is a case in point. More significantly, however, is that people working in the informal economy are mostly very poor and thus are forced to be prudent with their money. SEWU, in comparison to SEWA, did not offer members as comprehensive a set of support interventions. As noted above, ironically they were not able to do this because they did not have enough members. Membership numbers and support interventions to sustain membership are thus interrelated issues. A number of staff identified a problem with the ethos of the organisation where members saw SEWU as a 'charity' (i.e. an organisation offering handouts) rather than a trade union that belongs to them and was their responsibility to grow. This was partly a result of what some identified as recruiting shortcuts. The final problem was that of financial sustainability – SEWU was always dependent on donors.

Conclusion

Should SEWU be considered a social movement? In Chapter 1 social movements are defined as 'politically and/or socially directed collectives, often involving multiple organisations and networks, focused on changing one or more elements of the social, political and economic system in which they are located'. Tilly's definition of social movements as 'a series of demands or challenges to power holders in the name of a social category that lacks an established political position' is quoted.

In terms of objectives, SEWU focused on changing the environment in which its members operated and often challenged power holders in doing so. SEWU forged a collective identity; it united poorer women across political (and to a lesser extent racial barriers) around work-based issues. This was particularly remarkable in the KwaZulu-Natal branches in the early to mid-1990s at the time of the stark and often violent conflict between the ANC and Inkatha. Despite its founder being a well-known ANC Women's League member, SEWU had members who were Inkatha supporters – the long-standing support among some traditional medicine gatherers and traders being a case in point. On the basis of their objectives and this collective identity, those using a broad definition of social movements might be inclined to include SEWU. SEWU, however, did not have a high degree of popular participation nor a national profile. Although SEWU had strong relationships with other organisations – most notably SEWA in India – it did not involve multiple organisations or networks. It was formally constituted and explicitly saw itself as a union, a formation that Tilly defines social movements in contrast to. Therefore some may argue that SEWU was not a social movement.

Regardless of whether SEWU is regarded as a 'social movement' by those who seek to police the boundaries of the category, the SEWU case poses two challenges to many of the social movements that have emerged in the post-apartheid period – that of representation issues and gender. SEWU's democratic structures meant that there was a direct relationship between membership and representation. The organisation was structured to ensure that members were able to engage in political and policy processes themselves. Many social movements have yet to engage with these representational issues. Because there is not signed-up membership behind many social movements, there are no clear lines of representation and accountability, and it is easier for the leaders to talk on behalf of the poor, rather than as legitimate representatives of the poor. Further, SEWU had a specific gender agenda. The majority of supporters in many of the issue-driven social movements tend to be women, yet most of the leaders and strategic thinkers in these organisations continue to be men who do not position gender issues centrally. SEWU in contrast, as a union constituted specifically for women, had an empowering impact on members by allowing them to take up leadership roles that would often be filled by men in other organisations and to address the specific obstacles and bias that women face within market and government structures.

Note

1. For membership based in rural areas, there were cases in KwaZulu-Natal and the Eastern Cape of negotiations with traditional leaders, mainly about access to land.

References

Chandra,V. and B. Rajaratnam. 2001. 'Constraints to Growth and Employment in the Informal Sector: Evidence from the 1999 Informal Survey Firm'. Washington: World Bank.

Chen, M. 2001. 'Women in the Informal Sector: A Global Picture, the Global Movement'. SAIS Review XXI (1).

Chen, M., R. Jhabvala and F. Lund. 2002. 'Supporting Workers in the Informal Economy: A Policy Framework.' Paper prepared for the ILO task force on the informal economy. http://www.wiego.org.

Chen, M., R. Khurana and N. Mirani. 2004. 'Towards Women's Empowerment: The Impact of SEWA'. Unpublished draft.

Datta, R. 2003. 'From Development to Empowerment: The Self- Employed Women's Association in India'. *International Journal of Politics, Culture and Society* 16 (3).

Devey, R., C. Skinner and I. Valodia. 2003a. 'Informal Economy Employment Data in South Africa: A Critical Analysis'. Report prepared for the Employment Data Research Group, Human Sciences Research Council.

———. 2003b. 'Human Resource Development in the Informal Economy'. *Human Resource Development Biennial Directory*. Human Sciences Research Council.

Goldman, T. 2003. 'Organising in South Africa's Informal Economy: An Overview of Four Sectoral Case Studies'. Seed Working Paper No. 60. Geneva: International Labour Organisation.

International Labour Organisation (ILO). 2002. *Women and Men in the Informal Economy: A Statistical Picture*. Geneva: International Labour Office.

James, S. 1998. 'The Self-Employed Women's Union 1997 Membership Survey'. Durban: Self-Employed Women's Union.

Lund, F. and C. Skinner. 1999. 'Promoting the Interests of Women in the Informal Economy: An Analysis of Street Trade Organisations in South Africa'. CSDS Research Report No. 19. Durban: University of Natal.

Lund F., J. Nicholson and C. Skinner. 2000. *Street Trading*. Durban: University of Natal.

Marias, H. 1998. *South Africa: Limits to Change: The Political Economy of Transformation*. London: Zed Books.

Michie, J. and V. Padayachee. 1997. *The Political Economy of South Africa's Transition: Policy Perspectives in the late 1990s*. London: Dryden.

Nesvag, S. 2000. 'Street Trading From Apartheid to Post-Apartheid: More Birds the Cornfield?'. *International Journal of Sociology and Social Policy* 20 (3/4).

Rutherford, S. 1999. 'The Poor and their Money: An Essay about Financial Services for Poor People'. http://www.uncdf.org/mfdl/readings/PoorMoney.pdf.

Self-Employed Women's Association (SEWA). 2002. Annual Report 2002.

Self-Employed Women's Union (SEWU). 1994. The Constitution (last amended 2001).

———. Annual Reports – 1995; 1996; 1997; 1998; 1999; 2000; 2001; 2002; 2003.

Skinner, C. 2000. 'Securing Livelihoods: A Gendered Analysis of Support Interventions available to Street Traders in the Durban Metropolitan Area'. CSDS Research Report No. 34. Durban: University of Natal.

———. 2003. 'Constraints to Growth and Employment in the Greater Durban Metropolitan Area: Evidence from Informal Economy Survey'. Paper prepared for the World Bank and the Durban Unicity Council.

Standing, G. 1999. *Global Labour Flexibility: Seeking Distributive Justice*. London: MacMillan Press.

Statistics South Africa. 2004. Labour Force Survey, September 2003. Statistical Release PO210.

Thulare, P. 2004. 'Trading Democracy? Johannesburg Informal Traders and Citizenship'. Centre for Policy Studies, *Policy: Issues and Actors* 17 (1).

Valodia, I. 2001. 'Economic Policy and Women's Informal Work in South Africa'. *Development and Change* 32.

Vaux, T. and F. Lund. 2003. 'Working Women and Security: Self Employed Women's Association's Response to Crisis'. *Journal of Human Development* 4 (2).

Interviews

FSSC Co-ordinator, 29.06.04.

Horn, Pat. SEWU Founder, 27.02.04.

SEWU General Secretary, 12.02.04; 01.03.04; 22.06.04.

SEWU Member, 15.03.04.

SEWU Member, 16.03.04.

SEWU Member, 17.03.04.

SEWU National Education Secretary, 18.02.04.

SEWU Regional Organiser, 05.03.04.

13

From Economic Debt to Moral Debt

The Campaigns of Jubilee South Africa

Cyrus Rustomjee

We are a coalition, a network, an organisation, a movement. As long as we are a nascent formation, these things will tend to live together. Maybe in the future, the organisational tendency will tend to become more dominant, requiring a new definition of ourselves (Interview, Giyose, 07.10.04).

JUBILEE SOUTH AFRICA (JSA) is a growing new social movement, established as part of wider global Jubilee movement, representing 'not only a call for total, unconditional cancellation of developing countries' odious debts . . . but about general economic justice' (Gabriel in Ballenger 1999). This chapter seeks to trace the evolution of JSA, and its emergence from a global debt-based campaign, into a movement for broader global social and economic justice, yet with a distinctly South African flavour. In outlining JSA's objectives, activities, and alliances, the chapter aims to better understand how such a movement is forged and sustained. In particular, this chapter examines the movement's ties to anti-apartheid struggles, its relationship with government in democratic South Africa, and its relationship with wider Jubilee movements around the world.

Was JSA a domestically inspired social movement? The chairperson of JSA clarifies: 'JSA was really of native origin, in the sense that the problem of South African debt began to engage us before JSA was formed' (Interview, Giyose, 07.10.04). From mid-1997, a nucleus of individuals, largely based in Cape Town, pursued work on establishing the intellectual framework for a local Jubilee movement, culminating in JSA's launch the following year. George Dor, central to the establishment of JSA in 1998, observes:

... by 1998, there was a certain sense of concern around the post-1994 transition – concern with budgets, with social policies, with GEAR. At that stage there was no organisational structure to capture the issue. JSA stepped into that set of discussions and created a vehicle to discuss the apartheid debt issue, as a key obstacle to release the resources for development. JSA was also established as a platform to discuss macro-economic policy (Interview, Dor, 08.10.04).

JSA's focuses at its launch were multiple. Its founding statement cites apartheid debt, macro-economic policy, the international debt campaign, the implications of apartheid debt in southern Africa, and issues of economic and social justice as the areas in which JSA would work. Hence, while clearly inspired by local struggles, the movement would retain from the outset, as one element of its agenda, a focus on the international debt campaign.

Since its establishment, JSA has exhibited characteristics variously akin to an organisation, a network, a campaign and a movement. As it has grown and its campaigns broadened, JSA has assumed more formal organisational characteristics. The movement has its own National Executive Committee (NEC), comprising nine elected officials, who meet as often as necessary, and a National Council, comprising the NEC as well as two officials from each province, which meets three times a year. In addition to its national campaign, JSA has established branches throughout South Africa. As of September 1999, it had established organisational structures in eight provinces, and was expanding into the Northern Province (Ashley 1999). At the provincial level, members are elected to the Provincial Executive Committee.

The gradual shift toward a more defined organisational structure has been both difficult, with respect to the coalition that inspired JSA's establishment, and uneven, with the provincial structures evolving at different paces. Giyose explains that, at the launch of JSA, an executive committee was established, '[t]hen all the coalition partners went back. The NGOs went back to do development; the women's organisations went back to mobilise for women's issues; the youth organisations went back to work on youth issues. And the executive remained, holding the can. They did what executives would do first, which was to establish provincial organisations all around South Africa' (Interview, Giyose, 07.10.04).

Its status as a coalition has also meant that JSA has frequently grappled with the challenge of determining the rights and interests of the various partners. Some of JSA's campaigns have not always been fully supported by all coalition partners. Particularly strong divergences have arisen within the movement with regard to the issue of the reparations campaign, detailed below. Some, particularly church-based coalition partners, have perceived JSA's position to be excessively contrary to that of the South African government. As the chairperson of JSA notes:

> . . . [t]he reasons are probably connected with the politics of our country. The main issue has been the litigation issue, with some partners being influenced from the top to persuade JSA to change course . . . Government has a lot of influence over COSATU, less over the affairs of the churches. Yet the churches have strong connections with government (Interview, Giyose, 07.10.04).

While the different views regarding litigation have been significant, 'there is not a single coalition partner who wants to stay out of the movement' (Interview, Giyose, 07.10.04).

To cope with these evolving challenges, a dialogue emerged within the movement as to whether it should begin to assume the form of a formal organisation, rather than a coalition. As the provincial structures have established themselves, they have begun to establish campaigns in their own right; and have come to exert a stronger influence on the movement. A national planning strategy was developed in 2002, culminating in a decision to preserve the full rights of the coalition partners, while also recognising the growing influence of the provincial structures and their campaigns. As Dor notes, '[a]t the end, it was decided that we would be a bit of each of these' (Interview, Dor, 08.10.04). The planning strategy also observed that provincial preferences had emerged in the four years since the launch of JSA, which had not been fully recognised by the national structure. Consequently, provincial strategies have been developed, outlining the individual preferences and objectives of the various provinces. The exercise had revealed that the provincial structures differ from one another in terms of organisational capacity, focus and the nature of their campaigns.

JSA's support base has been closely reflective of its initial coalition character and has relied on an extensive network of support, both in terms of finance and campaigning. 'By far the most important groupings in terms of initial support were the faith-based groupings. There would not have been a JSA without their support' (Interview, Rudin, 04.10.04). Rudin notes that the support provided by faith-based organisations was both logistical and financial. This was particularly the case at the launch of JSA, when several key office bearers were seconded from the faith-based organisations to work full time on establishing JSA. Reliance on financial support has continued: '[f]aith-based finance remains a very important source' (Interview, Rudin, 04.10.04).

Since 1998, however, JSA's 'support base now is less faith-based'. We have come to rely more on other social movements, particularly for campaigning' (Interview, Rudin, 04.10.04). This support varies, depending on the theme and geographical location. For example, in the Free State, the provincial branch of JSA has been closely allied with a range of other environmental groups in campaigning for environmental justice, particularly focusing on the mining sector and the issue of ecological degradation (Interview, Nthako, 15.10.04), while the Gauteng provincial branch has jointly campaigned with the Soweto Electricity Crisis Committee (SECC) and more recently waged a campaign against the presence of the International Monetary Fund (IMF) and the World Bank (WB) in South Africa (SAPA 2004).

As a new social movement in South Africa, working to build an ' "Africa Consensus" on development for the continent' (Ashley 1999), JSA has received widespread domestic support since its launch, from such groups as the National Progressive Primary Health Care Network (NPPCHN), the Environmental Justice Networking Forum (EJNF) and the Environmental Monitoring Group (EMG), the latter two working particularly closely with the Free State provincial branch of JSA. JSA has also collaborated consistently with the Khulumani Support Group (KSG) and the Alternative Information and Development Centre (AIDC).

'Surely we have not forgotten the great wonders mass struggles can achieve?' (Harvey 1999). JSA has used a wide variety of modes of action, participation and protest. These have included small street protests, mass protests, contributing to the organisation of large national conferences (on reparations, for instance), objecting to the South African government's proposal in 2001 to borrow from the World Bank to finance hospital restructuring in South Africa (Dor 2001b), assisting in launching a major lawsuit in the US to seek reparations against multilateral corporations that transacted business in South Africa during the apartheid era (discussed below), and supporting other social movements in South Africa in their objectives. As Nthako states, 'you need to engage all the emerging international dimensions . . . viz. environmental, gender, democratic, working class, and gays and lesbian' (Interview, Nthako, 15.10.04).

Relationship with other Jubilee Movements

Two international Jubilee movements, the Jubilee 2000 Coalition (J2000) and Jubilee South (JS), have been influential in the development of JSA, although their objectives differed markedly. 'The Jubilee 2000 Coalition [did] not seek to write off every penny owing on 31 December 1999. Rather, it [sought] to have the inert, unpayable backlog of debt written off, and debts reduced to a level which [would] permit sustainable human, environmental and economic development' (Pettifor 1998: 121).

By contrast, the launch of JS marked a significant shift in the terms of discourse pertaining to developing country debt issues. The launch was marked by a strong sense among supporters of the new movement that J2000 and the multilateral debt relief initiatives that had been initiated by the large industrial countries – which came to be known as the Heavily Indebted Poor Country (HIPC) Debt Initiatives – had not adequately reflected the interests of the South, and that there was a need for a new movement espousing the needs and realities of majority world countries. 'We cannot . . . confine our Jubilee advocacy to the terms and framework largely dictated by the paradigm of debt. Rather, we are compelled to speak from the perspective of those who suffer the consequences of debt domination' (Jubilee South 2000).

With the objective of articulating a united position and agenda on the establishment of a broader South-South process (Jubilee South n.d.), 'Jubilee . . . is not a demand for relief or for cancellation. It is a demand for the respect for rights and human dignity' (Bandaña 1999). This process would include debt cancellation as a part of its objectives, but not as the sole purpose.

> We are not undertaking these campaigns and making these demands as short-term and single-issue events in isolation from broader struggles. We are only too aware that the forces that damaged us in the past can return to damage us again . . . We need to move beyond this system to one in which the upliftment of the lives of the poor takes centre stage.

This includes delivering on people's entitlement to jobs, land, food security, water, electricity, housing, transport, education, health and social security. But it is also far more than this. It is also about workers and the marginalised across the world coming together in social movements and political organisations and taking the lead in shaping their own future ('Reparations Towards Another World' 2001).

In general, however, JSA's stance since its launch has closely followed that of JS. JSA has focused on debt cancellation, not debt relief, its campaigns represent broader struggles for economic and social justice, and its objectives are more closely akin to those of JS.

Sustainability, while important in focusing on the impact that debt was having on poor countries and their capacity to attend to the basic needs of their people especially in the fields of education, health and social welfare, tended to deflect attention from the unequal and unjust relations that underpinned the indebtedness of Third World countries. Sustainability does not consider questions like what was the debt used for, who contracted the debt and on whose behalf, who benefited from and who suffered as a result (Ashley 2003).

Driving the distinction between illegitimate and unsustainable debt has enabled JSA to define its own specific framework and basis for struggle and to differentiate itself from J2000. Highlighting and building upon the concepts of illegitimacy and odiousness provided the catalyst for defining a new body of debt and past historical obligations and contracts more directly relevant to the South African case. Focusing on illegitimacy and odiousness also proved analytically convenient, enabling a cluster of concepts to be brought to bear – the historical concept of Jubilee, international norms of justice and morality, and restitution and international juridical precedents.

The shift in discourse, from sustainability to illegitimacy, has also served other purposes. Propelled by the South African case, the focus on the illegitimacy and odiousness of debt has offered the broader international Jubilee movement a new focus for action, providing a bridge from the time-bound J2000 campaign, to the broader and far more ambitious transformatory objectives pursued by JS; JSA has established and defined for itself a new agenda that has fed back into an international social movement.

A number of authors, including Della Porta and Tarrow (2005) and Keck and Sikkink (1998), have emphasised the importance of transnational advocacy networks and identities, which have contributed to strengthening local social movements. In the case of JSA, a local social movement, transnational advocacy networks have indeed proved important in supporting the domestic agenda of JSA; but JSA has taken these processes further, by defining and establishing new aspects of struggle, including its work on odious debt and on reparations, which have fed back into global social movements.

JSA and Apartheid Debt

> We're calling for the cancellation of apartheid debt, the reimbursement of debts already paid by democratic South Africa, and the return of company profits made during apartheid in the form of reparation payments. Reparations should also be paid to the people of southern Africa, who also suffered under apartheid (Gabriel in Rodoreda 2002).

Apartheid debt is considered to constitute the indebtedness incurred by pre-democratic-era apartheid governments in South Africa, and in other southern African countries. 'Our argument in the local chapter of Jubilee 2000 is that the apartheid government was undemocratic and that much of the money it borrowed was used to beef up its military power in order to conduct cross-border raids into Lesotho, Botswana, Mozambique, Swaziland, and Zimbabwe in pursuit of South African citizens who had sought refuge in those countries. Those loans did not benefit ordinary South Africans' (Mofokeng 2000). JSA argues that 'the loans made by the apartheid government were not used by the white apartheid government to uplift the living standards of its black section of the population, but to stamp its authority in the region [and] suppress the emerging struggle . . . for freedom' (Interview, Nthako, 15.10.04), and that the current democratic government, in accepting an obligation to repay such debt, is legitimising an illegitimate obligation.

In this way, JSA argues that the debts incurred during the apartheid era are odious. As Gabriel states, 'if there ever was an odious debt', it was that acquired under apartheid (Gabriel in Keeton 1998). The Doctrine of Odious Debt suggests that a debt has to meet two criteria to be odious: it must be contrary to the needs and wishes of the population; and creditors must recognise that the loans they provide have been acquired by illegitimate regimes for their own very narrow advantage (Ashley 2003; Khalfan, King and Thomas 2003). 'If apartheid was a crime against humanity, is the debt inherited from that terrible system not equally criminal? . . . We cannot allow our country to be held accountable for debt which we not only did not incur, but which was incurred to be used against us' (Harvey 1999).

The debt is also considered to be substantial, with JSA asserting that the stock of debt inherited from the apartheid era aggregates US$26 billion. Because of its magnitude, the stakes are high: 'If the campaign succeeds, it will release funds to enable the government to fulfil its promises to the electorate: accelerating delivery, poverty reduction, and job creation' (Harvey 1999). The campaign argues, for example, that reducing the interest servicing of approximately R40 billion on South Africa's national debt would free resources for social services. This is considered particularly appropriate because of the tight fiscal policies and in the context of the Growth, Employment and Redistribution (GEAR) macro-economic strategy of the post-1994 government. The argument has been consistently used to lobby support for the objective of unilateral debt cancellation.

In further arguing for the cancellation of apartheid debt, JSA asserts that adequate – indeed unnecessarily large – profits have already been made by creditors and, moreover, that there is a moral and conceptual linkage between apartheid reparations and compensation to victims of the holocaust: '[t]he World Bank and Pretoria's other international creditors made excellent profits from apartheid loans, and we won't allow them to dawdle for 50 years before repaying our democratic society, the way Swiss banks did with holocaust victims' (Giyose and Dor 2001). As Archbishop Ndungane states, 'We cannot wait 50 years [for reparations] like the victims of the holocaust' (KSG 2003).

The Government's Response to Apartheid Debt Cancellation

Crucial to the outcome of the campaign to cancel apartheid-era debt has been the government's stance. Initially, JSA adopted a cautiously optimistic approach, expecting tacit government support. As Dor notes, '[a]s we were calling for the cancellation of the debt, we wanted the quiet support of government' (Interview, Dor, 08.10.04).

While JSA recognised that the post-apartheid South African government would be in a difficult position in publicly accepting the validity of the debt cancellation argument, and that financial markets were likely to be adversely affected, at least initially, by governmental endorsement of the claim, to JSA such reasoning did not justify the lack of state support for 100 per cent debt cancellation. '[I]f our government's fears are well-founded, if it is the faceless financial markets, the selfish profit-seekers from abroad who ultimately tell our government what to do, then the struggle for national liberation has still to be won' (Ashley 1999). JSA also made sure to remind the democratically-elected ANC government of its apartheid-era debt position: that, in the 1980s, the ANC 'publicly condemned the banks' role in rescheduling the debt as an act of inhumanity and said that "when the time comes, the South African people will not be unmindful of the role of banks in making profit out of the misery of our people"' (Ashley 1999).

Clearly JSA hoped that a neutral stance would prevail, in which government neither committed itself publicly to the debt cancellation campaign nor rejected it. These hopes have been dashed. Government, through the National Treasury (NT), has rejected the claim that apartheid-era debt should be cancelled, challenged the claim that apartheid debt exists, and proclaimed that apartheid debt represents, if anything, a portion of the country's external indebtedness, asserting that '[f]oreign debt is only 5% of our total debt and most of this was borrowed after 1994' (in Rodoreda 2002); and that foreign debt accumulated by apartheid government's aggregates is 'at most 1% of government debt' (Kganyago in Eveleth 1998). With the largest share of foreign obligations argued to have been assumed after 1994, the NT's argument is that there is no apartheid debt (Ashley 2003).

Furthermore, if apartheid debt is defined to include domestic debt, the NT argues that there are valid arguments against its cancellation. When the claim to cancel apartheid debt was initially made in 1998, approximately a fifth of all government debt was held by private insurers (Kganyago in Eveleth 1998). The NT argues that cancelling the government's obligations to these private insurers would result in the cancellation of the 'investment of ordinary people who hold insurance policies' (Kganyago in Eveleth 1998).

Dor, citing the examples of Poland, which received debt cancellation, and more recently Iraq, which is seeking cancellation, observes that 'even within GEAR it is easy to maintain debt cancellation and still retain investor confidence' (Interview, Dor, 08.10.04). Giyose further notes that the NT has most recently accepted the principle of debt cancellation in the case of Iraq and that the same principle should inevitably apply to post-apartheid South Africa: '[t]he government appears to be half understanding the issue and half not' (Interview, Giyose, 07.10.04). Rudin observes that '[o]ur government's policy was desperate to attract foreign investment and anything like debt cancellation was seen as counter to that imperative' (Interview, Rudin, 04.10.04).

The Cancellation of Developing Country Debt

While failing to gain government support for the cancellation of apartheid debt, initially JSA appeared to be gaining government's support for debt cancellation elsewhere. At JSA's launch, the tone was upbeat, with JSA perceiving government to be directly supportive of the objective of debt cancellation:

> [d]emocratic South Africa has shown them (industrial country creditors) the way. Notwithstanding its own financial constraints, it cancelled the odious debts of Namibia incurred under South African occupation. In doing so, the ANC government did not consider whether unilateral debt cancellation could be 'afforded'; nor did it impose adjustments or other preconditions on its neighbour (Jubilee 2000 South Africa 1998).

Indeed, indirect support appeared to be forthcoming from the ANC parliamentary caucus for the call for international debt cancellation.

Subsequently, differences have arisen regarding the proposed scope of international debt cancellation. JSA has called for outright and complete cancellation of developing country debt, while government has supported the Enhanced HIPC Initiative. As Dor stated in response to the Initiative, '[t]here is progress, but we are a long way from victory on debt relief' (in Eveleth 1999). Harvey puts it more bluntly, stating, 'In the face of the enormous poverty, starvation and death in this country, Africa and the entire Third World rescheduling of debt or minor debt relief is a miserable concession. Total debt cancellation, which is not what President Thabo Mbeki called for . . . is the only appropriate remedy' (Harvey 1999).

From Apartheid Debt to Apartheid Reparations

More recently, the claim that apartheid-era debt should be cancelled has moderated and JSA has shifted strategic focus toward a second campaign – reparations for the victims of apartheid. In part, this may be due to recognition that the quantum of debt specifically contracted during the apartheid period, either by the South African government or by governments in southern Africa, is diminishing and being replaced by new debt instruments. As Ashley observes, '[a]s you may know, most of the apartheid debt has now been repaid. This has necessitated a shift in strategy by JSA' (Ashley 2003).

The passage of time and the diminution in the quantum of loans embraced by the original loan obligations has presented a significant challenge to JSA, as if there are no debts left to cancel, so a major platform of JSA is removed and its debt-related objectives and campaigns are obliged to focus on debt cancellation elsewhere. JSA's response has been to recognise this potential challenge and to devise a new strategy, focusing on reparations. The shift does not represent an abandonment of the claim for cancellation, and indeed is considered to be part of a logical progression in campaigning. As Rudin observes, '[r]eparations was presented as early as 1997 as one form of debt cancellation' (Interview, Rudin, 04.10.04). Furthermore, the linkage between debt and reparations offers important advantages for JSA:

> [l]inking debt and reparations simultaneously avoids duplication and potential divisiveness. Furthermore, the linkage ensures that each campaign concurrently builds on and strengthens the other so that the combined campaign exerts sufficient influence for each one to be taken seriously (Ashley 2003).

This strategy has been useful for JSA, providing an opportunity to shift focus at a moment when the national government has proved unwilling to accept JSA's claims regarding apartheid-era debt. This has enabled JSA to maintain momentum as well as both domestic and international support, while at the same time retaining the ability to resuscitate the claim for debt cancellation. It has also enabled JSA to ensure that a historically solid support base, the international anti-apartheid movement, does not disappear as the apartheid debt claim winds down. 'One of Jubilee's strengths in its apartheid debt campaign has been its ability to draw on the international anti-apartheid movements that played such an important role in the defeat of apartheid. The solidarity provided by these international groups can be expected in support of Jubilee's reparations campaign' (Ashley 2003).

That JSA has not abandoned, but essentially shifted its strategy is illustrated by the sentiment expressed by JSA's chairperson when referring to the issue of apartheid debt: 'Mr Manuel has never wanted to sit at a table to have a discussion. The days are coming when he or his successor will do so' (Interview, Rudin, 04.10.04).

Apartheid Reparations
US Litigation

> In this claim, we express our commitment to the future of apartheid's victims, to the protection of human rights, and to the rule of law (ARDC 2002b).

In the year of its launch, JSA embarked on an Apartheid Debt and Reparations Campaign (ADRC). The Reparations campaign can be summed up by its slogans 'Won't pay for Apartheid Twice! Cancel the Apartheid Debt!' (Ashley 1999), and 'Apartheid is ended, Mandela is free, sanctions are finished. But the people of the region cannot celebrate, because they are being asked to pay a second time for apartheid' (Hanlon 1998).

In late 2002, JSA, through the ADRC, and the KSG, instituted legal proceedings (KSG 2003). A US attorney, Michael Hausfeld, was engaged to proceed with the claims on behalf of the ADRC (ADRC 2002b). The purpose was to seek reparations from a group of banks and international corporations that conducted business in South Africa during the apartheid period and which were accused of having incurred secondary liability for the system of apartheid by having aided and abetted the system ('Summary of the Complaint' n.d.). The ADRC and KSG asserted that the lawsuits were filed 'after four years of failed attempts to get multi-national banks and businesses that propped up the apartheid state to account for their "odious profiteering"' (ADRC 2002b).

> The corporations aided and abetted a crime against humanity whose persistent social damage requires urgent repair . . . They made massive profits while the suffering of the victims of apartheid intensified. The banks and businesses have consistently ignored our attempts to engage in discussion about their role in supporting broad social programmes for the reconstruction and development of affected communities and in compensating specific individuals for the damage that the corporations made possible (ADRC 2002b).

The actual claimants cited in the lawsuit are individual members of the KSG, as well as the group itself, all of whom claim to have suffered injuries resulting from recognised categories of violations of customary international law. A third group of litigants in US courts has comprised a group of South Africans living in Connecticut, in the US, who claim to have been victims of apartheid.

Why the Litigation has been Pursued

The ADRC argues that there have been several opportunities, none of which have been taken up, for the relevant banks and corporations to seek amnesty from prosecution (ADRC 2002a). The first opportunity was the Truth and Reconciliation Commission (TRC), a key finding of whose final report is the direct assigning of blameworthiness to businesses operating during the apartheid period:

> Business was central to the economy that sustained the South African
> state during the apartheid years. Certain businesses, especially the mining
> industry, were involved in helping to design and implement apartheid
> policies. Other businesses benefited from cooperating with the security
> structures of the former state. Most businesses benefited from operating
> in a racially structured context ('Summary of the Complaint' n.d.).

The ADRC argues that despite this observation, none of the banks and corporations facing litigation came forward at the time of the TRC hearings. The ADRC acknowledges that the TRC provided opportunities for individual not institutional amnesty, but argues that 'this should not have precluded foreign corporations and banks to come forward and reveal their complicity with the Apartheid regime' (Abrahams 2002).

JSA notes that the second opportunity to come forward was presented by JSA's Cancel the Apartheid Debt campaign, which provided a clear opportunity for banks and corporations operating during the apartheid period to acknowledge their co-operation with the apartheid regime and to cancel their debts 'as an act of reparation in favour of the people of South Africa' (ADRC 2002a).

The extent of the claim for reparations lodged by the ADRC and KSG is significant, with the plaintiffs claiming the combined value of all loans made by

US banks and companies to the apartheid state, including the value of all loans already repaid, as well as the profits made by these institutions from these loans (Ashley 2003).

The ADRC statement emphasised that insufficient contributions had been made by South African corporations toward reparation funds for the victims of apartheid. While these corporations were complicit in and benefited from apartheid – '[t]hose that helped the apartheid government do its dirty work should be made to pay' (Mosikare in Friedman 2003) – the statement urged that the corporations be engaged through processes of national dialogue within the framework of the TRC. For South African corporations, reparations should be forthcoming through a process of dialogue and only as a last resort through court proceedings: '[w]hile we hope that SA corporations will consider dialogue, if there is no willingness on their part to do so, then Khulumani could consider adding SA corporations to its list of defendants' (Gabriel in Financial Services Correspondent 2003).

Clearly, JSA, the ADRC and KSG sought to adopt a dual strategy: foreign corporations would continue to be pursued through the courts while South African corporations would be pursued initially through dialogue. Firstly, South African corporations are likely to have been perceived to be more amenable to the provision of reparations and more likely to respond to dialogue. Archbishop Ndungane discusses how the lawsuits were filed out of 'sheer frustration' after calls for dialogue were not taken seriously (in SAPA 2003). Secondly, there is likely to have been some concern about the legal costs involved. Thirdly, both JSA and the ADRC are likely to have identified an opportunity to emphasise their broader intent to contribute to consensual approaches to societal change. Indeed, the latter reason appears to be discernible from the media statement: '[s]uch engagement will go a long way to avoid the negative consequences of long legal battles. It will also contribute to building a broad national consensus towards a new South African society, which the lawsuits cannot achieve in isolation' (ADRC 2003).

The Domestic Struggle for Reparations

While the US litigation by KSG does not include South African corporations, JSA makes it clear that domestic corporations share the blame. 'We call upon business, both local and foreign, to acknowledge their complicity in making profit out of apartheid and of protecting the regime for all but, in some instances, the terminal years of apartheid' (Giyose 2003).

JSA has also made specific demands on South African corporations, insisting that they enter into dialogue with the movement and other stakeholders, 'with a view to making contributions to a debt and reparations fund' (Giyose 2003). Reparations include not only monetary compensation, but also educational, human rights, justice, redistributive, and transformative dimensions as well (Giyose 2003).

Recently, there has been growing frustration at what the movement considers to be a lack of progress. In late 2003, the movement launched a new component of its domestic reparations strategy, involving the initiation of community-level hearings, at which communities express and define the scale and nature of reparations they feel are likely to adequately address the damage caused to them under apartheid. The process is envisaged to culminate in a People's Tribunal.

Government's Response

Government's response has focused on two issues: its response to the US lawsuits and its decision in respect of the compensation of the victims of apartheid, following the release of the final TRC report. In respect of the lawsuits, it has rejected these, refused to be a party to them and refused to accept any verdict that would compel government to act.

Instead it has asserted a pre-eminent claim to represent the sovereign interests of the country, with Minister of Justice and Constitutional Development Penuell Maduna sending an unsolicited affidavit directly to the US court, asserting the government's position that the lawsuits undermine South African sovereignty and asking the relevant courts not to adjudicate in the suits and instead to dismiss them (SAPA 2003). As Maduna stated, '[o]nce we decide international courts should decide for us, we impair our sovereignty and proclaim we are subservient to those countries' (in SAPA 2003). Elsewhere, President Mbeki has stated, '[w]e consider it completely unacceptable that matters that are central to the future of our country should be adjudicated in foreign courts' (in Friedman 2003).

By contrast, Khulumani's executive director, Ike Tlholwe, states, '[t]here is no intention of diminishing or nullifying the sovereignty of the government but rather a willingness to work with the rulers that we lived and died to put in office' (KSG 2003). The unsolicited affidavit was regarded as particularly antagonistic by JSA, and government was accused of interfering in the court process (Dor 2003).

Regarding compensation for apartheid victims, the TRC and JSA, on the one hand, and the government on the other, have differed significantly on the extent of compensation that should be granted to victims of apartheid. In its final report, the TRC recommended that victims be paid a total of R3 billion. To achieve this, the TRC recommended that government introduce a wealth tax on South African businesses to contribute to the payment for reparations. The government responded by indicating that it would pay R30 000 each (or about a fifth of the amount contained in the TRC's recommendations) (Zuma in Terreblanche 2004) to approximately 19 000 victims of apartheid identified by the TRC, with an aggregate compensation of R571.5 million (Mbeki in Wanneburg and Chege 2003). The government also rejected the TRC's recommendation to introduce a wealth tax, arguing that it would damage investor confidence (Sebelebele 2003).

JSA has criticised government for abandoning the victims of apartheid and having usurped the right of victims to speak for themselves: '[t]he TRC process will have given far more to perpetrators than to victims . . . Victims are still marginalised and socially excluded and are struggling to rebuild their lives. They do not accept the argument that the improvement of general infrastructure in the country is equivalent to the direct assistance they were promised' (KSG 2003).

Campaigns for Broader Economic and Social Justice

As observed by the movement's national secretary, JSA was established as part of wider global Jubilee movement, and that movement represents 'a call for economic justice' (Gabriel in Ballenger 1999). Along with many other new social movements, JSA cites an array of government policies to make the claim that there has been a decisive shift away from pro-poor policies toward a neo-liberal approach. Dor cites GEAR as a major reason for South Africa's public health crisis, stating, in reference to the proposed World Bank loan for public healthcare, '[t]he World Bank wrote the section in GEAR on cutting funds for social expenditure and ensured that this was implemented. Therefore, the government is turning to the same institution largely responsible for the crisis to bail us out' (Dor 2001b); there is 'no use asking the arsonist to put out the fire' (Giyose and Dor 2001).

The movement recognises the close nexus between debt, macro-economic policy, and basic needs, noting, 'Jubilee structures throughout the country have a lot of work to do to make the link between debt, GEAR and people's needs more tangible to workers and the poor and to develop a broad support base for the campaign' (Dor 2001a).

Consequently, throughout its campaigns, debt has been deployed as an instrument, not an end in itself: '[f]or those of us who were at the forefront of the formulation of Jubilee, the taking up of the issue of apartheid debt was a means by which we could expose and challenge this shift to neoliberalism and facilitate the coming into existence of a broader movement that could start challenging not just the apartheid debt but also neoliberalism' (Ashley 2003).

There have been several specific methods of intervention, including in particular working closely with the Congress of South African Trade Unions (COSATU), the South African Council of Churches (SACC) and the South African NGO Coalition (SANGOCO) in support of a People's Budget: 'A People's Budget entails the scrapping of the apartheid debt and appropriate levels of taxation for companies and higher income earners, thus releasing resources for social expenditure sufficient to meet people's basic needs and to stimulate the creation of jobs in the process' (People's Budget Coalition 2004). This involves continual work in making connections between debt, the budget, privatisation, and HIV/AIDS ('Jubilee South Meetings' 2004).

The movement's approach to contesting the arms deal has followed a similar approach, opting to work in conjunction with a broad group, in particular the Coalition Against Military Spending (CAMS), on the Ceasefire Campaign (CAMS 2000). Making the connection between debt, arms spending and social expenditure, Dor states, 'if the government scraps the apartheid debt and the R50 billion arms deal . . . it can do away with its GEAR policy and replace it with a policy that addresses people's health and social needs' (Dor 2001b). JSA asserts that apartheid precipitated enormous, wasteful expenditure on arms, and that the 'impact of the arms deal on the majority of South Africans is central to Jubilee 2000 South Africa's concern. The vast amounts being swallowed up by the deal represent vital resources that could be allocated to service delivery' (Press Statement n.d.). In this vein, JSA demands 'the prioritisation of the eradication of poverty before spending public funds on armaments' ('Declaration of Civil Society Anti-Corruption Summit' 2002).

JSA has also campaigned for a reversion back to a pre-1990 method of financing civil service pensions, as a means of freeing up financial resources to address the country's socio-economic challenges (Eveleth 1998). JSA argues that the government's interest bill, including on domestic debt, has increased significantly in the past decade and a half, in part as a result of a switch in 1990, from a pay-as-you-go system of funding civil service pensions, to an interest-based system, in which pension fund contributions are invested and the interest from the proceeds are used to finance the payment of pensions of retired civil servants (Eveleth 1998). The NT has publicly dismissed the demand to return to the previous system as 'irresponsible' (Ensor 2004).

Conclusion

In the six years since its launch, JSA has evolved from a coalition initially focused on debt-related issues, to a movement that has developed strong and effective campaigns for reparations on economic and social justice. JSA has managed to forge a movement that addresses apartheid-era injustices, as well as the struggles surrounding what it considers to be the broken promises of the post-apartheid era; the movement demonstrates this in its linkage of developing country debt with the apartheid state and its impact on South Africans and their neighbouring countries, further building on these links to strengthen the Doctrine of Odious Debt and the call for apartheid reparations. In this way, JSA has carved a distinctly South African campaign as part of a global movement that, on first glance, one might not associate with a country lacking the external debt burden associated with the call for Jubilee.

Although a relatively new movement with challenges ahead, JSA has so far proved adept in many respects. It has successfully switched priorities at defining moments, as in its shift in focus to reparations at a time when the quest for the cancellation of apartheid-era debt appeared to be flagging, while simultaneously building stronger provincial structures to later resume the apartheid debt campaign; it has utilised coalition support in struggling for economic and social justice; and established a new set of doctrines in regard to international debt. On the domestic front, JSA has demonstrated a willingness to engage government in order to create a 'new South African society' (ADRC 2003) that meets the needs of its citizens and is an example to the rest of the world in challenging the processes of neo-liberal globalisation (Ashley 2003). Throughout all of this, JSA has succeeded in maintaining and building support.

Nthako notes that Jubilee 'started as an international movement, but [that] the campaign can only be strengthened if national movements can be developed' (Interview, Nthako, 15.10.04). Effectively linking past apartheid struggles with present-day struggles for economic and social justice, JSA demonstrates the possibilities of collective action in democratic South Africa.

References

Abrahams, C.P. 2002. 'Briefing on the Reparations Lawsuit Facilitated by the Apartheid Debt and Reparations Campaign of Jubilee South Africa'. http://www/woek.de/pdf/kasa_klage_abrahams_briefing_nov_2002.pdf (accessed April 2004).

Apartheid Debt and Reparations Campaign (ADRC). 2002a. 'Briefing on the Apartheid Debt and Reparations Campaign'. http://www.africaaction.org/action/adrc0211.htm (accessed April 2004).

——. 2002b. 'Media Statement: Major Apartheid Reparations Suit Filed in US Court'. http://www.kosa.org/documents/ApartheidClaimFiled021112.doc (accessed April 2004).

——. 2003. 'Media Statement: Apartheid Reparation Lawsuits Against South African Corporations are Untimely'. http://www.kosa.org/documents/pressjubileesa030409.pdf (accessed 9 April 2004).

Ashley, B. 1999. 'Jubilee 2000 Campaign Intensifies'. Mail and Guardian 17 September.

——. 2003. 'Apartheid South Africa as a Case Study for Cancellation of Illegitimate Debt'. http://www.odiousdebts.org/odiousdebts/print.cfm?ContentID=8004 (accessed April 2004).

Ballenger, J. 1999. 'Jubilee 2000 Aims for New World Order'. Sunday Independent 25 April.

Bandaña, A. 1999. 'Jubilee South and the Call for a New Strategic Alliance'. http://www.jubileesouth.org/news/EpklpkuEFpHMyYYSXS.shtml (accessed April 2004).

Coalition Against Military Spending (CAMS). 2000. 'Background Information'. http://www.aktion-bundesschluss.de/camsbackground.htm (accessed June 2004).

'Declaration of Civil Society Anti-Corruption Summit'. 2002. http://www.jubileeusa.org/jubilee.cgi?path=/international_partners/declarations&page=anti-corruption.html (accessed June 2004).

Della Porta, D. and S. Tarrow. 2005. 'Transnational Processes and Social Activism: An Introduction'. In D. Della Porta and S. Tarrow (eds), Transnational Protest and Global Activism. Oxford: Rowman and Littlefield Publishers.

Dor, G. 2001a. 'Jubilee 2000 South Africa: Stop the Debt! Demand Reparations!'. Discussion paper on Strategy, Organization and Structure for Consideration at the National Conference, March. http://aidc.org.za/j2000/2nd_conference/discussion_paper.html (accessed April 2004).

——. 2001b. 'Move into Deep Debt'. The Sowetan 14 June.

——. 2003. 'Interference in Judicial Process Undemocratic'. Sunday Independent 3 August.

Ensor, L. 2004. 'State Rejects "Imprudent" Pension Plan'. Business Day 4 August.

Eveleth, A. 1998. 'Hard to Wipe SA's Slate Clean'. Mail and Guardian 30 October.

——. 1999. 'IMF Bullion Sale Would be a Drop in the Ocean'. Mail and Guardian 7 May.

Financial Services Correspondent. 2003. 'Reparations Case Kicks Off in New York'. Business Day 20 May.

Friedman, J.S. 2003. 'Paying for Apartheid'. The Nation 15 May.

Giyose, M.P. 2003. 'Jubilee, Reparations, and the Lawsuits Against Economic and Financial Backers of Apartheid'. Civil Society Conference on Reparations, 27 August. http://www.khulumani.net/reparations/civil/Giyose.doc (accessed October 2004).

Giyose, P. and G. Dor. 2001. 'No Use Asking the Arsonist to Put Out the Fire'. *Business Day* 3 July.

Hanlon, J. 1998. 'Free Nelson Mandela – and All Southern Africans – From the Chains of Debt'. http://www.jubilee2000uk.org/jubilee2000/news/nelson1.html (accessed April 2004).

Harvey, E. 1999. 'Support Debt Relief or Drop the Renaissance'. *Mail and Guardian* 1 October.

Jubilee South. n.d. 'Jubilee South – About Us'. http://www.jubileesouth.org/news?About_Us.shtml (accessed April 2004).

———. 2000. 'Jubilee South Manifesto Beyond Debt and 2000: Liberating Ourselves from Debt and Domination'. http://www.jubileesouth.org/news/EpklpAZlyEXFFpOWSm.shtml (accessed April 2004).

'Jubilee South Meetings in Mumbai, India – January 16th and January 21st, 2004'. n.d. http://www.jubileeusa.org/jubilee.cgi?path=/international_partners&page=wsf2.html (accessed April 2004).

Jubilee 2000 South Africa. 1998. 'Founding Declaration of the South African Jubilee 2000 Campaign'. http://www.aidc.org.za/j2000/launch/declaration.html (accessed April 2004).

———. 2001. 'No Sweet Fruit for the Majority!'. http://www.odiousdebts.org/odiousdebts/print.cfm?ContentID=1757 (accessed June 2004).

Keeton, C. 1998. 'Jubilee Wants SA Debt Scrapped'. *The Sowetan* 6 November.

Keck, M. and K. Sikkink. 1998. *Activists Beyond Borders: Transnational Activist Networks in International Politics*. Ithaca, NY: Cornell University Press.

Khalfan, A., J. King and B. Thomas. 2003. 'Advancing the Odious Debt Doctrine'. http://www.odiousdebts.org/odiousdebts/publications/Advancing_the_Odious_Debt_Doctrine.pdf (accessed March 2004).

Khulumani Support Group (KSG). 2003. 'Press Release: Apartheid Lawsuit Attorney for Khulumani, Michael D. Hausfeld Arrives for a 3 day Visit to South Africa'. http://www.khulumani.net/media/releases/201003_1.htm (accessed June 2004).

Mofokeng, L. 2000. 'SA's Poor are Squeezed by Odious Debt'. *Sunday World* 9 January.

People's Budget Coalition. 2004. 'Joint Summary for Submission to the Finance Minister's Budget Speech on the 18th February, 2004'. http://www.sangoco.org.za/index.php?option=news&task=viewarticle&sid=319 (accessed June 2004).

Pettifor, A. 1998. 'The Economic Bondage of Debt – and the Birth of a New Movement'. *New Left Review* 1 (230): 115–22.

Press Statement. n.d. 'No Loans for Weapons!' http://www.africafiles.org/printableversion.asp?id=351 (accessed June 2004).

'Reparations Towards Another World: Declaration of the Jubilee South Africa and Jubilee South Workshop'. 2001. http://www.jubileeusa.org/jubilee.cgi?path=/international_partners/declarations/reparations (accessed April 2004).

Rodoreda, G. 2002. 'Coughing up for Apartheid'. *Mail and Guardian* 8 December.

Sebelebele, M. 2003. 'Mbeki says no to Wealth Tax'. *BuaNews Online* 15 April. http://www.safrica.info/ess_info/sa_glance/constitution/wealthtax.htm (accessed October 2004).

South African Press Association (SAPA). 2003. 'Govt Opposed to Apartheid Lawsuits'. *Mail and Guardian* 27 August.

———. 2004. 'Anti-Debt Campaigners March on World Bank'. *Mail and Guardian* 7 October.

'Summary of the Complaint: Khulumani et al. vs. Barclays et al.'. n.d. http://www.cmht.com/casewatch/cases/cwapartheid4.html (accessed June 2004).

Terreblanche, C. 2002. 'Apartheid Victims Lasso "Cash Cowboy" Fagan'. *The Star* 23 July.

———. 2004. 'Zuma Dismissed Importance of Reparations'. *Pretoria News* 26 February.

Wanneburg, G. and W. Chege. 2003. 'Apartheid Victims will get R30 000 Payout'. Reuters 15 April.

Interviews

Dor, George. General Secretary, Jubilee South Africa, 08.10.04.

Giyose, M.P. Chairperson, Jubilee South Africa, 07.10.04.

Nthako, Brand. Jubilee Free State Secretariat (Questionnaire), 15.10.04.

Rudin, Jeff. Alternative Information and Development Centre, 04.10.04.

14

In the Absence of Citizenship

Congolese Refugee Struggle
and Organisation in South Africa

Baruti Amisi and Richard Ballard

THE POSITION OF refugees is instructive for understanding the meaning of citizenship. Bauman draws links between the position of the underclass and refugees both of whom do not enjoy full citizenship and are do not participate in circuits where the '"normal", the "complete" people live and move' (Bauman and Vecchi 2004: 39–40). Likewise, Simone suggests that the lives of some poor South Africans are 'analogous to those of refugee camps – an endless present unavailable to politics, unavailable to the elaboration of institutions and ways of life capable of marking a passage of time, of rendering what one does today in some larger framework of purpose and meaning' (2004: 3). Here Simone reminds us that there is no necessary overlap between having South African nationality and being a citizen in the full sense of the word. Indeed, as Mamdani (1996) has argued, the ongoing effects of a colonial history in which citizenship was denied should not be underestimated.

As studies in this volume and elsewhere demonstrate, one of the dominant features of post-apartheid social movements is the extensive use of the language of rights to articulate needs, make social demands and secure legally enforceable commitments from the government. Rights have become a way of defining fairness and social justice. The language of rights is used across the spectrum of social movements, including relatively militant ones who draw on this language to attach legitimacy to their illegal activities. It is even used to make claims regardless of whether there are actually legally encoded rights on the matter at hand (Greenstein 2003: 24). The appeal and power of the language of rights is that the end of apartheid has allowed the majority of the population for the first time to claim citizenship of South Africa, through which they can make demands on the state. Social movements are arguably a reflection of this new and growing claim to citizenship, something which becomes all the more evident when we examine groups that cannot, by definition, claim citizenship.

Of the 214 000 post-apartheid applications for asylum received by the Department of Home Affairs by 2005 (Parsley 2005: 5), the largest group is Congolese refugees who have fled what has become known as 'Africa's world war', responsible for the deaths of around 3 million people.[1] Refugees face considerable hardship in South Africa, with scant livelihood opportunities, inability to access services such as health and education, poor provision of documentation from the Department of Home Affairs and xenophobia experienced daily in institutions and public settings (Bhamjee and Klaaren 2004; Crush and Williams 2003; Danso and McDonald 2001; Groot 2004; Hunter and Skinner 2003; Landau 2004; Palmary 2003; Vawda 1999).

Despite these extensive hardships, refugees have by and large not organised as an aggregated group with a common political interest. Aside from a Gauteng-based non-governmental organisation (NGO), the Co-ordinating Body of Refugee Communities (CBRC), attempts to bring refugees together have failed. Congolese refugees have, instead, atomised into ethnic groupings, linked to the language group and corresponding province from which they originated. These ethnic groupings combine a focus on custom and tradition with saving schemes and other local level mechanisms to ameliorate material deprivation.[2] These groups call themselves 'tribes', 'families', 'mutuals' and 'networks' and are the basic unit of grassroots organisation.

While the discovery of Congolese tribes organising in South African cities may initially seem somewhat surprising, this needs to be located within the history of Congolese political identification. Any impression that ethnic groups are pre-colonial identities that have somehow survived into a modern age must be tempered with a recognition that ethnicity has been manipulated and promoted under colonialism (Mamdani 1996). In the Congo, as elsewhere in Africa, colonial authorities used traditional authorities to rule populations indirectly. This underpinned a structural exclusion of these 'tribal' populations from full citizenship. The era of independence initially threatened to dismantle these structures but has singularly failed to do so. Accounts of political organisation in the Congo suggest that in recent decades, local level ethnic networks have been prominent (De Boeck 1996). Even before the war of the mid-1990s, the failure of the Mobutu state killed the kinds of expectations citizens would normally have of their government. In response, local level ethnic organisation begins to function as what De Boeck described as 'local strategies of resilience' (De Boeck 1996: 99).

Displaced to South Africa, refugees find themselves once again in the familiar position of being unable to draw on their citizenship to make demands on the state. They express no intention of claiming citizenship in South Africa and see their time in the country as temporary and relatively undesirable. They express frustration, at times against the United Nations High Commission for Refugees (UNHCR), at times against NGOs, at times about the politics of the Democratic Republic of Congo (DRC), and against xenophobia. They generally do not, however, seek to organise to ensure that the conditions for the treatment of refugees laid out in the legislation are adhered to. The structural category of 'refugees' fails to translate into a political identity or basis of organisation. Instead, sustained organisation takes the form of ethnically-based local strategies of resilience.

The following discussion explores Congolese refugee grassroots mobilisation and organisation. The case we wish to make is that, despite considerable protest on the one hand, and considerable grassroots organisation on the other, the inability to draw on notions of citizenship pushes refugees away from demands on the South African government, notwithstanding the fact that the latter has signed up to the 1951 United Nations refugee convention and has undertaken to meet a variety of basic needs of refugees. The result is a splintered politics that proceeds from the heritage of ethnic identification in the Congo, political affiliation in the Congo, physical displacement to South Africa and a fatalistic belief that the South African government is not going to be of much help. Self-sufficiency and self-organisation along ethnic lines at the micro-level is seen as the basis for material and social security in the hostile South African environment. Yet the political identity of refugees is contradictory. Within this context, protests are an unambiguous expression of discontent and, at times, a tentative claim to rights.

Expressing Discontent

In order to provide a way into an analysis of Congolese refugees in relation to the questions that inform this broader assessment of social movements in South

Africa, it is useful to start with a review of refugees' recollections of and attitudes towards protest activity. Refugees in South Africa are not averse to protesting on various fronts. Reasons for protest can be grouped into four broad themes: protest in relation to the politics of the home country; protest against South African-dominated refugee forums and service providers; protest in relation to institutional exclusion and xenophobia in South Africa; and protests objecting to the asylum-granting process as administered by the Department of Home Affairs.

Some marches have related directly to the politics of the Congo. In 1998 there was a march to the Non-Aligned Movement meeting at the International Convention Centre in Durban, which was being attended by the new DRC leader Laurent Kabila (Interview, Anonymous, 19.11.03). This march was attended by around 300 people and was organised to show support for his 'banning of Ruandese' in the Congo. Such protests were expressions of political beliefs to the South African community, and it was hoped that this would have an impact in the Congo (Interview, Anonymous, 08.10.03). In 2001, the same venue was host to the UN Conference against Racism and Xenophobia. As well as using this as an opportunity to highlight xenophobia in South Africa, local refugees also used it as a platform to object to 'Tutsi occupation' of eastern regions of the Congo (Interview, Anonymous, 08.10.03). In Cape Town during the same year, refugees marched on the US and British embassies as well as parliament (Interview, Anonymous, 06.12.03b). This group had seen an e-mail from the DRC written in French that warned of the potential balkanisation of the DRC, and the Cape Town protesters wanted to oppose this. Permission for the protest had been granted by the authorities, and the purpose was to object to the proposed division of the Congo. There were more than 100 protesters, mostly from the east of the Congo.

Alongside these protests addressing the political situation in the DRC, there have been a series of events targeting service providers, mainly NGOs, who work with refugees in South Africa. Respondents in Durban remember having marched against the Durban Refugee Forum in April 2000 (Interview, Anonymous, 10.07.03; see also Daily News 2000a, 2000b). The Forum was a city-level initiative that attempted to bring together service providers and refugee representatives. The idea for the march originated at a meeting several weeks before it occurred. There was much anger over two problems with the Forum. One problem was that money donated by the UNHCR and intended for scholarships for refugees was only being allocated to some refugees. The other was that local NGOs were attempting to manipulate the appointment of a leader to the Durban Refugee Forum (Interviews, Anonymous, 09.10.03, 20.02.04). A woman participant recalled that at the meeting they were upset and decided they had to 'go to the road to show the government we were not happy' (Interview, Anonymous, 20.02.04). About 200 people attended the march and a statement was handed over. It stopped at the Durban Refugee Forum offices, which were stormed, chairs were broken and the telephone cable was pulled out. There was fighting and the police had to 'make peace'. The intention was to reform the Durban Refugee Forum but instead the Forum was closed. Similar protests have taken place elsewhere in the country. In Johannesburg, one leader said that in 2001, 40 people marched to the Jesuit Refugee Services as they had proof of stealing (Interview, Anonymous, 27.11.03).

The third category of protest is against xenophobia. In Cape Town a number of marches have resulted from murders of refugees in what are interpreted as xenophobic attacks. Respondents in Cape Town reported that in 2002 a Congolese person was killed for his cell phone (Interview, Anonymous, 03.12.03a). The community then marched with the body to parliament on the way to the cemetery. The decision to march came from the Congolese community, but the march was supported by a number of other refugee groupings. Leaders reported that there were approximately 700 people at this protest. When asked why they marched, the network elder said that protest shows dissatisfaction and that even if there is no immediate result, it is important to show the international community how badly they are treated in South Africa. He said that they were aware that Cape Town is an international tourist attraction and this is an opportunity to bring attention to problems. The leader said that protest is good as it is the only way in which weak people can express what is going on (Interview, Anonymous, 03.12.03a). There was also a protest following the death of an Angolan who had been burnt in 'Bangalore', a settlement in Cape Town (Interview, Anonymous, 03.12.03b). A variety of foreigners joined in this march and they were even, reportedly, joined by a South African woman who had been driving past and wanted to express sympathy when she heard why the march had been organised.

Finally, some marches have been directed against the Department of Home Affairs local offices. As the agency responsible for receiving asylum applications, granting refugee status and providing documentation, it is notoriously inept at doing so. In Durban several respondents remembered a march against Home Affairs in order to demand improvement in the way refugees are handled (Interviews, Anonymous, 05.09.03, 08.10.03). One said that it seemed Home Affairs had responded positively, with better assistance in terms of processing necessary applications and documentation. It seemed that refugee status was now easier to obtain and to extend.

Other centres have also experienced frustration with the Department of Home Affairs. There was a spontaneous riot at the Department of Home Affairs in Cape Town resulting from frustration that it was only processing about twenty people a day (see Sterken 2003 for a full description of the Cape Town refugee reception office). Refugees had to queue from 4 a.m. and were expected to bribe officials to get necessary documentation (Interview, Anonymous, 06.12.03b). One day there was a 'fight' and the waiting crowd pulled a gate down and started to break office equipment. Unlike other protests in Cape Town, which had been planned and which were legal, this was not a formal protest. A respondent described this as cumulative anger and said that 'enough is enough' (Interview, Anonymous, 07.12.03). The incident resulted in an investigation and the overhauling of systems at Home Affairs.

Protests, then, have addressed four themes: the politics of the DRC; local NGOs working with refugees; xenophobia; and the Department of Home Affairs.[3] Discussions about the efficacy of protests as a tool for achieving goals have resulted in a range of responses. Several respondents felt that marches should only be a last resort and that it is not a good way to solve a problem (Interviews, Anonymous, 20.11.03, 20.02.04). The Gauteng-based Co-ordinating Body of Refugee Communities wants to avoid marches altogether and limit itself to negotiation (Interview, Anonymous, 28.11.03a). Its intention is to relate to the South African government 'as fellow human beings' and attempt to raise sympathy in this way. Another respondent from the same organisation stated that he did 'not see marching as a solution as this has to come from the government. If you are a guest you can't revolt if you are ill treated. I have never been involved in a march. I would rather go elsewhere than protest' (Interview, Anonymous, 28.11.03b). He stated that he is not interested in struggling for improvements in the treatment of refugees in exile, and that the only way to solve their predicament is to fight to liberate the Congo. In a related argument, another respondent stated: 'The government can't do everything for its citizens, let alone refugees' (Interview, Anonymous, 06.12.03c; see also Sabet-Sharghi 2000: 69).

Fear of state repression is a major reason why some preferred to negotiate. One said that the police would treat foreigners badly, and that there is a level of fear amongst refugees (Interviews, Anonymous, 19.11.03, 20.11.03). The National Consortium for Refugee Affairs confirmed that those who have taken action have, at times, been victimised (Interview, Tlou, 27.11.03). One Johannesburg leader said that there were street marches in 1995 and that some people were deported as a result (Interview, Anonymous, 27.11.03). Since then, people have been scared to march.

Unlike the reticence of more formal lobby groups who felt that protest was to be avoided, many at a grassroots level expressed considerable faith in the potential of marching, and confirmed that it was something they should be doing (Interview, Anonymous, 05.09.03). Some felt justified in marching rather than talking to the government because the government has known for a long time about various problems, such as xenophobia, and has failed to solve them (Interview, Anonymous, 03.12.03a). It was believed that there is widespread frustration and that people were keen to do something about it. There was clearly an expressive element to marching. When asked why they marched, one leader indicated that they 'wanted to show the world what is in their hearts' (Interview, Anonymous, 30.08.03). Similarly, another said that it is a way for people to 'express their feelings' (Interview, Anonymous, 08.10.03). A third leader said marching is important 'when someone feels their rights have been violated and when other ways of mobilising are not working' (Interview, Anonymous, 09.10.03). A Cape Town leader indicated that at marches, refugees can express their anger and feeling in front of the world and this brings relief (Interview, Anonymous, 03.12.03b). Another simply said that it's 'better than just taking it' (Interview, Anonymous, 06.12.03a).

The idea for marches was said to come from 'informal organisation' and is sparked by the anger at the treatment of refugees here (Interview, Anonymous, 05.09.03). However, it was said that without an organiser, no march was likely to take place (Interview, Anonymous, 21.10.03). It was suggested that an absence of marching resulted from an absence of organisation rather than general satisfaction amongst refugees with their conditions (Interview, Anonymous, 09.10.03). In turn, this lack of protest was seen to lead to the further violation of rights. Those who are more organised were said to be more likely to receive assistance from organisations such as the UNHCR. One respondent exclaimed: 'We don't fight for our rights here in South Africa. We should initiate a movement of all refugees. We never organise' (Interview, Anonymous, 06.12.03c). Some respondents felt that refugees were not sufficiently aware of their rights, for example that they did not have to pay officials in order to acquire refugee status (Interview, Anonymous, 21.10.03). Refugees do not know the constitution and the legislation, and this makes it difficult for them to claim their rights.

On the question of whether refugees feared a repressive response, not all sided with the position that the South African government was going to respond repressively. Some were encouraged by earlier marches in which they 'stared down the South African army' (Interview, Anonymous, 05.09.03). Some informants even said that they did not fear being arrested. Many seemed to feel that protest is tolerated in South Africa and that people are not afraid to protest (Interview, Anonymous, 08.10.03). More than one respondent stated that the police are always very co-operative whenever there is a march and that it is usually possible to get permission to do so (Interviews, Anonymous, 03.12.03b, 09.10.03). A lack of participation might be explained not by fear, but rather by the inability to leave work or poor advertising of the march. Furthermore, some felt that refugees did not know that they had the right to march and did not know the constitution (Interview, Anonymous, 10.10.03). Some refugees said that they are not marching any more as they are tired of complaining (Interview, Anonymous, 10.10.03). Another said that the lack of progress after marches and protests has discouraged further efforts at protest.

From this survey of accounts of protest, and attitudes towards protest, three observations can be made. Firstly, the refugee community exhibits the same bifurcation that occurs in other marginalised communities attempting to express themselves politically, where the choice between engagement and opposition is a perennial theme (Greenstein 2003; Mamdani 1996; Saul 2002; and studies throughout this volume). Secondly, while refugees were willing to take to the streets on issues relating to the politics of the DRC, frustration with NGOs, and in relation to xenophobia, there is very little strategic use of refugee rights as encoded in South African legislation. While tentative reference is made to rights, claims are more frequently made on the UNHCR and the service providers it supports. Protest activity may also stem from general expressions of political affiliation in relation to the politics of the DRC. However, there are relatively few demands made on the South African government, despite the fact that it has committed itself to services such as the provision of education, healthcare and proper documentation for refugees. Thirdly, protests do not emanate from a consistent organisational source. They are reactive and, to some extent, free floating. In order to understand the fragmented form of refugee protest, the discussion now turns to forms of refugee political identification.

Political Identification: Organisation at the Grassroots
The civil society structures relating to refugees incorporate donors, their NGO recipients, unregistered refugee NGOs, churches and ethnic groupings. In South Africa the UNHCR essentially functions as a donor. Along with other donors it sponsors national NGOs such as Lawyers for Human Rights and the National Consortium for Refugee Affairs, which act as lobby groups, assist with individual cases, and attempt to confront xenophobia through awareness campaigns. Donors also support a variety of NGOs and service providers at the city level, which provide limited accommodation and some basic food supplies. Many NGOs that assist refugees are staffed by South Africans.

Attempts to bring together city-level service providers and refugee communities in the five main urban centres have essentially failed. Tensions arose in relation to the relative power of South African-dominated NGOs that, in some cases, prevented refugee representatives from having a vote on the Forums.[4] Since the collapse of Forums in Cape Town, Durban and Port Elizabeth, there have been no mechanisms for different refugee communities to meet. Feedback from refugees themselves confirmed that any engagement between different refugee communities remained informal and underground, and that there was no formal open network that was capable of effectively dealing with refugee problems (Interview, Anonymous, 30.08.03). One individual, who had been involved in the Durban Refugee Forum, said 'unity in the city is hard; in the camps this is forced' (Interview, Anonymous, 19.11.03).

Johannesburg is an exception to this pattern, where refugee representatives have grouped together to form the Co-ordinating Body of Refugee Communities. Preferring formal non-confrontational approaches, the CBRC has negotiated for the release of detainees from the notorious Lindela detention centre, negotiated access to free education for refugee children, partnered with banks on the provision of bank accounts and has even begun exploring potential links with unions.

With the exception of the CBRC, then, the category of 'refugee' has not been the basis for organising people into formal or informal groups. Instead there are a plethora of other bases for organisation: political parties, including would-be guerrilla organisations, churches, unregistered NGOs and projects, and women's organisations. Alongside these forms of grassroots organisation, ethnicity remains a vital basis for identification.

Initially, in the mid-1990s, there was little ethnic distinction and association took place between all Congolese refugees. However, as numbers grew individuals began associating more closely with members of their ethnic groups.[5] Some describe this as a more efficient way of organising, since the entire Congolese grouping in the city was too large to organise as a whole (Interview, Anonymous, 10.07.03). Ethnic structures appeared in Johannesburg and Durban from 1997 and in Cape Town from 2000. Reflecting on the origins of these networks, the founding members describe the motivation for their formation as being language, common nationality and the need to survive (Interviews, Anonymous, 30.08.03, 09.10.03, 27.11.03).

Refugees from the DRC estimate that, of the more than 412 ethnic groups in the Congo, there are around 17 different Congolese tribes in Durban and 11 in Cape Town. In Johannesburg it is likely that there are even more ethnic groupings than this given the size of the population, but because it is a relatively dispersed community it is difficult to obtain estimates. There was also some evidence that ethnic organisation was not seen as important in Johannesburg (Interview, Anonymous, 28.11.03b). In Durban these groups include: the Bembe; Anamongo (consisting of the related languages of Mongo, Kusu and Tetela, and considering themselves to have a common ancestor); the Kasongo Babanbwe (including Bango Bango, Binja and others); and Lega. In Cape Town, there are networks for the Bembe; Foliro; Vira; Rega; Baluba; Bashi; Bakongo; Kusu; Zimba; Bango Bango; and Zulua (Interview, Anonymous, 03.12.03a).

There were various triggers for the formation of the networks. In some cases, an individual set about contacting others of their ethnic grouping in the city and organising a meeting to establish a network (Interview, Anonymous, 20.11.03). In other cases, the trigger for the formation of some of the networks was a death in the community. It is seen as the responsibility of those who belong to the ethnic group of the deceased to organise the funeral (Interview, Anonymous, 09.10.03). In Cape Town, a network was formed specifically as a result of a xenophobic killing (Interview, Anonymous, 03.12.03b).

The invisibility of these organisations on any formal register of civil society organisations does not in any way mean that they are informal in their functioning. Ethnic networks are, in fact, highly organised and hold regular meetings. Each group has a formal executive committee elected by the membership. This committee has various portfolios, including a president, treasurer, secretary, communications, public relations, social and cultural affairs. Many of the groups also have constitutions, written by the executive but debated by the membership (Interview, Anonymous, 05.09.03). These are necessary, according to one leader, in order to have rules and regulations to help people meet and to sanction those who misbehave (Interview, Anonymous, 05.09.03).

These structures appear to be dominated by men, although most leaders interviewed indicated it was not impossible for women to be representatives. One group said that their previous vice-chair was a woman (Interview, Anonymous, 05.09.03). This was seen to be particularly useful in 'preserving culture' as it was possible to communicate required standards of behaviour to women. A group in Cape Town had a specific portfolio held by women for 'Women's Conditions' to deal with problems for women (Interview, Anonymous, 03.12.03a). One respondent stated that while women would be welcome in the executive structure, it was necessary to ensure that the group was chaired by a man (Interview, Anonymous, 09.10.03). They said that this reflects their patriarchal cultural background. In practical terms, this meant that women could not perform ceremonial roles at funerals and other cultural functions.

These networks can be understood as communities of support that provide both monetary assistance and knowledge, and encouragement to overcome local difficulties. One reason given for the formation of networks is to help newcomers who would otherwise have to sleep on the streets when they arrive (Interview, Anonymous, 10.07.03). As one put it, established refugees are the most knowledgeable to help newcomers with accommodation and job hunting (Interview, Anonymous, 05.09.03). A community leader stated that every person's problem belongs to the community as a whole (Interview, Anonymous, 30.08.03). In order to provide resources for solving problems, funds are collected from members.

Networks collect contributions from members ranging from R10 a month for larger groups to R50 a month for smaller groups. The money raised is used to pay for collective expenses such as funerals, or to help newcomers or members going through financial difficulties. Some groups levy special contributions from their members to deal with events on an *ad hoc* basis (Interview, Anonymous, 03.12.03a). The groups attempt to solve problems of accessing state services, for example accessing health and education, and dealing with the Department of Home Affairs. One group specifically mentioned arrests as something they would deal with (Interview, Anonymous, 03.12.03a).

If we take Swilling and Russell's distinction between developmentalist, survivalist and oppositional non-profit organisations (NPOs) (2002), Congolese networks might appear to sit primarily in the survivalist category. Lest survivalist organisations be mistakenly understood as focusing on materialism alone, it would be useful to bear in mind Simone's remarks in this regard:

> They must serve as affirmations that change is possible, that it is worth being engaged in efforts to try and change things. They must function with a sense that there is a wider world of possibilities for action and being that is not 'out there', far removed from the details of everyday life, but immediately accessible through the steps people take in local contexts (Simone 2001: 112; see also MacGaffey and Bazenguissa-Ganga 2000: 8; Young 2000: 167).

Simone argues that economic marginality in African cities results in a return to 'reinvented traditions of social cohesion' (2001: 104). Poor urban populations attempt to strike a balance between cohesion and opportunity, seeking on the one hand to embed themselves in networks of information and reciprocity, while at the same time attempting to find opportunities for themselves that might generate some kind of income. Although the march towards 'modern' conditions of individual citizenship may seem inevitable, collectives based on 'custom' often endure and flourish (Simone 2001: 112).

'Survivalist', then, may not be an adequate description of what is going on in refugee grassroots organisation. It would be a mistake to see them as mere savings groups focusing only on the material well-being of their members. As one informant said, they would meet anyway, even if they were not trying to deal with problems (Interview, Anonymous, 03.12.03a). The agenda of network meetings deals not only with everyday life in South Africa, but also ways of safeguarding culture and identity. One said that their organisation 'is trying to remind people where they come from' and that 'the feeling of belonging to a particular place is important' (Interview, Anonymous, 03.12.03a). They speak of the need to create an environment similar to home (Interview, Anonymous, 05.12.03) and say that the network 'provides a sense of safety' (Interview, Anonymous, 09.10.03). Leaders of these groups express a need to preserve their language, and say that they are proud of their ethnic group (Interviews, Anonymous, 30.08.03, 09.10.03, 06.12.03b). Several groups said that they keep traditions alive, such as songs and proverbs. Respondents have been circulating pamphlets of their proverbs and plan to write a book of proverbs (Interview, Anonymous, 20.11.03). Traditions also include the performance of rites and rituals at important events such as births, marriages and death (Interview, Anonymous, 19.11.03). Keeping traditions alive encompasses everyday conduct, such as 'how we eat and how we talk' (Interview, Anonymous, 19.11.03). Belonging to an ethnic group is seen to result in unity between members as a result of common language and common origins. It was said that having a common language gives 'a real connection' (Interview, Anonymous, 27.11.03). Group unity was associated with the mythological origins of the group.

There is a sense of incompatibility between refugee culture and local culture. At times there is outright antipathy towards local culture, which is seen to be permissive. South Africans are seen to be more western, resulting in a lack of respect towards elders (Interview, Anonymous, 19.11.03). Frequent mention was made of the way in which local women wear more revealing clothes, unmarried couples live together, and children disrespect their parents (Interviews, Anonymous, 05.09.03, 27.11.03). Concern was also expressed in relation to the commodification of *lobolo*, or bride price. One respondent said 'I don't want to sell my daughter' as they do in South Africa (Interview, Anonymous, 20.11.03).

Resistance to assimilation, therefore, comes through strongly as an objective of the networks. Many leaders and members express an extreme dislike for living in South Africa and say that they hope conditions in the Congo will one day allow them to return. Peberdy and Crush (1998) found that 'less than 4% of those interviewed intended on staying in South Africa' (cited in Hunter and Skinner 2001: 8; see also Sabet-Sharghi 2000: 70). One respondent said that he would not stay even if he was offered citizenship, and that it was impossible for him to be happy outside of his home country (Interview, Anonymous, 28.11.03b). Refugees' time in South Africa is therefore constructed as both temporary and undesirable. There is little interest in adopting and practising the cultural and national identity of their host country. One respondent stated that he had no ambitions to say that he was a proud South African and that he was still connected to his home country, which he remembers as peaceful (Interview, Anonymous, 09.10.03). Whereas he would be well established in his home country, he feels that in a foreign country he is without respect, hope or a future. The intention to return home provides even greater imperative not to abandon ethnic identity. Many perceive a need to guard against the tendency for people to drop their culture once they leave their land (Interview, Anonymous, 28.11.03b). There is much concern about children born outside of their homeland as they do not know their culture (Interview, Anonymous, 27.11.03). Regardless of whether or not this perception of transience will translate into an actual return, or whether this is simply first generation migrants' inevitable sense of displacement and longing for home, the key point for this research is the impact it has on claims to the state by contemporary refugee groups. Specifically, the avoidance of assimilation prevents claims to rights and citizenship and forces an ethnic structuring of civil society.

Although the primary unit of organisation is the ethnic group, there are mechanisms that ensure that all Congolese engage with one other. When there is a funeral, for example, all ethnic networks are expected to contribute towards the costs. Furthermore, all Congolese are expected to attend funerals even for deceased from another network. On particular occasions, people will even travel from other cities to attend funerals, thus enabling communication nationally. Aside from these cultural events, there is currently no formal forum in which the leaders of various ethnic networks can gather and address issues affecting the entire Congolese group.

Various opinions were offered as to whether an ethnic identity was more important than the national identity. Some suggested that the ethnic identity was more important because it 'came before the Congolese identity' and that while the Congolese identity may change, the ethnic identity will remain constant (Interview, Anonymous, 09.10.03).[6] One representative stated that, even though he was a Congolese nationalist and opposed ethnic chauvinism, his ethnicity was more important than the Congolese identity as it was his family group (Interview, Anonymous, 28.11.03a). However, even where ethnic identities are seen to be strong, the Congolese identity is also seen as extremely important. Some respondents resisted temptations to prioritise Congolese or ethnic identity saying that it was impossible to separate the two (Interview, Anonymous, 03.12.03b). 'To be Anamongo is a base to be Congolese' said one respondent of their ethnic identity (Interview, Anonymous, 20.02.04). Ethnic identities appear not to be at odds with a national identity and indeed specific ethnic identities and broader Congolese are understood to be mutually constitutive.

In order to properly understand the relationship between ethnicity and nationalism, it is useful to briefly consider how these functioned in the Congo before the refugees took flight. Mamdani argues that the relationship between nationalism and ethnicity has to be located within the colonial practice of indirect rule. The appearance of unmediated pre-colonial ethnicity is entirely false given that colonial authorities manipulated ethnicity in order to control populations. Belgian colonial authorities implemented the policy of indirect rule in the Congo from the 1920s, thereby reproducing the approach of the French, Portuguese and British throughout Africa (Mamdani 1996: 86). Rather than directly ruling all people as citizens within a nation state territory, colonialists gained the co-operation of ethnic leaders, or installed co-operative ethnic leaders where there were none available, who continued to rule a 'free peasantry' as subjects. Since the advent of independence, the legacy of ethnic engineering has had a profound impact on African identity despite various attempts at reform (Fanon 1967: 128). Although some chiefs were chased from office after independence, Mobutu restored chiefs to office (De Boeck 1996: 82). Reforms in the 1970s failed to dislodge chiefs as central power brokers in Zaire, and the increasingly clientelist post-colonial state maintained an ambivalent relationship towards chiefs as both a means for exerting power and a threat.

In parallel to this constant reinvention of ethnicity, a discourse of independence and self-support has emerged in recent decades. The reclamation of agency became important given the way in which Zairians had been subject to Belgian colonial and post-colonial influence, Mobutu's rule and increasing state collapse, and the austerity resulting from the International Monetary Fund (IMF) intervention (De Boeck 1996; see also MacGaffey and Bazenguissa-Ganga 2000). Ritual was idealised and reinvigorated, and ethnic identity gained renewed significance. Constructions of 'tradition' have become a compass for the organisation of everyday life. De Boeck asks whether, in the context of state collapse, 'order, morality and social control [are] relegated to local-level village, kinship and co-operative units' (1996: 76).

The ethnic 'mutuals' or networks that have been emerging amongst South African Congolese refugees, therefore, are not particular to the local context but have their origins in the Congo. This is confirmed by respondents who describe these structures as a normal part of life. Some Congolese refugees said that they remember their parents having formal monthly meetings about a range of issues pertinent to their community (Interview, Anonymous, 06.12.03a). Several groups explained that the state has not functioned properly for many decades in the Congo, and that people have long relied on their own networks of support (Interviews, Anonymous, 09.10.03, 06.12.03a). If a person moved to another province within the Congo, they would seek out individuals from their ethnic group and organise a support network (Interview, Anonymous, 06.12.03b). The war has, in effect, created diasporas of the Congo's ethnic groups all over the world. Networks are connected to the Congo and at times senior leaders in the ethnic groupings send messages that have to be followed (Interviews, Anonymous, 19.11.03, 06.12.03a). Members of an ethnic group visit one another in different cities from time to time. One group had been in telephone contact with refugees in Belgium whom they had known from the Congo (Interview, Anonymous, 05.09.03). Such networks can be called upon for financial or even legal assistance. All assist one another in the improvement of life conditions.

Networks, of course, change when they travel (Hart 2002: 169) and it would be a mistake to see formations in South Africa as being the same as those in the Congo. What is relevant here is that the heritage of political identity, which refugees bring with them, has a fundamental impact on the way in which they organise and make claims on the state. This is a heritage in which concepts of democracy and civil society have decreasing appropriateness. De Boeck states that 'analysis of central issues forgrounded in the Zairean crisis – issues concerning representation, identity, ethnicity, nationalism, violence, strategies of survival and resilience, the role of the media, the notion of citizenship and civil society – no longer benefits from an explanatory frame that presupposes the "state"' (De Boeck 1996: 93). Similarly, it is inappropriate, in the context of the Congo, to conceive of 'local strategies of resilience' only as opposition to the state (De Boeck 1996: 99). This resilience can simply be attempts by groups of people to insert themselves into political and economic realms. We can, now, better situate comments from refugees such as the following:

> The South African government should teach the population to work
> for themselves and avoid a paternalist attitude. Since Mobutu, we have

learned not to expect anything from the government. We know that we are refugees. We just want to survive here. [We find it strange] to see people marching here demanding (Interview, Anonymous, 28.11.03a).

The Political Nature of Ethnic Identities

The absence of a socialist agenda, or claims to citizenship, may well push refugee ethnic groupings outside of the realm of 'social movement'. The idea of a social movement is certainly one that would seem alien to these Congolese groupings whose English words to describe their groups include 'tribe', 'family' and 'network'. However, these groupings do represent political identities. One respondent said that although their organisation was not a political party it worked like a political party (Interview, Anonymous, 27.11.03). He said that it had a political culture that reflected the political and ethnic organisation at home.

The fact that these kinds of organisations are now no longer located in the Congo means that their politics takes on new dimensions. At one level this is a banal and somewhat obvious point. Not unlike first generation migrants all over the world, Congolese refugees in South Africa retain a strong attachment to their ethnic origins and resist assimilation into the host environment. The decision not to assimilate is arguably not so much a choice as it is a response to the unwelcoming host environment (Bauman 2001: 141). If a sense of belonging to a moral community is taken to be a relatively generic human need (Bauman and Vecchi 2004: 47; Hetherington 1998: 63; Simone 2001: 113), then the understandable response to an environment where one feels one does not belong is to create a community of one's own. Belonging and identification are based upon a sense of similarity – common elements that unite a group of people. Since the South African social environment responded to the arrival of refugees by telling them they were unwelcome and different, the option of assimilating into the host country became immensely difficult. A sense of belonging, then, was to be achieved by linking with 'others like me'. The emotional effect of such groupings should be recognised as an end in itself and should not be diminished in relation to political effects (Hetherington 1998: 63).

As much as these organisational forms are intended for internal con-sumption,[7] the South African context fundamentally transforms their meaning. Hetherington says cultural movements are often just as much about assuming or creating a new identity, of embracing marginality, and being openly and proactively different. These identities play with the idea of margins and marginalisation (1998:16).

What Hetherington had in mind was anti-essentialist identity politics conceptualised as the use of hybrid and multiple identities to unsettle the dominant notions of essentialised unitary identity (1998:25). Spivak's notion of strategic essentialism requires any adherence to an identity to be accompanied by a critique of the possibility of that identity being somehow immutable (quoted in Bonnett 2000: 139–40). Yet this kind of politics is arguably not typical of group-based social movements that are frequently characterised by essentialist understandings of themselves (Young 2000: 87). As we have seen, ethnic networks amongst Congolese refugees assert a kind of uncritical ethnic essentialism based in a sense of historical rootedness and authenticity. However, this is not a reproduction of a pre-colonial ethnic identity. It is the result of both colonial and post-colonial manipulations of ethnic identity, and local-level interest in traditional forms of association. In South Africa these are marginal identities that function as 'a source of empowerment and resistance' (Hetherington 1998: 22). In the face of xenophobic hostility, Congolese refugees respond with defiant pride in their culture – something they believe is not only valid but is actually *better* than their new cultural environment. Rather than accepting the denigration heaped on them, they reverse the hierarchy of inferiority placing themselves at the apex (cf. Young 2000: 165–6). In effect, they create, in the words of MacGaffey and Bazenguissa-Ganga describing Congolese migrants to Paris, a 'society outside society, a world of their own' that rejects 'both the activities and the value system of mainstream society' (2000: 7).

Refusing to assimilate or conform is itself a kind of politics. As De Certeau (1984: 30) says of a migrant in Paris:

Without leaving the place where he has no choice but to live and which lays down its law for him, he establishes within it a degree of *plurality* and creativity. By an art of being in between, he draws unexpected results from his situation.

As one leader stated: 'Our presence here is an eye-opener for local people' (Interview, Anonymous, 03.12.03a). For example, he said, they see that foreigners do what is required to survive and this forces local people to consider new possibilities for their own survival. The very cosmopolitanism introduced by refugees is itself transformative. It presents a challenge to ethnic chauvinism of those South Africans who are hostile not only to migrants from beyond the borders but to other South Africans of different ethnic origin. It also challenges the nationalism being promoted by the government (Landau 2004). It forces the recognition of social diversity beyond South African nationals and therefore creates the possibility of the creation of a more open and accommodating society.

In addition to the political challenge of diversity, a 'politics of recognition', as Young calls it, 'usually is part of or a means to claims for political and social inclusion or an end to structural inequalities that disadvantage them' (Young 2000: 104–5). In this way, an apparent 'identity'-based movement or formation interfaces with material disadvantages experienced by the poor. Refugees' politics in South Africa therefore bring together aspects of material survival and cultural recognition.

The notion of new social movements has been criticised for the way it defies its own multiplicity and cannot deal with the specificity of particular formations (Hetherington 1998: 10). Social movements are often loaded with the responsibility of being agents of massive social change – the 'hinge' around which society can be diverted in a new direction (Hetherington 1998: 10). As the present case suggests, however, political formations in response to marginalisation are better imagined as housing an assortment of political, social and cultural functions that do not always conform to orthodox social movement ideologies or even basic claims to citizenship and inclusion.

Conclusion

Refugee communities will by and large fail to register in a scan for what would be considered to be conventional social movements. Yet in the absence of more recognisable political expressions, there is not simply a void. There is both a high degree of grassroots organisation on the one hand, and a considerable amount of protest activity on the other. These formations are neither irrelevant nor are they to be uncritically romanticised on the landscape of social movements in contemporary South Africa. They are an understandable response to the circumstances refugees find themselves in. They are a political response as well as being about survival and culture.

In material terms, survivalist organisations are attempting to help refugees meet their basic needs of housing and finding a livelihood. They operate as communities of support in which people subjected to similar forms of exclusion attempt to work out how to deal with it. It is striking that ethnic identity and organisation for material support organise into the same structures. Economic marginality is, therefore, not the primary 'sub identity' which forms the basis for these networks (Hetherington 1998: 15).[8] This is not to say, of course, that members of these groups are not highly marginalised or that this position is not of concern to the leadership of these networks. However, were this to be the basis for organisation, we would expect organisation at the broader level of 'refugee' or, at the very least, 'Congolese refugees'. Instead we find that the preference is to organise in a somewhat atomised way along cultural lines, at times co-operating with other networks and refugee groupings to address combined concerns, but not within the framework of an institutionalised meeting of leaderships, for example.

Along with material support, these structures function to maintain national or ethnic cultural identity. In response to xenophobia, through which the host South African society pathologises and stigmatises refugees' foreignness, many refugees respond with attempts to preserve their own cultures. Ethnic organisation represents, to use Mamdani's (1996) analysis, ambiguous potential. Although this national or ethnic pride is essentialist, the cultural plurality that results can be seen as a kind of defiance, and a kind of resistance with transformative potential. It adds cosmopolitanism to South African cities and introduces unapologetic otherness that forces host populations to begin engaging with social difference. As a politics of recognition, it also represents a concern about the structural inequality experienced by refugees. Its drawback, of course, is the inability to transcend ethnic identities and to organise either as Congolese or as refugees as a whole (see Bauman 2001: 77 on the pitfalls of sectarianism).

Grassroots ethnic organisations have indeed been the platform for a number of street marches. Even here, however, the thrust of protest is fractured. Protests have confronted the poor service delivery of the Department of Home Affairs and various other government agencies. They have been directed at other refugee representative bodies (for example, the Durban Refugee Forum) deemed not to be effectively representing refugees. Protests have also addressed xenophobia.

However, they are not limited to the adverse conditions in South Africa. A number of protests were concerned with the politics of the Congo. The complex nature of refugee marginality therefore results in various grassroots organisational formations and various political impulses expressed in a range of modalities.

The forms of mobilisation and organisation that have been reviewed here can largely be explained through the absence of citizenship in two senses. In narrow terms it is the result of being refugees; the technical legal status of being foreign and therefore having inferior claims on the state. In broad terms, the absence of citizenship is inherited from the Congo, where there were few expectations on government and people were not used to making any claims on it. This was the result of the colonial history of indirect rule that deprived many of citizenship, and the failure of independent governments to transcend this. The result is a situation in which it makes no sense either to fight for extended citizenship or to pursue counter-hegemonic political projects. Local-level ethnic organisation functions both in the Congo and in South Africa as a substitute for national citizenship, where cultural norms, laws and hierarchies are strongly defined and underpin the structure of everyday life.

Notes

1. This study does not represent all refugee political activity. Congolese refugees were chosen partly because they are the largest group and also because they have been particularly vocal in expressing frustration. For research on Somali groups in inner city Johannesburg see Dykes (2004).

2. Such structures are by no means alien to South Africa. Migrant workers living in cities in the 1930s and 1940s often organised into 'homeboy' networks based on their rural origin (Mamdani 1996: 193). As well as assuming cultural forms, many of these organisations had survivalist imperatives, organising saving schemes in stokvels or burial societies to help cover the costs of large expenses. Furthermore, they operated as political conduits, not only bringing consciousness of the ANC, PAC and SACP to migrant workers in the city, but allowing migrant workers to anchor resistance against authorities in the rural home.

3. Lawyers for Human Rights reports that there was little involvement of refugee civil society in the drafting of refugee and migration legislation and that the feedback process was dominated by the South African-run NGOs. One exception was in 1996 where a group of refugees organised themselves and had a sit-in in the Union Buildings in order to object to the lack of attention being given to refugees (Interview, Van ger Gerden, 27.11.03). This was broadcast on television and the President's Office then began engaging over the issue.

4. There is a complicated tension here between service providers and refugees. On the one hand, service providers point to the divided nature of the refugee community and the difficulties in achieving

consensus on leadership. On the other, refugees themselves point to the way in which South African-dominated service providers, especially at the city level, attempt to monopolise access to resources.

5. See also Muzaliwa's (2004) account.

6. In conjunction with ethnic distinction, another important cleavage in this community is a division between supporters of Mobutu and Kabila (Parsley 2005: 40).

7. It may be possible to argue that their inward orientation disqualifies them from the terrain of civil society or social movements. Young (2000: 160) expresses concern that 'self-regarding' *private associations* whose activities are orientated to the members alone do not contribute to civil society as such in the way that outwardly focused *civic* and *political associations* do. Young's observations are an effective critique of Putnam's indiscriminate celebration of all voluntary association. Young argues that while it might be possible to recognise 'soccer clubs' and 'bowling leagues' as enriching society, such organisations do little to enhance democracy (Young 2000: 162). Congolese ethnic networks certainly do take on the functions of 'light sociability, personal caretaking, consumption, entertainment, grieving, and spiritual renewal' that characterise private associations (Young 2000: 160). They even fit into Young's assessment that they 'care little for outsiders, and indeed may be hostile to others' (Young 2000: 162). It might well be appropriate to conclude that their prevalence in the absence of more outward focused civic associations is indicative of weak democracy and is 'depoliticising' (Young 2000: 162). Despite this apparent match with Young's classification, applying her assessment to the current case is complicated. There is no neutral choice between private and civic activity, and opting for the former needs to be contextualised within the unavailability of democracy and citizenship to members of these organisations. Furthermore, this unavailability results in a blurring of the boundaries between private and civic associations – a possibility that Young (2000: 163) concedes – such that ethnic networks have, at times, broken from an inward focus into more collective engagement.

8. Young (2000: 98) distinguishes between structural groups and cultural groups. Structural groups experience impaired life opportunities as a result of social structures and while these often overlap with cultural groups there is no necessary parity between the two. In this case, all refugees might be said to experience shared structural disadvantage in society. Yet the basis for identification is groupings within the category of refugee, namely ethnic groupings.

References

Bauman, Z. 2001. *Community: Seeking Safety in an Insecure World*. Cambridge: Polity.

Bauman, Z. and B. Vecchi. 2004. *Identity*. Cambridge: Polity.

Bhamjee, A. and J. Klaaren. 2004. 'Legal Problems Facing Refugees in Johannesburg'. In L. Landau (ed.), *Forced Migrants in the New Johannesburg: Towards a Local Government Response*. Johannesburg: Forced Migration Studies Programme, University of the Witwatersrand.

Bonnett, A. 2000. *White Identities: Historical and International Perspectives*. London: Prentice Hall.

Crush, J. and V. Williams. 2003. 'Criminal Tendencies: Immigrants and Illegality in South Africa'. South African Migration Project, Migration Policy Brief 10.

Daily News. 2000a. 'Refugees Fight Forum Election Process'. 1 May.

———. 2000b. 'Forum Denies Misusing Donor Funds for Refugees'. 10 May.

Danso, R. and D. McDonald. 2001. 'Writing Xenophobia: Immigration and the Print Media in Post Apartheid South Africa'. *Africa Today* 48 (3): 115–38.

De Boeck, F. 1996. 'Postcolonialism, Power and Identity: Local and Global Perspectives from Zaire'. In R. Werbner and T. Ranger (eds), *Postcolonial Identities in Africa*. London: Zed Books.

De Certeau, M. 1984. *The Practice of Everyday Life*. London: University of California Press.

Dykes, K. 2004. 'New Urban Social Movements in Cape Town and Johannesburg'. *Urban Forum* 15(2): 162–79.

Fanon, F. 1967. *The Wretched of the Earth*. Harmondsworth: Penguin Books.

Greenstein, R. 2003. 'Civil Society, Social Movements and Power in South Africa'. Unpublished RAU Sociology seminar paper.

Groot, F. 2004. 'Challenges of the UNHCR's Programme for Urban Refugees in South Africa'. In L. Landau (ed.), *Forced Migrants in the New Johannesburg: Towards a Local Government Response*. Johannesburg: Forced Migration Studies Programme, University of the Witwatersrand.

Hart, G. 2002. *Disabling Globalization: Places of Power in Post-Apartheid South Africa*. Pietermaritzburg: University of Natal Press.

Hetherington, K. 1998. *Expressions of Identity: Space, Performance, Politics*. London: Sage.

Hunter, N. and C. Skinner. 2001. 'Foreign Street Traders Working in Inner City Durban: Survey Results and Policy Dilemmas'. Research Report No. 49. Durban: School of Development Studies.

——. 2003. 'Foreigners Working on the Streets of Durban: Local Government Policy Challenges'. *Urban Forum* 14 (4).

Landau, L. 2004. 'The Laws of (In)Hospitality: Black Africans in South Africa'. Paper prepared for 'The Promise of Freedom and its Practice: Global Perspectives on South Africa's Decade of Democracy', Wits Institute for Social and Economic Research, University of the Witwatersrand, Johannesburg, 17 May.

Mamdani, M. 1996. *Citizen and Subject: Contemporary Africa and the Legacy of Late Colonialism*. Princeton NJ: Princeton University Press.

MacGaffey, J. and R. Bazenguissa-Ganga. 2000. *Congo-Paris: Transnational Traders on the Margins of the Law*. The International African Institute with Oxford: James Curry and Bloomington: Indiana University Press.

Muzaliwa, R.M. 2004. 'Refugees from the DR Congo in Durban: Survival Strategies and Social Networks in a South African City'. Masters dissertation, Politics Department, University of KwaZulu-Natal, Durban.

Palmary, I. 2004. 'Coty Policing and Forced Migrants in Johannesburg'. In L. Landau (ed.), *Forced Migrants in the New Johannesburg: Towards a Local Government Response*. Johannesburg: Forced Migration Studies Programme, University of the Witwatersrand.

Parsley, J. 2005. 'Displaced and Discarded: The Role of Civil Society Organisations in Promoting Socio-Economic Rights for Refugees and Asylum Seekers in South Africa'. Unpublished report submitted for the Centre for Civil Society grant programme, University of KwaZulu-Natal.

Peberdy, S. and J. Crush. 1998. 'Trading Places: Cross-Border Traders and the South African Informal Sector'. SAMP Migration Policy Series No. 6.

Sabet-Sharghi, F. 2000. 'The Social, Economic and Political Circumstances of Congolese Refugees in Durban'. Master's dissertation, School of Development Studies, University of Natal.

Saul, J. 2002. 'Starting from Scratch?: A Reply to Jeremy S. Cronin'. *Monthly Review* 54 (7).

Simone, A. 2001. 'Straddling the Divides: Remaking Associational Life in the Informal African City'. *International Journal of Urban and Regional Research* 25 (1): 102–17.

——. 2004. 'South African Urbanism: Between the Modern and the Refugee Camp'. Dark Roast Occasional Paper Series No. 17. Cape Town: Isandla Institute.

Sterken, S.J. 2003. 'Two Weeks at the Cape Town Refugee Reception Office'. *Botshabelo* 6 (2): 4–6.

Swilling, M. and B. Russell. 2002. *The Size and Scope of the Non-Profit Sector in South Africa*. Durban and Johannesburg: Centre for Civil Society, University of Natal, and the Graduate School of Public and Development Management, University of the Witwatersrand.

Vawda, S. 1999. 'Foreign Migrants, Governance and Local Development Strategies: A Case Study of International African Migrants in Durban'. Paper presented at the 4th International Congress of Ales Hrdlicka World Anthropology at the Turn of the Centuries, 31 August – 4 September, Prague.

Young, I.M. 2000. *Inclusion and Democracy*. Oxford: Oxford University Press.

Interviews

Anonymous, 10.07.03, 30.08.03, 05.09.03, 08.10.03, 09.10.03, 10.10.03, 21.10.03, 19.11.03, 20.11.03, 27.11.03, 28.11.03a, 28.11.03b, 03.12.03a, 03.12.03b, 05.12.03, 06.12.03a, 06.12.03b, 06.12.03c, 07.12.03, 20.02.04.

Tlou, Joyce. National Consortium for Refugee Affairs, 27.11.03.

Van ger Gerden, Jacob. Lawyers for Human Rights, 27.11.03.

15

The Problem of Identities

The Lesbian, Gay, Bisexual, Transgender and Intersex Social Movement in South Africa

Teresa Dirsuweit

IN 2000 A GROUP of lesbians was gang-raped as they left the official after-party of the Gay and Lesbian Pride march in Braamfontein. Euphemistically termed 'corrective rape', lesbians are often raped as a means of 'curing' them of their lesbianism. Recent research (Reid and Dirsuweit 2002) indicates that black lesbians and gay men in townships are particularly vulnerable to these types of corrective-rape incidents and may be subjected to them more than once in their lives. While the Lesbian, Gay, Bisexual, Transgender and Intersex (LGBTI) movement reacted with concern and condemned the crime, very little attention was given to the incident in the media. The most extraordinary aspect of the incident, however, is that it took place in a country that had just passed the most progressive constitution in the world with regard to gay rights.

These hate crimes are a critical hinge for this discussion on the LGBTI movement in South Africa for they highlight a number of factors that characterise the movement. The LGBTI movement in South Africa is small but has gained enormous ground with regard to the legal standing of gay citizens. At the same time, the movement has struggled to stabilise itself internally over the past ten years. LGBTI governance has not been exempt from painful exclusionary politics with tensions existing along race, class and gender fractures. However, together, this politics and a focus on getting the basic legal framework of South Africa aligned with its constitution has been of enormous benefit to those who have access to the institutions that enforce these rights. It has also meant that more vulnerable sections of the gay community have faced increasing levels of violence related to their sexual lifestyle choices as the gay community becomes more visible. Recently, however, the social movement organisations (SMOs) that make up the movement have reflected on their position and value in poorer township communities and there has been a shift in focus to address the systemic violence that affects these communities on a day-to-day basis.

At the same time there are a number of lasting tensions that relate to how the LGBTI movement has been theorised: the conflicts between social consumption and political citizenship that have beset gay identity politics internationally have found their way into the LGBTI movement locally. This chapter will also explore tensions around the definition of the LGBTI movement in South Africa that respond to a theoretical question about how identity-based movements fit into broader-based struggles around distributional issues. The third lasting tension is exemplified in a comment made in an article by Jara and Lapinsky (1998: 55) that 'an authentic South African gay identity needs to be consciously constructed and that partisan choices need to be made'. The LGBTI movement, as with all identity-based movements, however, is marked by difference and how it deals with these differences is explored in this chapter.

Habermas (1981) first theorises a set of protest movements that do not fall within the ambit of traditional social protest motivated by distributional issues. Briefly, these movements do not have at their core issues of distribution, but rather are concerned with what Habermas terms 'the grammar and form of everyday life'. While Habermas writes very little on social movements, he has had extraordinary influence on the post-socialist left, particularly on issues of social justice and citizenship. At the core of these discussions is the call for the recognition of identity. A political and theoretical binary has evolved out of this call for inclusion of identity recognition as a means of understanding social protest. Often placed at odds with one another, the theoretical debate around recognition politics and distributional politics has raged. Fraser (1997: 3–4), however, critiques the split between recognition and distribution politics:

> These, I maintain, are false antitheses . . . critical theorists should rebut the claim that we must make an either/or choice between the politics of redistribution and the politics of recognition. We should aim instead to identify the emancipatory dimensions of both problematics and to integrate them into a single, comprehensive framework.

Arguing that 'economic injustice and cultural injustice are usually inter-imbricated so as to reinforce each other dialectically', Fraser (1997: 15) suggests that socialist economics combined with deconstructive identity politics provide a substantive model for the transformation of both cultural and social inequities. But Fraser also acknowledges that there is 'no neat theoretical move' that forms a critical theory of recognition and redistribution. She resolves the problem by presenting a *prima facie* match of the transformative politics of socialism with radical cultural deconstruction. Young presents a slightly different model of social justice that recognises both forms of politics, but emphasises that the acknowledgement of cultural difference is necessary to the promotion of social justice:

> The achievement of formal equality does not eliminate social differences, and the rhetorical commitment to the sameness of persons makes it impossible even to name how those differences presently structure privilege and oppression (1990: 164).

Young suggests a radical democratic pluralism (which she is careful to clearly differentiate from liberal pluralism) that acknowledges and affirms social group differences as a means of ensuring their inclusion in social and political institutions:

> Both liberal humanist and leftist political organizations and movements have found it difficult to accept this principle of group autonomy. In a humanist emancipatory politics, if a group is subject to injustice, then all those interested in a just society should unite to combat the powers that perpetuate that injustice. If many groups are subject to injustice, moreover, then they should unite to work for a just society. The politics of difference is certainly not against coalition, nor does it hold that, for example, white should not work against racial injustice or men against sexist injustice. The politics of group assertion, however, takes as a basic principle that members of oppressed groups need separate organizations that exclude other, especially those from privileged groups . . . In discussions within autonomous organizations, group members can determine their specific needs and interests . . . contemporary emancipatory social movements have found autonomy an important

vehicle for empowerment and the development of a group-specific voice and perspective (Young 1990: 167–8).

Fraser (1997) argues that while Young's model of social justice accounts for both aspects of the recognition-redistribution dilemma, it overemphasises the politics of recognition. In later work, however, Young (2002: 85), in taking issue with the notion that the politics of difference have 'splintered progressive politics into separatist enclaves', draws a distinction between identity and difference. Here she argues for a relational approach to social group differentiation – social groups are the sum of similarity and difference as they interact with endogenous and exogenous factors. In this way Young offers a definitional move that allows for a far greater potential to break down the binary between recognition and redistribution.

The recognition-distribution binary haunts the LGBTI social movement in South Africa and is confounded by the post-apartheid political landscape. Overwhelmingly, LGBTI SMOs in South Africa struggle between meeting both distribution and recognition needs and are profoundly ambiguous about how they are situated between the two. Gerald Kraak (1998: ii) summarised the dilemma soon after the inclusion of the equality clause in the constitution:

> In South Africa, identity politics have been given impetus by the rights-based political culture that emerged after apartheid, and a constitutional order that protects a range of human rights. People have begun to organise to secure these . . . From a Marxist and socialist perspective, questions have also been asked about the effectiveness of identity politics because they minimise the importance of class struggle as a vehicle for change . . . This argument points to a potential contradiction of identity politics. In societies as divided as those of Southern Africa, can identity politics lead to change? . . . Marxists and socialists would argue that organisation based on identity is hostage to domination by the interests of the middle class.

The LGBTI movement is one of the few that can boast a pre- and post-apartheid history. Indeed it is this very history that forms the basis of many of the cleavages and theoretical tensions within the movement. The gay and lesbian lobby in South Africa found its roots in the mid-1960s. The subsequent history of the

LGBTI movement has become increasingly solidified in the accounts of gay activists (Gevisser 1994; Jara and Lapinsky 1998; Kraak n.d.): gay politics was dominated in the eighties by the Gay Association of South Africa (GASA). Gay and lesbian politics was firmly established as a white, predominantly male and middle-class form of activism (Gevisser 1994; Jara and Lapinsky 1998). A number of accounts exist of the bitter racial alienation experienced by black gay activists, notably in the case of Simon Nkoli, in predominantly white organisations and social spaces.

> Thus, in the period leading to South Africa's political transition, the gay movement here was crossed by several persistent fault lines – the dominance of white middle class men (irrespective of political persuasion); a faltering black presence; and tension between organisations' social support and political roles (Jara and Lapinsky 1998).

Unlike gender, homosexuality failed to become a significant point of rally within the anti-apartheid movement (Gevisser 1994, 2000; Kraak n.d.). So a further fault-line should be added to Jara and Lapinsky's (1998) statement: while there were many gay anti-apartheid activists, gay politics came late to the political field. LGBTI issues eventually found a significant foothold within the ranks of the broad-based mass mobilisation of the anti-apartheid movement as exemplified by the United Democratic Front (UDF) and LGBTI rights were included in the ANC constitution in 1991. However, the long absence (or lack of recognition) of gay politics had an interesting consequence; while many organisations aligned themselves or distanced themselves from particular political discourse, apart from the small exceptional organisation (for instance, the Organisation of Lesbian and Gay Activists or OLGA), the LGBTI movement had not established a clear progressive political framework that could be considered, debated and revisited. Furthermore, the development of a complex debate on the positioning of progressive gay and lesbian politics in South Africa was further confounded by the general conservatism of the gay community.

Formed in 1994, the primary mandate of the National Coalition for Gay and Lesbian Equality (NCGLE) was the inclusion of the equality clause within the constitution. In the NCGLE leadership a number of anti-apartheid activists aimed to create an umbrella organisation to represent a broad band of lesbian and gay (LG) organisations. For a time the NCGLE was enormously successful and many were awestruck by its greatest victory, ensuring the inclusion of gay rights in the equality clause of the constitution. At its peak, the NCGLE had over 80 organisations affiliated to it. After a number of victories in parliament and the courts, the movement turned its attention to the building and solidification of a LGBTI movement. It seems that at this point, the political expectations and the realities of lesbian and gay life where somewhat irreconcilable:

> . . . the needs were to do with building a movement, a movement made up of cadres, made up of activists on the ground, addressing issues on the ground. We were not that. There were those expectations that we were that, but we were not that (Interview, Former Activist Leader, 2004).

Once it had achieved its primary mandate, the NCGLE began to encounter a number of difficulties. Many of the organisations affiliated to it were founded on the basis of a few social events. There was an enormous resource drain in terms of assisting organisations with funding and a competition to get funding developed between the different organisations despite the fact that 'it was never a consortium to feed the periphery with resources' (Interview, Activist, 2004). There was also a more generalised reason for the stresses on the organisation as 'South Africa experienced a massive imploding of the non-governmental sector' (Knoesen 2002). Many of the member organisations simply did not survive this process. Furthermore, a conflict within the movement about the political affiliation of NCGLE had developed:

> . . . the NC[GLE] made a serious engagement to be as inclusive as possible. The range of organisations was from across the country, but what became clear over time was that such a coalition was really quite unsustainable. As the organisation grew, as it started developing networks and contacts with a whole range of progressive organisations that were not exclusively LGBT oriented, it reached a point where tensions were exposed. These tensions came out prior to the elections of 1999, in particular at an election forum organised by NC[GLE] in Pretoria which got quite heated (Interview, Activist, 2004).

In 1999, recognising that 'a more institutional approach within the progressive movement' was required, the NCGLE was restructured resulting in the Equality Project and the separation of the different organisations (Knoesen 2002, n.d.). Despite the problems of the NCGLE, LGBTI activists speak of the legal gains that the organisation made with deep respect. And as the older leadership of the NCGLE (many of whom are still prominent on the boards of the main organisations that make up the LGBTI movement in South Africa) gives way to a fresh set of leaders, the problems that the NCGLE encountered have been transformed into lessons:

> I've heard from quite a few people that the coalition was too pushy as far as the politics go, and that that is not how an organisation should be. So I mean there were negatives to the coalition (Interview, Activist, 2004).

Post-NCGLE, one of the striking features of LGBTI politics is how few people are involved in them. Ironically, the inclusion of the equality clause in the constitution has resulted in a sense of lulled apathy within the LGBTI community.

> Some of major battles had been fought and won . . . things were going quite smoothly, so there was a lot of apathy especially among people who thought everything was going fine for them (Interview, Activist, 2004).

Curiously, as the state continues to gain legitimacy within the LGBTI community with regard to its promotion of LGBTI rights, the everyday politics of homophobia have become secondary. A stasis has developed in the LGBTI politics worldwide in relation to increased acceptance of LG sexuality. It is a painful paradox that as the state introduces the institutions to establish and maintain gay rights, LGBTI members face increasing levels of homophobic violence. This violence, however, is more dominant in poorer communities and it is a bitter realisation for many that

> . . . people aren't willing to go to rallies, to write letters, to do things because they think, well, I'm okay, so why should I bother. And the fact of the matter is I think those people are very narrow in their perception

of what their community is, because our community is much larger than what we see (Interview, Activist, 2004).

But the 'seeing' of this quote is critical for vulnerable LGBTI communities are also amongst the most hidden. In many instances apathy can be explained in terms of a lack of awareness. While there is some (scant) media coverage of corrective rape, following similar stories in the international media, online magazines and other media, they are saturated with stories regarding the recognition of LG marriages.

> We're still in a situation where our rights are being advanced. So I think if we are ever in a situation where there was an attempt to push back those rights, then you would see the emergence of a social movement (Interview, Activist, 2004).

A more cynical view of apathy must, however, be entertained. This can be seen in terms of the LGBTI community being so fractured along lines of race, class, gender and sexual identity, and that one part of the community simply does not care what happens to other parts of the community.

> Because of lots of legal successes in LGBTI issues, there is some sense of complacency, and it is not easy to mobilise people. Anger and opposition do wonders to bring people together, since there are issues to fight for, but these are now the very issues which divide . . . (Interview, Activist, 2004).

The Problem of Identities
Race
Racism has for a long time been a crisis within the LGBTI community. The experiences of racism of black gay activists in the eighties have continued to plague the gay community, particularly in social clubbing spaces where there has been a long history of racism. Nkoli related his experiences of alienation at the one white club that would allow him entry during the eighties (Gevisser 1994) and in April 1993 the Association for Bisexuals, Gays and Lesbians (ABIGALE) picketed outside the club Strawbs in protest of their racist exclusions (Gevisser 1994). Recently, a club was taken to the equality court with regard to their racist entry policies by a group of Cape Town LGBTI members. The court

founded in favour of the group and the club was asked to apologise to the people concerned. The money that was given to the group by the club was used to set up a new organisation (Siyazenzela) in May 2004. In the July 2004 edition of the gay newspaper *Exit* yet another appallingly racist incident in the LGBTI community was reported. Furthermore, in many instances racism has a far more subtle manifestation:

> . . . gay places are very dominated by white males. And even if it's not directly said that black people can't come in – the whole culture, the whole feel of it is extremely exclusionary. I feel excluded from it – it's not a free and open space for everyone (Interview, Activist, 2004).

> There is this sort of underlying racism and I think when it comes to Pride that is extremely pronounced (Interview, Activist, 2004).

The response of the LGBTI movement has ranged from allowing the issue to turn the movement in on itself to an extracted apathy:

> . . . the fact that race and class was an issue was denied by many. That was a very big problem (Interview, Activist, 2004).

While many of the interviewees described racism within the community, few could provide an adequate explanation apart from 'you can't expect the issues which apply to society not to apply to lesbian and gay society. But I think they do more or less apply everywhere' (Interview, Activist, 2004). Racism within the LGBTI community, however, seems to be particularly blatant and vicious and it is very perturbing that these incidents should be encountered in the social spaces of the gay community for these act as the 'bonding-agents of community – the sports clubs, counselling centres, religious groups, bars, clubs and social networks' (Gevisser 1994). Sexual identity in South Africa cuts across a vast range of difference and draws it into small social networks and an even smaller number of social spaces that not only reflect broader tensions in South Africa, but also make them more potent. What makes racism within the LGBTI community more poignant (and indeed may even explain the vociferousness), however, is that the general rejection and lack of affirmation most LGBTI people experience in broader society is re-enacted through racial prejudice.

Class

Coupled to race is the issue of class as a dominant weakness in the LGBTI community. Class prejudices have surprised many of the activists within the LGBTI community, but as the black middle class has grown in the past ten years so classist dynamics have appeared and become solidified.

> But, we're at the point now where sexual orientation is no longer what unifies us. We're so happy that we are all gay, but after a while – there is a divide that is not only racial. When I look at the guys, how many choose groups to hang out at a social, students will be together – [they form groups around] race and class (Interview, Activist, 2004).

> White clubs in Pretoria are racist, that you can know. Even to the extreme level of . . . if you are black and you have Diesel on you can come in but if you are black and you are a bit poorer it's a different issue (Interview, Activist, 2004).

> . . . many black lesbians that won't assert don't have that power. The ones who do have the power tend to . . . kind of merge into the white lesbian community. So, you'll have your yuppie type, your educated, they have good jobs . . . But there's a divide between them and the lesbian who lives in Hillbrow or Yeoville or the townships . . . you have your type, your middle to upper/middle professional – educated – and they don't really mix . . . (Interview, Activist, 2004).

Class dramatically skews the experiences of LGBTI people:

> I think there are huge numbers of . . . economically active, happy middle-class gay and lesbian couples, for example, who consider that they have all the rights they need and that there is no more to do. There is no more struggle, there's no more changes to be made . . . (Interview, Activist, 2004).

The experiences of operationalising gay rights in working-class and middle-class communities are different. In one of the interviews, an activist claimed that class also skewed the ways in which activism was perceived. Specifically, outreach strategies were criticised for being too superficial in their approach:

. . . they are liberals; declaring love to a black person is sufficient; or black people who are liberals themselves . . . (Interview, Activist, 2004).

Here the smoothness around the activist strategies described earlier in the chapter may indeed be less coherent than it appears. While the strategies of economically empowering poorer LGBTI communities are similar, the meaning and intention of empowerment in terms of class politics may be very different.

Gender

Women are well represented on most of the boards of the different organisations, but gender inequalities occurred at the intersection of race, class and gender. Black lesbians are not well represented on the boards of the different SMOs and lesbians from poorer communities are rare indeed.

There's visibility, which is another big issue for black lesbians. They're not visible in the movement. We're not visible in women's organisations and we're not visible in the LGBT organisation. So, that's a big issue (Interview, Activist, 2004).

Once again LGBTI social spaces were the focus of a number of exclusionary incidents:

All the clubs in Braamfontein are owned by white gay men. So, any kind of space that we could claim is controlled by white gay men . . . We don't want black women here; it's just that the posters that you have on the wall is the language that you speak, the music that you play, it excludes black lesbians, you know (Interview, Activist, 2004).

Strategically, two approaches emerged from the interviews. The Forum for the Empowerment of Women (FEW) emphasises the economic empowerment of lesbians coupled with an increased sense of confidence and entitlement.

. . . space, I think, is something that comes with power and black lesbians don't have power in South Africa, they don't have power in the LGBT movement. And that's power from a purely economic point of view. Economic I suppose, social power if you define social power as having the self-confidence to go out there and claim things, which comes with economic power, it comes with education, it comes with independence. And many black lesbians that won't assert don't have that power (Interview, Activist, 2004).

The Equality Project endorsed this approach, but in line with their broader strategies emphasised the building of alliances with the broader South African feminist community:

On a very personal and basic human level, there is an opportunity for specifically black lesbians to form some kind of strong movement in this country with an alliance with other women's organisations – or other heterosexual women individuals who are working in these organisations – and I think there is room, and an absolute need, for that . . . (Interview, Activist, 2004).

One of the strengths of the LGBTI movement is its increasing recognition of and commitment to the needs of black lesbians. There is also a strong commitment to empowering working-class black lesbians and to, in the long term, increasing the presence and visibility of black women within leadership structures in the LGBTI movement. More importantly, these commitments find their way into the daily praxis of the different organisations through regular workshops, training opportunities and social events.

Sexual Identity

At the centre of the LGBTI movement are the rights of lesbians and gay men. The bisexual, transgender and intersex part of the movement, however, receives little attention. In alignment with international trends, the South African LGBTI community has recently added the intersex 'i', but there was little by way of lobbying for the rights of intersex people. Notably, the Equality Project was integral in reforming the law in terms of recognising transgender, transsexual and intersex people in the form of the Alteration of Sex Description and Sex Status Act No. 49 of 2003 (Equality Project 2004). But apart from the odd support group for transgender people, there is very little by way of active organisation around these communities. Within the LGBTI community, these sexual identities are abjected by those who see themselves as the normal gay majority. The response to media coverage of Pride (which generally focuses only on drag queens) is very often one of anger that more 'normal' gays and lesbians are not shown in the media more often.

> At every single Gay Pride event there are our transsexuals that do parade and I have no problem with that . . . some people of the community might have . . . but there's place for all of us. It's the bisexual, lesbian, gay, transgendered and intersexed community . . . and the media has focused on the wrong side of the gay community . . . I mean that's not what we're all about (Interview, Activist, 2004).

> . . . if we look at our mission, lesbian and gay comes first, transgender comes second (Interview, Activist, 2004).

> . . . because I think that for anyone at the moment, in the organisation, to understand transgendered issues . . . that would be wrong. What needs to happen is transgendered people need to be brought on board in some sort of organisational way . . . (Interview, Activist, 2004).

A number of enclaves exist within the South African LGBTI community. On the face of it, it often appears that sexuality simply is not enough to weave these sub-cultures of the LGBTI community together. Indeed, should one even speak of an LGBTI community in the singular?

> Identity is not enough, as a gay man I don't necessarily have much in common with others who share my identity as such (Interview, Activist, 2004).

However, in itself the existence of these differences within the community is potentially a strength. Enabling a cross-section of people from different communities to organise around a set of issues is a powerful political tool. But perhaps this vision of inclusivity is naïve:

> Identity politics – the real issues are not so much identity issues, as access to services and resources, and about how do the poor get access to the law. These are not easy issues to fit into identity (Interview, Activist, 2004).

There is a powerful perception within the LGBTI community that there is a split between identity needs and socio-economic needs and the movement is actively shaping itself to meet the needs of the most vulnerable within the community. To a large extent, the politically active community has abandoned the issues of race, class, sexism and intolerance of sexual difference within the broader LGBTI community. However, there is a real danger that a culture of isolationism could develop within the LGBTI community. Examples of well-established LGBTI movements internationally show that LGBTI communities are beset with cleavages around these weak points. However, for the LGBTI movement to strengthen, a culture of inclusivity needs to be established. To go back to the introduction of the chapter, at the core of this issue of inclusivity is that both distributional and recognition issues are of equal importance. There is still an open theoretical discussion then as to how these two needs should be forged.

Consumers and Citizens

Both the international and local literature on LGBTI movements identify the tensions between the social and the political aspects of gay organisations (Kriesi 1995). In Gevisser's (1994) documentation of the emergence of the LGBTI movement in South Africa, this has been one of the key dilemmas troubling the LG movement in South Africa from its inception:

> But while most white middle-class gay people stay away, so too do most black working-class gays and lesbians. And this points, most strongly, to the dilemma in which current progressive lesbian and gay politics now finds itself: its expressly liberationist ideology alienates the conservative white gay subculture while its expressly political profile does not take directly to the interests of recently unclosetted gay men and lesbians from the townships who need social space and support (Gevisser 1994: 82).

As the LGBTI community in South Africa has developed in a dispensation that promises legal freedom, and as it has been introduced to global trends, these politics have become far more complex. One of the defining (and certainly the most public) features of the LGBTI community has been a culture of conspicuous consumption of gay signifiers, hence the excitement over the potential of the pink rand. In this conspicuous consumption lies a conundrum about the form and content of LGBTI activism. Activism in its more classical formation finds its expression in a series of advocacy and protest actions against the state and hegemonic structures. In gay politics, however, this form of political action is often less apparent.

In South Africa the state is clearly in alignment with the principle of ensuring LGBTI rights, and gay politics is increasingly about shifting homophobic hegemonic discourse. The face of gay politics in South Africa, however, is increasingly most visible in a series of spectacle events in which conspicuous consumption is displayed. Key examples of this are the Mother City Queer Project which hosts an annual themed costume party and the Gay Pride event which, like similar events in New York and Sydney, has increasingly shifted from being a political march to a festive Mardi Gras. This emphasis on the conspicuous consumption as a means of affirming identity, and by extension asserting LGBTI cultural identity, is the basis of a conundrum in which the politics of consumption and the politics of production and counter-hegemony jostle to achieve a similar political end. Aldridge (2003: 100) summarises the tensions within the conundrum:

> *Citizenship* is presented as a means of escape from the evil of passivity. Citizens are actively engaged in public life, whereas stupefied customers wallow or flounder in private enclaves. Obsessed with their needy worries about service delivery, consumers are childishly ignorant of political and economic realities . . . What consumers want is a fix: a better service now. The citizen, in contrast, is aware that these symptoms have complex causes . . .

Nevertheless, within South African LGBTI politics, conspicuous consumption has drawn far more people into the project of affirming and asserting LGBTI identity. As Aldridge's (2003) quote suggests, this type of consumption has certainly split the LGBTI community into political activists and gay consumers (or as they are more commonly called: muscle marys). Similarly a divide has developed between those who apolitically consume and those who are politically engaged in the community.

A case in point is the transformation of the annual Gay Pride march from a political protest event to a commercial endeavour. Gay Pride is a key event for the gay community and provides a forum for activism as well as self-identification.

The first Gay Pride march left from Braamfontein in the inner city of Johannesburg on 10 October 1990. The first marches were clearly a forum for gay and lesbian activism, lobbying for the recognition of gay and lesbian rights in the changing political landscape of South Africa. With the inclusion of gay rights within the constitution, Gay Pride changed its name from 'march' to 'festival'. This transformation is not unique to South Africa; the politics of consumption has transformed Pride marches worldwide. Subsequently, LGBTI social movements have struggled with the ambiguity of Gay Pride. Pride in South Africa has been particularly fraught with a series of bitter politics and power struggles.

> . . . when you read the papers the following Monday morning, and the lesbian and gay community is presented as the slim, beautiful, white gay boys. And that's all that people see. And it's just the wrong picture. The majority of people in this country are black – it then makes sense that the majority of lesbian and gay people will be black. And Pride doesn't bring that out. It continues on an exclusionary route that it has taken in terms of restricting people even to parties – after-parties for Pride (Interview, Activist, 2004).

The reason for this huge shift is that over the years there has been the enormous stress that Pride presents for the organisers of the event. Pride has consistently run at a loss, except in 2001. It also is a thankless task with bitter personal and political struggles amongst the members of the committee – many of whom leave, with only a few remaining to continue the organisation of the event. Interviewees also reported minimal interest and support from the different LGBTI SMOs. In 2002, an entrepreneur registered Pride as a closed corporation (Pride Communications) and began to treat the event as a commercial spectacle. With this change in organisation management, the route of Pride was shifted from the (poorer and much maligned) inner city to the affluent northern suburbs and has taken place there since. On the one hand, the shift was necessary for the promotion of sponsorship from a conservative business community. On the other hand, this was a moment when the power of consumption politics clearly overwhelmed the workings of community politics. The changing of the route has carved out the two spheres of the LGBTI community and placed them into powerful relief:

. . . I wrote some sort of letter to *Exit,* for a lot of people from township communities for example, they walk the streets of Soweto every day, taking a risk, because they face homophobia from their communities. And all we're asking people is to take one day to walk downtown, with 12 000 other gay people so the risk is minimal, but that is what they said. It was unsafe to go downtown. Well, its unsafe to be a lesbian or gay person living in a township community, you expect those people to do that every day, you can't do it for one single day to show your solidarity (Interview, Activist, 2004).

People may say that we go past businesses and we're not going past people we want to get the message to, but what is the message at the end of the day that we want to get across . . . (Interview, Gay Business involved in Pride, 2004).

For South Africa and the establishment of post-apartheid progressive politics, Pride is an extraordinary case study because it highlights many of the tensions that SMOs experience in terms of their role in the transformation of South African socio-economic dynamics into those that provide social justice to a broad range of interest groups. In this case, the crisis of legitimacy does not lie with the state; the state in many respects is highly productive in the delivery of gay rights. There is rather a tension between different parts of the community about who may speak for the community and where the power of the community lies. These tensions are raised within SMOs with regard to the terms upon which a social movement could legitimately represent the needs of the LGBTI community.

However, the politics of consumption may be a bit more complex. Aldridge (2003: 102) draws our attention to the political potential of the *radically conspicuous* consumption of culturally weighted signifiers, '. . . consumption, for them, is a vehicle of liberation and self-expression . . .' Therefore, radically conspicuous consumption makes use of the power of the fun economy of late capitalism to achieve recognition and affirmation of identity through social networks (whether they be physical or virtual). At first glance, albeit unintentional, this is an ostensibly powerful form of activism. However, those who are excluded from or those who choose not to be a part of the economy are subsequently deeply peripheralised through a combination of a lack of community acceptance, a lack of access to institutional justice, and economic constraints to entering consumption culture. Furthermore, in its current form, the social relations within the platforms of radically conspicuous consumption reinforce bitter racial, gender and class cleavages within the LGBTI community. There is, however, a complex discussion around legitimacy here for many seek the sense of community that the social spaces of consumption provide.

Movement Politics

Is this a Movement?

While the LGBTI social movement is young, it is apparent that some thought has gone into theorising the movement politically. A lot of this thought, though, has been centred on finding a defining model of social movements that the SMOs can work towards fulfilling, and while LGBTI politics fulfil Habermas's criteria for a social movement, many of the SMOs have sought to model themselves on a more classical Marxist model of coalition politics. Subsequently, many of the leaders in the movement do not define their organisations and the role of their organisations as that of being a social movement.

> It took some time for people to realise you can't be in this work and not be political. The movement is moving towards the left. I think it is an emerging movement, I don't think it's ever been a movement. It may yet become one (Interview, Former Activist Leader, 2004).

At the same time it must be recognised that alliance-building strategies, while promoting the socio-economic empowerment of the most vulnerable portions of the LGBTI community, may result in the needs of the LGBTI community being peripheralised:

> A movement is what you would see as a strict Marxist revolutionary movement. With some movements your goal is to create a majority. But some movements you can't, you'll always be a structural minority. You may get some support from that majority but you are not part of that majority, I don't think. I think that some movements sort of have a . . . populist movement . . . I don't know, this is a decidedly unpopular movement (Interview, Activist, 2004).

Establishing the LGBTI Movement

The key resource-oriented challenges that the LGBTI movement faces are leadership and funding. Many of the SMOs interviewed were well funded, but there was some concern about how to sustain funding in the long term, particularly since most of the funding was received from foreign donors. A small portion of funding was received from internal funding structures such as the national lottery, but very little funding was received from the LGBTI community itself. In the past, many of the organisations engaged in unhealthy competition to secure funding. However, it was noted that since SMOs received funds generously from funders, a lot of the tensions that had beset the movement had become diluted. Furthermore, many of the funding organisations also provided a development framework for the different organisations for SMOs that also had a positive effect on the way in which the movement was developing.

> . . . the healthy component of that is that you need to look very hard at what you do and what is special about what you do. And grow that. You need to be selling, to some extent, a unique product, or if you're not, you need to be working in collaboration with others, rather than against others. And that is the healthy part of it, I think, you've got to continuously re-check yourself, you've got to be relevant, you've got to be doing what you do well and you've got to be able to prove it (Interview, Activist, 2004).

Funders have a lot of say in the way the LGBTI movement develops and for the most part the funders' vision and intervention was beneficial: 'What I would like to see as a consequence of the intervention is an actual, visible and organised black lesbian and gay community' (Interview 2004). While this type of clarity carried through the different organisations and their endeavours, sometimes activists expressed anxieties about the reaction of funders to increasing the scope of their organisations into economic development work and indeed this was the cause of some tension within organisations.

The dissolution of the NCGLE left a vacuum of well-connected, seasoned political leadership in the LGBTI movement:

> . . . there's been quite a large shift . . . when I first arrived there were some very heavyweight people working in lesbian and gay activism, with

> very good connections to unions and political parties and government.
> It seemed a lot more solid (Interview, Activist, 2004).

> There was no real leadership initiative, since the organisation was very
> tied to the individuals who were there and making things go (Interview,
> Activist, 2004).

Many of the leaders of the NCGLE sit on the boards of the different
organisations, but see their participation in the different organisations as
receding:

> I think there is space for new leadership to emerge. Now organisations
> which are there, the subjective factor has to come in that way, whereby
> we get a core of comrades, who can think about where the movement
> should be going, about how the movement should be built. [Older
> activists] have a role to play but I think we need to give space to new
> people. Otherwise you end up with dinosaurs (Interview, Activist, 2004).

The new generation of post-1999 leaders have expressed a number of anxieties
about their youth and their lack of experience, while at the same time
recognising that their presence within the different organisations had freshened
approaches to LGBTI activism, as well as providing the different organisations
with a greater range of flexibility:

> We're not all experienced. And I think that also if you look at current
> leadership in organisations, although the current leadership does have
> some history, we're very young – extremely young . . . If you look at the
> idea that these are the leaders within the actual NGO sector within a
> particular movement . . . There is a kind of an alarm bell . . . we're an
> extremely young group of leaders, facing a particularly difficult piece of
> work . . . (Interview, Activist, 2004).

In terms of strategising to continue establishing and growing the LGBTI
movement, again there emerged two subtly different understandings of the
roles of the SMOs and the activists in them. In the first instance there is an
emphasis on the formation of an allied popular movement and drawing on
this allied community as a means to strengthen the LGBTI movement:

LGBT issues are not hugely popular, and the way to become seen as legitimate is by how you get involved in other human rights struggles and how you position your work as part of broader issues. Pre-1994 was a lesson; there were broader issues which caused change. Now there is an isolationism developing (Interview, Activist, 2004).

For me the question is, is there a need for a movement? Speaking to some activist friends of mine, who are not necessarily from the lesbian and gay community, I have come to the conclusion that a strict lesbian and gay movement is not going to work . . . If any kind of social movement that will deal with sexual orientation issues will be formed, it's going to be much broader than homosexuality (Interview, Activist, 2004).

The second position is in general agreement with the strategy of alliance building, but approaches it from a position of needing to settle, strengthen and grow the LGBTI movement first. Another activist spoke of equating the issue of orientation with issues such as poverty, and even suggested that gay and lesbian issues should be presented as 'greater' than other issues (Interview, Activist, 2004).

Within this particular narrative of how a progressive LGBTI social movement should develop were also some concerns about how one maintains an inclusive culture drawing upon the richness of the LGBTI community:

. . . there is no one gay identity, though society often sees it as one . . . (Interview, Activist, 2004).

We have to be less interventionist and rather allow it to grow . . . (Interview, Activist, 2004).

. . . so I think it's very important that we start on a civil movement and an inclusivity campaign . . . (Interview, Activist, 2004).

There is strong agreement within the LGBTI movement around its objectives: there is a clear sense that the needs of vulnerable LGBTI communities have to be addressed. The LGBTI movement has moved past a simple call for recognition into a call for socio-economic justice. In order to achieve this objective, the

LGBTI movement has identified the need to form linkages with other social movement groups that are not primarily concerned with LGBTI politics. This may take the form of coalition politics or it may take the form of a looser set of strategic partnerships or consultative forums. Furthermore, some of the organisations within the LGBTI movement may make firmer alliances than others. While critical for the ongoing growth of the LGBTI movement, these linkages will effectively intensify the recognition-redistribution dilemma as the movement asserts its position within broader social movement politics, particularly since the recognition work of the LGBTI movement is not complete.

There are simply no clean political solutions to the messy matrix of LGBTI internal and external politics. These can only be managed in a responsive manner that allows for a flexible and relational accounting for changing exogenous and endogenous factors. In the last ten years the LGBTI movement has claimed a substantive political and social space within post-apartheid democracy. To maintain this position and to open up further space, there is one overarching challenge: the continued strengthening of the movement internally so that it is able to assert itself as an important actor in a stronger democracy.

> But the measurements for that is not going to be in the number of counselling centres that we see around the country, but, in a general sense, how much pride we see in the gay and lesbian community. Movement: a sense of voices, that we see them in the media, that there's a sense of, presence . . . (Interview, Activist, 2004).

References

Aldridge, A. 2003. *Consumption.* Cambridge: Polity.

Equality Project. 2004. 'Commentary on the Alteration of Sex Description and Sex Status Act No. 49 of 2003'. http:///www.equality.org.za.

Fraser, N. 1997. *Justice Interruptus: Critical Reflections on the 'Postsocialist' Condition.* New York: Routledge.

Gevisser, M. 1994. 'A Different Fight for Freedom: A History of South African Lesbian and Gay organisations – the 1950s to the 1990s'. In M. Gevisser and E. Cameron (eds), *Defiant Desire: Gay and Lesbian Lives in South Africa.* Johannesburg: Ravan Press.

――――. 2000. 'Mandela's Stepchildren: Homosexual Identity in Post-Apartheid South Africa'. In P. Drucker (ed.), *Different Rainbows.* London: Gay Men's Press.

Habermas, J. 1981. 'New Social Movements'. *Telos* 49: 33–7.

Jara, M. and S. Lapinsky, 1998. 'Forging a Representative Gay Liberation Movement in South Africa'. *Development Update* 2: 44–55.

Knoesen, E. 2002. 'Presentation to Amnesty International Global Conference on Lesbian and Gay Rights, Sydney 2002'. www.equality.org.za/archive/2002/lgepsydney.php.

———. n.d. 'State of the Nation: Evert Knoesen (in interview with Luiz DeBarros'. www.mambaonline.co.za/feature/feature_state_project_02.php.

Kraak, G. 1998. 'Class, Race, Nationalism and the Politics of Identity: A Perspective from the South'. *Development Update* 2: i–xii.

———. n.d. 'Homosexuality and the South African Left: The Ambiguities of Exile'. Unpublished seminar paper presented at Wits Institute of Social and Economic Research.

Kriesi, H. 1995. *New Social Movements in Western Europe: A Comparative Analysis*. Minneapolis: University of Minnesota Press.

Reid, G. and T. Dirsuweit. 2002. 'Understanding Systemic Violence'. *Urban Forum* 31 (3): 99–126.

Young, I.M. 1990. *Justice and the Politics of Difference*. Princeton: Princeton University Press.

———. 2002. *Inclusion and Democracy*. Oxford: Oxford University Press.

Interviews

Research participants have been assured anonymity. No interview list is provided as a result of the sensitivity of interview content, and for the protection of research participants. This is to prevent any possibility of the speakers' identities being deduced by linking statements quoted in various parts of the text.

16

The Challenges of Inclusion and Transformation

The Women's Movement in Democratic South Africa

Shireen Hassim

THE WOMEN'S MOVEMENT in South Africa is widely considered to be a success, with many feminist observers drawing attention to the constitutional commitments to gender equality, the array of progressive legislation and policies dealing with various forms of gender inequality and, not least, the large number of women occupying elected political positions. In examining the South African women's movement, this chapter seeks to understand what strategies have been employed by women's organisations to negotiate power *vis-à-vis* the state and other social movements, how these strategies have been shaped by the context of democracy, and what kinds of equality outcomes can be claimed as the product of women's activism in the democratic period.

This chapter argues that the South African women's movement must be understood as comprising heterogeneous organisations, rather than being viewed through the lens of a single organisation. It seeks to examine the extent to which this heterogeneous movement is able to ensure that the gains made in the transitional period of the early 1990s, when the post-apartheid state was designed, will be made real. This assessment of the women's movements is made against a particular definition of a 'strong' social movement. A strong social movement has the capacity to articulate the particular interests of its constituencies, to mobilise those constituencies in defence of those interests and is able to develop independent strategies to achieve its aims while holding open the possibilities of alliance with other progressive movements. This definition suggests that a strong social movement requires a degree of political autonomy in order to retain its relative power within any alliance. In addition to these organisational capabilities, the ideological influences of feminism are vital in building robust women's movements. A long-term view of the South African women's movement against this definition of movement strength suggests that the movement is relatively weak, apart from a brief moment in the early 1990s.

The argument proceeds by firstly outlining the theoretical and strategic debates relating to definitions of the term 'women's movement' in the South African context. I then map the current terrain of the women's movement, identifying and classifying different forms of organisations and strategies. The chapter concludes by addressing the relationships between social movements, the democratic state and the women's movement, examining in particular the impact of the institutionalisation of gender on the women's movement.

Inclusion and Transformation: Classifying the South African Women's Movement

Attempts to define 'women's movement' raise a peculiar set of considerations, as this is not a movement in which subjects, interests and ideological forms are self-evident. Firstly and perhaps most obviously, women do not mobilise as women simply because they are women. They may frame their actions in terms of a range of identities, whether as worker, student, African, white and so on. In other words, there is not a stable subject for mobilisation. Indeed, as several theorists have pointed out, attempts to disaggregate gender identity are near futile, as the cultural meanings of 'woman' shift in relation to the numerous other markers of identity and in different contexts. Secondly, there is contestation over how to define the notion of 'women's interests' given the interactions between race, class and other objective and subjective interests. Gender is simultaneously everywhere, in that gender differences are inscribed in practically all human relationships as well as in the ordering of the social, political and economic structures of all societies, and nowhere, in that it is difficult to apprehend as an independent variable. And finally, the women's movement takes different forms in different contexts, operating at some moments as a formalised structure and at others as a loose network. This variety of organisational forms is accompanied by a range of tactics used, from assimilative to confrontational and even violent.

As Mohanty (1991) and other post-colonial scholars have argued, women's movements need to be understood in their particular historical and political contexts. Women's movements are not homogeneous entities characterised by singular and coherent sets of demands. Rather, by their nature they tend to be diverse, embracing multiple organisational forms, ideologies and even at times contradictory demands. Indeed, some activists prefer to speak about the existence of many women's movements in South Africa, reflecting these different tendencies (Fester 1997). Despite these diversities, however, it is possible to name and loosely bind together organisations that mobilise women collectively on the basis of their gender identity as a women's movement. Like other social movements, women's movements wax and wane in the context of particular political, economic and social crises. What needs to be understood is why and when women's organisations act in a co-ordinated way – that is, defining at what moment disparate groups within the movement coalesce in such a way that they *act* as a *movement*, distinct from other political forces.

In this chapter, I contrast a 'transformational' feminist approach with an 'inclusionary' feminist approach, in order to elicit a set of criteria by which to assess the challenges of the South African women's movement. In defining the transformational approach I draw on Maxine Molyneux's conceptual distinction between 'strategic gender interests' and 'practical gender needs'. Molyneux defines 'practical gender needs' as those which arise from the everyday responsibilities of women based on a gendered division of labour, while 'strategic gender interests' are those interests that women share in overthrowing power inequalities based on gender (Molyneux 1985). While Molyneux (1998) acknowledges that these distinctions might be difficult to pin down in practice, her conceptualisation of women's movements recognises the diversity of women's interests, while allowing feminists to distinguish those strategies that are likely to lead to radical change. In Molyneux's approach, the task of feminism is to examine the particular ways in which power operates within and between the political, social and economic spheres of specific societies – in effect, this is a political project of transformation.

The inclusionary approach defines women's interests as more limited, focusing only on women's relationships to formal political institutions. In this view, the most stable interest that cuts across the range of differences between women is women's exclusion (or at least marginalisation) from the political arena as conventionally understood (Phillips 1995; Baldez 2002). Regardless of race, class, ethnicity, etc., women are consistently defined as political outsiders or as second-class citizens, whose entry into the public sphere is either anachronistic and short term, or conditional upon their maternal social roles. Here the emphasis is on women's interest in accessing arenas of public power, and less on debating the policy outcomes of such engagements. The task of feminism, in this more constrained approach, is to challenge exclusion. The political projects that are associated with this approach are, for example, women's enfranchisement, struggles focused on women's representation in national parliaments and the emphasis on electoral systems, quotas and other mechanisms for breaking political-systemic blockages. Inclusionary feminism – or equality feminism – may be seen to create some of the necessary conditions for the removal of gender inequalities but it is reluctant to tamper with the structural basis of inequalities. This reluctance stems in part from a strategic imperative to maintain minimal conditions for unity among women and in part from the ideological underpinnings of liberalism, which regards family and market as lying outside the realm of state action.

Like the distinction between women's practical needs and strategic gender interests, the transformatory and the inclusionary approaches to defining women's interests are not mutually exclusive. Rather, they need to be seen as part of a continuum of women's struggles for full citizenship, which may take a linear historical form (that is, a shift from inclusionary demands to transformative demands over time) or may be present within a single movement at a given moment with some sectors pursuing alliances with political elites for inclusion and others pushing towards a more radical set of demands. As I will discuss below, in South Africa both these approaches have been used in order to advance gender-equality claims, at times with striking synergy. However, although these approaches may co-exist within women's movements, they are many ways in which they are in tension with one another. It is important to note that each approach has long-term implications for what *kinds* of political alliances are built, which may in turn impact on internal relations within the women's movement. In the case of the inclusionary approach, women's movements need access to political power to pursue the interests of representation effectively. Although they can gain this access through effective mobilisation, they also need linkages with power brokers within political parties in order to ensure ongoing attention to the political system. Consequently there is a tendency for inclusionary politics to become increasingly elite-based.

Transformatory feminism, on the other hand, is more likely to be conducted in alliance with other social movements aiming at structural transformation, such as social movements of the poor. This kind of politics may bring certain sections of the women's movement into contestation with elite and party-oriented members, as it is a form of politics that is likely to take a more confrontational approach over party manifestoes and state policies. The outcome of such alliances may be a marginalisation of these actors from the state and political parties.

The inclusionary approach in South Africa has its most immediate roots in the strategic approach adopted by the Women's National Coalition (WNC) during the early 1990s. A lasting consequence of the transitional period was the emphasis in women's organisations on the issue of inclusion, and a slow marginalisation of the politics of transformation. In the WNC, both strategies were held together as complementary and indeed mutually dependent. This is most clearly exemplified in the Women's Charter for Effective Equality, adopted by the WNC in February 1994, which calls for increased access to arenas of decision-making as well as for structural transformation. The strategy of inclusion had broad support among women activists as it was seen as a means to the goal of changing the conditions of women's lives. It was an implicit questioning of the extent to which non-elite groups could expect democracy to increase their access to power and was the basis on which to launch a questioning of the assumptions of the political transition. The demand for quotas was supported because it was seen as an instrument to facilitate women's access to decision-making and to create a political space to articulate a transformatory ideal of citizenship. Representation was not conceived as an end in itself but as part of a broader agenda of redistribution of social and economic power.

For these reasons, as well, the women's movement participated in shaping the design of the national machinery for women, a set of institutions inside and around the state that would create the mechanisms to articulate women's particular policy interests and hold the state accountable to its broad commitments to gender equality. The South African women's movement thus exemplified the strongest and most progressive version of inclusionary feminism. However, the new emphasis on the state had contradictory outcomes. On the one hand, loss of leadership and strategic vision weakened the structures of the women's movement. On the other hand, the move into the state undoubtedly created room for integrating gender concerns into key law reform and social policy processes.

Mapping the Women's Movement in Post-Apartheid South Africa

One of the most notable changes in the landscape of the women's movement in the post-1994 period was the fragmentation and stratification of women's organisations in civil society. The political centre of the WNC did not survive as the layer of the top leadership of women's organisations shifted into positions in the state and bureaucracy. The new stratifications that emerged reflected a disaggregation of the movement into a diversity of arenas, some of which (such as those closely tied to policy-making processes) were strengthened by new approaches to civil society within the state, whereas other levels reverted to the more familiar community-based forms of organisations.

The post-apartheid women's movement can be characterised as having three distinct arenas:
* national policy advocates;
* networks and coalitions; and
* community-based organisations.

Two aspects of women's political activism fall outside of this characterisation, but are important to analyse, given my definition of the women's movement as a broad umbrella encompassing diverse organisations and occupying a variety of spaces. The first set of activities is the highly prominent participation of women in political parties in the period since 1994. The second lies at the other end of the spectrum – women's participation in other social movements, albeit as members rather than as leaders and albeit that the mobilisation of their gendered identities is muted (which is not to say that it is not a valid explanation for why women have joined those movements). I will return to the arenas of political parties and other social movements below.

Looking at the first level of the pyramid, it is evident that there has been a strengthening of non-governmental organisations (NGOs) that act as advocacy agents and are tied in to state policy processes (for example, the Gender Advocacy Programme, NISAA and the Gender Research Project at the Centre for Applied Legal Studies). These organisations have the expertise, and in a relative sense, the funding, to intervene in legal and policy debates and public consultations. They remain extremely active in public debate and have found spaces in the new governance system. Their primary role is to ensure the implementation and elaboration of the rights-based democratic framework, in itself an important political task given the advanced formal rights that were secured in the constitution. At this level, organisations can make effective links between other allies in civil society, such as the gay and lesbian rights movement, to mutually reinforce democratic agendas and share strategies. They are easily accessible to the state as well as external donors, and may be seen to play a strategic rather than representative role in civil society. Indeed, a concern about this level is the tension between the relatively high degree of access to decision-makers and the relative distance from constituencies of women (and particularly poor, rural women). At this level, the difficulty for policy advocates is maintaining 'reality checks' to ensure that what they are advocating is likely to be meaningful to the constituencies they seek to assist (Interview, Serote, 20.11.03).

However, keeping close relationships with constituencies is demanding when funding and gender expertise is thinly spread, making it difficult to 'listen' to how interests are being articulated at the grassroots level. To exacerbate this problem, there is insufficient capacity to ensure that information about what is happening at the advocacy level flows downwards to constituencies of women who are directly affected by particular policies. Although some NGOs in other sectors have developed this relationship to a mass base (for example, the relationship between the Aids Law Project and the Treatment Action Campaign), this has not happened within the women's movement. As a result, the gap between the high level of access to information and also awareness of women's rights among the urban elite and the marginality of poor women is exacerbated. Even where victories are scored, for example in the passage of the Maintenance Act, poor women do not always know about these or, as the Women's Legal Centre pointed out, government departments do not immediately implement the new rulings (Interviews, Ndatshe, 06.04.04; Serote, 20.11.03).

Operating in this relationship to the state, women's organisations at this level employ a set of tactics that does not rely on mass mobilisation or confrontation. Rather, tactics, demands and rhetoric might be moderated to fit the discourses of the state in order to make incremental gains and to retain hard-won openings into the state. A number of crucial legislative and policy gains have been made as a result of this strategy. A notable example is the success in legalising abortion, despite the deep opposition to this in civil society and in the rank-and-file membership of political parties. Using a carefully argued strategic approach, feminists were able to frame the demand within the more acceptable terms of health rather than as an overt right to bodily integrity.

Even so, it was only the ANC's strong support for the Termination of Pregnancy Act and its refusal to allow its members of parliament a free vote that made possible the passage of the legislation in 1996. In this case, a partnership between women's advocacy organisations and a strong political party ally resulted in an undoubted victory for women, entrenching women's reproductive rights in ways that are still not politically possible in many older democracies.

The alliance between political parties and advocacy groups is a form of upward political linkage. Equally important are downward linkages between advocacy groups and other social movement allies. There have been relatively few instances where advocacy and mass mobilisation have effectively combined around common issues. In one of the few examples of women's collective action in defence of their interests in the past ten years, poor women organised under the banner of the New Women's Movement mobilised against the Lund Committee's recommended reforms of the state maintenance grant. Their allies were experienced advocacy activists in the Black Sash. Interestingly, however, they were opposed by the ANC Women's League in the Western Cape, who argued that organisations such as the New Women's Movement and the Black Sash represented the interests of relatively privileged coloured women. The ANC Women's League stood by the ANC Minister of Welfare, Geraldine Fraser-Moleketi, under whose aegis the cutbacks in grants were being proposed. The opposition alliance of women's organisations was successful in ensuring that the amount of the child support grant increased fairly rapidly (although still not anywhere near the level required to have a poverty-reducing effect). This example shows that pressure from below can strengthen advocacy work and act as a critical lever in re-shaping the priorities of the state (Hassim 2003).

However, the need to retain allies in political parties and the state (the upward linkage) can at times work against the process of retaining downward linkages within the women's movement. One of the political costs of working primarily with parties and the state is the emergence of gaps between advocacy groups and those constituencies of poor women who have sought to demand their rights to basic services such as water or electricity through direct action. Direct action tactics have tended to bring social movements into conflict with the state in ways that have created new lines of fracture in the political terrain. In certain cases, particular forms of direct action (such as informal reconnections to the electricity grid) have been deemed criminal by the ANC government. In this context the choice of retaining credibility with state actors may, over time, reinforce the elite bias of this level of politics as access to decision-making via party-political and bureaucratic allies becomes more important than pressure from below. The moderate feminist discourses that characterise this sector and which allow access to political decision-making can thus act as limits to the women's movement, by gradually constraining the range of potential strategies (and, possibly, citizenship claims) that are considered legitimate.

At the next level, there are a number of new, issue-based networks which have emerged, and which coalesce on common issues (such as the Network Against Violence Against Women and the Reproductive Rights Alliance). The networks straddle the advocacy and policy roles of the first category, but are more likely to have identifiable constituencies. Like the advocacy organisations, the networks tend to be urban-based, with a bias towards location in Cape Town and Johannesburg. While they are primarily funded by foreign donors, many have also gained support from the local business sector on specific campaigns, particularly in the area of violence against women (for example, the white ribbon campaign). The remarkable aspect of these networks is that they are characterised by attention to issues that would in the 1980s have been regarded as 'feminist' and problematic – that is, to issues of women's sexual and reproductive autonomy. This may be a function of the discursive shift from nationalism to citizenship as exemplified by the constitution, as a result of which women's organisations feel less constrained in the types of issues that they can take into the national political domain. The new democracy, despite its weaknesses, has opened the possibilities for women's organisations to take up issues that are outside of the conventional definitions of political action, and to demand attention by the state to issues that states have generally been reluctant to regulate (that is, regulating and mitigating men's power in the private sphere).

The challenge for these networks is to hold together organisations that are in some respects competing for similar resources and operating on the same terrain. While they are most effective when they speak with one voice on issues of critical concern, such as gender-based violence, and are able to articulate and lobby for policy alternatives, they are the hardest type of organisation to keep alive. They often lack funding to support the networking office, or when they are too well funded, their constituent members may feel resentful that more funding is not being channelled to the actual work on the ground. Coalitions are by their nature fragile structures, having to constantly negotiate the terms of the relationships between members. Where there are scarce resources or where there is some jockeying among organisations to be seen as the representative voice on an issue, coalitions are at their most vulnerable. This problem is exacerbated by the fact that the most experienced activists and organisations in this sector are white women, and black women activists entering the field of violence against women have come up against relatively well-established funding and advocacy networks. As a result there has been considerable racial tension in this sector. It was no surprise, therefore, to find that the networks are the most unstable form of organisation in the women's movement.

Least visible, but most numerous, is the layer of women's organisations at local community level. Women's organisations have always existed at this level but have been weakly tied in to national networks. The period of the early 1980s was exceptional for the extent to which community-level organising was incorporated into a national political project, and women's organisations shaped and were shaped by the political visions of feminism. However, by the mid-1980s, the United Democratic Front (UDF) dominated strategic decision-making and women's organisations lost their capacities for independent political action. Twenty years later, women's community organisations appear again to be adrift from any politically cohesive project. Yet community-based organisations are the most numerous type of organisation in civil society, according to a study of the size and scope of the non-profit sector in South Africa (Swilling and Russell 2002). The bulk of the non-profit sector is made up of culture and recreation, social services, and development and housing. These areas of work are also gendered, according to the study. Culture and recreation is a sector that includes sport and is not surprisingly dominated by men. Education and research, social services and development and housing are sectors dominated by women. The study notes that 'this type of organisation, of which there was a substantial number, is involved in supporting and improving the lives of ordinary people through associations, development organisations, and co-operatives. Anecdotally, these types of activities tend more frequently to be carried out by women' (Swilling and Russell 2002: 26).

This level of women's organisations has been most distant from the state and even women's NGOs and networks that engage the state. A major part of the work at this level is concerned with women's practical needs, particularly in the face of the HIV crisis. It ranges from welfare work, caring for the ill, organising and financing funerals to mobilising at community level against rapists (and particularly men who rape children). In a number of respects, it is women who have been the shock absorbers of high levels of unemployment and of the failure of the state to provide a comprehensive and efficient system of social security and healthcare. The emphasis on the cultural value of caring in government policy frameworks (such as the White Paper on Social Welfare) in effect shifts the burden of caring for the young, the sick and the elderly onto women (and increasingly onto children as well), without financial compensation for their time and without effective backing up by the state. Yet these increasing burdens are not without political opportunities. In performing caring tasks for people dying of AIDS, women often have to cross cultural barriers of privacy and respect. As one carer noted, 'it is hard to *hlonipha* [respect] your brother-in-law in the old way when you clean his sores and the private parts. He respects me now and I have grown to respect and understand his needs' (Interview, Maria, 18.06.04). In her view, dignity and respect have had to be re-negotiated in everyday actions within the household. These cultural negotiations and re-definitions of social roles challenge the commonplace assumption that women are simply victims of the HIV/AIDS crisis. They also challenge the view of the Moral Regeneration Movement, led from The Presidency, that the emphasis should be on reconstructing the traditional values within families (Albertyn and Hassim 2003).

At the community level women have also discovered other forms of agency. Many are participants in the emerging social movements that are challenging the cost-recovery basis on which basic services are delivered. In the presence of perceived weaknesses in the justice system in dealing with violence against women, they have at times effected 'citizen's arrests'. Although direct action, such as marching to police stations with rapists in tow, is not widespread, it occurs often enough to remind observers of the enormous degree of agency that vests at this level. Political ideologies in this arena may be characterised as being within a maternalist tradition, in the strong and positive sense of maternalism. At this level, perhaps ironically the most vibrant and creative forms of collective solidarity are emerging as women seek to address everyday crises with few resources. Yet community-level women's organisations often do not have the time, expertise or resources to address decision-makers, and women within other social movements do not as yet appear to have inserted a gender analysis into the conceptualisation of their struggles.

These three levels within the women's movement should ideally add up to a strong and diverse social movement. In a democratically effective state they should work together to ensure that poor and vulnerable people are an important constituency for politicians, that there is accountability in public spending, that the constitutional values of equality and social justice are upheld and that both the public and private spheres are increasingly governed by democratic norms. This has not yet happened in South Africa. In the next section I explore reasons for this, re-focusing attention on the balance between inclusionary feminism and transformatory feminism. I argue that the most visible gender politics has centred on issues of representation (that is, equality/inclusionary feminism) rather than on policy outcomes. The challenge is to create the necessary synergies between the different levels – a difficult task in the absence of a mobilised feminist component within the movement. I analyse the possibilities for a stronger versions of feminism in the context of the current environments of social movements and the state.

Relationships between Women's Movements and Other Social Movements

Social movements in South Africa have generally been collapsed into the term 'civil society' – language that very often elides the significant differences between those movements that seek to transform society and those organisational forms that represent market or conservative society interests. In post-apartheid South Africa, a much clearer sense of social movements as both distinct from civil society and politically progressive is emerging. McKinley (2004: 20), for example, sees the new social movements as having effected a radical break with the '"traditional" progressive forces', standing on the side of 'principled inter-nationalism, a socialist vision, and an independent, mass-based mobilisation and struggle as an ideological and organisational alternative to the capitalist ANC'. This formulation conceives of social movements as oppositional to the state, independent (at least formally) of political parties, explicitly political in nature and implicitly democratic. The state thus is seen as the sphere of repression; social movements, by contrast, constitute the sphere of justice. Gordon White's characterisation of this view of civil society resonates in South Africa. Civil society functions as 'an idealized counter-image, an embodiment of social virtue confronting political vice: the realm of freedom versus the realm of coercion, of participation versus hierarchy, pluralism versus conformity, spontaneity versus manipulation, purity versus corruption' (White 1994: 377).

It is a powerful counter-image, and the binary dichotomy of state versus social movements has a rhetorical appeal that has a mobilising intent.

Yet the binary opposition of state and society is a difficult one to sustain from a feminist perspective. Neither the state nor social movements have been entirely welcoming spaces for women. Looking firstly at social movements, the conception of these arenas as fundamentally democratic and transformative is in many respects an idealisation that feminists have challenged for some time. In the 1980s, this idealisation pushed to the margins struggles to deal with aspects of and institutions in civil society that are inimical to the values of equality and justice. The narrow understanding of what constituted 'political' action within the mainstream left over a long period of time meant that issues of culture and tradition were not engaged by social movements. Relations of power within social movements have been masked, and questions of who has voice and agency within social movements remain very often obscured. The new social movements that have emerged since 1994 have very often relied on the mobilisation of women on the basis of their practical needs (for example, for electricity, land and housing) but have rarely linked these to issues of the pernicious gender division of labour. Internal tensions of race and gender within the social movements have rarely been directly examined. As Dawn Paley (2004) has pointed out, more than half of the activists in the Anti-Privatisation Forum are women, 'yet it [is] men's voices that overwhelmingly dominated' at a meeting she recently attended. She questions, 'how is it that Black women can make up the bulk of the membership of the movements against neo-liberal policies and be so marginalised in the functioning of these organisations?' One of her informants suggests boldly that women are being used. Similar comments were made to me in relation to other organisations where women (as in the UDF, interestingly) were foot soldiers while men assumed the role of generals.

This is not meant to suggest that social movements are arenas of action that should be avoided by women. As demonstrated earlier, there is a long tradition of women organising in alliance with other progressive political forces and there is much to be gained strategically from linking struggles against class and race oppression to those against gender oppression. However, it needs to be recognised that social movements in South Africa are profoundly gendered and unequal, and as yet far from inclusionary in their practices or even their visions for transformation to the extent that these do not explicitly address male social and cultural power.

The Women's Movement and the Democratic State: New Challenges, New Relationships

If the women's movement's relationship to other progressive social movements has always been fraught, its relationship to the state is equally contradictory. The period of transitional government, leading up to the first national elections and into the first two years of government, was a time of great optimism in South Africa. There was an expectation among many sectors of civil society that the democratic state would have the will and the capacity to deliver on the ANC's election manifesto (the Reconstruction and Development Programme or RDP) and to the constituencies of women and poor people. In the case of the women's movement particularly, this optimism was fuelled by the receptiveness of the ANC to gender issues. Many gender activists who moved into the state saw their new roles as an extension of their activism in a new arena, rather than an abandonment of the women's movement and many described the new relationship as a form of partnership or synergy. As gender activist and former ANC MP Pregs Govender (2004) commented, 'in the first few years, many of us in the ANC were very clear about the mandate and priorities that our budget needed to reflect. It had been the right time to assert the interests of poor women . . .' Thenjiwe Mtintso (2003: 577) has argued strongly that women need to be present in parliament and the state:

> Women have got to challenge the socially constructed divide between the private and the public spheres. Entering Parliament is one way of making the private political. Consistent and conscious efforts have to be made to bring women and gender interests to centre stage in decision-making spheres like Parliament.

For the democratic state, too, civil society remained important albeit in a new guise as the third partner in the development triad of state, market and society (Greenstein 2003). The ANC has argued that it is the most legitimate representative of the interests of poor people, counterposing the state as the arena of democracy to social movements as the arena of mobilisation. This formulation is the inverse of the idealised notion of state as site of repression/ social movements as site of justice discussed above. On the one hand, this conceptualisation serves to shift popular mobilisation outside of the institutionalised processes of party competition into the non-democratic (or even anarchic) realm.[1] On the other hand, it reinforces popular notions that there is only one politically legitimate vehicle for the representation of poor people's interests, and that vehicle is the party of national liberation. In this version of state-social movement relations, those parts of civil society that are engaged in a partnership with the state are treated as democratically effective, whereas those that challenge the state threaten to undermine democracy.

Reforms in the mechanisms of governance have reinforced this new view of the role of civil society as development partner. The new democratic government has changed the nature of public decision-making to incorporate a high degree of public participation and consultation, including women as a distinct constituency. These governance reforms were driven by the view that civil society has a role to play in the development process itself, both in service delivery in the context of a state whose institutional reach has been limited by apartheid, as well as in ensuring government accountability in periods between general elections. Drafts of policy, in the shape of the Green and White Papers, are formulated with the involvement of key 'stakeholders' in civil society and often draw on the expertise of academics and lawyers from outside the state. Portfolio committees in parliament, responsible for oversight of government departments, have regular public hearings on particular aspects of administration. Parliament itself is open to the public at all times. Access has been created for women's organisations and the national machinery to debate the content of policies and examine their gender sensitivity at early stages in policy formulation.

It is clear that in many respects women in particular have benefited from the new institutional and procedural arrangements in the state. Women are treated as a constituency with special interests that need to be represented in policy-making. The national gender machinery was designed to provide a bridge between different sectors of the state as well as between state and society. Thus in formal terms, the state has been made more permeable to the influence of organised constituencies of women. In practice, as is the case with national machineries worldwide, the South African institutions are elite driven, under-resourced and dependent to a high degree on donor funding. Expertise within the state to mainstream gender is thin; as a result many of the gains made in relation to gender equality are in those areas where policy addresses women directly as a category (for example, termination of pregnancy and maternal health) while those aspects of policy in which the relationships between women and men have to be addressed (for example, customary law, land) have been much harder to define (Albertyn and Hassim 2003; Hassim 2004).

Inclusion of women in the formal institutions of the state, and of the term gender equality in policy documents, has not led to redistribution of resources and power in ways that change the structural forces on which women's oppression rests. Inclusion has rather been an avenue for reinforcing elite women's access to the formal political system while not (as yet) translating clearly into policies that address the needs of poor women. The reasons for this are complicated, and have their roots in part in the tense relationship between feminism and the nationalist movement and in part in the elite biases of the democratic model adopted during the transition. Key actors within the state, as well as in the women's movement, remained suspicious of the intentions of middle-class (mostly white) feminists. In addition, they were (correctly) concerned with allowing a far more diverse set of voices to be heard in defining policy goals. The combination of these factors meant that more experienced feminist activists were often bypassed in order to reach poor women within communities. As I have argued above, however, this level of women's organisation is least mobilised and far more likely to be dominated by approaches that stress maternalism as a frame for gender recognition. In her study of the Commission on Gender Equality, Gay Seidman shows how pro-poor rhetoric itself marginalised transformatory goals. She comments:

> During the first five years of South Africa's democratic experience, gender policymakers appeared so insistent on representing the concerns of poor women that they seemed to undermine the likelihood that already mobilised feminists could participate at all in policymaking discussions – perhaps replacing the risk that democratization would undermine links between grassroots women's groups and the professional feminists who staff new state institutions with a different problem. Instead, it seemed likely that privileging grassroots and popular gender concerns would undermine the state's ability to take up more controversial or complicated feminist issues (Seidman 2003: 560).

Where feminists did have technicist expertise that could not easily be bypassed (for example, feminist lawyers) or where women's advocacy groups were politically well connected or run by black women (such as the Gender Advocacy Programme), state openness to women facilitated progressive outcomes. Within the constraints of the terms of reference set by bureaucrats,[2] feminists were able to make long-term gains in embedding gender equality in overarching policy frameworks, and ensuring that in many cases the details of legislation (such as the Employment Equity Act and the local government policy framework) specified gender equality as a criterion. Catherine Albertyn (2003: 604) notes that 'by 2000, women in South Africa enjoyed unprecedented political and legal equality in the form of political participation and entrenched human and legal rights'.

Despite these formal gains, policy vacillation, resource constraints, infrastructural weaknesses and bureaucratic inadequacies have combined to limit the impact of pro-poor policies of the government. This creates tension for those feminists who entered the state on the assumption that it would be a site of strategic intervention. As former ANC MP and Commission on Gender Equality chairperson, Thenjiwe Mtintso, puts it, 'when I visit ANC constituencies I experience a feeling of guilt about my privileged position and about my claim to represent their interests as women. I have grappled with my feminism and have questioned the extent to which it articulates the urgent needs of poor women' (2003: 573). For Pregs Govender, ANC MP and chairperson of the highly effective Joint Monitoring Committee on Women, the tensions between state and party constraints and her vision for transformation became untenable, and she resigned her seat in parliament in 2002.

Notwithstanding these tensions, there have indeed been many gains from the inclusionary strategy. This form of feminism sought to change existing inegalitarian laws and policies and to entrench the notion of equality in new frameworks. This emphasis was by the coincidence of the emergence of a critical mass of women in the new parliament at the very moment in which a wholesale legislative reform was implemented that sought to overturn racist laws. However, the emphasis of equality feminism on engaging the state had three key unintended and unforeseen consequences for the women's movement. The first lies in the impact of institutionalisation of interests on the politics of interest articulation. Creating a set of specialised institutions for the consideration of gender shifted the issues of gender inequality out of the realm of politics and into the technical realm of policy-making. As Banaszak, Beckwith and Rucht (2003: 6) point out, this is increasingly a problem with national machineries around the world: 'women's movements have been presented with an increasingly depoliticised and remote set of policy-making agencies at the national level . . . The relocation of responsibility to nonelected state bodies eventually reduces social movement influence.' In the administration, gender-equality concerns have fallen hostage to a range of institutional hierarchies and systemic blockages that are hard to deal with from outside the bureaucracy. The second consequence of the dominant focus on reforming the state is that very few women's organisations are dealing with issues of cultural norms and everyday practices, which may indeed limit the implementation and impact of legislative reforms. Finally, most activists who moved into the state assumed that public resources would be directed in a concerted fashion towards the reduction of the massive inequalities inherited from apartheid. Instead, anti-poverty policies have been mostly ineffective. While quotas for women have been written into state initiatives such as the Community Based Public Works Programme, the racial and gendered biases in the economy remain intact. Black women are still more likely to be unemployed, to be paid less than men when employed, and to perform unpaid labour (Seidman-Makgetla 2004).

The most notable attempt to engage the state outside of the equality feminist considerations of political and civil rights was the Women's Budget Initiative, which sought to track the ways in which spending had gendered impacts. The project had real possibilities to raise fundamental questions about spending priorities and to highlight the ways in which women were benefiting (or not) from particular policy approaches. However, within a few years the Ministry of Finance, which had initially embraced the Women's Budget Initiative, downgraded the project and it is now virtually moribund at the national level.

These comments should not be read as meaning that engaging the state was a misguided strategy for the women's movement, or that alliances with political parties necessarily lead to co-option. Rather, what needs to be considered is *how* the state should be engaged, what kinds of legal and institutional reforms should be promoted and how to build a women's movement that is sufficiently mobilised to support a critical engagement with the state. Poor women in South Africa would undoubtedly be better served by a strong state with the infrastructural capacities to implement functional health, welfare and basic service delivery. Removing formal inequalities is also important as it creates the normative and enabling environment in which women's claims to full citizenship can be pursued. However, it is self-limiting for the women's movement to pursue inclusion in the state in a piecemeal and depoliticised fashion, seeking to include women into existing policy frameworks without questioning whether the overall policy directions are appropriate for poor women, or how to put new areas of policy- or law-making on the agenda. For example, Seidman-Makgetla points to the limits of law reform in addressing economic inequalities. She argues that 'the laws on equity . . . did not directly address the economic context of high levels of unemployment and women's lack of economic assets. Nor did they engage persistent inequalities in homes, communities and schools.' What is needed, she argues, is structural trans-formation 'rather than just better enforcement of anti-discrimination measures' (Seidman-Makgetla 2004: 1).

Changing inequities in social and economic power will require not just the increased representation of women within the state, but also the increased and assertive representation of *poor* women within the state. It requires that those elected into power pursue redistributional policies and that a vibrant social movement will act to ensure accountability to the interests of marginal and vulnerable groupings. The roles of interest articulation (rather than merely group representation) and accountability require a different form of social movement of women. The reduction of the women's movement to a 'development partner' has long-term costs for democracy as it reduces the ability of the movement to debate the underpinning norms and values of policy directions *as well as* within other social movements and in civil society more generally. These cultural inequalities can only partially be dealt with by more equitable and gender-sensitive policies; they often reflect power relations that cannot be 'remedied' by state action. Rather, they demand that state policies be supplemented by a vibrant debate in the public sphere about the nature of society. They require a type of social movement that is not merely seeking to make piecemeal interventions in the policy and legislative processes of the state, but is engaged with norm-setting at the broadest level. In strategic terms, this also requires a movement that will form appropriate alliances and seek to influence the norms and procedures of alliance partners, whether these are political parties or social movements.

Conclusion

The South African women's movement does not easily meet the criteria of movement's strength identified in the first section of the chapter. Although South Africa is notable for the extent to which women's collective action resulted in gender equality being inscribed in its constitution and in the design of new state institutions and policy-making procedures, this chapter shows that the women's movement is currently too weak to ensure that these commitments are acted upon in ways that will remove gender inequalities. The understanding that race, class and gender are intertwined forms of oppression has privileged strategic alliances with other, more powerful political movements such as the ANC and the UDF. While this was an advantage, in that it gave gender activists (over time) entry points into the highest levels of political power, it also served to limit the extent to which the movement was able to develop independent goals and strategies. Since the 1990s, this limitation has translated into a movement dominated by a politics of inclusion directed at political elites (first outside and then within the state). In the context of a weakly mobilised movement and without clear and coherent leadership, the effect of this inclusionary politics has been the neglect, or even marginalisation, of those forms of politics that aimed at more fundamental transformations of gender relations of power in the economy and society. In other words, the leadership of the women's movement has tended to operate with an overly narrow conception of the 'political', being focused on the public sphere of the state while ignoring for the most part the spheres of economy and society. While participation in the national liberation movement was a catalyst for women's political involvement, women's collective action was rarely utilised as the basis to build a strong mass movement of women. This has had consequences for the post-apartheid period, as the emphasis on inclusion in the democratic state has produced an elite-oriented leadership within the movement. Economic restructuring and social crises, most notably HIV/AIDS, have paradoxically created openings for new forms of politics to emerge within communities. However, these localised forms of action have not yet been effectively linked to a feminist political project. As a result, the synergistic relationship between inclusionary and transformatory approaches to gender politics that was envisioned by the Women's National Coalition and that it embodied in the Women's Charter for Effective Equality has not developed. While the first decade of democracy has laid down the basis for progressive policy frameworks and enabling legislation in a number of areas, the next few years will test the ability of the women's movement to ensure that these are implemented in ways that address the needs of poor women.

Notes

1. For example, see Michael Sachs' comment on the 2004 election results (Sachs 2004).
2. An example of this is the ways in which the members of the Lund Committee of Inquiry, among whom were a number of prominent feminists, were restricted by a very narrow budgetary allocation for child-support grants (Hassim 2003).

References

Albertyn, C. 2003. 'Contesting Democracy: HIV/AIDS and the Achievement of Gender Equality in South Africa'. *Feminist Studies* 29 (3).

Albertyn, C. and S. Hassim. 2003. 'The Boundaries of Democracy: Gender, HIV and Culture'. In D. Everatt and V. Maphai (eds), *The Real State of the Nation: South Africa after 1990*. Johannesburg: Interfund.

Baldez, L. 2002. *Why Women Protest: Women's Movements in Chile*. Cambridge: Cambridge University Press.

Banaszak, L.A., K. Beckwith and D. Rucht (eds). 2003. *Women's Movements Facing the Reconfigured State*. Cambridge: Cambridge University Press.

Fester, G. 1997. 'Women's Organisations in the Western Cape: Vehicles for Gender Struggle or Instruments of Subordination?'. *Agenda* 34.

Govender, P. 2004. 'The Power of Love and Courage'. Ruth First Memorial Lecture, April. University of the Witwatersrand.

Greenstein, R. 2003. 'State, Civil Society and the Reconfiguration of Power in Post-Apartheid South Africa'. Occasional paper, Centre for Civil Society, University of Natal, Durban.

Hassim, S. 2003. 'The Gender Pact and Democratic Consolidation: Institutionalising Gender Equality in the South African State'. *Feminist Studies* 29 (3).

———. 2004. 'A Virtuous Circle of Representation? Gender Equality in South Africa'. In J. Daniel, J. Lutchman and R. Southall (eds), *The State of the Nation 2004*. Pretoria: HSRC.

McKinley, D. 2004. 'The Rise of Social Movements in South Africa'. *Debate: Voices from the South African Left* May.

Mtintso, T. 2003. 'Representivity: False Sisterhood or Universal Women's Interests? The South African Experience'. *Feminist Studies* 29 (3).

Mohanty, C.T. 1991. 'Under Western Eyes'. In C.T. Mohanty, A. Russo and L. Torres (eds), *Third World Women and the Politics of Feminism*. Bloomington, Indiana: Indiana University Press.

Molyneux, M. 1985. 'Mobilization without Emancipation? Women's Interests, the State and Revolution in Nicaragua'. *Feminist Studies* 11.

———. 1998. 'Analysing Women's Movements'. *Development and Change* 29 (1).

Paley, D. 2004. 'Women Pushed aside as Men Seek Power'. http://www.rabblenews.ca/news_full-story.shtml?x-=31275.

Phillips, A. 1995. *The Politics of Presence*. London: Polity Press.

Sachs, M. 2004. 'The Poor Believe in the Poll'. *Mail and Guardian* 21–28 May.

Seidman, G. 2003. 'Institutional Dilemmas: Representation versus Mobilisation in the South African Gender Commission'. *Feminist Studies* 29 (3).

Seidman-Makgetla, N. 2004. 'Women and the Economy'. Paper prepared for the Genderstats project. www.womensnet.org.za/genderstats/economy.

Swilling, M. and B. Russell. 2002. *The Size and Scope of the Non-Profit Sector in South Africa*. Durban and Johannesburg: Centre for Civil Society, University of Natal, and Graduate School of Public Development Management, University of the Witwatersrand.

White, G. 1994. 'Civil Society, Democratization and Development: Clearing the Analytical Ground'. *Democratization* 1 (3).

Interviews

Maria. Home-Based Carer, Diepsloot, 18.06.04.
Serote, Pethu. Director, GENNET, Cape Town, 20.11.03.
Ndatshe, Sibongile. Women's Legal Centre, Cape Town, 06.04.04.

17

The Cape of Good Dope?

A Post-Apartheid
Story of Gangs and Vigilantes

Ashwin Desai

The Event

PEOPLE AGAINST GANGSTERISM and Drugs (PAGAD) entered the South African political landscape in dramatic fashion. On the night of 4 August 1996, PAGAD drove in convoy from the Gatesville Mosque to the house of the head of the Hard Livings gang, Rashaad Staggie. He was not home, but in an act of bravado, arrived. Already shots had been fired between PAGAD and those inside Staggie's Salt River home. While trying to alight from his vehicle, he was shot in the head. As he fell out of his bakkie 'his inert body, apparently dead, was kicked, jumped on, hit with the butt of a shotgun and shot several more times before a petrol bomb was hurled at the body. Miraculously, this revived the mortally wounded man and he rose and tried to run away, only to be brought down by a volley of gunfire from the crowd' (*Sunday Tribune* 11 August 1996).

All this happened in the full glare of the media and with the police present. It was one of the first times a movement in post-apartheid South Africa acted with such impunity and with such directness in respect of their aims and objectives. PAGAD wanted to rid the Cape Flats of gangs and drugs. Participants in its first big mass march had just killed a leading gangster and known drug dealer.

Five years later PAGAD was involved in another dramatic incident in the city centre:

Shots were fired and pedestrians scrambled for cover as policemen engaged in a shootout with seven men who escaped from court in Cape Town . . . The seven members of PAGAD's G-Force faced urban terrorism charges. They apparently overpowered a policeman in the high court's holding cells during a lunch break and seized his gun . . . scaled a gate to reach Queen Victoria Street, and were then involved in a shootout with the police in the after-lunch traffic in the city centre (*Mercury* 5 October 2001).

What had happened in the five years that turned PAGAD from being an organisation seeking to rid the Cape Flats of drug lords into fugitives from the law?

The Style

PAGAD developed a particular repertoire of mobilising tactics. The march on Staggie's headquarters became emblematic of how PAGAD confronted drug lords. A meeting would be held outside the mosque. From there marchers, some hidden behind scarves, would arrive outside the shop or house of a drug dealer and demonstrate. They would deliver a first and final warning that they had to put an end to their drug dealing or answer to the people. In the demonstration there was a deliberate attempt at shaming. According to Keenan this strategy is mostly successful in an environment where there is 'exposure to others and susceptibility to their gaze . . .' (2004: 437). However, more often than not, the drug dealer was 'embedded' in social networks in the community that legitimised his 'business' and assuaged any feelings of guilt and shame. In any case the local drug dealer was beholden to a drug lord and clearly could not meet the 'first and final warning of the people'. The answer of 'the people' would be a bullet. Some of the leading gangsters and drug dealers were eliminated, creating fear and pandemonium in the ranks of the underworld.

Those who decided to confess would have to do this in public. On the Cape Flats a home-grown localised version of the Truth and Reconciliation Commission (TRC) was enacted. Archbishop Desmond Tutu's stricture that the process of reconciliation is 'not about being cosy; it is not about pretending that things were other than they were . . . reconciliation based on falsehood, on not facing up to reality is not true reconciliation' was taken seriously (quoted in Eze 2004: 765). The drug dealers would be forced to pay their profits into

PAGAD bank accounts, to be used ostensibly for PAGAD's drug rehabilitation programmes. PAGAD here was prefiguring the state's own forfeiture assets unit and bypassing it when it came into existence.

We see here the instrumental and rational aspects at work in PAGAD's *modus operandi*. PAGAD's tactics were instrumentally designed to isolate and create fear in the world of the gangsters and drug lords while also creating opportunities for them to make a 'clean break'. However, once the bombing campaign started, then one witnesses the consummatory aspects. In this campaign there was always the potential that 'innocent' bystanders would become victims. Part of this slide, as will be shown, happened as PAGAD faced increased repression, and so it retreated into smaller secretive cells.

Leadership and Social Composition

As it became more powerful as a movement, so PAGAD was accused by those within the Muslim community and government of being a front for Qibla. During the liberation struggle Qibla kept aloof from the Congress movement and allied itself to the Pan-Africanist Congress (PAC). The association between PAGAD and Qibla was heightened when Muhammed Ali 'Phantom' Parker, PAGAD's chief commander, warned of Qibla trying to take over control of PAGAD. Parker was expelled, followed by Farouk Jaffer and Moegamat Nadthime Edries. Jaffer was chief co-ordinator and Edries was involved in security.

People like Parker claimed that the radicals in Qibla had taken over the organisation. But a perusal of newspaper articles of the time demonstrates that, while Parker was the main voice of PAGAD, he was prone to make the most outlandish statements. Soon after Staggie's killing, he said that Cape Town should prepare for suicide bombings and warned gangs:

> If they are not going to listen then I will pack myself full of explosives and pay somebody a visit. Then they will know. If they dare to burn mosques, if they burn just one mosque, there will be Jihad. Africa will smoulder (*Mercury* 6 August 1996).

Things started to change when the police turned on the heat. Edries was arrested for the murder of Staggie (the charges were subsequently withdrawn) and asked Parker and Jaffer to come in for questioning. It was at this time that Parker and others took to blaming the radicalisation of PAGAD on Qibla, their own statements seemingly forgotten.

Qibla's Achmat Cassiem argued that there was no direct link between PAGAD and Qibla (Derek Watts speaks to Achmat Cassiem, 'Carte Blanche', 28 September 2001). A PAGAD spokesperson, AR, explains the Qibla issue (the identity of respondents is protected as a result of the sensitivity of the content of the interviews):

> People will work with any organisation which has the same aims and objectives as us. It wasn't because of Qibla's involvement that there was incitement of people. Qibla had no bearing on the decisions of PAGAD (Interview, AR, October, 2003).

Christopher Clohessy, a Roman Catholic priest and at the time a member of PAGAD, held that 'despite allegations that PAGAD has been manipulated by Qibla infiltration, the agenda appears to have remained the same: to confront. I myself know nothing substantial about Qibla: if, as is being claimed, PAGAD was from its inception a Qibla initiative, this does not make the initiative any less noble or legitimate' (Clohessy 1996: 70).

According to Cassiem, Qibla 'was formed specifically to present an Islamic perspective on the liberation struggle, because most of the parties that were involved did not cater for an Islamic perspective, and as a result most of the Muslims joined the nearest organisation that opposed the regime, but a liberation struggle fights not only against certain things, it also fights for certain things, and what we are fighting for is a just social order' (Derek Watts speaks to Achmat Cassiem, 'Carte Blanche', 28 September 2001).

While Cassiem might not have had a direct influence on PAGAD, his ideas did make inroads into Muslim thinking in the Cape – thinking influenced by the Iranian revolution.

Inscribed in Cassiem's position is the *umma*, the global community of believers. 'For a Muslim, the fundamental attachment is not to the *watan* (homeland), but to the *umma*, or community of believers, all made equal in their submission to Allah. This universal confraternity supersedes the institutions of the nation-state, which is seen as a source of division among believers' (Castells 1997: 15). The idea of a global *umma* is what PAGAD's Amir, or spiritual leader, was referring to when he proclaimed that 'the government poses a definite danger to our community and the police are nothing but legal gangsters in uniform . . . this is the same scenario to be found in Bosnia, Algeria, Egypt, and all over the world, where governments are discriminating against Muslims' (Pillay 2003: 296). This global identity of Islam that fed into PAGAD and helped fuel its emergence was facilitated by the ending of South Africa's international isolation. These developments were linked locally into fluidity within the Cape Muslim community. Changing circumstances were making it difficult for the *Imam*, who is traditionally at the centre of the Muslim community, to maintain the dominance he would normally expect. Implicated here is the declining relevance of traditional modes of addressing social problems, as a PAGAD representative told Dixon and Johns:

> I don't think that (the traditional, mosque-based system) was working throughout . . . It's based on very small types of societies. You basically have a community, a mosque, the Imam at the head of the mosque and everybody being loyal and obedient or at least paying allegiance to the mosque. That model actually goes back to the nineteenth century . . . and I think the problem we . . . faced at the end of the 1980s (was) that the mosque system was not sufficient, partly because of the fact that the community (was) growing very big and we have a much larger society than the small little communities living next door (Dixon and Johns 2001: 11).

Imams, who often had a monopoly of leadership in communities, found PAGAD difficult to contend with (Tayob 1996: 33). Certainly for PAGAD, there was a challenge to the traditional leadership. 'At the time of our formation, there was no proper Islamic leadership. Those who stood on the *mimbar* (pulpit) and preached did not use the opportunity to address the social ills in the community. They felt threatened by us and tried to cut us off from mosques. We had to fight them to fight the gangsters' (Interview, AR, October 2003).

This begs the question of the social composition of PAGAD. It would appear that the initial impetus of the movement drew on 'sections of the middle-class neighbourhood watches of the Cape Flats, especially the predominantly Muslim residential areas' (Jeppie 1996: 15). Parts of the rationale for this lay in the fact that middle-class youth were increasingly attracted to crack cocaine. However, while the leadership and membership of PAGAD were almost exclusively coloured and Muslim, the movement soon transcended class divides. This was because, as Jeppie puts it, 'class and locality do not fit together . . . simplistically . . . the middle class drug consumer market and gangster activity are connected and overlap. Peddlers . . . are actually the "contracted" distributors for much bigger drug-lords who are gang bosses. Petty crime such as burglaries and car thefts are often the result of indebtedness to a "merchant" or the result of having to procure substances to satisfy a bad habit' (Jeppie 1996: 14).

Both middle- and working-class people were integrally involved in PAGAD. Those I met while doing fieldwork ranged from flower-sellers and carpenters to owners of construction companies and medical doctors. In its early days PAGAD's leadership was not aligned politically, and included 'an African National Congress (ANC) branch executive member, a carpenter and an alarm fitter . . .' (Manjra 1996: 40). A critical commentator on PAGAD from its earliest days, Farid Esack, who saw in PAGAD the 'rise of conservative religio-ideological forces seeking to protect the new South Africa from the "scourge of democracy and liberalism"', noted the 'myriad of seemingly discordant voices coming from the public PAGAD . . . A number of strands converge . . . without any coherent distinction between them, one can simultaneously belong to more than one stream' (Esack 1996: 24–5). Those streams could range from Africanists alienated from the PAC to those 'who believe that the values of the liberal democratic state (are) repugnant to human decency and subversive of all religious values and there are those who believe that there is only one solution for South Africa and the world, an "Islamic" revolution along the lines of the Iranian experience. At all of these levels, the discourse is essentially an anti-state one which feeds on deeply felt community concerns' (Esack 1996: 25).

Women were integrally involved in the PAGAD upsurge, 'aggrieved and angered by the abuses waged upon them and their families by the men in leather jackets and fast cars who rule the streets of their neighbourhoods' (Dodd 1996: 64). The spokesperson of PAGAD is a housewife, Abieda Roberts, while at the level of activity, PAGAD member, Fatima Zahra, points out that in delegations of ten who confronted drug merchants, there were always three or four women. Yet another woman member, Fasiegha Arendse, argues that their presence goes unreported by the media because 'women are always conveniently written out of history of these things' (quoted in Dodd 1996: 67).

S is a Woodstock mother. She became involved with PAGAD by default when her brother R, who was involved in the organisation, got arrested. She works at Independent Newspapers and is not shy or quiet about her PAGAD association. S says, 'Drug dealers felt safe because their neighbours didn't do anything about them. People were cowered into a space of apathy. I suppose that's how I initially reacted until my parents' home was bombed.' This happened, S says, because her brother was active in PAGAD's operations and became a headache for the gangsters. Her parents lived in Athlone, and have since moved to a safer area. S's brother was 29 at the time, and she says his arrest followed a shooting at a gangster's home.

S continues: 'PAGAD empowered me in a way. I was able to make a meaningful contribution to my community. My brother was fired from his job and my parents lived in virtual fear of their lives. We could either sit back and allow the drug dealers and gangsters to take over our lives, or do something about it. All we did was pass on the message. People had to know that there were others in the same predicament as them. Working in a newspaper environment and having had the opportunity of seeing things from both sides, it became clear to me that the media were lazy to write the real stories about PAGAD and their activities. I would call the journalists and give them information about PAGAD's activities, but they would simply sit on their telephones and take down a police report.'

S was initially sceptical of organisations involved in the community. She did not want to get involved with PAGAD at its inception in 1995. 'I wanted to make a meaningful contribution. I hated organisations. Most of the organisations which sprung up from the 80s and 90s were playing power games and I was not prepared to subscribe to that mentality.'

Then, when S was 21 years old, her life changed, when she came face to face with the harshest and most violent brush with gangsterism: 'On my way home, I was raped. In a train by seven men. I was helpless. Each of these dirty, angry but young men raped me one by one. I was on my way home.' But S was not prepared to be a victim. She fought back. 'I joined a trauma centre and started giving voluntary counselling to people. I realised there were other women like myself who kept quiet. Cape Town is such a dangerous place. Some parents don't give a damn about their children. My community activism was all the power I had. I was walking the streets to tell the youth not to permit the gangster culture to take over their lives. Then came PAGAD. At first I watched and waited. And then when R got arrested, I had to do something.'

S was cautious about what she accepted from her PAGAD leaders and stood up and questioned at every opportunity when she found something was not appropriate to her: 'There was a faction among the leadership which became too militant. It was "Phantom" Parker and his group and I repeatedly asked about the significance of all the violence associated with our marches. Personally I feel we could have solely mobilised around local issues instead of bringing the Palestine and Afghanistan problems to our struggle. There was too much emotion put into fighting than common sense. We should have moved away from the fundamentalist tag that was given to us.'

Asked if her mind had been changed towards the organisation, she said: 'I have not forsaken PAGAD. I don't want to stop marching and this is the view of many people. It's a pity that the organisation has been stereotyped as Muslim. I live alongside white neighbours and they believe in PAGAD' (Interview, October 2003).

The Framing

PAGAD describes itself as a 'broadly-based multi-faith movement', that is 'non-aligned, non-affiliated to any political movement' (Interview AR, October 2003). Despite this, the label 'Muslim movement' has stuck. Part of this lay in the fact that 'its rhetoric and grassroots support expressed unmistakable Islamic characteristics. Its marches, scarves and slogans evoked scenes from international Islamic movements' (Tayob 1996: 30). As Jeppie points out, 'PAGAD members would march – for the occasion, men in *kaffiyehs*, women in black *hijab* – through the main streets to the homes of alleged drug dealers. They marched after late night mass meetings at mosques, followed by prayers and *dhikirs*, so that marchers could be physically and collectively prepared to "confront the enemy"' (2000: 227).

The fact that the meeting place was outside the mosque (most often the Gatesville Mosque), reinforced the label 'Muslim movement'. Some have taken on this issue of Muslim as a positive. Na'eem Jeenah saw PAGAD continuing past traditions: 'From the arrival of Muslims on these shores, Muslims have been engaged in a struggle against oppression and dictatorship . . . Muslims have striven with might to achieve justice here . . . the PAGAD phenomenon is just a continuation of this heritage' (Jeenah 1996: 18).

The language of the meetings was dominated by an Islamic discourse. 'Quranic verses of struggle and slogans, introduced first by the Muslim Youth

Movement from Egypt and Pakistan, reverberated at the end of PAGAD meetings. More directly, reflecting Achmat Cassiem's Islamist version, the Quranic verse appealing for unity, "Hold on fast to the rope of God and be not divided" (3: 103), was recited at the end of every meeting with members holding hands over their heads . . . Unity, togetherness and standing up for truth and justice charged and overwhelmed PAGAD meetings. The atmosphere and motivation was certainly and unmistakably Islamist' (Tayob 1996: 32).

Initially, the slogans at meetings were drawn from the days of the liberation struggle: 'Kill the drug merchant, kill!' drew on the ANC Youth League president, Peter Mokaba's, 'Kill the Boer, kill the farmer', and the PAC slogan, 'One Settler, One Bullet!'. But in time this also got an Islamic inflection captured in the slogan 'One Solution, Islamic Revolution'. Statements by leadership also reflected Islamic orientation. Witness the words of Salie Abader, the PAGAD security chief who faced charges of killing Rashaad Staggie: 'Whether you have a legal or illegal firearm, they (the gangsters and drug dealers) must be removed. If you take a firearm and see a merchant, don't tell them they are rubbish or criminals. Call out the name of God and let Allah guide the bullet' (*Cape Argus* 14 December 2000).

The 'global' also impacted on identity. One of the ways of understanding this impact is through images portrayed in the media. Gabeba Baderoon argues that the South African media, unable to make sense of the PAGAD phenomenon and without an understanding of Islamic iconography, came to rely on an Orientalist discourse, readymade with the backing of international precedent. So the *Argus* and *Cape Times* in one week 'referred to "holy war", "suicide bombers", "militant", "extremist", "jihad", "death threats", and "vigilante group" in potent combination with images associated not only with PAGAD, but with Islam . . . In a reduced vocabulary, the connection of PAGAD to Islam, Islam to violence, and violence, therefore to all Muslims was made' (Baderoon 2003: 333). Baderoon also points out PAGAD's own culpability. While suspicious of the media and sometimes hostile, PAGAD also fed the media certain images 'because it learned the advantages of playing to the stereotypes which drew the most attention' (2003: 333).

Identity and organisation reinforced each other. In this context PAGAD's strength lay in its ability to call on pre-existing networks. These centred around the Muslim community. But this strength was also to prove to be PAGAD's Achilles heel, for by not breaking out of the mould of 'Muslim', PAGAD could not reach the majority of coloureds who were not Muslim. This 'narrowness' impacted on the two ways social scientists have distinguished vigilantism, viz. social control and crime control (Johnston 1996: 228). In PAGAD, social control (for example, raging against homosexuality) and crime control tended to overlap, which limited a broader appeal. In response, non-Muslims could be mobilised against PAGAD on the basis of pre-existing religious, ethnic and class divides.

The State

The relationship between PAGAD and the state changed over the years. At the beginning, the ANC saw possibilities for itself in the movement. It had lost the Western Cape to the New National Party (NNP) and was on the lookout for opportunities to make inroads into the coloured constituency. In the immediate aftermath of the Staggie killing, the Minister of Justice, Dullah Omar, effused that PAGAD had 'wakened the soul of the community' (quoted in Jeenah 1996: 17). On the other hand, local police were virulently against PAGAD. In the aftermath of the killing of Staggie, police spokesperson, Superintendent John Sterrenberg, said that PAGAD 'members can no longer be considered victims of crime, but as criminals themselves . . . We are combating a gang war here. This is a war between two gangs. The actions of PAGAD are exacerbating the problem, as we now have to take action against them as well as trying to stamp out criminality in all its forms' (*Natal Witness* 6 August 1996). PAGAD countered that the police were infested with rogue policemen and were intent on 'criminalising' PAGAD. Inscribed in PAGAD's repertoire was the public indictment of police collaborating with gangsters.

Safety and Security Minister, Sydney Mufamadi, was equally condemnatory of PAGAD. However, at a national level, the police took a more conciliatory stance. The National Police Commissioner, George Fivaz, met with PAGAD and called for PAGAD to work with the police (Shaw 2002: 35). PAGAD, it seemed, was also open to talking to politicians. It marched to parliament on 11 May 1996 and presented Minister of Justice, Dullah Omar, with a list of demands. But attitudes started to harden.

According to PAGAD's website, the 'government's failure to respond to PAGAD's plea to bring an end to the disease that the society was plagued by, made the people lose whatever little hope they had in the system . . . The government's inability to act, forced the people to take action themselves'.

This position was reinforced by AR: 'PAGAD was eager to work with the justice and safety and security departments. However, over time we were labelled an illegitimate, vigilante organisation by the state. We were demonised. At the same time there was disillusionment with the state's inability or unwillingness to respond to repeated demands for action against the gangsters' (Interview, AR, October 2003).

As PAGAD got more militant in its attacks on gangsters and its criticism of government, so the state began to attack PAGAD. Gangs also started to fight back. PAGAD member, Faizel Ryklief, was shot after a march on the American's gang in Bridgetown. According to PAGAD, the police enforcement that marchers could not cover their faces (invoking the 1969 Prohibition of Disguises Act) made their members vulnerable. The open carrying of firearms was also seized upon by police and banned. With echoes of Fanon (1989 [1959]), some women turned to veils, which they did not normally wear, to disguise themselves from gangsters, the veils ensuring they remained visible and noticed (Fatima Zahra in Dodd 1996: 66; Pike 1997).

The attacks facilitated PAGAD's drift into small, secretive cells that came to be known as the G-Force. 'Their task was to protect – the "G", purportedly standing for guard – the leadership, but they became the only way that PAGAD could operate' (Jeppie 2000: 228).

This was a different PAGAD from that described by Father Christopher Clohessy who 'always perceived the leadership to be in tune with the people. And at times when the leadership appeared to be losing focus, the response of the people appeared sufficient to bring them back' (Clohessy 1996: 74) Despite Clohessy's belief that it was 'inconceivable' that there could be two PAGADs, this was to become a reality. An above- and underground PAGAD were born.

Mansoer Manuel, a member of PAGAD's Grassy Park G-Force cell, who became a National Intelligence Agency (NIA) informer, gave some insights into G-Force operations when giving evidence in court. He told the court that Abdus Salaam Ebrahim (PAGAD's chief co-ordinator) referred to G-Force as *Hizbollah*, the Army of Allah. The *amier* (spiritual leader) of his G-Force cell was H. Those who disobeyed the *amier* faced certain death. The G-Force of Grassy Park had twenty members. Orders would come after a 'masoera', a strategic planning meeting. Words from the *Quran* were often used as a code. For example, when they spoke of the *azaan* (call to prayer) starting, it meant there had to be a pipe-bomb attack.

Manuel spoke about an attack on the Wynberg Synagogue: 'In December 1998, Mr Ebrahim sent word that the Grassy Park cell needed to work as they were very quiet. At first, we were ordered to bomb the Sea Point Synagogue. But the cell felt it was too dangerous and decided instead to bomb the Wynberg Synagogue.' He described the unfolding of the operation: 'We referred to the making of a pipe bomb as "baking a cake". The bomb used in the synagogue attack was rectangular and the smallest bomb we ever made. They prayed on their way to their target. Faried Mohammed (40) detonated the bomb after struggling to light the cracker fuse . . . The first three months after the NIA agents had recruited me, they telephoned me at least once a week for information. I eventually gave them information and was paid R3 000 every month' (*Cape Argus* 10 October 2000).

Even more startling were the revelations of the trial of the 'PAGAD Four' who appeared in the Oudtshoorn Regional Court on explosives, theft and weapons charges in February 1999. One of the four, Ayob Mungalee, revealed himself to be an NIA agent. This claim was verified by Superintendent Henry Beukes. A NIA spokesman, Helmut Schlenter, revealed that Mungalee was an informant not an agent. Police maintained that Mungalee was an acting NIA member who had been instructed to courier explosives to Cape Town (*Mercury* 10 March 1999). PAGAD spokesman, Abdus Salaam Ebrahim, responding to the exposé of Mungalee, held that the explosives belonged to the NIA: 'They did not belong to PAGAD. They will try to frame people now. They want to cover their backs' (*Natal Witness* 25 February 1999).

The Mungalee affair led to a revealing address by Intelligence Minister Joe Nhlanhla to a special sitting of parliament on 9 March 1999. Nhlanhla pointed to both corruption and collusion in the South African Police Service (SAPS) that led to the leaking of information to gangs before important operations. This was made worse by elements of the 'Third Force who continue to use their old networks, including people in the security forces. To be able to succeed we need the security services to rid themselves of these elements through arrests that lead to their puppet-masters' (*Mercury* 10 March 1999).

The state not only recruited informers, but also took to arming PAGAD operatives. In one case, made public in 1997 (before the spate of bombings), the Western Cape attorney general, Frank Kahn, was reported to want to charge two police officers. These charges were a response to 'a sting operation last year in which police handed back a dud hand grenade to People Against Gangsterism and Drugs (PAGAD), who used it in an attack on an alleged drug dealer. Both sides in the conflict used grenades from the same batch in attacks on the Cape Flats earlier this year . . . Intelligence operatives say such sting operations are common in attempts to infiltrate the ranks of vigilantes and gangsters . . . The dud grenade failed to explode when it was used to attack an alleged drug dealer in Crawford. But a pregnant woman was killed in another attack where a grenade from the same batch was used . . .' (*Mail and Guardian* 21 November 1997).

Alongside this, the provincial ANC also entered the fray and attempted both to get *Imams* to condemn PAGAD, while trying to delegitimise the movement in the media and with potential funders, like the Iranian government. Just as suddenly, a different kind of violence was laid at the door of PAGAD – a series of bomb attacks between August 1998 and August 2000. The state pointed the finger at PAGAD. PAGAD denied culpability.

PAGAD tried to point to other suspects. PAGAD leader Abdus Salaam Ebrahim made allegations that former Vlakplaas commander and NIA agent, Dirk Coetzee, and a notorious company boss, Cyril Beeka (who was on trial for the murder of a Chinese national), were behind the bombing at the Waterfront as part of a move to control the security network in the area (*Daily News* 2 October 2000). But the state persisted in laying the blame on PAGAD. By now it had become 'common sense' that PAGAD was behind the 'urban terror' campaign. This was despite the fact that the minister in charge of intelligence had pointed to corruption and Third Force elements in the justice system.

If the spate of bombings was directed by PAGAD, then why the change of tactics from confronting gangsters and those with political power to anonymous bomb attacks? Mark Shaw, in similar vein to a number of other commentators, holds that 'from mid-1998, the targets chosen reflected a combination of state institutions, such as police stations or magistrates' courts, tourist locations like the city's popular waterfront, a series of restaurants in crowded nightspots, and, targets with their particular symbolic connotations such as a gay bar and a synagogue . . . The PAGAD case illustrates how initially vigilante responses to crime can assume a much more anti-government stance. In fact PAGAD could now be defined less as a vigilante organisation than a terror group with particular motives, although these are difficult to discern' (Shaw 2002: 98-9).

Was PAGAD responding to the increasing attacks on 'Muslim' targets by the United States? Was this the work of state agents, trying to draw PAGAD out?

Was it the result of a cell of the G-force acting independently, given the arrest and/or surveillance of the leadership of PAGAD?

Interviews with G-Force members like MB, while giving valuable insights, provide no answers in this regard. MB was imprisoned for more than four years for charges including car theft, possession of pipe bombs, attempted murder. He was acquitted when the state case fell apart. He will not comment on whether the accusation that PAGAD is responsible for the Cape urban terror is true, or whether the organisation is responsible for the assassination of more than a dozen leading gangsters in 1998. He does, though, talk of his work as a G-Force member. The members of the security department operate in cell structures. The cells are responsible for protecting the areas where PAGAD members live. Every cell has a commander who is accountable to the security department. Each geographic area thus has its own structure and co-ordinator. This is where MB fitted in.

MB said that none of the members in G-Force knew each other. 'When we attended meetings at Gatesville or any other mosques, we would meet, not knowing what our backgrounds were.' He is from Grassy Park, a mixed coloured and Indian area in Cape Town. He worked as a builder and ran a fairly successful company until his arrest. He has a wife and four children and while working as a builder supplements his income by fixing cell phones. He has spent over R200 000 of his savings on his appeal. PAGAD does not pay for appeal matters.

Clearly MB is streetwise, and knows who the gangsters are and where they operate from. 'Policemen stand with the gangsters. They are corrupt. Before I joined PAGAD we would complain to the police only to be told that they need evidence before they can take action. As a cell we would meet in the mosque, separate from the Gatesville congregation, and talk about issues. I studied Arabic and would lead the meetings. If I had to say something people believed in me and would not question it.' He and his cell members were confident and strong and were able to defend themselves: 'We would not tolerate the gangsters' nonsense. We met them with force head on.' In 1998 MB was arrested, then released, arrested again in 1999 and was finally released and acquitted in 2002.

Would he still want to be involved with PAGAD after the long period in jail and the money he had to pay to defend himself? 'PAGAD as an organisation still operates. But people who were part of my cell don't want to come to the fore any longer. They fear for their lives and those of their families. Even some PAGAD ex-prisoners don't want to get involved. Actually, my personal view, even though I am a member of PAGAD's working committee, is that the organisation is only surviving because it has to. Once all the court cases are finalised, there will no longer be a PAGAD.'

MB dismisses all claims that PAGAD's security department has an agenda to overthrow the government or any other political agendas: 'PAGAD stands for a good cause. We never wanted to engage in an armed struggle. All we wanted to do was to stop the drug dealers. We had to deal with the root of crime.' For him these were the dealers in drugs.

MB is critical about the role of the Muslim Judicial Council (MJC), which controls almost all the mosques around the country. He suggests political aspirations of the MJC leaders, who are close allies to the ANC, as the reason the MJC called for a clampdown on PAGAD. 'Because we had shown up ANC leaders for their inefficiencies as government ministers' (Interview, MB, October 2003).

The 'Crack'

In Soweto students took on the gangs and routed many of them in 1976, forcing a decline in gang activity and fostering a politicised 'alternative youth culture' (Glaser 2000: 179). But the challenge did not happen on the Cape Flats, allowing gangs to keep growing in their attraction to young people and increasing their power in communities. In fact, there are stories that Umkhonto we Sizwe (MK) units had to negotiate with the Cape Flats gangs for safe passage in the 1980s.

The proliferation of gangs and crime was facilitated by apartheid policing: 'Black people were policed for control and not crime prevention, the police aimed to prevent crime in white areas not by reducing it in black areas but by preventing the uncontrolled movement of black people, who were considered to be its perpetrators. Thus the police spent an inordinate amount of resources on arresting people for apartheid administrative offences . . . but seldom confronted criminal violence in the township themselves' (Shaw 2002: 1).

By 1994, the two most influential gangs were the Hard Livings and the Americans, spread out across the Cape Flats into cells of fifteen to twenty members. The Americans had a loose alliance with the Sexy Boys while the Hard Livings were allied to myriad smaller gangs (Schärf and Vale 1996: 31). In the 1980s, gangs like the Hard Livings were still limited to their neighbourhoods. Money, in addition to drugs, came from gambling and extortion. The gangs did not only rely on naked force and fear to embed themselves in communities. Often they would distribute food parcels to the needy and give assistance at funerals. Many in the community would also rely on the gangs to buy 'cheap' television sets, VCRs and the like. There were cruder tactics too. Rashaad Staggie, for example, would drive through the streets and throw money from his car (Kinnes 2000: 7).

The fall of apartheid met neo-liberal globalisation, with its accompanying paradigm of deregulation, dropping of exchange controls and privatisation, facilitating the porousness of borders. And so the flow of illegal substances was facilitated into South Africa. There were also other factors at play. The transition saw the coming together of eleven former police forces into the SAPS, providing all kinds of co-ordination problems. At the same time, 'international syndicates saw South Africa as an accessible new market. The drug markets in the western world were levelling off and South Africa was not only a potentially large market in its own right, but its transport and communications infrastructure, together with the weakness of the state and the venality of its officials, made it ideal for new trans-shipment routes to other destinations, at least in the short term. Drugs poured into the country and the criminal justice system offered little resistance' (Schärf and Vale 1996: 33).

Crack made its appearance: 'the poor man's cocaine'. Crack was soon to replace mandrax as the drug of choice on the Cape Flats. To this must be added cheaper forms of alcohol. Illegal distillers were starting to put alcohol on the market at cheap prices. The alcohol would have a familiar tinge of Smirnoff vodka for example. Like crack, its effects on the body were devastating. As a social worker put it, it 'slowly eats up the body, picking bits off like a vulture' (Interview, December 2003).

This changing environment cannot be decontextualised from the apartheid state's willingness in the 1970s and 1980s to sanction covert groups who bypassed South African laws. Inscribed in the state operations were widespread smuggling and the undermining of international sanctions. One outcome of this was the fact that covert state bodies became adept at running 'illegal businesses'. Some individuals made the transition in post-apartheid South Africa to using this knowledge and old networks to facilitate the emergence of South Africa as a trans-shipment point for illegal goods. Alongside illegal smuggling rackets, the apartheid state co-opted vigilante groups and street gangs into dealing with anti-apartheid mobilisation. With the changing political environment, the drug lords of the Cape Flats 'that developed criminal ties with key members of the apartheid security forces have been in a prime position to profit from illicit enterprise . . .' (Standing 2004: 38). Gang structures responded to the new opportunities:

> . . . with the opening up of South Africa's borders after the 1994 election, and with the realization that foreign crime syndicates were likely to exploit the new situation, most of the Western Cape syndicates decided to establish a cartel. Their aim was to reduce turf battles, to order bulk shipments, to distribute the drugs in pre-arranged proportions at agreed prices, and to allocate distribution areas in terms of a set of agreed principles. In many senses of course this reflected the monopolies of South African capitalism. Called 'The Firm', the cartel substantially changed the nature of organised crime in the Western Cape after 1994 . . . Most of the local leaders of Hard Livings were provided with seed capital and cars to run their own drug trade. The role of the leadership of Hard Livings became one of merely collecting the money and co-ordinating activities. The developments . . . reflect a progression of a common criminal gang moving up the ladder of sophistication on its way to become a well-organised criminal group (Shaw 2002: 75–6).

What is clear is that a criminal elite emerged. Many have moved into the formerly white suburbs and rely on local 'strong-men' to maintain their 'business interests'. By 1996, for example, police could reveal that Colin Stanfield had assets worth R30 million (Schärf 1996: 60).

But it is important not to paint the gangs on the Cape Flats with one brush. There are the bigger, better-organised gangs, as well as myriad smaller gangs. While many are involved in drug peddling, they are not the conduits for bringing drugs into the community. For many young people gangs are a 'way of life'. This has been variously labelled as 'defiant individualism', 'carnalismo' (brotherhood) and 'machismo' (masculinity) (Valdez 2003: 17).

'The Man'

On almost every street corner, at the bottom of the stairs of flats, boys and young men congregate. Often talk is of violent escapades, not only of fighting other gangsters, but also of violence perpetrated against sexual partners and rape. Imbricated in this talk is the showing off of 'sexual conquest'. Of the eleven top gangster arrests highlighted in the *Cape Argus* (22 October 2003), four of the eleven were charged or convicted of rape, and eight were charged with assault, attempted murder or murder.

Permeating the language of street-level gangsters is the idea of respect. But respect cannot come from having a job and providing economically for one's family. It is not a weapon that can be used to demand control over wives and children. In fact, women on the Cape Flats have taken jobs in the service sector, in supermarkets as packers and cashiers, and as office support staff. For most men these are 'sissies" jobs, and most baulk at working under the supervision of women or pushing carts around offices delivering tea and coffee. Many of the men live off the earnings of their lovers and wives. Are tales of sexual conquest seen as one way of retrieving masculine dignity in the face of economic dependence? And is rape part of this pursuit too?

To get to the heart of this requires 'deep' ethnographic work that can enter the shaping of family organisation, intimacy, gender power relationships and so on. This is beyond the scope of this study. Phillipe Bourgois' ethnographic accounts of inner-city Puerto Rican men in New York points in one direction. He holds that the men 'confined to the margins of the nation . . . that no longer requires their labour power, reconstruct their notions of masculine dignity around interpersonal violence, economic parasitism, and sexual domination. Increasingly large proportions of frustrated, desperate men have taken refuge in a street culture of resistance that roots its material base and its ideological appeal in the growing drug economy, which offers a concrete alternative to exclusion from the legal economy . . . rather than being mere pawns of larger social structural and ideological forces, drug dealers who participate in street culture are active agents seeking dignity – even if violently and self-destructively' (Bourgois 1996: 414). Bourgois is careful not to legitimate violence, by also holding that the drug dealers, while 'victims from a social structural perspective, . . . are also agents of destruction in their daily lives. They wreak havoc on their loved ones and on the larger community'. But he keeps reminding that behind this in the United States lies 'the *de facto* apartheid ideology that legitimates a public "common sense" tolerating rising levels of immiseration among the working poor' (Bourgois 1996: 425).

There prevails also a masculine identity that emphasises money, designer clothes, jewellery and flashy cars. Part of this 'conspicuous consumption' is related to the emergence of a new black elite both of the 'underworld variety' and those operating in the 'open economy' under the prerequisites of black economic empowerment. This new elite with its extravagant lifestyle has unleashed a form of what Veblen has called 'pecuniary emulation'. Through the concept of emulation Veblen argued that those lower down the class hierarchy will try to emulate those of higher income, status and power rather than struggling and organising to create a different society predicated on the elimination of the 'leisure class'. In looking at the actual and aspiring consumption patterns of gang members on the Cape Flats one can see the veracity of Veblen's theory (Veblen 1953; Dowd 2002).

The Denouement?

How much of the criminalisation of PAGAD and its labelling as 'terrorist' was a political act by the state? The state adopted a range of measures to weaken PAGAD. Firstly, it used existing legislation to stop PAGAD members wearing any scarves to disguise their identity, refused the public display of firearms and insisted on the long bureaucratic mechanisms for marches to be allowed. This, of course, negated the surprise element in confronting drug lords. Secondly, it used state agents to infiltrate the organisation, or turned PAGAD members into state agents. This created paranoia and facilitated PAGAD drifting into smaller cells. At the same time, PAGAD was openly labelled 'criminal' and 'terrorist' by the state. The ANC co-ordinated a programme to 'squeeze' PAGAD from meeting spaces in mosques and encourage leading Muslims to denounce PAGAD. In the words of the state, 'war had been declared on PAGAD'. Thirdly, it tied the PAGAD members into a number of cases. In many instances the members walked free, but it consumed resources and time and scared away potential supporters. Crucially, the state then went after the PAGAD leadership. 'The state relentlessly pursued the PAGAD leadership through the legal channels. PAGAD was exhausted through the lengthy and expensive court cases. Key figures were apprehended, and eventually a number of them were found guilty and incarcerated. The movement was neutered in this way' (Vahed and Jeppie 2004: 259).

Part of understanding the heightened repression against PAGAD is that, unlike other movements with the label 'vigilante', PAGAD was making direct attacks on the ANC and publicly labelling ANC leaders as 'gangsters' and political criminals. In a province where it was vital that the ANC broaden its support base on the Cape Flats, PAGAD was a threat and, unlike other 'vigilante' groups who act as a form of social control, PAGAD was questioning the state's willingness to fight crime, bypassing the corporatist structures set up by the state, managing at the same time to sustain mass mobilisation, embarrassing Muslims who were ANC leaders and questioning the very legitimacy of the state.

Fourthly, the identity that made PAGAD strong also made it weak, and the state was able to play on this. PAGAD's mainly Muslim base and its organising around the precincts of mosques gave it an existing network, but in order to establish hegemony or at least appear to, it had to either subsume existing organisations or, if the voices were critical, to turn on them. As *Imams* and the MJC expressed criticism of PAGAD, PAGAD was tempted into battles that created tensions in its primary base. And once the bombing started and the focus shifted to PAGAD and Muslims, many saw the need to overtly create a distance from PAGAD.

The state, by labelling PAGAD as criminals and terrorists and hounding them through arrests, was able to isolate the organisation. When PAGAD turned to the *Imams* for support, the doors of the mosque were closed to them as an organisation but open to them as individual worshippers beholden to the *Imam* and, if not beholden, at least silent about the re-assertion of the leadership and legitimacy of the MJC. If PAGAD turned to smaller, secretive cells that took to isolated acts of terror, it was precisely the state's infiltration, repression and sowing of divisions that forced it into that route. PAGAD, by conflating the gangsters and the government as a common enemy, cut itself off from any engagement with the state. Whatever success it had in pushing back the stranglehold of the gangs, it was not able to consolidate those gains. In the absence of engagement with the state, it needed to maintain hegemony over the space it had de-territorialised from the gangs. This PAGAD was not able to achieve. The state was able to undermine PAGAD by using its repressive arsenal, allowing the gangs to re-territorialise some areas. Earlier in PAGAD's history, Jeenah argued that 'partnerships are now possible between the community and the state to together combat the threats to peace and stability. It is true that peace cannot exist without justice, but the struggle for justice does not have to be a struggle for the overthrow of the state' (1996: 21). As shown, PAGAD was not able to develop a working relationship with the state, let alone any kind of partnership.

People count costs in joining an organisation. And the costs for those involved kept mounting. Families of those jailed are a reminder of this. This militates against a revival of PAGAD. Also the changing identity of PAGAD creates its own limitations. PAGAD started out as a broad-based movement that looked beyond the confines of a 'Muslim identity'. But as the repression of PAGAD increased, PAGAD turned to an organisation, while not explicitly, implicitly composing itself as a Muslim organisation. The PAGAD 'experience' illustrates that an identity of a social movement is not static. This 'Islamisation' of PAGAD impacts on attempts to revive the organisation as it feeds into a growing turn to a more inward-looking Islam and the creation of what Vahed and Jeppie call 'liberated zones'. This 'does not imply animosity to the state nor is there a serious proselytising to it' (Vahed and Jeppie 2004: 268). Examples of 'liberated zones' include shariah-based law, finance and investment, education and media. The use of the term 'liberated zone' is somewhat of a misnomer because in these zones there is an attempt to create islands of 'Muslim world' that is highly policed often by reference to a conservative and non-debateable reading of Islamic texts. This is an inward-looking Islam. These factors militate against a revival of PAGAD.

Ultimately, PAGAD could not sustain the mobilisation necessary to keep up the pressure on a number of fronts – gangsters, the state and the policing of internal boundaries. It tried to move beyond the Cape in order to broaden its base. But PAGAD could not break out of the identity of 'Muslim organisation' and could not sustain any significant presence. In any case there was strong current to keep PAGAD 'Islamic'. At the same time the state was able to hive off the MJC, as well as other 'moderate' voices in the Muslim community in the Cape, from PAGAD, while using its repressive arsenal to curtail PAGAD's operations, exhausting the energy and resources of the organisation.

In the case of PAGAD, we see the truth of McAdam, Tarrow and Tilly's assertion that 'a combination of exhaustion, sectarianisation, and cooptation' is central in eroding the ability of a movement to continue mounting protest actions (2003: 66). The gangs seem to have done much better than PAGAD. Traditionally one could only 'pick up' a gang number while in prison. But, now one can 'be taught' the number outside jail (Steinberg 2004). This has enabled the 26s and 28s to grow considerably. The gangs have not only remained on the Cape Flats but have moved into Woodstock and Sea Point. While PAGAD, if the allegations are true, tried to bomb its way into the city centre, the gangs moved quietly and with more success. There are pointers that foreign syndicates, the Chinese Triads (perlemoen and shark fin), the Nigerians (heroin and cocaine) and the Pakistani mafia (mandrax and crack) are becoming more visible.

Are the social forces discussed here – vigilantes, gangs – not manifestations of the effects of the commodification of more and more aspects of life? A response to deepening marginalisation and poverty? A process of what Castells calls 'perverse integration', where sections 'of the socially excluded population, along with individuals who choose far more profitable, if risky ways to make a living, constitute an increasingly populated underworld . . .' (2000: 73). This, of course, is happening exactly at the time that the traditional organisations that defend the poor, trade unions and the state, find themselves unable or unwilling to provide a safety net for those without defence.

PAGAD was an organisation that in its initial orientation set out to fill this vacuum, and in the process came to be defined as a vigilante movement (Ero 2000; Shaw 2002). Johnston has defined vigilantism as 'a social movement giving rise to premeditated acts of force – or threatened force – by autonomous citizens. It arises as a reaction to the transgression of institutionalised norms by individuals or groups – or to their potential or imputed transgression. Such acts are focussed upon crime control and/or social control and aim to offer assurances (or "guarantees") of security both to its participants and to other members of a given established order' (Johnston 1996: 232). Autonomous citizens are those engaged in voluntary activity 'without the state's authority or support' (Johnston 1996: 226).

Keeping within this framework, there is veracity to defining PAGAD as a 'vigilante movement'. However, what we also see is that a vigilante movement that is born pressing a very narrow grievance or demand can rapidly radicalise and grow into a movement that questions the legitimacy of the entire social and political order, should it, in pursuing its original demand, come to the view that the social and political order has an interest in denying it its narrow and, at first glance, reasonable demand. Some have argued that PAGAD was predisposed to be anti-systemic in its methods and rhetoric because it was the brainchild of Islamic radicals (housed within Qibla) to exploit perceptions of the ANC's being soft on crime as a basis for a wider push towards Islamic revolution. While this charge is given some credence by PAGAD's later trajectory where a series of expulsions and 'defections' took place that were blamed on the growing influence of Qibla on PAGAD, this is too narrow a view. It neglects the very powerful, if latent, desires in communities where PAGAD came to operate that are, literally, infested with gangsterism, to which PAGAD gave expression.

As Shuaib Manjra put it, 'PAGAD gave hope to these people where they saw none . . . PAGAD represents the response of civil society who clearly feel alienated from the political process. Past structures campaigning for the political and civil rights of communities in the hegemonic battle against the apartheid regime disappeared with the onset of a democratic government. This vacuum and widespread disillusionment made fertile ground for militant mass struggles led by whoever is prepared to take up this popular cause' (Manjra 1996: 38–9). Qibla did not need to form PAGAD. PAGAD was waiting to be born. If the ANC-led government had anything to do with what PAGAD was to become, it was in its reaction to the organisation. For the state PAGAD became a 'terrorist' organisation and for the police just another gang.

What the PAGAD story indicates is that while one might mobilise 'autonomous citizens', civil society is not autonomous from the state. This is especially so in contexts where a post-liberation state has tremendous legitimacy. As Neera Chandhoke points out:

> civil societies operate on the terrain of the state. Or that setting and institutionalising the framework for civil society gives to the state immense power to define which civil society organisation is permissible . . . Within the frontiers of what is politically permissible, civil society actors can do what they like: exercise vigilance against arbitrary power, demand accountability, and insist that the state delivers what it promises. But groups which transgress these boundaries are likely to be interned to a space beyond the pale of law or civil rights . . . Consider the fate of Naxalites or for that matter any individual/group which dares challenge the boundaries of state power (2004: 2–3).

For the Naxalites in India read PAGAD in South Africa.

References

Baderoon, G. 2003. 'Covering the East – Veils and Masks: Orientalism in South African Media'. In H. Wasserman and S. Jacobs (eds), *Shifting Selves*. Cape Town: Kwela Books.

Bourgois, P. 1996. 'In Search of Masculinity'. *British Journal of Criminology* 36 (3).

Castells, M. 1997. *The Power of Identity, Volume 2*. Oxford: Blackwell.

——. 2000. *End of Millennium, Volume 3*. Oxford: Blackwell.

Chandhoke, N. 2004 'The Taming of Civil Society'. www. India-seminar.com.

Clohessy, C. 1996. 'Thoughts on PAGAD'. In R. Galant and F. Gamieldien (eds), *Drugs, Gangs, People's Power: Exploring the PAGAD Phenomenon*. Cape Town: Claremont Main Road Masjid.

Dixon, B. and L. Johns. 2001. 'Gangs, PAGAD and the State: Vigilantism and Revenge Violence in the Western Cape'. *Violence and Transition* 2 (May).

Dodd, A. 1996. 'The Women of PAGAD'. In R. Galant and F. Gamieldien (eds), *Drugs, Gangs, People's Power: Exploring the PAGAD Phenomenon*. Cape Town: Claremont Main Road Masjid.

Dowd, D. 2002. 'Thorstein Veblen: The Evolution of Capitalism from Economic and Political to Social Dominance; Economics as its Faithful Servant'. In D. Dowd (ed.), *Understanding Capitalism*. London: Pluto Press.

Ero, C. 2000. 'Vigilantes, Civil Defence Forces and Militia Groups: The Other Side of the Privatisation of Security in Africa'. *Conflict Trends* 1/2000.

Esack, F. 1996. 'PAGAD: Its Location in the New South Africa'. In R. Galant and F. Gamieldien (eds), *Drugs, Gangs, People's Power: Exploring the PAGAD Phenomenon*. Cape Town: Claremont Main Road Masjid.

Eze, E. 2004 'Transition and the Reasons of Memory'. *The South Atlantic Quarterly* 103 (4).

Fanon, F. 1989 [1959]. *Studies in a Dying Colonialism*. London: Earthscan.

Glaser, C. 2000. *Bo-Tsotsi: The Youth Gangs of Soweto, 1935–1976*. Cape Town: David Philip.

Jeenah, N. 1996. 'PAGAD, Aluta Continua'. In R. Galant and F. Gamieldien (eds), *Drugs, Gangs, People's Power: Exploring the PAGAD Phenomenon*. Cape Town: Claremont Main Road Masjid.

Jeppie, J. 1996. 'Introduction'. In R. Galant and F. Gamieldien (eds), *Drugs, Gangs, People's Power: Exploring the PAGAD Phenomenon*. Cape Town: Claremont Main Road Masjid.

Jeppie, S. 2000. 'Islam, Narcotics and Defiance in the Western Cape, South Africa'. In T. Salter and K. King (eds), *Africa, Islam and Development in Africa: African Islam, African Development*. Edinburgh: Centre of African Studies, University of Edinburgh.

Johnston, L. 1996. 'What is Vigilantism?' *British Journal of Criminology* 36 (2).

Keenan, T. 2004. 'Mobilizing Shame'. *The South Atlantic Quarterly* 103 (2/3).

Kinnes, I. 2000. 'From Urban Street Gangs to Criminal Empires: The Changing Face of Gangs in the Western Cape'. ISS Monograph Series No. 48. Pretoria: Institute of Security Studies.

Manjra, S. 1996. 'Battle Plans in the PAGAD Struggle: Political Fascism vs. Democracy'. In R. Galant and F. Gamieldien (eds), *Drugs, Gangs, People's Power: Exploring the PAGAD Phenomenon*. Cape Town: Claremont Main Road Masjid.

McAdam, D., S. Tarrow and C. Tilly. 2003. *Dynamics of Contention*. Cambridge: Cambridge University Press.

Pillay, S. 2003. 'Experts, Terrorists, Gangsters: Problematising Public Discourse on a Post-Apartheid Showdown'. In H. Wasserman and S. Jacobs (eds), *Shifting Selves*. Cape Town: Kwela Books.

Pike, S. 1997. 'Opposition, Political Identities and Spaces of Resistance'. In S. Pile and M. Keith (eds), *Geographies of Resistance*. London: Routledge.

Schärf, W. 1996. 'Organised Crime Comes of Age: During Transition to Democracy'. In R. Galant and F. Gamieldien (eds), *Drugs, Gangs, People's Power: Exploring the PAGAD Phenomenon*. Cape Town: Claremont Main Road Masjid.

Schärf, W. and C. Vale. 1996. 'The Firm: Organised Crime Comes of Age During the Transition to Democracy'. *Social Dynamics* 22 (2).

Shaw, M. 2002. *Crime and Policing in Post-Apartheid South Africa*. Cape Town: David Philip.

Standing, A. 2004. 'Out of the Mainstream: Critical Reflections on Organised Crime in the Western Cape'. In B. Dixon and E. van der Spuy (eds), *Justice Gained? Crime and Crime Control in South Africa's Transition*. Cape Town: University of Cape Town Press.

Steinberg, J. 2004. *The Number*. Johannesburg and Cape Town: Jonathan Ball Publishers.

Tayob, A. 1996. 'Islamism and PAGAD: Finding the Connection'. In R. Galant and F. Gamieldien (eds), *Drugs, Gangs, People's Power: Exploring the PAGAD Phenomenon*. Cape Town: Claremont Main Road Masjid.

Vahed, G. and S. Jeppie. 2004. 'Multiple Communities: Muslims in Post-Apartheid South Africa'. In J. Daniel, R. Southall and J. Lutchman (eds), *The State of the Nation 2004–2005*. Cape Town: HSRC Press.

Valdez, A. 2003. 'Towards a Typology of Contemporary Mexican American Youth Gangs'. In L. Kontos, D. Brotherton and L. Barnos (eds), *Gangs and Society*. New York: Columbia University Press.

Veblen, T. 1953. *The Theory of the Leisure Class*. New York: Mentor.

Interviews

Between the end of 2003 and July 2004 nine members of PAGAD (four were lapsed members but still supporters of the organisation) were interviewed. In addition two members of the Americans and one member of the Hard Livings gang were interviewed between April and June 2004. These interviews were supplemented with numerous informal 'conversations' with PAGAD and gang members.

18

Conclusion

Making Sense of Post-Apartheid South Africa's Voices of Protest

Richard Ballard, Adam Habib and Imraan Valodia

WHAT, THEN, ARE the principal findings of and lessons emanating from the preceding studies? What is the impact of contemporary social movements on the political and socio-economic scene in South Africa? What is their impact on the country's development trajectory and the future of its democratic political system? These questions, and the answers to them, would be of interest to a diverse set of stakeholders including academics, social movement activists and even public officials. While we recognise and address our findings to all three stakeholders, we do not structure the presentation of findings and the analysis thereof in a form that treats these stakeholders as distinct constituencies. After all, these roles often overlap, and the thematic issues are of interest to readers across the academic and non-academic divide.

It is also important to note that a study of this scale generates innumerable findings, not all of which can be captured in an overall thematic conclusion such as this. This chapter thus focuses on highlighting and reflecting upon six principal overlapping issues emanating from a number of the movements under study that speak to themes aggregated to the national or international level. There are numerous other findings directed at the level of the individual movement or thematic area, which can only be comprehended with a close reading of the empirically rich chapter case studies on which this conclusion is founded. In any case, six principal issues are the focus of attention in this chapter. Three of these reflect on the character, tactics and leadership of social movements in post-apartheid South Africa. Two consider how the South African cases speak to contemporary social movement theory elsewhere in the world. And the final one is a reflection on the implications of the existence of these movements and their operations for development and democratic consolidation in South Africa.

Social Movements in South Africa

It may be useful to begin these concluding reflections on social movements in South Africa with the obvious and perhaps banal remark that these institutions are essentially the products of the post-apartheid moment. This is not to suggest that they emerge from a vacuum. Obviously their strategies, activities and orientations draw on the experiences, repertoires and other rich heritage of struggle in South Africa. Nevertheless, the post-apartheid moment imparts to them a particular character. Whether it is the economic crisis of post-apartheid South Africa, as is manifested in its unemployment and poverty rates, or the cost-recovery initiatives of the local state, made mandatory by the policy choices of post-1994 state elites, or the democratic and essentially liberalised political environment of this period, all crucially influenced the genesis of these movements, their evolution and their strategies and tactics. But this is where their similarity ends. And this is important to note. For often in the emotive atmosphere within which political debate occurs, these movements are implicitly projected by both state elites and public officials, and social movement activists themselves, as a coherent homogenous entity. Some political leaders and public officials have intimated that these movements undermine democracy because of their engagement in extra-institutional action. Some social movement activists and intellectuals, on the other hand, portray these movements in romanticised terms, describing them as arenas of free democratic debate and participation epitomised in a 'principled internationalism, a socialist vision, and an independent mass-based mobilisation and struggle as an ideological and organisational alternative to the capitalist ANC' (McKinley 2004: 20).

The case studies reflected in the preceding chapters challenge the assumption of homogeneity underlying both these views, for not only do they speak to a somewhat hypothetical ideal rather than to the current reality of social movements, but they also generalise the respective ideal as characteristic of all within the social movement universe. As a way of reminding ourselves of the heterogeneity and overlapping models of grassroots activism, it is useful to undertake a typology of what it is that social movements in South Africa are opposing. First, much activism in South Africa is directed against government policy on distributional issues, particularly with regards to the inability of many poor South Africans to access basic services. Privatisation and cost recovery are perceived as the key elements debilitating delivery. Movements that reflect such campaigns include among others the Soweto Electricity Crisis Committee (SECC), the Anti-Privatisation Forum (APF), the former Concerned Citizens Forum (CCF), the now divided Western Cape Anti-Eviction Campaign (AEC) and the Treatment Action Campaign (TAC). Second, some movements oppose the state, banks and private landlords through opposition to evictions and attempts to secure land tenure. Movements that have taken up such struggles are the Landless People's Movement (LPM), Concerned Citizens Forum (CCF), and the AEC.

Third, there is a base of familiar unions in post-apartheid South Africa that target government policy on employment conditions as well as the labour practices of businesses. Most of these unions are housed within the Congress of South African Trade Unions (COSATU), which, although in alliance with the current government, has nevertheless continued to engage in adversarial mass action. The limitation of these formal sector unions so far, however, has been their inability to deal with the changing nature of work and the growing layer of informal workers. This challenge has been taken up by a new set of nascent campaigns like the Self-Employed Women's Union (SEWU), which target the local state on accommodating workers and traders rather than targeting 'bosses' on conditions of service. Notwithstanding SEWU's demise in 2004, its agenda continues to impact on mainstream unions.

Fourth, there is a significant component of activism that is directed against corporations and the government on issues of pollution and the environment. One such action, sustained over a long period of time has been the community action in South Durban. In addition, the Environmental Justice Networking Forum (EJNF) represents a group of organisations that has been instrumental in shifting popular environmental consciousness from green conservation to brown issues that emphasise social justice in the human environment. Fifth, some organisations have sought to counter various forms of social prejudice against refugees, sexual minorities and women, especially through reforms of government's policy infrastructure. Finally, there are movements, notably Jubilee South Africa (JSA), that oppose multilateral organisations and foreign corporations in relation to unpayable or odious debt, or in terms of claiming compensation from businesses that operated in South Africa during apartheid.

They have also lobbied the current South African government to take a stronger social justice approach, particularly in relation to reparations for victims identified through the Truth and Reconciliation Commission (TRC).

Character

These six categories are not exhaustive but begin to show the range of political projects assumed by various movements. Some of these overlap or are allied projects. What is distinctive about the movements in this period is that unlike their anti-apartheid counterparts, they do not collectively share a common counter-hegemonic political project with a focus on state capture. Instead, the political projects of contemporary social movements can be taken in one of two directions: rights-based opposition and counter-hegemonic opposition. There is a tension between the two idealised positions of wanting fundamental transformation on the one hand and deepened claims to citizenship within existing structures on the other. In the latter position, rights-based opposition attempts to hold the government to constitutionally enshrined rights within the current liberal order. The primary problem is understood to be one of either a deficient government policy or its compromised implementation. As Young argues, '[c]alls for inclusion arise from experiences of exclusion . . . Some of the most powerful and successful social movements of this century have mobilized around demands for oppressed and marginalized people to be included as full and equal citizens in their polities' (2000: 7).

Alternatively, there are activists that articulate their project as a counter-hegemonic one. The scale of focus is broadened from a particular policy to the state's economic path. Many of these movements suggest that they draw from class-based ideologies with notable self-descriptions such as: anti-neoliberal, anti-capital, anti-GEAR, anti-globalisation, anti-market, socialist and Trotskyist. Such ideologies are frequently expressed in the Social Movements Indaba, which was originally convened in response to the World Summit for Sustainable Development in Johannesburg in 2002, and continues to meet on a regular basis. The Indaba includes movements such as the APF, AEC, LPM, CCF and others. While these are all ostensibly issue-based campaigns, they can become vehicles for articulating broader challenges against the state's economic path and have, at times, supported the need for a socialist alternative. One delegate at the Social Movements Indaba meeting of March 2004 referred to their collective as the 'socialist movements'.

There is a sense within the Social Movements Indaba that its movements constitute the 'real' social movements of the country in contrast to more collaborationist and reformist organisations. Ngwane differentiates between 'good' and 'bad' social movements, and says flatly that 'social movements . . . have to fight the state, destroy it and replace it with a workers' state' (2003: 32). This is not simply a view of a small group of activists. Indeed, it is a view advanced within the academy itself. Bond, for instance, distinguishes between organisations

> that emerge in the implementation of formal social policies (such as welfare agencies or implementation-oriented NGOs) or the reproduction of daily life (mutual aid groupings) – and *movements*. The latter are both protest-oriented and utopian, in the sense of attempting to construct the community of a future society in the decay of the old (2004: 9–10; original emphasis).

Drawing on Tironi, Bond sets the desire for participation against the objective of breaking the social system, or its rupture (Bond 2004: 11). In this sense, social movements are imagined, in Hetherington's characterisation, as the 'hinge' on which society can be diverted in a new direction (1998: 10). Collaboration with the state is seen as pointless as it represents bourgeois interests, as was demonstrated in the case studies of the APF and the AEC. The test of an authentic movement, from this perspective, is whether it holds a vision for a socialist alternative or at least opposes the state's neo-liberal growth path. Successes in relation to particular issues such as the provision of HIV treatment are not unambiguously good for such activists, unless they are attached to this broader counter-hegemonic project. Indeed, success is sometimes perceived as harmful. As indicated in Chapter 2, leaders of the TAC are derided for their simultaneous criticism of the government's failure to deliver HIV treatment, and proclaiming to be loyal card-carrying members of the ANC. The decision to work with the government on the delivery of anti-retrovirals – now that it has decided to supply them – is seen not as a success, but rather as having compromised their ability to vociferously oppose the state in the future.

These critics are, however, ignoring the large percentage of the members of their own organisations that continue to support the ANC. This flags a contradiction between ideological hope and empirical reality. Ideological hope thrusts responsibility for a utopian future upon local-level struggles by the poor.

While it might be possible to say that community struggles are – by default – anti-neoliberal, it does not follow that they set out with this ideology in mind. Mark Heywood of the TAC suggested at a conference in Durban in 2004 that revolutionary social movements as defined by the left were a figment of their imagination. While his sentiments created a stir, they did bring to the fore, as Haffajee (2004) has noted, the necessity to distinguish between ideal types and reality on the ground. As Harvey recognised, there is no necessary link between what he calls 'insurgent movements against accumulation by dispossession' and a socialist political programme. Many such movements would, in fact, resent being 'co-opted by socialist developmentalism' (Harvey 2003: 166).

The choice between participation with a view to improving the state and opposition with a view to rupture is, to some extent, academic. Struggles in post-apartheid South Africa respond, in the first instance, to particular manifestations of exclusion, poverty and marginality. They are very often local and immediate; they are pragmatic and quite logical responses to everyday hardships (Barchiesi 2004; Desai 2003; McKinley and Naidoo 2004). Activists operate to achieve direct relief for marginalised groupings on particular issues. Such activists do not focus primarily on opposing the state's economic path, although they may do so by default. This is not to say that they necessarily agree with the current national programme, but rather that they choose to focus their attention on particular gains on specific issues. In such situations, engagement with the state may indeed be on the cards. The country has, after all, installed a democratically elected government and given it an overwhelming mandate to pursue its programmes for overcoming the injustices of apartheid. Regardless of the effectiveness of these programmes, rhetorical interest in resolving poverty in South Africa allows considerable room for activists to manoeuvre. They recognise that the current situation allows many opportunities to nudge, coerce or force the state and other institutions to address various aspects of marginality. In particular, movements make extensive and flexible use of the discourse of rights to add legitimacy to their activities (Greenstein 2003). Even the more militant movements that engage in technically illegal activities, such as reconnections and land occupations, use the language of rights to invest their activities with a sense that they are endorsed by a higher code of 'good'.

Does engagement necessarily reduce activists to nothing more than collaborators with bourgeois interests? Is it necessarily the case that progressive politics is impossible in the absence of a long-term objective to 'overthrow the capitalist system' (Ngwane cited in Bond 2004: 29)? Some question whether the objective of the seizure of state power should be the benchmark of radical action; the qualifying indicator of being truly progressive. For Mngxitama (2004), '[r]evolutionary theory as we know it has become suspect, together with the old answers it prescribed'. Greenstein (2003) deploys some of the writings of post-Marxists such as Laclau and Mouffe to reflect anew on movements that do not position themselves as revolutionary. His question: is it possible to achieve counter-hegemonic goals outside of the traditional trajectory specified by socialism? His answer: such movements can claim to be progressive in as much as they challenge existing power relations, although such challenges are not cast as a political revolutionary project. They therefore seek to challenge state power without merely 'replacing one set of relations of domination with another' (Greenstein 2003: 16). Or rather, they do not imagine that the only way to oppose state power is to seek to overthrow it. Cock argues in her study in Chapter 10 that the contemporary forms of mobilisation are best described by William's phrase, 'militant particularisms'. To quote Barchiesi, the politics of the multitude is 'non-teleological' and seeks to 'open up previously unchartered terrains of political possibility and lines of advance' (2004: 6–7).

For many radicals, then, it does not follow that the absence of a socialist programme renders one unprogressive. While local struggles often focus on particular sites or situations, they are not confined to them and can expose and contribute to broader struggles (Low and Lawrence-Zúñiga 2003: 18). Small-scale, locally embedded actions can contest broader relations of dominance and subordination. As Laclau and Mouffe have argued, the political nature of struggles is not confined to parties and the state, but is rather any 'type of action whose objective is the transformation of a social relation which constructs a subject in a relationship of subordination' (1985: 153). The existence of a range of struggles, even if not co-ordinated in a national liberation movement, can result in a 'chain of equivalence' that confronts and transforms relations with dominant powers.

Socialists such as Harvey believe that the innovation of embedded politics is an inadequate replacement for macro-politics.

The danger . . . is of seeing all such struggles against dispossession as by definition 'progressive' or, even worse, of placing them under some homogenizing banner like that of Hardt and Negri's 'multitude' that will magically rise up to inherit the earth. This, I think, is where the real political difficulty lies (Harvey 2003: 168–9).

Similarly, Ngwane argues against 'autonomism' that attempts to break with the hierarchy of the traditional left which is seen as a kind of militancy without politics (cited in Bond 2004; see also Bauman and Vecchi 2004: 35–6).

While acknowledging the validity of their argument, that not all struggles have equal counter-hegemonic potential, one need not reduce the definition of counter-hegemonic to state capture. After all, there is a long debate within the left about the relationship between reform and revolution (see Habib and Kotze 2003). Moreover, in the South African context, while neither side might always acknowledge it, both sides actually require each other, a lesson abundantly evident in the preceding chapters. The counter-hegemonic movements' engagements tend to create crises, which more rights-based campaigns can capitalise on to influence policy and government practice. Zuern's study in Chapter 9 demonstrates that the SECC's decision to illegally reconnect the electricity of disconnected households created a legitimacy crisis that forced government to get Eskom to write off electricity debts in Soweto. While many are critical of the credit going to the South African National Civics Organisation (SANCO), one could argue that the potential created by the SECC may never have been realised had it not been possible to strike a deal within the concessionary space close to the ruling Alliance occupied by the civic movement. The women's movement demonstrates this lesson in a negative way. Hassim, in Chapter 16, concludes that there has been immense success in inserting gender into government policy and increasing institutional gender representivity. Nevertheless, in the absence of grassroots mobilisation and more radical action, the lives of many poor women remain extremely marginalised.

Tactics

These examples suggest, then, that the issue of tactics is crucial for social movements. These are, of course, not only shaped by a movement's ideology, but also by the character and evolution of its campaign, its own access to resources, including leadership, and by the opportunities and constraints generated by the post-1994 political environment. The new political, economic and social order is underwritten by a constitution that enshrines first- and second-generation rights; clauses that have been used by a number of social movements to either defend themselves or advance their campaigns. Social movements' engagements with the state fall on a continuum between in-system collaborative interactions on the one extreme, and out-of-system adversarial relations on the other. Relatively few movements can be clearly placed in a single camp. The Homeless People's Alliance (HPA) is one of the exceptions, as Khan and Pieterse explain in Chapter 8, preferring to pursue a 'politics of patience' with a high degree of 'bureaucratic intimacy'. Another is the APF, which by contrast, prefers to avoid engagement (see Chapter 4). Even in this case, however, there are internal discussions around the merits of non-engagement and adversarialism. There is a lack of consensus within many movements over the best strategic approach. Oldfield and Stokke's study in Chapter 6 shows that the community organisations that make up the AEC diverge significantly from one another, with some choosing to engage, while others fear co-optation and therefore wish to avoid collaboration. Most deploy a variety of strategies in order to achieve their goals. This deployment of a diverse set of strategies is best exhibited by the TAC which has sided with the government against pharmaceutical companies, negotiated with the government to provide treatment through the National Economic Development and Labour Council (NEDLAC), taken the government to court when it proved intransigent, and even pursued a defiance campaign. These tactics represent moments in a constantly evolving relationship between the movement and the government.

A variety of movements have chosen to make extensive use of the wide range of democratic spaces afforded by South Africa's post-apartheid political system. As Dirsuweit's study in Chapter 15 shows, the Lesbian and Gay Equality Project claims as a core success the fact that legislation that affected sexual minorities has been changed in the last ten years. The AEC is using courts, not because it necessarily wants to operate within formal institutions or has any particular faith in them, but because it can frustrate the local government and finance institutions in their attempts to evict. Most of all, it can use courts to buy a little time for families who would otherwise be on the streets.

The state has undeniably opened up since 1994. There is much more democratic engagement with various societal forums. Increasingly, instruments and spaces have become available for the state to engage with civil society, and indeed, for civil society actors to challenge the state. NEDLAC, media, courts, constitution, formalised attempts to have public input into most policies, and even rhetorical support for mass demonstrations, provide a significant repertoire of 'in-system' mechanisms for influencing policy and challenging the government. Given this existence of institutionalised avenues of action, movements recognise that the most belligerent tactics may not be the most expedient way of achieving immediate material goals and it is often useful to apply 'friendly' pressure, which gains the co-operation of the state, rather than the kind of action that puts the state in a position of bending only under duress.

However, other movements do not consider immediate material gains to be their primary target, and seek to confront the state at a more systemic level. These movements have been engaging the state on more adversarial terms. In November 2003 the LPM announced a 'no land no vote' campaign in response to the state's attempts to register voters. The campaign capitalised on the fact that voters could only register by giving a residential address and this was impossible while they were under threat of eviction. This campaign was later endorsed by most other social movements that attended the Social Movements Indaba meeting in March 2004. Other extra-institutional tactics included illegal strategies of land invasions, water and electricity reconnections, and public protests not granted official permission.

It needs to be stressed that no simple distinction can be drawn between movements that practise in-system tactics and those that undertake extra-institutional action. We might expect that, in their effort to avoid collaboration, movements that frame their operations in explicitly counter-hegemonic terms would adopt a mix of strategies, but in-system strategies would often be used as a supplement to more extra-institutional action. Conversely, movements with an explicitly rights-based agenda would be at the in-system pole of the continuum, practising a mix of strategies with extra-institutional action often used to supplement in-system strategies (cf. Guha 2000: 4). In practice, however, it is very difficult to discern such a dichotomy. Indeed, all the movements studied tended to practise an ill-defined mix of in-system and extra-institutional strategies. The use of conventional avenues of engaging the state did not necessarily amount to collaboration, and the TAC, CCF and AEC studies all provide examples of extreme antagonism playing itself out through courts or other formal institutions. Where there would perhaps be a clear dividing line is on the issue of policy formulation. It is certainly the case that there is a set of organisations that would be prepared to engage the government on policy, while another would not consider this a worthwhile exercise. Even here, however, the dividing lines can be blurred. The LPM, for instance, has for some time been calling for a land summit in order to engage the state over a solution on the land question.

State response is, of course, itself a determinant of tactics taken up by movements. Where organisations have operated illegally, it has not been their original intention. Rather, state reaction and circumstances tended to facilitate the resort to extra-institutional protest. Desai's study in Chapter 17 demonstrates that PAGAD's (People Against Gangsterism and Drugs) initial intentions were for a positive engagement with the state, but the government's treatment of it as a political threat drove it underground. In March 2004 an application for the APF to march on the opening of the constitutional court was declined and their decision to proceed resulted in the arrests of 52 people, some of whom were simply members of the public who happened to be wearing red T-shirts. On election day in April 2004, 62 members of the LPM were arrested for undertaking a picket too close to a polling station. And, there is growing concern among social movement leaders and human rights activists about the stigmatisation of the 'ultra left' and the desire to repress protests (Cronin 2002; Desai 2003; Greenstein 2003: 30–1; Saul 2001, 2002; Vally 2003). Commentators aligned with the ruling party, however, maintain that whereas illegal tactics were justified under apartheid, such behaviour should be redundant under the tenure of a legitimate democratic regime (Sachs 2003: 26).

Leadership

Aside from the influence of ideology, the opportunity structure and the response of the state, how do actual choices of tactics get to be made? Of course, the democratic character of these movements can vary widely, but in almost all cases leadership and a vanguard cadre play a crucial role. This then takes us to the final notable feature of these movements, namely the role of the leadership in their genesis, definition and evolution. This should not be surprising. After all, the international literature has for long pointed out the indispensable role of human capacity and resources in the establishment of social movements (see Chapter 1). And despite the fact that some social movement activists may be reluctant to acknowledge the centrality of leadership and a vanguard cadre, we would be remiss if we did not recognise that none of these movements would be what they are without their leadership and vanguard cadre and the resources these individuals were able to broker from a variety of institutional settings.

This must not be interpreted to mean that the leadership is a small, manipulative, undemocratic clique. Neither does it suggest that these movements are undemocratic. Rather, it is a recognition that deprivation on its own cannot lead to social action. It must be used by a cadre and leadership to mobilise and build sustainable organisation and/or campaigns. The fact that this cadre and leadership is regularly from a middle-class environment, and therefore often not African, is sometimes used in attempts to discredit the movement. As Friedman and Mottiar (Chapter 2) remind us, the Minister of Health attempted to discredit the leadership of the TAC on the basis of race. In this case, the accusations did not succeed in creating divisions within the TAC. A more serious critique, however, comes from within the social movement universe. Andile Mngxitama (2004) has in a recent intervention criticised the dominance of white leftist individuals who he argues skew the political agenda of these movements in a particularly negative direction. Aside from the accuracy or not of these allegations, Mngxitama's remarks suggest that these movements are contested spaces where the wider debates of the South African transition are played out. This is of specific significance given the fact that these movements are committed to achieving greater levels of democracy, and realising an alternative, less exploitative future.

Many of these leadership figures do indeed emerge from middle-class backgrounds, whose locations in different institutional settings enable them to broker resources and legitimacy for these movements. Examples from the case studies abound in this regard. Zackie Achmat is the public face of the TAC and was able to utilise connections with prominent members of the ANC, including Jacob Zuma and Nelson Mandela, to build engagement with the state. His connections with the gay rights movement were also used to generate resources for and legitimise the demands of the TAC. Fatima Meer and Ashwin Desai used their location at the Institute of Black Research to establish and support the CCF. The leadership of the APF was formed largely from a group of disaffected COSATU personnel who were able, for a time, to use the resource base of the union federation to establish the movement. The SECC is supported by Patrick Bond and Trevor Ngwane, who were located at the relevant time at the University of the Witwatersrand and the Alternative Information Development Centre respectively. The role of well-resourced, connected individuals is a matter that is – to some extent – beyond a choice for social movements. These leaders do indeed have a decisive impact on the direction of their movements. But beyond this, the very existence of these movements may depend on this leadership and cadre involvement. Their involvement opens up possibilities that help the movement to thrive, as well as introducing challenges that have to be negotiated along the way.

Some Reflections for Theory Building

For some years now there has been an international literature developing on social movements, some of which has been identified and reflected upon in the Introduction, with the explicit agenda of uniting disparate theories and bringing them together in a comprehensive explanation of the genesis, operations and impact of social movements. We would of course be remiss if we were not to comment on this literature and how the South African cases speak to the debates and issues relevant to this theory-building project. Two issues emanating from the South African case studies need to be reflected upon by these scholars. First, we need to look at how these case studies speak to the assertion by some scholars, mainly those associated with the new social movement theories (see Chapter 1), that identity-based struggles now supersede distributional politics in post-industrial societies. This view has been most recently echoed by the noted sociologist Michael Buroway who insists that '[i]n the postcommunist era progressive struggles have moved away from distributional politics to focus on identity politics or what Nancy Fraser calls a politics of recognition' (Burawoy 2003: 242).

South Africa is, of course, not a post-industrial society, and so it may seem unfair to respond to this assertion from a context that is so socio-economically different. But we believe the South African cases may highlight issues worth noting if only because this is a society that is an interesting hybrid, reflecting both humanity's post-industrial and developing worlds. In any case, the case studies in the preceding chapters suggest that distributional issues are still central in South Africa. Indeed, a good proportion of the movements emerged as a response to the economic crisis and its manifestations, and they deliberately founded on effecting a redistribution of scarce resources in favour of marginalised communities. This is the explicit intent of movements as diverse as the TAC, the LPM, the AEC, the CCF and the SECC.

But perhaps even more relevant for these theories is how distributional issues colour the politics within explicitly identity-based movements. The case studies of the gay, environmental, women's and refugees' movements in the preceding chapters make it clear that even while identity is an important driver within these movements, distributional questions are by no means marginalised. In fact, these case studies demonstrate that a huge contestation exists within these movements on distributional issues. So as Dirsuweit points out in Chapter 15, the gay movement is divided over the distributional questions raised by the poverty of a significant proportion of their members, as is the environmental movement that is increasingly being forced to take on 'brown' rather than 'green' issues, thereby addressing the socio-economic concerns of marginalised communities, and bringing to the fore the principle of environmental justice.

These case studies, then, suggest that identity-based social movements in South Africa, typical of those in the industrialised world, are being driven by an intricate mix of identity and distributional pressures. And there is no reason to assume that this is a peculiarly South African phenomenon. Indeed, Dirsuweit's chapter, which reflects on the writings of Young (1990) and Fraser (1997), suggests that a similar mix of pressures defines movements in the industrialised world. After all, there is increasing evidence that inequality and poverty is rising across the globe, including in the industrialised countries. This, together with the fact that a large part of the world where social movements are active are developing contexts, suggests that distributional issues need to be an explicit component of the theory-building agenda of social movement scholars.

The second issue that the South African case studies speak to is the increasingly widely held belief among both scholars and activists that the fulcrum of mobilisation and anti-hegemonic political activity is shifting from the realm of production to that of consumption. Again, Buroway's recent intervention makes this assertion explicit. Drawing on Polanyi (1957), he suggests that counter-hegemonic potential lies not only in the realm of production, as classically understood, but in the domain of consumption and the market:

> Everyone suffers from the market in as much as unrestrained it leads to the destruction of the environment, global warming, toxic wastes, the colonization of free time, and so forth . . . Whereas alienated and degraded labour may excite a limited alternative, it does not have the universalism of the market that touches everyone in multiple ways. It is the market, therefore, that offers possible grounds for counterhegemony.

We see this everywhere but especially in the amalgam of movements against the many guises of globalization (Buroway 2003: 231).

And he is not alone in the academy in holding this view. Harvey (2003), in his recent work *The New Imperialism*, arrives at a similar conclusion on the basis of his analysis of neo-liberalism, which he argues is capital's response to the problems of over-accumulation that emerged in the last three decades of the twentieth century. His analysis holds that the dominant logic of capital accumulation in the contemporary period is what he calls, following Rosa Luxemburg, 'accumulation by dispossession', which forces 'the costs of devaluations of surplus capitals upon the weakest and most vulnerable territories and populations' (Harvey 2003: 184–5). The result is an explosion of struggles outside the arena of production around the privatisation of basic services and the displacement of poor and marginalised peoples. Harvey's conclusion: greater attention needs to be paid to the struggles occasioned by accumulation through dispossession, and links need to be forged between these and proletarian struggles at the point of production.

While there is not much that can be disputed in Harvey's carefully constructed and nuanced conclusion, the more extreme readings of these processes both within the academy and among social movement activists must be questioned. In the case of the latter, a growing perception has been that unions have lost their potential to serve as institutional agents for counter-hegemonic struggle, and the only hope now remains in a range of radical social movements located in the arena of reproduction. Ashwin Desai has explicitly expressed this view on multiple occasions, as has Richard Pithouse who, following Hardt and Negri (2000), asserts, that 'the idea of the multitude has freed many from both the fetish of the proletariat as the only viable agent of challenge to capital and the fetish of the nation as defender against capital. Given the reality that most resistances in contemporary South Africa are at the point of consumption (basic services, housing, healthcare, education, etc.) rather than production, and are largely community rather than union driven, as well as the complete immersion of the South African elite into the transnational elite, these are very welcome releases' (Pithouse 2004: 182).

Implicit in this view is the suggestion of union impotence in the face of a resurgent community activism to represent the interest of marginalised communities. But the South African case studies suggest that this is too easy a read of contemporary developments. After all, even in the pre-1994 era, community struggles composed a significant portion, if not a majority, of the struggles against the apartheid state from as far back as the 1950s (Mamdani 1996). Even more important is the fact that the union movement today is a very vibrant component of the social movement universe, notwithstanding its alliance with the ruling party. COSATU may not phrase its agenda and activities in counter-hegemonic terms, but, as Habib and Valodia in Chapter 11 demonstrate, this has not completely disarmed the federation. After all, its recent strikes and its struggles against GEAR, AIDS and Zimbabwe suggest that it is still a political force that needs to be reckoned with. Some social movements, like the TAC, have of course recognised this and explicitly entered an alliance with this social movement located in the realm of production. Moreover, it also needs to be noted that in pure membership terms, COSATU dwarfs almost all other social movements combined.

The problem, of course, is the impression created by the union federation's alliance with the ANC. This alliance has at times placed the federation on the defensive, forcing it to conduct some struggles within the institutional parameters of the Tripartite Alliance. But the combativity of the movement resurfaces every so often, and this together with the social movement orientation of COSATU, suggests that unions are still very much relevant and alive to the struggle to represent marginalised communities. Again this suggests, if only because our socio-economic context is so similar to much of the developing world, that the realm of production cannot be ignored as an arena of mobilisation and organisation of counter-hegemonic struggle, and that as a result unions must be retained as one of the institutional agencies capable of conducting and leading these struggles. The South African case studies therefore imply that that arena of production is as relevant as that of consumption in understanding various responses to the manifestations of globalisation.

Social Movements, Development and Democracy in South Africa

What, then, is the impact of these movements on the development trajectory and the consolidation of democracy in South Africa? As has been indicated earlier, some have argued that these movements undermine the democratic project by explicitly challenging, through extra-institutional action, a legitimate democratically elected government. The essential problem with these interpretations is that they conflate and confuse the stated aims of social movements with their immediate systemic effect. Whatever the ultimate distant goals of these movements, their impact needs to be assessed in relation to their immediate systemic effects. And the most obvious tangible effect of social movements on the political landscape of this country is that they represent the interests of the poor and marginalised, and apply pressure on the government to pay greater attention to the welfare of these groups. Social movements are thus an avenue for marginalised people and those concerned about their interests to impact on material distribution, and social exclusion, and to claim a certain degree of influence and power over the state itself. In a context where the formal political system has failed to produce a significant political party to the left of the ANC to more directly champion the cause of the poor, social movements contribute to the restoration of political plurality in the political system.

This then raises the more significant contribution of contemporary social movements in South Africa. The fundamental purpose of a democracy is to make state elites accountable to the citizenry. This is the only way to effect not only public participation, but also to guarantee a development trajectory in the interests of all the citizenry, including its most marginalised and dispossessed. Such accountability is founded on the emergence of substantive uncertainty in the political system. Political uncertainty is, of course, the essence of democracy. It takes one of two distinct forms; institutional and substantive. Institutional uncertainty – the uncertainty about the *rules* of the game – implies the vulnerability of the democratic system to anti-democratic forces. Substantive uncertainty – the uncertainty of the *outcomes* of the game – is about the perceptions of ruling political elites in a democratic system on whether they will be returned to office (Schedler 2001: 19). The former – institutional uncertainty – is bad for democracy as it raises the prospect of the return to authoritarianism in the 'Third Wave' of democracies. The latter – substantive uncertainty – is good for democracy for it keeps politicians on their toes and makes them responsive to their citizenry.

There has been much investigation into and reflection on institutional uncertainty (O'Donnell and Schmitter 1986; O'Donnell 1993; Huntington 1991), but there is surprisingly little work on substantive uncertainty. This should not be surprising given that researchers and activists concerned with democratisation have been preoccupied with the business of transcending authoritarian regimes and institutionalising democratic ones. Nevertheless, the lack of attention to substantive uncertainty has significant political costs. Indeed, the weakness of many contemporary democracies lies precisely in this arena. Despite the presence of institutional mechanisms that are intended to promote substantive uncertainty – legislative elections, separation of powers, civil liberties, opposition political parties, an independent press – this goal still eludes much of what Huntington (1991) has called the 'Third Wave' of democracies. One reason for this is the shift in power from the legislature to the executive of governments across the globe in the last two decades. Another emanates from the inclination of democratisers and democratisation scholars to not rock the boat in societies undergoing democratic transitions. Fearful of the very real danger of a reversion to authoritarianism, these actors have focused on procedural aspects of democratisation and made significant political and institutional concessions to the state and economic elites of the authoritarian order. Finally, it can be explained by the honeymoon phenomenon where citizens are reluctant to vote against liberation parties who were responsible for co-ordinating the popular rebellions that brought down authoritarian regimes (Fanon 1967: 137; Mamdani 1996: 21; Mbembe 2001: 104).

As a result of some of these developments, and peculiar contextual factors, such as the racialised or ethnic character of South Africa's principal opposition parties – the Democratic Alliance (DA), Inkatha Freedom Party (IFP) and the now defunct New National Party (NNP) – the ANC has not been seriously threatened at the polls. This lack of substantive uncertainty has eroded the citizenry's leverage *vis-à-vis* state elites. The ANC, as the dominant party in the liberation movement, came to office with an overwhelming electoral mandate but despite this its policy concessions over the last decade have been largely to foreign investors and domestic capital (both black and white). This is because it has been able to take the citizenry's vote for granted. Policy concessions in favour of capital are most graphically reflected in the abandonment of the Reconstruction and Development Programme (RDP) and the adoption of the Growth, Employment and Redistribution (GEAR) strategy. The net effect has been a transition that has deracialised the apex of the class structure and has economically favoured the upper echelons and strata of South African society (Whiteford and Van Seventer 2000).

The antidote to this state of affairs is the reintroduction of substantive uncertainty into the political system. Of course there could be much debate on the precise institutional mechanisms that could facilitate substantive uncertainty.

Some may maintain that it need only involve electoral reform and the emergence of social movements (Mattes and Southall 2004; Ballard, Habib and Valodia 2006), while others would suggest that in addition to this, it would require the break-up of the Tripartite Alliance and the abandonment of corporatist institutions (Habib and Taylor 2001; Desai and Habib 1997). All of this could facilitate uncertainty, and this is necessary for loosening up the existing configuration of power in South African society. What is important to note in this debate, however, is that none of the other elements except the presence of social movements exists at present, or is likely to emerge in the foreseeable future. Thus, for now at least, social movements are our only hope for introducing substantive uncertainty, and thereby facilitating the accountability of state elites to our citizenry.

It is instructive to note that the South African government's recent shift to a more state interventionist and expansive economic policy with a more welfarist orientation, coincided with the emergence and heightened activity of social movements in South Africa. While it would be difficult to establish direct causality between the shift in state policy and the emergence of social movements, very few observers of the South African scene would deny that social movements have contributed to the emergence of a political climate that encourages state elites to become more responsive to the country's most marginalised citizenry. This shift in state policy is not without problems and has as yet not gone far enough (Habib 2004). It could also be argued that such shifts are the enlightened twin of the strategy of repression. For Harvey, drawing on Gramsci, '[t]he power of the hegemon . . . is fashioned out of and expressed through an ever-shifting balance between coercion and consensus' (Harvey 2003: 37–8). Realising that it has opened the door for others to gain support through more explicitly worded anti-poverty manifestos, the ANC government shifted to re-capture this ground in the build-up to the 2004 election. Recognition of this enables us to conclude that the effective operations of social movements is a necessary, if not a sufficient, political condition for prompting a sustainable shift in state policy in the interests of South Africa's poor and marginalised. A more human-centred development trajectory and the consolidation of democracy thus require in part the systemic presence and effective functioning of contemporary social movements in South Africa.

References

Ballard, R., A. Habib and I. Valodia. 2006. 'Social Movements in South Africa: Promoting Crisis or Creating Stability'. In V. Padayachee (ed.), *The Developing Decade? Economic and Social Change in South Africa, 1994–2004*. Cape Town: HSRC Press.

Barchiesi, F. 2004. 'Classes, Multitudes and the Politics of Community: Movements in Post-Apartheid South Africa'. Paper presented at How Class Works Conference, State University of New York, 10–12 June, Stony Brook, and at the annual Congress of the South African Sociological Association, University of the Free State, 27–30 June, Bloemfontein.

Bauman, Z. and B. Vecchi. 2004. *Identity*. Cambridge, UK: Polity.

Bond, P. 2004. *South Africa's Resurgent Urban Social Movements: The Case of Johannesburg, 1984, 1994, 2004*. Centre for Civil Society Research Report No. 22, Durban: University of KwaZulu-Natal.

Burawoy, M. 2003. 'For a Sociological Marxism: The Complementary Convergence of Antonio Gransci and Karl Polanyi'. *Politics and Society* 31 (2): 193–261.

Cronin, J. 2002. 'Post-Apartheid South Africa: A Reply to John S. Saul'. *Monthly Review* 54 (7).

Desai, A. 2003. 'Neoliberalism and Resistance in South Africa'. *Monthly Review* 54 (8).

Desai, A. and A. Habib. 1997. 'Labour Relations in Transition: The Rise of Corporatism in South Africa's Automobile Industry'. *Journal of Modern African Studies* 35 (3).

Fanon, F. 1967. *The Wretched of the Earth*. Harmondsworth: Penguin.

Fraser, N. 1997. *Justice Interruptus: Critical Reflections on the 'Postsocialist' Condition*. New York: Routledge.

Greenstein, R. 2003. 'Civil Society, Social Movements and Power in South Africa'. Unpublished RAU Sociology seminar paper. http://general.rau.ac.za/sociology/Greenstein.pdf .

Guha, R. 2000. 'On Some Aspects of the Historiography of Colonial India'. In V. Chaturvedi (ed.), *Mapping Subaltern Studies and the Postcolonial*. London and New York: Verso.

Habib, A. 2004. 'The Politics of Economic Policy-Making: Substantive Uncertainty, Political Leverage, and Human Development'. *Transformation* 56.

Habib, A. and H. Kotze. 2003. 'Civil Society, Governance and Development in an Era of Globalisation'. In O. Edigheji and G. Mhone (eds), *Governance in the New South Africa*. Cape Town: University of Cape Town Press.

Habib, A. and R. Taylor. 2001. 'Political Alliances and Parliamentary Opposition in Post-Apartheid South Africa'. *Democratization* 8 (1).

Haffajee, F. 2004. 'Fact, Fiction and the New Left'. *Mail and Guardian* 11–17 June.

Hardt, M. and A. Negri. 2000. *Empire*. Cambridge, MA: Harvard University Press.

Harvey, D. 2003. *The New Imperialism*. Oxford: Oxford University Press.

Hetherington, K. 1998. *Expressions of Identity: Space, Performance, Politics*. London: Sage.

Huntington, S. 1991. *The Third Wave: Democratization in the late Twentieth Century*. Oklahoma: University of Oklahoma Press.

Laclau, E. and C. Mouffe. 1985. *Hegemony and Socialist Strategy: Towards a Radical Democratic Politics*. London and New York: Verso.

Low, S.M. and D. Lawrence-Zúñiga. 2003. 'Locating Culture'. In S.M. Low and D. Lawrence-Zúñiga (eds), *The Anthropology of Space and Place: Locating Culture*. Malden, MA: Blackwell.

Mamdani, M. 1996. *Citizen and Subject: Contemporary Africa and the Legacy of Late Colonialism*. Princeton, NJ: Princeton University Press.

Mattes, R. and R. Southall. 2004. 'Popular Attitudes toward the South African Electoral System'. *Democratisation* 11 (1).

Mbembe, A. 2001. *On the Postcolony.* Berkeley and Los Angeles: University of California Press.

McKinley, D. 2004. 'The Rise of Social Movements in South Africa'. *Debate: Voices from the South African Left* May: 17–21.

McKinley, D. and P. Naidoo. 2004. 'New Social Movements in South Africa: A Story in Creation'. *Development Update* 5 (2): 9–22.

Mngxitama, A. 2004. 'Let Black Voices Speak for the Voiceless'. *Mail and Guardian* 22 June.

Ngwane, T. 2003. 'The Anti-Privatisation Forum (APF)'. *South African Labour Bulletin* 27 (3): 31–2.

O'Donnell, G. 1993. 'On the State, Democratization and some Conceptual Problems: A Latin American View with Glances at some Post-Communist Countries'. *World Development* 21 (8).

O'Donnell, G. and P. Schmitter. 1986. *Transitions from Authoritarian Rule: Tentative Conclusions about Uncertain Democracies.* Vol. 4. Baltimore: Johns Hopkins University Press.

Pithouse, R. 2004. 'Solidarity, Co-option and Assimilation: The Necessity, Promises and Pitfalls of Global Linkages for South African Movements'. *Development Update* 5 (3): 169–99.

Polanyi, K. 1957. *The Great Transformation.* Boston: Beacon Press.

Sachs, M. 2003. '"We Don't Want the Fucking Vote": Social Movements and Demagogues in South Africa's Young Democracy'. *South African Labour Bulletin* (37) 6: 23–7.

Saul, J. 2001. 'Cry for the Beloved Country: The Post-Apartheid Denouement'. *Montly Review* 52 (8): 1–51.

———. 2002. 'Starting from Scratch?: A Reply to Jeremy S. Cronin'. *Monthly Review* 54 (7).

Schedler, A. 2001. 'Taking Uncertainty Seriously: The Blurred Boundaries of Democratic Transition and Consolidation'. *Democratization* 8 (4).

Vally, S. 2003. 'The Iron Fist and the Velvet Glove'. *Mail and Guardian* 20 December: 24.

Whiteford, A. and D.E. van Seventer. 2000. 'South Africa's Changing Income Distribution in the 1990s'. *Studies in Economics and Econometrics* 24 (3): 7–30.

Young, I.M. 1990. *Justice and the Politics of Difference.* Princeton, NJ: Princeton University Press.

———. 2000. *Inclusion and Democracy.* Oxford: Oxford University Press.

Contributors

Baruti Amisi is a researcher at the Centre for Civil Society at the University of KwaZulu-Natal. His research interests include peasant identity in the Democratic Republic of the Congo, and refugee livelihoods and organisation in South Africa.

Richard Ballard is a research fellow at the Centre for Civil Society and School of Development Studies at the University of KwaZulu-Natal. His research interests include refugee social organisation, social movements, urban desegregation, and urban governance.

Sakhela Buhlungu teaches sociology and is a deputy director of the Sociology of Work Unit (SWOP) at the University of the Witwatersrand. He has done research and published widely on work, labour and activism in South Africa. He serves on the governing board of the National Labour and Economic Development Institute (NALEDI) and is a member of the editorial board of the journals *Labour History* and *South African Review of Sociology*.

Jacklyn Cock is a professor of sociology at the University of the Witwatersrand. She is active in the environmental movement and has written extensively on gender, militarisation and environmental issues. Her current research interests are focused on environmental justice and in particular the grassroots struggles against the pollution of the air and groundwater around Vanderbijlpark by Iscor, now part of the largest steel company in the world.

Ashwin Desai is an independent researcher based in Durban. His published works include *We Are the Poors: Community Struggles in Post-Apartheid South Africa* (2002) and interventions in journals such as *African Sociological Review, Historical Materialism,*

Journal of Asian and African Studies, Monthly Review and *South Atlantic Quarterly*. He has been active in union and community struggles since the 1980s.

Annie Devenish is a lecturer in the Department of Historical Studies at the University of Cape Town. She has worked as a researcher at the School of Development Studies, University of KwaZulu-Natal, on informal economy, professionalisation of traditional medicine and the Self-Employed Women's Union. Her research interests include the history of indigenous medicine in South Africa and social and cultural issues relating to HIV/AIDS.

Teresa Dirsuweit is a lecturer in the Department of Geography, Archaeology and Environmental Studies at the University of the Witwatersrand. Her research interests focus on African cities in transition, and on the theorisation of the relationship between space and identity.

Peter Dwyer completed a PhD on political participation by COSATU members in the liberation struggle and then as members of government post-1994. He subsequently undertook a one-year Postdoctoral Fellowship at the Centre for Civil Society at the University of KwaZulu-Natal. He currently works on the Right Work campaign in the Education and Campaigns Unit at the Alternative Information and Development Centre (AIDC) in Cape Town.

Anthony Egan S.J. teaches applied ethics at St Augustine College of South Africa, having studied history and politics at the universities of Cape Town and the Witwatersrand, philosophy at the University of London, and theology at Weston Jesuit School of Theology, Cambridge, Massachusetts.

Steven Friedman is a research associate at the Institute for Democracy in South Africa and visiting professor of politics at Rhodes University. He has edited two books on South Africa's negotiated transition and is the author of a study of the South African labour movement. He has written many monographs, book chapters and newspaper articles on democratisation and related issues. He is currently studying the relationship between inequality and democratic politics.

Shauna Mottiar is a researcher whose interests lie in the field of democratic consolidation in South Africa. She has worked on issues of democratic elections, political parties, civil society, service delivery and local government and has a Master's degree in political studies from the University of the Witwatersrand.

Stephen Greenberg is an independent researcher with a particular interest in the politics of land, agriculture and food. He has worked in a number of rural and environmental non-governmental organisations and has worked closely with the Landless People's Movement in Gauteng. He is an honorary research associate in the School of Geography, Archaeology and Environmental Studies at the University of the Witwatersrand.

Adam Habib is executive director of the Democracy and Governance Programme at the Human Sciences Research Council, and an honorary research professor of the Centre for Civil Society and School of Development Studies at the University of KwaZulu-Natal. He is the former founding director of the Centre for Civil Society, prior to which he served on the tenured faculty of the University of Durban-Westville. He is a well-known researcher on South Africa in a diverse set of thematic areas, including political economy, institutional reform, civil society and foreign policy. At present, he manages three national research projects on The State of Giving and its Impact on Development, Race and Redress, and South Africa's Engagement in Africa.

Firoz Khan is a lecturer at the School of Public Management and Planning at the University of Stellenbosch. He has published in the areas of globalisation, local economic development, urban restructuring, institutional transformation, informality and poverty eradication, and housing praxis. More recently, he edited and contributed to Interfund's *Development Update* special edition (2004). His current research is focused on the political economy of housing policy and practice.

Shireen Hassim is associate professor in political studies at the University of the Witwatersrand. She is co-editor of *No Shortcuts to Power: African Women in Politics and Policy-Making* (2003), and author of *Women's Organizations and Democracy in South Africa: Contesting Authority* (2006). She has published widely in the areas of feminist politics, political institutions and social policy.

Sophie Oldfield is a senior lecturer in human geography in the Department of Environmental and Geographical Science at the University of Cape Town. Her research interests focus on post-apartheid intra-urban social, political change and urban development.

Kristian Stokke is professor of human geography at the University of Oslo (Norway), specialising in movement politics and democratisation in South Africa and nationalist conflict and conflict transformation in Sri Lanka. His recent publications include *Politicising Democracy: The New Local Politics of Democratisation* (2004), and *Democratising Development: The Politics of Socio-Economic Rights in South Africa* (2005).

Edgar Pieterse is special adviser to the premier of the Western Cape on development policy. He is a visiting associate professor in the Department of Public Management and Planning at the University of Stellenbosch and an associate of Isandla Institute. He is co-editor of *Voices of the Transition: The Politics, Poetics and Practices of Social Change in South Africa* (2004). His current research is focused on international urban development policy and the cultural politics of urban integration.

Cyrus Rustomjee is an independent researcher. His research interests include governance of global financial institutions, capacity utilisation and financial sector stability.

Caroline Skinner is a research fellow at the School of Development Studies at the University of KwaZulu-Natal. Her work has been an iterative process between research, advocacy and policy concerned broadly with the nature of the informal economy in South Africa in the post-apartheid period. A cross-cutting theme has been a critical analysis of the state's response to this phenomena and the role of collective action in strengthening often precarious livelihoods.

Imraan Valodia is a senior research fellow in the School of Development Studies at the University of KwaZulu-Natal. His research interests include trade and industrial policy, gender and economics, globalisation and labour markets. He has worked extensively on the informal economy, critically examining informal economic statistics; on conducting industry-level studies of informalisation; and on linking informal employment to broader labour market trends in South Africa. He has recently begun work on time-use data, exploring the links between time use, gender and employment in South Africa.

Alex Wafer is a researcher at the Independent Development Trust, and is part of the French Institute of South Africa's Fear and Security in Sub-Saharan Africa research project. He has a Master's degree in urban geography from the University of the Witwatersrand.

Elke Zuern is an assistant professor of politics at Sarah Lawrence College in New York. Her publications address the role of social movements in new democracies, institutional and extra-institutional mechanisms of protest, popular responses to poverty and inequality, state-civil society alliances, and the role of violence in processes of democratisation.

Index